Skills for Using Theory in Social Work

Using theory, research evidence, and experiential knowledge is a critical component of good social work. This unique text is designed to help social work students and practitioners to integrate theorizing into practice, demonstrating how to search for, select, and translate academic knowledge for practical use in helping people improve their lives and environments.

Presenting 32 core skills, *Skills for Using Theory in Social Work* provides a conceptual foundation, a vocabulary, and a set of skills to aid competent social work theorizing. Each chapter outlines the knowledge and action components of the skill and its relationship to core practice behaviors, along with learning and reflection activities. The lessons are divided into four parts:

- Section one discusses foundational material, including self-identification as a theorist-practitioner, the deliberate use of the term *theory*, and a social work approach to the selection of knowledge.
- Section two focuses on the adept use of theorizing skills. It covers identifying assumptions, using concepts, formulating propositions, organizing theory elements inductively or deductively, summarizing and displaying the elements of a theory, gathering and organizing assessment information, and communicating with clients and colleagues about tentative theories.
- Section three includes lessons preparing social workers for the construction of useful middle-range theories, including causal theories and interpretive theories, and for testing and sharing these practical theories.
- Section four presents skills to develop critical thinking about theoretical knowledge. These include avoiding the misuse of theory, judging a theory using scientific standards, judging a theory by professional standards, critiquing theory in its cultural and historical context, and making judgments about the likely long-term impact of a theory.

This key text will help readers to demonstrate their expertise in reflective, competent, and theory-informed practice. It is suitable for all social work students and practitioners, particularly those taking courses in practice, theory, and human behaviour in the social environment.

James A. Forte is Professor of Social Work at Salisbury University, Maryland, USA.

Skills for Using Theory in Social Work

32 lessons for evidence-informed practice

James A. Forte

Routledge
Taylor & Francis Group

LONDON AND NEW YORK

First published 2014
by Routledge
2 Park Square, Milton Park, Abingdon, Oxon, OX14 4RN

and by Routledge
711 Third Avenue, New York, NY 10017

Routledge is an imprint of the Taylor & Francis Group, an informa business

British Library Cataloguing in Publication Data
A catalogue record for this book is available from the British Library

Library of Congress Cataloging-in-Publication Data
Forte, James A.
Skills for using theory in social work : 32 lessons for evidence-informed practice / James A. Forte.
      pages cm
   1. Social service. 2. Social service – Philosophy. I. Title.
   HV40.F6724 2014
   361.3´2–dc23   2013032545

ISBN13: 978-0-415-72683-2 (hbk)
ISBN13: 978-0-415-72684-9 (pbk)
ISBN13: 978-1-315-85604-9 (ebk)

Typeset in Sabon by
HWA Text and Data Management, London

To some of the practical theorists, theoretical thinkers, and theorizing practitioners who have inspired this project

David D. Franks, Grace Harris, Joseph Healey, Stephan Lenton, Martin Schwartz, Marvin Tossey, and Manny Tropp

Contents

Figures

Tables

Foreword

Malcolm Payne, author of *Modern Social Work Theory*

Let me tell you a secret: I feel a bit of a theory fraud. I've been working on and worrying about social work theory for getting on for 40 years. That's because when I was doing social work I used to hear about theories that I never had time to explore fully. When I started in the 1970s having to contribute to a lecture and seminar series on social work theory and practice, I thought: "Oh good, if I'm going to have to explain theory, I'll have to read the books and then I'll understand it better." Later, I was pressurized by a publisher's editor into turning something I was writing into a social work theory textbook called *Modern Social Work Theory* and, a quarter of a century later, it has come out in four editions (Payne, 2014, 4th edn, Chicago: Lyceum), so people expect me to be an expert. As a result, I've been writing, teaching, giving lectures and presenting papers to social workers and students about theory in many parts of the world.

Why do I feel a fraud, then? When I was first a student at university, philosophers and theoreticians seemed to have this special skill and technique for teasing out and understanding every minuscule bit of complexity in things that I'd obviously never thought through adequately. It seemed very daunting. Now people call me a "theoretician" and I still don't think I can hack that sort of expertise. I've realized that you can study theory for ever, and never really feel on top of it. As you practice, something happens and all the theory you thought you could use turns to jelly or doesn't seem to apply at all. New books or journal articles that you read seem to add to the profusion of ideas that are available. Even when they mostly seem to repeat what you know, you find that it makes you feel that you have not quite understood what you thought you had a grasp of.

If you feel like that sometimes, too, James Forte's new book is for you, because it shows that it should not be our aim to know and understand all social work theory. He makes it absolutely clear that you have to *do* it, not learn it. Using this book, instead, everyone learns to be their own theorizer, and they theorize with their colleagues and team mates and with their clients too. It's also clear that not only do we do it, we *have* to do it, because theorizing is an essential part of doing social work (doing anything, actually, but this book is about how theorizing helps you to do social work well).

I have my doubts about books that try to make theory practical, because I think you have to interact and grapple with the ideas that are contained in everything that you do. But this book tries to help you do both. It says: "Theory is not a burger, put together by someone else for you to take away and eat from the package. You do theory, and you do it all the time: you just hadn't realized." This book is not totally free from fast food, because you'll probably already have noticed that it comes in nice bite-sized chunks, with lots of helpful tables and pictures that might be good for you if your mind works in structured or graphical ways. In that way, it recognizes that there is not just one way of doing theory, there is the way that works for you.

Because it's about how to incorporate theorizing into your thinking and practising, you can use the book alongside many other texts that try to explain particular theories or offer models of practice. It will help you to use them better. And it's not over-simplified: it shows how being a professional social worker means thinking through and working out the detail of how you practise. This is not easy, but it can be immensely satisfying, and adds to your security as a practising social worker because it makes you an accountable professional in working with your colleagues, your managers and your clients.

I hope you find it as useful and stimulating as I did.

Malcolm Payne

Introduction

Theoretical knowledge and its competent use are central features of professional social work. In his classic examination of the aspirations of social work at the beginning of the twentieth century, Abraham Flexner (1915/2001) defined a profession by reference to theoretical knowledge. He stated that the "the intellectual character of professional activity involves the working up of ideas into practice" (p. 154). Flexner argued that professionals "derive their raw materials from science and learning" (p. 156). He emphasized the practical aspect of theory use by adding the clause "this material they work up to a practical and definite end" (p. 156). Flexner had doubts about an affirmative answer to the question, "Is social work a profession?" Yet, he acknowledged that social work met an important criterion for professionalism. Social work derived its knowledge base from science and the world of learning.

Mary Richmond, a pioneering leader of social work, also valued theory and theorizing. In her paper, *The Training of Charity Workers* (1897/1971), she recommended the training of social workers in a "course of instruction which will combine theory and practice under leaders who are skilled in both" (p. 90). She appreciated the importance of theory-practice integration and characterized ideal workers as men and women who have "learned to apply reasonable theory to many concrete needs and then to modify the theory by results" (p. 94). Her list of attributes of the trained charity workers included a capacity for strenuous thinking and the ability to think for themselves: each an important component of evidence-informed practical theorizing.

Greenwood (1976) conducted a masterful analysis of the features of professions. He concluded that professionals use practice skills that "flow from and are supported by a fund of knowledge that has been organized into an internally consistent system, called a *body of theory*" (p. 304, emphasis in original). In a review of approaches to professionalism, Jones and Ross

(1995) noted a common theme: "[T]he nature and application of knowledge (and understanding) is still held to be a key dimension of professional work" (p. 21). They added that this knowledge should include a theoretical orientation, a set of systematic underpinning theories, and a practice theory: a guide to the application of the theoretical knowledge.

Contemporary claims by social work leaders for the distinction of professional status and for professional jurisdiction in many fields of service include the assertion of specialized knowledge. The Council on Social Work Education (CSWE) mandates that graduates of accredited programs be able "to apply *theories* and knowledge from the liberal arts to understand biological, social, cultural, psychological, and spiritual development" (CSWE, 2013, p. 6; emphasis added). The Canadian Association of Social Workers (2011; emphasis added) asserts that "the uniqueness of social work practice is in the blend of some particular values, knowledge and skills" and "social work education consists of *theoretical courses and practical training* at the undergraduate or graduate level." The International Federation of Social Workers (2011a) declares in its introduction to social work that social workers are dedicated to "the development and disciplined use of scientific knowledge regarding human behaviour and society" (original spelling) and the Federation (2011b; emphasis added) gives central place to theory in its definition – "the social work profession *draws on theories* of human development and behaviour and social systems to analyse complex situations and to facilitate individual, organisational, social and cultural changes" (original spelling). The British Association of Social Workers (2009, p. 1) includes as one of its objectives "to improve the professional and technological knowledge of its members)." The Association of Social Work Boards (2011) provides detailed information about examination content for professional licensure in its "Knowledge, Skills and Abilities Statement." At each license level, content related to theoretical frameworks is explicitly and prominently included.

If we think of a social worker metaphorically and refer to the body parts of a typical practitioner, the heart is prominent. Professional social workers are characterized by empathy, compassion, and fellow feeling: sentiments associated with caring dispositions. The hand is also important. Social workers are characterized as lending a helping hand to persons and groups facing life difficulties and needing support. Professional social workers also have steady nerves and are characterized as possessing the courage and persistence to fight for needy clients and just causes. One attribute receives less attention. Professional social workers also need a brain. Assume the scarecrow in the Wizard of Oz became a social worker. He would attract few clients and gain little support while he was lamenting: If I only had a brain. Theoretical knowledge, theorizing competencies, and the theorizing skills to apply this knowledge are like nutritious food, and, if digested regularly, they help build healthy social workers with all the necessary parts and attributes: heart (tender), nerves (brave), hand (strong), and brain (thoughtful).

The council on social work education and professional competencies

Whom are you going to call? If you need a doctor for a family member, you call the best. If there's something strange in your home or neighborhood you call the qualified Ghostbusters. If you need to help people in their environments, you call a professional social worker.

In the last decade, a "competencies movement" has worked to ensure that social workers who hear the call, pick up the phone, or respond to a text message are accomplished and responsible practitioners. Leaders of this movement set the expectation that professions develop explicit standards for appraising the ability of its members to act competently (Gehart, 2010). Lewis (1982), an expert on social work, identified the key components of a competent performance. These are knowledge (the social worker is informed and acts based on the best available knowledge); values (the social worker acts intentionally and in ways that affirm values and ethical standards); skills (the social worker adeptly uses knowledge and implements effectively the procedures and methods required by the situation); and style (the social worker develops a distinctive approach to job performance, an approach that fits with his or her personality, with the agency or business context of practice, and with the profession). Accountable and effective professional practitioners must be able to demonstrate in observable action their adept integration of these four components.

The CSWE expects educators to prepare social work students for careers as practitioners who can demonstrate expertise in reflective, competent, evidence-informed action. Like Lewis (1982), the CSWE defines competencies multi-dimensionally as "measurable practice behaviors that are comprised of knowledge, values, and skills" (CSWE, 2013, p. 3). The CSWE has also developed guidelines for educational programs. These identify ten core competencies. The competent graduate of an accredited social work program can demonstrate mastery in the following realms: professional identity and conduct, the use of ethical principles, critical thinking, the engagement of diversity, the advancement of rights and justice, research usage, knowledge application, policy practice, responsiveness to practice contexts, and the use of the planned change process. The CSWE has defined each competency and identified the specific practice behaviors associated with the ten competencies. For example, Educational Policy and Accreditation Standard (EPAS) 2.1.7—knowledge application—mandates that social workers achieve the competency necessary "to apply theories and knowledge from the liberal arts to understand biological, social, cultural, psychological, and spiritual development" (p. 6). Such mastery should be demonstrated by two identified practice behaviors: utilize conceptual frameworks to guide the processes of assessment, intervention, and evaluation, and critique and apply knowledge to understand person and environment. The Council doesn't provide details on the specific knowledge, skills, techniques, and attitudes that constitute each practice behavior, an omission that will be remedied to some extent in this book.

Sailing guide for navigating practical theorizing

In relation to the CSWE standards, professional socialization might be compared to a trek up the steps of a Mexican or Central American pyramid. Aztec, Mayan, and other indigenous peoples constructed these buildings more than 600 years ago (See Figure 0.1). The steps of a typical structure lead to the temple's platform near the top of the pyramid. Many pyramids had different areas of worship on this platform. From the shrine areas, pointed or circular structures would rise toward the sky. The pinnacles or spires represent the core competencies and the highest place, one near the gods. The pyramids were very high. The shrine areas or platforms represent the practice behaviors. Each lesson in this book is like a step by which the devoted social worker climbs toward the platform of demonstrable practice behavior and there reaches for the apex of theorizing competency. Professional competence seems a lofty objective for many practitioners. In this book, I also provide a conceptual foundation, a vocabulary, and a set of skills to aid the practitioner climbing steadily toward competent social work theorizing.

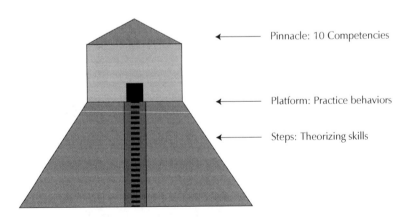

Figure 0.1 Representation of Mayan temple and the path toward excellence

Practical theorizing—the use of theoretical, research, and personal knowledge for professional purposes—is a critical component of social work practice and central to the ten core competencies. After culling the literature on scientific theorizing and reflecting on my own career, I have created 32 lessons describing 21 core theorizing skills directly relevant to practice and the associated knowledge for their use (See Figure 0.2).

I have also identified eight advanced theorizing skills (See Figure 0.3). Ambitious readers might attempt to use the 32 lessons to master these skills and supplement the lessons with instruction from theory experts (supervisors, seasoned practitioners, social work educators) to refine their performance of the advanced skills.

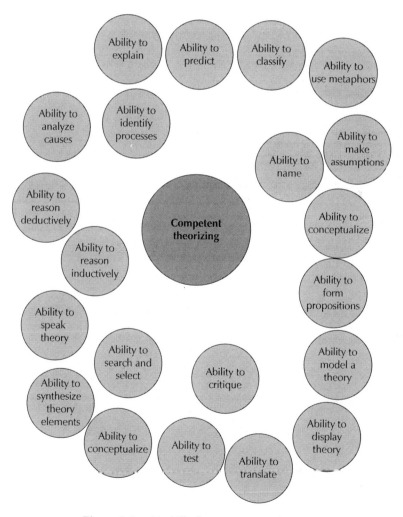

Figure 0.2 21 skills for competent theorizing

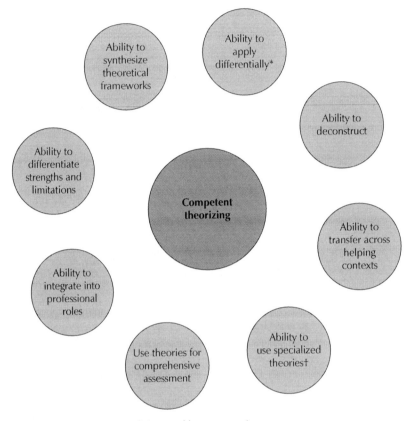

* By culture, life stage, population, problem, system size
† Of loss, prevention, stressors, substance abuse, etc.

Figure 0.3   Eight advanced skills for competent theorizing

Purpose of the book

Your use of this book can help you achieve a variety of important objectives. Three objectives are directly related to CSWE practice behaviors associated with Competency 2.1.7.

Objective one

The book will increase the reader's adept use of theorizing skills in the application of knowledge (Competency 2.1.7, Practice Behavior 2b). For example, the book will help you develop a vocabulary of scientific terms for practical theorizing and the basic skills needed for knowledge application.

Objective two

The book will increase the reader's adept use of a critical thinking approach to theorizing and the application of knowledge (Competency 2.1.7, Practice Behavior 2a). For example, social workers are consumers of theoretical knowledge. The book will help you judge the quality of the theories and theoretical models you consider for practical use. Social workers also reconstruct existing theories to fit specific practice circumstances and sometimes create their own theories. The book will help you do so with consideration of scientific, practical, and professional standards of excellence.

Objective three

The book will increase the reader's adept use of theorizing skills to guide several important phases of the helping process (Competency 2.1.7, Practice Behavior 1). For example, you will find new ways to use theorizing skills in a reflective and competent way to understand and explain personal and public problems. The book will also help you understand the relationship between theory, theorizing, practice choices, outcomes, and effectiveness and, thus, the book will help you engage in theory-guided, evidence-informed practice.

Objective four

The book will help readers understand some of the basic strategies for producing a theory, summarizing and diagramming a theory, testing out a theory, and sharing a theory with other professionals. Thus, the book will help the reader add to the social work knowledge base. The set of theorizing lessons will enhance specifically your ability to develop theories for practical use in work with client systems. For some of these readers, the book will help you write about your theory so it is included in the profession's library of useful knowledge. Later in your career, you may even contribute your practical theory-informed case studies, articles showing how to use theory practically to understand particular person-in-environment configurations, your written critiques of contemporary theory with suggestions for improvements, your workshop slides that share your theoretical ideas and applications, and your books on an innovative explanatory or practice theory.

This book can be a starting point for novices: students beginning social work careers and eager to climb the steps toward mastery of the core competencies necessary for critical, reflective, and evidence-informed theorizing. Additionally, professionals determined to increase their theorizing competency and appreciation of the centrality of theorizing to social work will benefit from the book. Last, expert social workers interested in enacting better their teaching roles, research roles, supervising roles, or theory-building roles can use the book's lessons as tools for promoting advanced theorizing by your students, researchers, supervisees, or theorizing colleagues.

Practical theorizing lessons

This book includes 32 theorizing lessons. Each lesson is focused on a particular theorizing skill, knowledge combined with a set of actions designed to accomplish a particular outcome (Sheafor & Horesji, 2008). Some cover multiple skills. Each of the 32 lessons provides information about the knowledge and action components of the skill while referencing the relevant practice behavior(s) attached to the CSWE's core competencies.

Each lesson includes a title, a commentary synthesizing necessary information about the skill, learning and reflection activities, and related references. The title includes a skill name. The title also includes a number, and linkage to the core competencies/practice behaviors addressed by the lesson. The commentary provides the knowledge necessary to understand the skill and to use it effectively. I have worked hard to synthesize the best information about each theorizing topic from the social work literature and the literature of closely related fields such as nursing, psychology, and sociology. Lessons in sections 2 and 3 focus on the deconstruction and reconstruction of theoretical frameworks and models, capabilities central to effective social work practice.

I agree with Swedberg (2012, p. 16) that "One becomes good at theorizing through practice; to theorize is also a reflexive activity. One gradually teaches oneself how to theorize by repeatedly doing it, and thinking about what one does." Following each commentary, I include learning/reflection activities. However, I would suggest supplementing solo reflection with collective reflection. Reading the commentary and doing the reflection activities with fellow students, colleagues, mentors, or teachers can provide the practice necessary to transform the skills into habitual ways of thinking and acting. Practicing the skills with more expert social workers can help the reader develop the professional attitudes (commitments to continual reflection, critical thinking, and scientific, evidence-based practice, for examples) for their adept use in specific practice circumstances.

Each lesson includes a set of references for further exploration of the relevant knowledge and skill information. Key terms are also included in the lessons, printed in italics, and defined. Many lessons include a figure or table to enhance the reader's understanding of the lesson's content.

Organization of the book

The organization of the book is tied to the book's objectives. The lessons in Section 1 introduce the reader to the nature and importance of theorizing, the meanings of the term *theory* and the major styles of theorizing, and the basics of searching for, selecting, and differentially using theoretical knowledge for social work purposes. These lessons will contribute to achievement of the four objectives.

I have broken the CSWE practice behavior, *critique and apply knowledge to understand person and environment*, into two separate behaviors. In Section 2, I start with lessons related to the second part of the practice behavior, theory application (objective one). This starting point is a logical predecessor to theory critique. The section includes lessons designed to enhance the reader's knowledge, skills, and attitudes related to the practice behavior: *"apply knowledge to understand person and environment."* For example, readers can learn a systematic process for theorizing and try theorizing reflection activities related to specifying the theoretical puzzle, learning from the great theoretical traditions and the exemplars of theorizing, considering root metaphors and foundational assumptions, formulating concepts and propositions, deductive reasoning, inductive reasoning, and summarizing a theory's elements in narrative and visual form. Section 2 also focuses on theory deconstruction and reconstruction.

Section 3 includes lessons preparing social workers for the construction of useful middle-range theories including causal theories and interpretive theories and for testing and sharing these practical theories (objective four). The skills in sections 2 and 3 are presented in a sequence that a practitioner could follow from the initiation to the conclusion of their theorizing project. However, each skill might also be used independently as appropriate to the practitioner's needs.

Together, sections 2 and 3 also provide learning content and experiences useful to mastering the practice behavior: *"utilize conceptual frameworks to guide the processes of assessment, intervention, and evaluation"* (objective three) This book prioritizes the information-gathering and assessment-formulation aspects of the planned change process. A companion book, *An Introduction to Using Theory in Social Work Practice*, provides additional strategies and lessons for using fourteen theoretical frameworks to guide engagement, goal setting, information gathering, assessment formulation, intervention selection and implementation, evaluation, and ending work with clients.

Section 4 addresses objective two and provides lessons related to the CSWE practice behavior: *"critique knowledge used to understand person and environment."* The lessons provide opportunities useful in mastering the knowledge, skill, and attitudes associated with this practice behavior. Lessons focus on topics such as critical thinking about theory; the appraisal of theory by the standards of science such as explanatory power, parsimony, and usefulness; and the appraisal of theory by social work standards such as ethics, diversity, and justice.

The book concludes with a coda. This summarizes my approach to practical theorizing and theorizing skill. The coda identifies major themes that might stimulate your own thinking about how you would like to meet the challenge of theory-practice integration. It also includes a table showing the lessons associated with each theorizing skill.

Theorizing lessons and set of core competencies

Theorizing is a critical component of all social work activity. Therefore, as I see it, each of the Council's ten core competencies and many of the related practice behaviors include theory use or critique components. Here are some illustrations. EPAS 2.1, *identify as a professional social worker*, for example, calls for the use of supervision, a primary arena for theory-practice integration. EPAS 2.1.2, *apply social work ethical principles*, requires familiarity with the major ethical theories and the different principles derived from each theory. EPAS 2.1.5, *advance human rights*, explicitly requires that social workers become knowledgeable about theories of justice. EPAS 2.1.9, *respond to contexts that shape practice*, calls on social workers to attend to changing scientific developments and implicitly the contextual factors influencing changes in theory preference and theory development. In relationship to the ten core competencies, then, theoretical knowledge and theorizing cut across the competency-oriented social work curriculum and have relevance to practice, research, policy, human behavior, ethics, and diversity courses. As stated earlier, the book prioritizes Competency 2.1.7, but each theorizing lesson includes reference to the relevant competencies and practice behaviors. The book will help readers advance in their mastery of the set of ten competencies.

Suggestions for using this book

Unlike books of fiction and many textbooks that are read from the front page to the last page, this book can be approached in many different ways. Of course, you can read and practice the theorizing activities in order from one to 32. Or you might design your own competency mastery program. For example, you might begin by assessing your proficiency for each of theorizing skills and then identify those that you haven't fully mastered. Then, you could read about and practice the skills related to areas for desired improvement. Additionally, you could work on the theorizing lessons in your preferred order and then return to those that you believe merit repeated practice.

Educators using this book might select the lessons most relevant to a particular social work course. In my social work program, my colleagues and I have selected applying (Section 2), constructing (Section 3), and critiquing lessons (Section 4) to accompany the content in our HBSE I (Human Development) course. Over a semester, students learn to critique the conventional human development theories (Section 4), to develop all the elements of a theory of a developing adolescent (Section 2), and to construct their own theory integrating these elements (Section 3).

Educators might incorporate lessons into the curriculum in creative ways. In the field placement, the lessons and the reflection activities could be the topics for a reflective journal linking field and the HBSE class. Process-recording formats could be modified to include student reports on theorizing application and critique skills used during the helping process. In the field seminar, students could present a case study based on an internship experience and report on the use of a set of theorizing skills and on evidence of effectiveness. In the HBSE classroom, the lessons and selected learning activities could be transformed into classroom experiences and discussions that expand on theoretical content. Students could role-play the use of particular theorizing skills. In the practice class, students might complete a term paper reporting on both the proposed application of a practice theory and the identification of the planned use of theorizing skills. Mastery of the knowledge component of each theorizing skill could be appraised by conventional quizzes and tests.

Additionally, there are several ways to approach each theorizing lesson. If you believe that you know much about the lesson's topic, you might complete the learning activities and reflections first and then read the commentary. For beginners in the lesson's area, however, I suggest that you read the commentary once, respond to the learning activities, and return to the commentary as needed for clarification.

I believe that much learning about theorizing occurs in cooperative social settings. My approach to theorizing mastery assumes that the study and practice of each skill in classroom, field, or practice settings can reinforce the book's content. Additionally such study and practice will deepen each aspect of the practitioner's theorizing competency. As discussed earlier, these aspects include knowledge enhancement via reviews of the commentaries that provide the information necessary for understanding each theorizing skill; skill enhancement by completion of the learning activities and reflections (work that can be viewed as mental rehearsals of the thinking and action necessary for the use of the theorizing skill); value and attitude socialization-enhancement via feedback from teachers, supervisors and others informing the practitioner about how to use the skill intentionally and in ways affirming social work standards; and style enhancement via reflective experimentation with the varied theorizing skills in ways that result in the learner's fitting each theorizing skill with his or her own personality, practice context, and professional identity preferences.

The reader of this book might work on theorizing lessons with fellow students, colleagues, or supervisors. I have been piloting these lessons in my classes. In face-to-face sections, we use theorizing lessons to supplement theory content, and students work on one lesson during each class. During group discussions, students share with their peers any difficulties and insights that emerged while reading the commentary and doing the learning activities. In my hybrid section (televised live lectures to distant sites with online supplemental activities), students participate in a discussion board, and each theorizing lesson is a topic for the week. Students offer their own detailed reflections in response to several assigned learning/reflection activities, and they are rewarded for exchanging additional ideas with their peers. As the moderator, I preview the theorizing lesson at the beginning of the week, and I review the shared and unique themes in the participants' comments the following week.

Theory and theorizing: the profession's ambivalence and antagonism

I remember my master's- and doctoral-level studies. For our theory survey course, we used a book heavy enough to weigh down the strongest backpack. The syllabus listing supplemental readings on major theories was constructed of a tree's worth of paper. We were expected to learn dozens of explanatory theories and practice theories. Not once did we discuss theorizing or learn any of the theorizing competencies identified in this book. This approach is very common in social work education and is called "the pedagogy of theory." It left me dissatisfied.

Professionals need knowledge, and I am pleased that my medical doctor knows the latest theories and research related to my health conditions. Competent medicine and social work, however, require more than the memorization of theoretical and research knowledge. The book takes a different approach from books offering surveys of major theoretical traditions. Based on the "pedagogy of theorizing" (Segall, 2008), the book provides lessons that will increase your ability to apply knowledge, critique knowledge using evidence and other standards, and use knowledge to guide the planned change process.

Unfortunately, many members of our profession avoid theory and theorizing entirely and are ambivalent, or even antagonistic, about expectations to become adept theorist-practitioners. Hearn (1982) commented on a "well entrenched sense of ambivalence or even antagonism towards theory from certain types of social worker or styles of social work" (p. 96). Borden (2010), an expert on theoretical perspectives in social work, contends "theory is often marginalized in social work education as a result of perceived conflicts with the practical concerns of the profession; the emergence of generalist, skills-based courses of study, and the growing emphasis on evidence-based practice" (p. xi).

As indicated earlier, many major social work professional associations do identify theory, its application, and its development as ingredients of the social work identity. However, the record indicates that theorizing is not a priority for the profession of social work. Thus, there are few resources for social workers committed to the steady improvement of theorizing skills. For example, the CSWE (Gutiérrez, 2011) includes nothing related to the mastery of theorizing competencies in its ten top scholarship priorities. The profession of social work lacks an organization dedicated to theory and theorizing, comparable to the American Sociological Association's Theory Section or The Society for Theoretical and Philosophical Psychology.

Professional social workers assign low value to theoretical materials. In a national survey of American social workers, Cha, Huo, & Marsh (2006) found that "information about theoretical perspectives" was ranked eight of ten types of information for usefulness. Regarding sources of information, the item "theoretical articles and books" was ranked seven of eight for usefulness. Only an item on "articles and books by non-social workers' ranked lower. Items regarding the usefulness of information and information sources related to theorizing and theorizing skills weren't even included in the study.

Unlike nursing, psychology, and sociology, our professional library includes few books about how to theorize. Search *amazon.com* or *barnesandnoble. com*, and you will find few or no social work books using key words such as "learning to theorize," "theorizing," "theory construction," "theory application," "theory toolbox," or "theory use." The few books with any of these words in their titles generally provide a chapter or less of content on theorizing processes and skills. The social work profession doesn't have a journal dedicated to theorizing and theory topics such as *The Journal of Theory Construction & Testing* in nursing, *Theory and Psychology* in psychology, or *Sociological Theory* in sociology. Though some social work journals include mission statements emphasizing the coverage or advancement of theory— *British Journal of Social Work, Clinical Social Work Journal, Journal of Social Work,* and *The Journal of Human Behavior in the Social Environment*—no social work journal to my knowledge focuses intentionally on theorizing or the mastery of theorizing skills.

Our knowledge base has a minimal representation of theorizing articles and few articles on theory. My professional background is group work, for example. The pattern of neglect is apparent in *Social Work with Groups* (Forte, 2009a). This journal is the main vehicle for communication among social workers committed to using the group method and the flagship journal for the *International Association for Social Work with Groups.* Titles and abstracts are posted at the journal's website. From 1993 to the first issue of 2007, there have been only three article titles including the word *theory*. Not one article included the keyword *theorizing* in its title or abstract. Check your library's search engine, *Social Work Abstracts*, as I have. This database is the repository of article information from major social work journals since 1977 and its more than 45,000 records. You will find little evidence of a professional concern with theorizing. Our encyclopedias and handbooks—the National Association of Social Workers *Encyclopedia of Social Work* and the four-volume, *Comprehensive Handbook of Social Work and Social Welfare*, for examples—include some content on theory but minimal content on theorizing. Our human behavior textbooks include little on recent advances in theoretical content and almost nothing on theorizing skills with the exception of those related to the critical appraisal of theory (Forte, 2009b). Our published articles are anemic in the area of theorizing. Daley and his colleagues (Daley et al, 2007; Decker et al, 2007; Gentle-Gennity et al, 2007) conducted a series of studies of articles in professional journals. They concluded that social work articles make minimal use of theory. The few articles that do include theory provide discussion of theory use and theory progression at a low-quality level. They also noted that there was little evidence that social workers theorize consciously when making practice decisions. Finally, they noted that there was some coverage of theory and theorizing in HBSE and practice articles but little in areas related to the field, ethics, diversity, populations at risk, and justice

Our major annual conferences, the Annual Program Meeting of the Council on Social Work Education or the Baccalaureate Program Directors Conference, generally include very few workshops on theory and no workshops on theorizing. Their programs for the last four years include presentations on many topics but rarely on theorizing. Our educational programs seem to be shy about teaching theorizing. In my review of 44 HBSE syllabi (Forte, 2009b), there were some very general statements about theory-related objectives such as "learn to critically appraise theories" (eighteen syllabi) and "learn how to apply theories" (eleven syllabi) but attention to specific theorizing skills such as middle-range theorizing, identifying and understanding concepts, parsing the elements of a theory, and using theory to describe, explain, predict, and communicate were not indicated. Theorizing content is not integrated systematically into social work curricula. Though educators have attempted to infuse curricula with topics such as aging, evidence-informed practice, domestic violence, spirituality, cultural diversity, and technology use, I have found no social work curricula that infused content and learning activities supporting the mastery of theorizing competencies. Few social work educators teach theorizing. In our department, senior faculty members conduct classroom observations of new faculty members. In the last ten years, I have seen minimal evidence of these educators' including theorizing content in their lectures. In contrast, some research knowledge, much practice wisdom, and lots of common sense were apparent in these lectures and associated PowerPoint slideshows.

Whom are social workers going to call if they want to master theorizing competencies? Unfortunately, the profession doesn't provide many resources to facilitate career-long learning about how to apply theoretical knowledge to unique practice circumstances, how to solve theoretical puzzles presented by our clients, how to construct new theories grounded in social worker and client experiences, or how to judge critically the suitability of theories for use.

Theory and practice: dichotomies or distinctions with unity

In the next few sections, I will identify some of the likely sources of the mixed or negative feelings toward theory and theorizing. I will also offer suggestions for transforming these dispositions. My major theme is that members of the social work profession are prone to dichotomous or dualistic thinking. This kind of thinking conceives of theory and practice as opposites separated by a divide, a gap, or a gulf. Theory and practice exist in different and mutually exclusive realms with a constant tension between the two, and the practitioner should choose one or the other—either theory or practice. The orientation of this book is holistic and rejects the notion of an inevitable theory-practice divide. Theory and practice are distinct, yet words such as *linked, connected*, and *related* characterize these overlapping processes better than words preferred by dualists. Theory and practice are essential parts of a whole, and the practitioner should choose a both/and, dialectic, and integrative view of their inseparable nature. Images of polarities (positive and negative) on one indivisible circuit and of a continuum that can't broken into distinct sections are apt.

Academic theory and practice knowledge: distinction with unity

Why are many social work leaders, educators, and students indifferent, ambivalent, or hostile when it comes to theoretical knowledge? First, I suspect that social workers believe that they are taught too much academic theory and too little practical theory. Academic theory has several distinctive and problematic features (Alexander, 2010; Dreyfus & Dreyfus, 2009; Hill & Morf, 2000, Thompson, 2000).

Academic theory

Academic theory is knowledge created by contemplative academicians and researchers, not practitioners. This knowledge has been developed in universities and laboratories distant from the helping settings inhabited by social workers and their clients. Academic theory prioritizes abstract, universal, and context-free understandings of person and environment configurations. This differs significantly from the situated understandings preferred by social workers. Academic theory is the result of a search for truthful explanations, not for useful solutions. If practicality is considered at all, academic theorists assume that their ideas can be applied without modification in technical, rational ways during professional problem-solving efforts. Academic theory often involves exploration of questions related to "knowing why" (the causes of human disease, system dysfunction, or recurrent patterns of behavior, for examples) and "knowing that" (sequencing that certain events or processes follow from other events or processes). These questions have relevance to social workers. However, "Knowing how to," a critical and central demand for practitioners, guides fewer theoretical projects. Academic theory is usually judged for its novelty, elegance, and generality. The adherence to rigorous scientific standards in the formalization of the academic theory is also important. Criteria related to relevance to practice by social workers or effectiveness in ameliorating personal and social problems are minimally important.

Practice knowledge

Practitioners often prefer the practical knowledge derived from reflection on practice experiences. This includes knowledge based on intuition, on practice wisdom obtained via experiential learning on the job, and on one's personal and subjective life lessons. Practice knowledge helps practitioners fulfill their role obligations and meet the daily challenges that arise in the workplace (Cornelissen, 2000). It is geared to resolving the ordinary problems of living experienced by our clients (Hearn, 1982). Method takes priority over theory. Practice knowledge deals with "knowing how" and is used by practitioners to make things happen (Hill & Morf, 2000). Practice knowledge is developed often in interactions with supervisors, colleagues, and clients. This kind of knowledge is often tacit and difficult to articulate rather than publicly described, fragmented rather than systematic, validated by usefulness rather than by the source of origin—academy or research site (Spong, 2007; Zundel & Kokkalis, 2010). Practice knowledge doesn't accumulate into new theory and isn't contributed to the scientific knowledge base. Concerns about the "official" standards and conventions for judging theoretical knowledge are minimal.

The potential unity of academic and practical knowledge

Yes, there are differences in the ways that many conceive of theoretical knowledge and practice knowledge. It is regrettable but understandable that many practitioners make little use of theories from the behavioral and social sciences and fail to see the benefit of theoretical knowledge (Englehart, 2001). As Jacoby (1977) noted, however, "[T]heory is not to be reduced to practice nor severed from it" (p. 120). Scientific theories are a resource that can and should enrich our practice. How might we stitch together academic and practical knowledge?

First, we might persuade university theorists and field researchers to develop knowledge with greater attention to its future usefulness. Such practical theory would focus on client systems and their action patterns in the real world. This kind of theorizing is an engaged and creative process drawing from the theorist's subjectivity but attentive to unmet human needs and embedded in particular membership contexts. The development of this strategy is a project for a different book.

Second, we might select those theories that are more practical than others (Craig, 1996b). Such theoretical knowledge is presented in narrative fashion rather than in the terms of formal logic or the symbols of mathematics. Such theories organize information situated in specific social contexts rather than general contexts, and such theories prioritize guidance in changing individual and collective processes rather than explaining their abstract qualities.

Third, we can translate academic knowledge for practical use. This starts with a new way of thinking. Hearn (1982) characterized this stance:

> [T]heory is not a set of sterile axioms, concepts, models, value or whatever, but an attempt to make a statement of relevance to changing practice; and practice itself is not a series of atheoretical actions to experiences, but an attempt to act in relation to developing and changing theory (p. 109).

We might deconstruct a theoretical tradition into a set of discrete instrumentalities—theoretical concepts, propositions, models, and displays—and make creative use of these tools in our problem solving enterprises (Barge, 2004; Cronen, 2001). Specifically, theorizing practitioners can create partnerships with clients to adapt or reconstruct a-priori scientific theories and their elements and to construct, sometimes, original middle-range theories. Academic and ad hoc theories become part of the practitioner's intellectual tool kit increasing the resources for solving practical problems.

Theorist and practitioner: distinction with unity

There is a second dichotomy contributing to the indifference, ambivalence, or antagonism of social workers to theory and theorizing: the artificial division of the roles of theorist and practitioner. In their historical review, Kirk and Reid (2002) note "as professional education migrated into universities, a division arose between theoretical and practical learning and between those who were primarily involved in the development and refinement of professional knowledge and those who were practitioners," and they add that this "ushered in a new structural problem, namely, how to connect the methodology of science and the abstract world of theory to the practitioner's helping specific clients with their idiosyncratic human troubles" (p. 10).

Dichotomous stereotypes regarding theorists and practitioners

There are many either/or characterizations of the roles of theorist and practitioner (Hill & Morf, 2000; Kessels & Korthagen, 2001; Korthagen, 1999; Lobkowicz, 1977; Zundel & Kokkalis, 2010). Some describe different intellectual orientations. Theorists prioritize thinking while practitioners prioritize doing. Theorists seek universal principles, but practitioners seek situated insights. Theorists deal with abstractions and other worldly topics; practitioners grapple with case particulars and concrete problems. Theorists are committed to their theoretical traditions and paradigms and rigorous scientific methods, but practitioners are at ease muddling through and improvising independently of science and its historical accomplishments.

Theorists want knowledge for its own sake; practitioners acquire knowledge for use.

Some of these stereotypes describe different personal and social inclinations. Theorists maintain their objectivity and avoid the contaminating influence of emotion, but practitioners appreciate and use their emotions. Theorists trust their heads: reasoning and science-derived conclusions. In contrast, practitioners trust their self-awareness and their hearts: emotions and intuitions.

Others describe the role occupant's orientation to the larger environment. Theorists are distant and detached from the streets, the households, and the other life spaces of service recipients, but practitioners try to learn about and engage with community members in these natural places. Theorists are spectators and contemplators such as the philosophers and lovers of wisdom of ancient Greece whereas practitioners are makers and shakers. They are more like the politician and engaged citizen of the Greek polity in their focus on dealing with the daily problems and their determination to improve the prospects of the community and its members.

Some stereotypes deal with issues of social worth. Theorists belong to an "all men's club." Excluded from the club, females become practitioners. Theorists are high-status scientists contributing in special ways to the overall society, but practitioners are low-status social servants doing society's dirty work. Theorists write the cookbooks whereas practitioners stay in the kitchen and follow the steps outlined in the cookbooks.

The potential unity of theorists and practitioners

Though academic settings and human service organizations are typically aligned with different cultures or social worlds, theorists and practitioners shouldn't be treated as unlike planets with orbits that never intersect. We may find some truth in a stereotype, but the overall portrait of the stereotyped group is always inadequate.

Dualists emphasize the differences between theorists and practitioners, but there are many areas of overlap (Zundel & Kokkalis, 2010). Theorists and practitioners both endeavor to cope with tasks at hand. The coping activities of theorists and practitioners are embedded in and influenced by the organizational context of their work and its rules. Theorists and practitioners aim to contribute to the common good. As Dewey (1929/1960) asserted, we should "conceive of *both* knowledge and practice as means of making goods–excellencies of all kinds-secure in experienced existence" (p. 37, italics in original). Theorists and practitioners both engage in "practices," the practices of the science-oriented academy and the practices of the service-oriented agency.

Instead of considering theorists and practitioners as antagonists, we can and should view them as members of a team (Hill & Morf, 2000). The team may require a division of labor among members based on special talents and knowledge. However, each member of the team is a partner in a collaborative project devoted to human betterment. Each can bring the perspectives and resources from his or her home institution to the work of the team. Moreover, as members interact together, barriers to team communication and cooperation lessen and team unity increases. Theorists and practitioners learn about one another's role specialties. They begin to see the connectedness of theoretical and practical knowledge. They learn to talk with one anther despite different languages, and they learn to negotiate differences for the collective enterprise. Common interests become central. At times, theorists even apply knowledge, and practitioners create theories for the sake of the team. Hearn (1982) shares this holistic approach to theorists and practitioners. He argues that theorists in organizations such as colleges and universities prioritizing theory development and practitioners in agencies prioritizing service delivery have divergent interests, but areas for negotiation can be established and inter-organizational relationships improved.

Let's consider one final way to affirm the unity of theorists and practitioners. Cribb's quotation (2011) articulates this stance: "[T]here is clearly no sharp line between theorists and practitioners. There is nothing to stop someone being both" (p. 384). A social worker can become a theorizing practitioner (the many proponents of evidence-informed practice use a similar term, *scientific practitioner*, but they emphasize the merger of the researcher and practitioner roles). The theorizing practitioner engages with academic theories and insights. He or she decides which theories to use, how to translate and deconstruct impractical theories for practical use, and how to adapt and reconstruct scientific theory with an awareness of social work contexts and purposes (Hearn, 1982). Theoretical knowledge in conjunction with practice wisdom, refined intuition, and relevant evidence is adapted after translation for application in particular cases. The responsible and energetic theorizing practitioner might communicate with academy-based theorists about the strengths and limitations of the applied theory (Cornelissen, 2000). If we accept that social work has a craft and a professional component (and that scholars of the past indulged in sexist language), Mills's (1959) recommendation is still relevant: "Let every man be his own methodologist; let every man be his own theorist; let theory and method again become part of the practice of a craft" (p. 224).

Metaphors of theorist-practitioner unity

Several metaphors may increase our readiness to merge theorist and practitioner in one person: the theorizing practitioner (other possible appellations include the theory-based practitioner, the practical theoretician, or the theory-guided, evidence-informed practitioner). Boero, Pedemonte, and Robotti (1998) draw from the work of Mikhail Bakhtin and compare the mental processes of a theorizing practitioner to polyphony. *Polyphony* is a concept from music referring to the playing of two or more melodic lines simultaneously. In this approach to science, voices are the verbal and nonverbal expressions produced by historical and contemporary scientists to build and communicate theoretical knowledge. The theorizing practitioner learns to listen to and integrate into practice the voices of academic theorists and, also, the voices of researchers, colleagues, clients, and teachers. Each of these voices has its own perspective, its own validity, and its own narrative weight. The theorizing practitioner can engage in imaginary interaction with the speakers of each type of voice (interactions that transcend time, place, and culture), listen to their voiced utterances, and use these interactions to create new musical scores: for social workers, solutions to theoretical puzzles instead of the creative response to sonic impulses of composers. As theorizing practitioners internalize these voices in their minds, inner orchestral halls, they become capable of producing their own echoes or playlists of influential voices. An echo is a link to a scientific voice that a speaker can use in private conversations and can share explicitly in public discourse. Resonant echoes, for example, are the theorizing practitioner's appropriation of the voices of preferred scientific theorists to represent the person-in-environment difficulties presented by the client. Echoes facilitate the use of theoretical content, of methods of theoretical inquiry, and of theoretical languages to create solutions to complex practice problems.

Second, we might think about unification with a metaphor related to eyesight (Mullen, Greenlee, & Bruner, 2005). The theorizing practitioner looks at every helping situation through special glasses. The glasses have a frame and two lenses. The left lens is the viewpoint of theorist, and the right lens is the viewpoint of practitioner (I would amend the metaphor by suggesting three lenses: theorist, researcher, and practitioner). With practice, a theorizing practitioner learns to merge the images produced by the different lenses into one whole picture of the viewed person-in-environment configuration. In special circumstances, the theorizing practitioner can alternate and close one eye after another to view from the theorist lens, the researcher lens, and then from the practitioner lens. Then, he or she returns to the unified vision derived from the distinct perspectives. If one lens is damaged or not used, seeing is impaired. For effective sight, the frame of the lens must be solid, keeping each lens separate yet attached to the glasses. Additionally, each lens must be equally powerful and focused or vision will be distorted.

Teaching theory and teaching theorizing: distinction with unity

I suspect that most social workers have been socialized by teachers committed to the pedagogy of theory but not to the pedagogy of theorizing (Segall, 2008; Swedberg, 2010). According to Boero, Pedemonte, and Robotti (1998), for example,

In Italy as in other countries, mathematics and science theories are "explained" by the teacher to students as from the 10th grade; the students' job is to understand them, to repeat them in verbal or written tests and to apply them in easy problem situations. The results are well known: for most students, theories are only tools for solving school exercises and do not influence their deep conceptions and ways of reasoning. (p. 81)

Similar learning histories contribute to professionals' reactions of aversion, ambivalence, indifference, and irritation to theory and to calls for theory-practice integration.

The pedagogy of theory

Guided by educators committed to the pedagogy of theory, students learn in a classroom what theorists have written. The teacher requires students to read extensively, and students study textbooks and articles by the famous theorists and commentaries about classic theories written by theory specialists. The literature's relevance to social work practice is assumed rather than demonstrated, and the fact that millennial-generation students don't read complicated academic texts is ignored.

Students learn from the teacher, the expert interpreter of the theoretical tradition and its language, and the student, a novice theoretical language user, must accept the expert's interpretation. Little time is spent, however, translating complex theoretical terms into everyday English or teaching students the grammar of a theory.

When the pedagogy of theory governs, much theory learning occurs alone in solo reading and writing activities. Theorizing as a verb and theorizing methodology are downplayed. Barnard (2004) notes about social work theory education, "Rarely is the how-to-do-it knowledge needed to build and apply theory extensively articulated" (p. 983).

Using the pedagogy of theory, the learners focus on creating an end product: the written representation of a theory, not on the process leading to that creation. Theory is a noun. Grades depend more on skills in organizing and presenting ideas in a clear, well-written argument than on the power of the theory application.

The pedagogy of theorizing

This pedagogy is different. The convictions that theory is an object separate from the real world and that theory can be learned in a classroom with impermeable boundaries are rejected. The emphasis is on theorizing as process situated in the world of practice and on education that consistently relates class and field (Doane & Varcoe, 2005). Rather than assuming that specialists create theory, educators allied with the pedagogy of theorizing assume that every social worker can think theoretically and theorize (Swedberg, 2010; Thompson, 2010).

Educators also share Weick's conviction (1989, p. 516): "Theory cannot be improved until we improve the theorizing process, and we cannot improve the theorizing process until we describe it more explicitly, operate it more self-consciously, and de-couple it from validation more deliberately." Classroom activities focus on teaching the process of theorizing and theorizing skills.

Students learn theory and theorizing skills in both academic settings and field settings. They become members of connected learning communities. Through reciprocal socialization, they learn theorizing skills as part of urgent attempts to solve theoretical puzzles and to improve theorizing efforts for the sake of service recipients.

Students improve in theory mastery and theorizing competencies by doing exercises and repeating these experiences over and over again: adjusting their performance according to feedback and personal reflections. Students are active participants in experiential learning and encouraged by teachers who serve as models of practical theorists. Though theory is someone else's product, theorizing becomes the student's own accomplishment.

Theorizing is a verb, and the classroom shows this. Theory learning is structured as a collaborative process involving theorizers (teachers, supervisors, students, clients, researchers) with different levels of expertise but with a shared interest in theorizing excellence. Theory as written is a product frozen in time in the pedagogy of theory (a misunderstanding of the provisional nature of all good theory). Theorizing is never finished according to the pedagogy of theorizing, and students can always improve their theorizing capabilities.

Theorizing-oriented educators don't restrict judgments of a student's progress to tests assessing memorization of theoretical content or term papers assessing the assembly of theoretical knowledge in support of a thesis. The quality of theorizing is appraised. Is the novice theorizing practitioner demonstrating that she or he can theorize in a creative, reflective, critical, and evidence-informed way?

The potential unity of the pedagogies of theory and theorizing

Theory and theorizing are related. The term *theorizing*, for example, can refer to the creation of new theory but it also involves the activation of thinking and acting processes necessary to make use of existing theoretical knowledge. Effective theorizing, Solomon (2007) adds, requires "a complex knowledge of theories and their application in various fields" (p. 108). Spong (2007) agrees and notes that adept theorizers make choices about which preexisting theories and theoretical ideas to adapt for use in particular circumstances. This requires a breadth of theoretical knowledge.

The social constructionist approach to science offers a way of reconciling theorizing and theory. Theorizing requires deconstruction work. Theory deconstruction involves separating and identifying the elements of a theory and their relationships (theoretical concepts, statements, models, and diagrams) to better understand and use the theory (Walker & Avant, 1995). Theory deconstructionists are like the volunteers at my local Habitat for Humanity, *Restore*. They take apart abandoned buildings and bring the parts—doors, windows, hinges, wood, and so on—to a warehouse for sale at low cost. Previously unnoticed and undervalued elements of houses are used once again but for new purposes.

Theorizing also involves reconstruction work. Theory reconstruction involves reforming a theory's elements and arrangements in new ways as building blocks for creating knowledge closer to the lived experiences and ecological contexts of our clients than knowledge provided by most academicians and researchers. Reconstruction is the bringing together and arranging of the theory elements (concepts, constructs and their definitions, for instance) in a new form to represent a puzzling event, process, system, or set of systems in a way meaningful to the worker and client (Beard, 1995). Like Habitat volunteers, theory reconstructionists build something with suitable resources tailored to a particular client planning to live in a particular place.

From the holistic stance, the ideal classroom, field practicum, or other site of professional socialization achieves an appropriate balance between theorizing and theory, process and product, a-priori theory and ad hoc theory, doing theory and writing theory down, theory deconstruction and theory reconstruction. In such sites, teaching by using theorizing lessons and reflection activities can bring theory alive and increase learners' interest while teaching by theoretical content can provide the information that serves as essential materials for social work construction projects (Swedberg, 2010). This book is my attempt to strike a balance between theory and theorizing. Each of the 32 lessons in this book assumes the importance of learning theory and learning theorizing, and many will help you dissolve the conceptual barriers and emotional dispositions contributing to dualisms, and often to a rejection of the theorizing aspect of practice.

A pragmatist model for practical theorizing

In the last three sections, I have made the case that social workers will approach theory and practice more positively if dualistic thinking is replaced by holistic thinking. In this book, I start from the pragmatist position that separations between theory and practice, theorist and practitioner, teaching theory and teaching theorizing are artificial (Biesta & Burbules, 2003; Craig, 1996b; Doane & Varcoe, 2005). Craig (1996a, 1996b) provides the informative notion of a theory-practice continuum. All helping action includes theoretical and practical elements. These are combined in varying proportions depending on the circumstances.

The theory end of the continuum

At the theoretical end of the continuum, the pure theorist develops relatively formal and systematic conceptual frameworks that provide knowledge not restricted to local contexts but applicable across a range of situations. Minimal attention is given to practical concerns. At this end, the theorist emphasizes the search for understanding. The "armchair" theorist is like an architect who never lifted a hammer, assembled pieces of a structure, or visited a building site. However, the continuum approach asserts that every theory is an intellectual tool or instrumentality for achieving some desired end (Andrew, 1977). Practicality is relevant even at this end point.

The practice end of the continuum

At the practice end of the continuum, the pure practitioner acts in ways relatively unconstrained by an explicit conceptual system with judgments bound to a particular and local context and prioritizing change. Minimal attention is given to scientific theories and theoretical reflection. The practitioner emphasizes the search for problem-solving actions and acts with no or little reflection. The practitioner is like an impulsive carpenter who never read directions for using a power saw, never imagines the sequence of steps for a building project, and never consults an architectural blueprint. However, the continuum approach asserts that all practice is intentional behavior expressed in symbolic language and, therefore, involves some degree of thinking and some degree of doing. Thinking and theorizing are relevant even at this end point.

The middle of the continuum: practical theorizing

The unity of theory and practice, theorist and practitioner, theoretical knowledge and theorizing skills becomes most apparent in the middle of the continuum. Excessive emphasis on the theory end of the continuum constrains theory use and development because theoretical knowledge is not enriched by real world experiences. Excessive emphasis on the practice end of the continuum limits the depth of understanding and range of choices that a practitioner brings to the helping situation. The theorizing practitioner alternates purposefully between moments of theorizing (conceptual thought and critical reflection) and moments of practicing (acting in the immediate situation). Theorizing guides practice, and practice grounds theorizing. Theory reflects and organizes practice actions while practice manifests and enriches theoretical thinking.

The middle of the continuum might be referred to as practical theorizing, an important supplement to scientific, evidence-informed practice. Dewey (1900), for instance, identified science as the means for overcoming theory-practice dichotomies:

> The real essence of the problem (the legitimate division of labor between the general educational theorist and the actual instructor) is found in an *organic* connection between the two extreme terms-between the theorist and the practical worker-through the medium of the linking science. The decisive matter is the extent to which the ideas of the theorist actually project themselves, through the kind offices of the middleman, into the consciousness of the practitioner. (p. 67, italics in original)

Every moment in the scientific helping process becomes an opportunity to deconstruct, reconstruct, or critique theoretical knowledge by reflecting on evidence regarding its empirical support and the likely consequences of its use (Doane & Varcoe, 2005). Theory helps practitioners gather information and use concepts, propositions, and theoretical models to explain "person-interacting in an environment" problems and processes (knowing why and knowing that), and to formulate comprehensive assessments. Practice helps in the refinement of this process of developing explanatory hypotheses for particular cases in specific places.

Theory helps practitioners identify and choose from varied possible interventions (research suggests the relative quality of the interventions). Practice helps with the implementation of the selected interventions and improvisatory adjustments for unanticipated contingencies (knowing how). Theory helps practitioners test their explanatory and intervention hypotheses and evaluate critically the overall results of episodes of helping work. Practice helps in the wise appraisal of the strengths and limitations of the applied theory.

Theory also helps the practitioner increase his or her ability to articulate the perceptions, actions, and thoughts relevant to scientific problem solving (Maclean & Harrison, 2008). The theorizing practitioner can fluently communicate how and why a set of theories was selected, what other theories were considered, and why these alternative theories weren't used. The theorizing practitioner can discuss with clients, colleagues, supervisors, and theory creators how theoretical and research knowledge guided the process of scientific inquiry and provided a rationale for intervention selection and implementation. The theorizing practitioner can explicate how well the use of theoretical knowledge worked to achieve desired outcomes and talk about the evidence supporting such claims. The theorizing practitioner can contribute to larger scientific conversations by sharing with experts and laypersons how the theoretical knowledge might be refined and employed differently in the future. Practice experience contributes to the eloquence and persuasiveness of theory talk.

Conclusion

I join Harris Chaiklin, the social work educator (2004), in railing "against anyone denying that theory is related to practice" (p. 95). Table 0.1 summarizes the discussion in the last three sections that pits theory against practice by emphasizing differences in roles, purposes, venues, preferences, applications, and audiences.

Table 0.2 summarizes the argument for the synthesis of theory and practice in acts of practical theorizing. By describing the theorizing skills essential to social work competency, I hope to provide tools for social workers committed to competent practice: practice in helping roles informed by purposeful and

Table 0.1 Theory versus practice

Feature	Theory	Practice
Role	develop and test theories in academy	use practice wisdom and intuition in field
Purpose	advance solutions to conceptual puzzles	provide practical solutions to practical problems
Venue	communicate and debate in journals	communicate at meetings and conferences
Preferences	abstract, explicit, formal theory	concrete, implicit, narrative knowledge
Application	action directed by theory and elements	action directed by cookbook and agency policy
Audience	only theorists, specialists, experts	only practitioners, colleagues, clients, public

Based on: Craig 1996a, 1996b; Hill & Morf, 2000; Wilson, 2000

Table 0.2 Theory and practice: practical theorizing*

Feature	Theory and Practice = Practical Theorizing
Role	deconstruct, reconstruct, and critique knowledge for practical use
Purpose	guide scientific helping processes to achieve agreed-on goals
Venue	talk theory in academy, laboratory, field, natural sites
Preferences	knowledge from multiple sources that can be adapted and used
Application	critical and reflective use of theoretical principles and emergent theory
Audience	theorists and practitioners, specialists and generalists, experts and laypersons

*Based on: Craig 1996a, 1996b; Hill & Morf, 2000; Wilson, 2000

practical theorizing; practice that transcends different sites of knowledge production and synthesizes knowledge from diverse sources; and practice that reconstructs theoretical knowledge in reflective, evidence-informed ways for the needs of our clients, colleagues, and communities.

When I was in high school, I spent hours at the Catholic Youth Organization's basketball court. When alone, I would practice dribbling, passing (by bouncing the ball off the wall), layups, jump shots, foul shots, and so on. In pick-up games and in league play, I synthesized these skills into the behaviors necessary for competition. Eventually, I became a competent player on our "Justice League of America" intramural basketball team.

The same learning process applies to other areas of human excellence. Chambliss (1989), an ethnographer, studied world-class swimmers for years. He concluded that "superb performance is really a confluence of dozens of small skills or activities, each one learned or stumbled upon, which have been carefully drilled into a habit and then fitted together in a synthesized whole" (p. 81). I hope that readers studying and practicing the 32 lessons for practical theorizing in my book will integrate the included knowledge, skills, and attitudes and become first-rate and award-winning theorizing practitioners.

References

Alexander, E. R. (2010). Introduction: Does planning theory affect practice, and if so, how? *Planning Theory, 9*(2), 99–107.

Andrew, E. (1977). The unity of theory and practice: The science of Marx and Nietzsche. In T. Ball (Ed.), *Political theory and praxis: New perspectives* (pp. 117–137). Minneapolis, MN: University of Minnesota Press.

Association of Social Work Boards. (2007). ASWB exam information. Retrieved June 4, 2007, from www.aswb.org/exam_info_NEW_content_outlines.shtml

Association of Social Work Boards. (2011). Knowledge, skills, and abilities statements. Retrieved September 23, 2011, from www.aswb.org/pdfs/2011KSAs.pdf

Barge, J. K. (2004). Articulating CMM as a practical theory. *Human Systems: The Journal of Systemic Consultation & Management, 15*(X), 187–198.

Barnard, P. J. (2004). Bridging between basic theory and clinical practice. *Behavior Research and Therapy, 42*, 977–1000.

Beard, M. T. (1995). Theory construction and testing: An introduction and overview. In M. T. Beard (Ed.), *Theory construction and testing* (pp. 1–18). Lisle, IL: Tucker Publications.

Biesta, G. J. J., & Burbules, N. C. (2003). *Pragmatism and educational research.* Lanham, MD: Rowman & Littlefield.

Boero, P., Pedemonte, B., & Robotti, E. (1998). Approaching theoretical knowledge through voices and echoes: A Vygotskian perspective. In E. Pehkonen (Ed.), *Proceedings of the 21st International Conference of the Psychology of Mathematics Education* (Vol. 2, pp. 81–88). Lahti, Finland: University of Helsinki.

Borden, W. (2010). Introduction. In W. Borden (Ed.), *Reshaping theory in contemporary social work practice: Toward a critical pluralism in clinical practice* (pp. xi–xviii). New York: Columbia University Press.

British Association of Social Workers. (2009). Memorandum articles and bye-laws. Retrieved February 12, 2013, from http://cdn.basw.co.uk/documents/governance/Memorandum-Articles-2009-revised.pdf

Canadian Association of Social Workers (2011). What is social work? Retrieved September 23, 2011, from www.casw-acts.ca/en/what-social-work

Cha, T., Huo, E., & Marsh, J. (2006). Useful knowledge for social work practice. *Social Work and Society*, 4(1), 1–6. Retrieved July 17, 2013, from www.socwork.net/sws/article/view/180/240

Chaiklin, H. (2004). Problem formulation, conceptualization, and theory development. In A. R. Roberts & K. R. Yeager (Eds), *Evidence-based practice manual: Research and outcome measures in health and human services* (pp. 95–101). New York: Oxford University Press.

Chambliss, D. F. (1989). The mundanity of excellence. *Sociological Theory*, 7, 70–86.

Cornelissen, J. P. (2000). Toward an understanding of the use of academic theories in public relations practice. *Public Relations Review*, 26(3), 315–326.

Council on Social Work Education. (2013). *2008 Educational policy and accreditation standards*. Retrieved July 17, 2013, from www.cswe.org/File.aspx?id=13780

Craig, R. T. (1996a). Practical-theoretical argumentation. *Argumentation*, 10, 461–474.

Craig, R. T. (1996b). Practical theory: A reply to Sandelands. *Journal for the Theory of Social Behaviour*, 26(1), 65–79.

Cribb, A. (2011). Beyond the classroom wall: Theorist-practitioner relationship and extra-mural ethics. *Ethical Theory and Moral Practice*, 14(4), 383–396.

Cronen, V. R. (2001). Practical theory, practical art, and the pragmatic-systemic account of inquiry. *Communication Theory*, 11(1), 14–35.

Daley, J. G., Peters, J., Taylor, R., Hanson, V., & Hill, D. (2007). Theory discussion in social work journals: A preliminary study. *Advances in Social Work*, 7(1), 1–19.

Decker, V. D., Suman, P. D., Burge, B. J., Deka, A., Harris, M., Hymans, D. J., Marcussen, M., Pittman, D., Wilkerson, D., & Daley, J. G. (2007). Analysis of social work theory progression published in 2004. *Advances in Social Work*, 8(1), 81–103.

Dewey, J. (1900). Psychology and social practice. *Psychological Review*, 7, 105–124.

Dewey, J. (1929 / 1960). *The quest for certainty: A study of the relation of knowledge and action*. New York: Capricorn.

Doane, G. H., & Varcoe, C. (2005). Toward compassionate action: Pragmatism and the inseparability of theory/practice. *Advances in Nursing Science*, 28(1), 81–90.

Dreyfus, H. L., & Dreyfus, S. E. (2009). The relationship of theory and practice in the acquisition of skill. In P. Benner, C. A. Tanner, & C. A. Chesla (Eds), *Expertise in nursing practice: Caring, clinical judgment and ethics* (pp. 1–23). New York: Springer.

Englehart, J. K. (2001). The marriage between theory and practice. *Public Administration Review*, 61(3), 371–374.

Flexner, A. (1915/2001). Is social work a profession? *Research on Social Work Practice*, 11(2), 152–165. Originally published in National Conference of Charities and Corrections, Proceedings of the National Conference of Charities and Corrections at the Forty-second annual session held in Baltimore, Maryland, May 12–19, 1915. Chicago: Hildmann.

Forte, J. A. (2009a). Adding the "symbolic" to interactionist practice: A theoretical elaboration of William Schwartz' legacy to group workers. *Social Work with Groups*, 32(1/2), 80–95.

Forte, J. A. (2009b). Teaching human development: Current theoretical deficits and a theory-enriched "Models, metaphors, and maps" remedy. *Journal of Human Behavior in the Social Environment*, 19(7), 932–954.

Gehart, D. (2010). *Mastering competencies in family therapy: A practical approach to theories and clinical case documentation*. Belmont, CA: Brooks/Cole Cengage.

Gentle-Gennity, C. S., Gregory, V., Pfahler, C., Thomas, M., Lewis, L., Campbell, K., Ballard, K., Compton, K., & Daley, J. C. (2007). A critical review of theory in social work journals: A replication study. *Advances in Social Work*, 8(1), 62–80.

Greenwood, E. (1976). Attributes of a profession. In N. Gilbert & H. Specht (Eds), *The emergence of social welfare and social work* (pp. 302–318). Itasca, IL: Peacock.

Gutiérrez, L. (2011). Scholarship on social work education in the 2010s: An invitation to our readers. *Journal of Social Work Education*, 47(1), 1–3.

Hearn, J. (1982). The problem(s) of theory and practice in social work and social work education. *Issues in Social Work Education*, 2(2), 95–118.

Hill, D. B., & Morf, M. E. (2000). Undoing theory/practice dualism: Joint action and knowing from within. *Journal of Theoretical and Philosophical Psychology*, 20(2), 208–224.

International Federation of Social Workers. (2011a). Introduction. Retrieved September 23, 2011, from www.ifsw.org/p38000002.html

International Federation of Social Workers. (2011b). Definition of social work. Retrieved September 23, 2011, www.ifsw.org/f38000138.html

Jacoby, R. (1977). *Social amnesia: A critique of contemporary psychology*. Hassocks, UK: Harvester.

Jones, S., & Ross, R. (1995). Models of professionalism. In M. Yelloly & M. Henkel (Eds), *Learning and teaching in social work: Towards reflective practice* (pp. 15–33). London: Jessica Kingsley Publishers.

Kessels, J., & Korthagen, F. (2001). The relation between theory and practice: Back to the classics. In F. A. J. Korthagen (Ed.), *Linking practice and theory: The pedagogy of realistic teacher education* (pp. 20–31). Mahwah, NJ: Lawrence Erlbaum.

Kirk, S. A., & and Reid, W. J. (2002). *Science and social work: A critical appraisal*. New York: Columbia University Press.

Korthagen, F. (1999). Linking theory to practice: Changing the pedagogy of teacher education. *Educational Researcher*, 28(4), 4–17.

Lewis, H. (1982). *The intellectual base of social work practice: Tools for thought in a helping profession*. New York: The Haworth Press.

Lobkowicz, N. (1977). On the history of theory and praxis. In T. Ball (Ed.), *Political theory and praxis: New perspectives* (pp. 13–27). Minneapolis, MN: University of Minnesota Press.

Maclean, S., & Harrison, R. (2008). *Social work theory: A straightforward guide for practice assessors and placement supervisors*. Rugeley, UK: Kirwin Maclean Associates Ltd.

Mills, C. W. (1959). *The sociological imagination*. New York: Oxford University Press.

Mullen, C. A., Greenlee, B. J., & Bruner, D. Y. (2005). Exploring the theory-practice relationship in educational leadership curriculum through metaphor. *International Journal of Teaching and Learning in Higher Education*, 17(1), 1–14.

Richmond, M. (1897/1971). The training of charity workers. In A. Greer (Ed.), *Mary Richmond's the long view* (pp. 86–98). Dubuque, IA: Brown Reprints.

Segall, A. (2008). Why teaching critical social theory as "theory" might not be enough. In J. Diem & R. J. Helfenbein (Eds), *Unsettling beliefs: Teaching theory to teachers* (pp. 13–30). Charlotte, NC: Information Age Publishing.

Sheafor, B. W., & Horesji, C. R. (2008). *Techniques and guidelines for social work practice* (5th ed.). Boston, MA: Pearson/Allyn and Bacon.

Solomon, B. (2007). Taking "guilty knowledge" seriously: Theorizing, everyday inquiry, and action as "social caretaking." In S. L. Witkin & D. Saleeby (Eds), *Social work dialogues: Transforming the canon in inquiry, practice, and education* (pp. 94–112). Alexandria, VA: Council on Social Work Education.

Spong, S. (2007). Skepticism and belief: Unravelling the relationship between theory and practice in counselling and psychotherapy. In S. R. Smith (Ed.), *Applying theory to policy and practice: Issues for critical reflection* (pp. 55–70). Aldershot, UK: Ashgate.

Swedberg, R. (2010). From theory to theorizing. *Perspectives: Newsletter of the ASA Theory Section, 32*(2), 1, 8–9.

Swedberg, R. (2012). Theorizing in sociology and social science: Turning to the context of discovery. *Theory and Society, 41*, 1–40.

Thompson, N. (2000). *Theory and practice in human services.* Buckingham, UK: Open University Press.

Thompson, N. (2010). *Theorizing social work practice.* Basingstoke, UK: Palgrave Macmillan.

Walker, L. O., & Avant, K. C. (1995). *Strategies for theory construction in nursing* (3rd ed.). Norwalk, CT: Appleton.

Weick, K. E. (1989). Theory construction as disciplined imagination. *Academy of Management Review, 14*(1), 516–531.

Wilson, E. J. III (2000). How social science can help policymakers: The relevance of theory. In M. Nincic & J Lepgold (Eds), *Being useful: Policy relevance and international relations theory* (pp. 109–128). Ann Arbor, MI: The University of Michigan Press.

Zundel, M., & Kokkalis, P. (2010). Theorizing as engaged practice. *Organization Studies, 31*(09/10), 1209–1227.

<table>
<tr><td>SECTION

1</td><td># Theorizing basics</td></tr>
</table>

The lessons in Section 1 introduce the reader to the nature and importance of theorizing, the meanings of the term *theory*, and the major styles of theorizing, the basics of searching for, selecting, and differentially using theoretical knowledge for social work purposes, the major sources of knowledge, and the notion that theorizing differs by level of abstraction and theories may be suited to a specific system level.

LESSON	
1	# Identify and act as theorist engaged in theoretical thinking

(EPAS 2.1.1 Identify as a Professional Social Worker;
EPAS 2.1.3 Apply Critical Thinking;
EPAS 2.1.5 Engage in Research-Informed Practice;
EPAS 2.1.7 Apply Knowledge)

Theorizing is a process of making empirical observations and then constructing meaningful patterns that organize the acquired information in the form of a theoretical explanation, interpretation, or critique (Jorgensen, 1989). Those enacting the role of theorist show concern with theories, theorize to make sense of puzzling situations, share the products of their theorizing with others in the scientific or professional community, and become very familiar with the theories and research in the knowledge domain relevant to their profession. Social work theorists might theorize about complex aspects of their helping work by deconstructing and reconstructing useful scientific theories: theories of the client's cultural and social groups, theories to explain a focal individual or public problem, theories specifying the elements and processes of change, or theories articulating and justifying logically a particular program or intervention. Social work theorists might also make use of existing theories to better understand and cope with workplace challenges. For instance, systems theory might help a theorizing practitioner employed in an agency troubled by conflict and turmoil following the departure of a respected leader. Some social work theorists even theorize and construct their own middle-range theories to contribute to the professional archive of human behavior and practice theories.

Professional social work and the role of theorist

Training in generalist social work prepares novice social workers to enact responsibly and effectively many different helping roles. You are probably familiar with some of these roles: advocate, broker, counselor, case manager, educator, practice evaluator, mediator, and researcher. Advanced education and training equips social workers for specialty roles such as lobbyist, politician, program evaluator, or therapist. Why add the role of theorist to your repertoire of roles?

As a theorist, you will refine and develop your theoretical, research, and critical thinking skills. These are essential to all aspects of effective social work. As a theorist, you can access varied perspectives on human behavior and the environment, assorted theorizing techniques, and diverse scientific vocabularies. Such knowledge and tools will enhance your ability to serve many different clients, explain varied person-in-environment (PIE) challenges, and generate a list of creative intervention strategies. In the role of theorist, you will increase your insights into the positions of your colleagues on interdisciplinary and inter-professional teams and become better able to argue for your preferred approach to inquiry and action planning. Mastering the theorist role will improve your ability to understand and transform difficult and confusing situations in your professional and personal life. For some of you, learning the role of theorist will reflect your commitment to contribute knowledge to the social work profession. Benefits of such intellectual service include accolades added to your resume, financial support for travel to distant conferences, and the satisfaction of leaving a mark on social work history.

Several social work experts have made the case that social workers should incorporate the role of theorist into their identity as professionals. Brennan (1973) pioneered the idea of practitioner as "theoretician," arguing that skillful theorizing is

> recognized as aiding the social worker in focusing more systematically on essential factors or variables, in expanding the scope of his perspectives, in explaining underlying causal dynamics, in providing leads for practice strategies, and in formulating predictive statements about the probable outcomes of various treatment modalities. (p. 5)

Barsky (2010) suggested "the ability to apply specific theories to practice is one of the key ways that professional social workers differ from lay helpers (i.e. families, friends, peers, and others without professional education)" (pp. 30–31). Boisen and Syers (2004) made a similar point, "competent social work is grounded in the intentional use of theory. Practice informed by theory distinguishes professional social work from informal forms of helping" (p. 205). In this book, I am providing knowledge and resources to help you learn and become adept at enacting this vital, distinctive role.

Only a few social workers aspire to become famous theory creators. However, each social worker can attempt to develop theorizing competencies for the theorist role in some of the areas included in the 2008 Council on Social Work Education set of core competencies. Relevant competencies include using theories as tools for understanding persons and their behavior in environmental contexts (EPAS 2.1.7); judging the adequacy of theories for use under specific practice conditions by thinking critically (EPAS 2.1.3) and considering evidence (EPAS 2.1.5); using theories for guiding the planned change process (EPAS 2.1.10); and enhancing knowledge accumulation (at least at the agency and community level) by suggesting practice-informed theoretical reformulations and by alerting theory specialists to under-theorized client problems and practice challenges (EPAS 2.1.1).

Knowledge, skill, and attitudes for effective theorizing

In this section, I will present a profile of the components of the ideal theorist, the ingredients that will make effective theorizing possible. I will organize this presentation in terms of knowledge, skills, and attitudes.

Knowledge

The ideal social work theorist has a sound and general intellectual foundation for helping action including knowledge obtained from disciplines such as anthropology, biology, economics, history, philosophy, psychology, political science, sociology, and religion. This is the liberal arts base on which social work careers are built. Unifying this knowledge is the understanding of and commitment to science and to scientific, evidence-informed practice.

The ideal social work theorist acquires much specialized knowledge. This knowledge is specific to the social work profession. Students master the information presented in major curriculum areas including human behavior and the social environment, social policy, practice, and research. Students also learn the themes central to our profession such as a commitment to ethical practice, an appreciation for diversity, a dedication to the advancement of justice and the elimination of poverty, and an emphasis on the promotion of human strengths and community potentials. Social workers who enroll in graduate school or participate in advanced training after graduation will acquire knowledge that deepens their performance as theorists and refines their theorizing skills. Such specialized knowledge may relate to modality (casework, family therapy, group work, community organizing, and so on), field of practice (child welfare, aging, corrections, health, or others), helping role (therapist, advocate, researcher), client population (military veterans, the homeless, migrant workers, abused children), or theoretical perspective (cognitive-behavioral, feminist, or symbolic interactionism, for examples).

Scientific knowledge is central to professionalism. Wieck (1999) reminds us that scientific paradigms, theoretical traditions, theoretical models, and other forms of theoretical knowledge are the heavy gear carried by all theorists. However, he adds that the successful practitioner also remembers to carry and use survival gear beyond scientific knowledge including their life history, practice experiences, empathic inclinations, intuitive hunches, and capacities for attentive observation and listening. The ideal social worker draws on many ways of knowing when preparing to engage in competent theorizing.

Most important, the theorizing practitioner can demonstrate mastery of theoretical knowledge and theorizing skills in each phase of the planned change process. Theory can guide information gathering, assessment, intervention planning and the use of theory-guided, evidence-informed interventions, ending work, and effectiveness evaluation. Zetterberg (1962) offers a concise summary of this defining characteristic of the core capability of a competent theory-informed practitioner. He refers to the professional's ability to make "use of scientific knowledge in solving problems repeatedly encountered in his occupation" (p. 18).

Skills

The ideal social worker has developed the skills necessary for thinking theoretically. Practical theorizing requires *theoretical thinking*, the process of conceiving of ideas and reflecting on them in a way "serious in purpose, careful in reasoning, and cautious in reaching conclusions" (Lutz, 1992, p. 8). Theoretical thinking is similar to everyday thinking—Einstein wrote, "the whole of science is nothing more than a refinement of every day thinking" (1936, p. 349)—but the refinement means that theoretical thinking requires more skill and awareness than the thinking that helps us act daily in our roles (Sierpinska, 2005). Figure 1.1 summarizes these differences.

In everyday thinking, our thought processes help us understand what is going on in concrete reality and to act effectively. Thinking results in statements of fact and decisions about preferred courses of action. Practical

Everyday Thinking	Practical Theorizing
To act	To understand and reflect on action
Automatic or voluntary	Voluntary and purposeful
One level – thought and aim	Two levels – thought (concept use) and aim with critical/reflective reasoning about concept use
Guided by social meanings	Guided by scientific and social meanings
Immersed in experienced situation	Alternate distancing and immersion
Influences and changes events, objects, people	Influences and changes events, objects, people and theories
Judged by result of action	Judged by coherence, consistency and results of theorizing acts

Figure 1.1 From everyday thinking to practical theorizing

theorizing facilitates action—helping actions, for instance—but also involves the effort to reflect on and understand our actions in an orderly way. Practical theorizing also includes the acquisition of conceptual frameworks (theories) that transcend specific situations and help us solve a range of similar problems. Practical theorizing results in hypotheses and other theoretical tools.

Much daily action occurs with minimal or automatic thinking; our routines and habits enable us to cope with ordinary life tasks. Cooking a meal or driving the car to work can be mindless activities. Practical theorizing is most useful when customary action patterns fail. It requires an act of volition (I must choose to theorize about an obstacle that emerges as I help a difficult member of a family system, for example) and practical theorizing is purposeful (I theorize to describe, categorize, explain, predict, or change some aspect of the "family–interacting-in-an-environment" configuration).

In everyday thinking, thought and aim are on the same level. For instance, I think to figure out how to respond best to a recall notice from the Toyota car manufacturer. Practical theorizing occurs at two levels. I might use concepts to make sense of an odd interaction between family members convened for a helping session. This is the first level, but I also reflect critically on the quality of my reasoning and I consider evidence about the effectiveness of my concept use. This is the second level and adds to everyday thinking a concern with devising better tools for thinking.

Everyday thinking is guided by meanings shared by societal members. Americans have similar understandings of a "defective car part recall notice." Practical theorizing is guided by common and shared social meanings but also by the scientific meanings specific to the relevant disciplinary, professional, or theoretical community. Think of the varied family systems concepts with their technical meanings that I might bring to bear when working as a family social worker. Moreover, practical theorizing uses concepts that have meaning within a specific thought system or network of concepts, a theory.

During everyday thinking, the person is immersed in the experienced situation. The stream of thought is one aspect of a holistic transaction with the environment: my fairly effortless call to the Toyota dealer to obtain clarification regarding the recall process. Practical theorizing requires intentional shifting back and forth between immersion in the situation and distance from the situation. I meet with the family for a session. I step away and confer with my supervisor after the meeting to think about the helping work, identify areas for improvement, and plan for the next session. Then, I join with the family again at the next family conference.

We think everyday in ways that enable us to influence the events, objects, people, and matters that are important to us. After brief mental preparation, I contacted my Toyota representative, learned of the required steps, and scheduled an appointment to replace my airbag assembly. In practical theorizing, I also use my thinking skills to influence the events, objects, people, and matters that are part of a clientele and agency context.

However, I am trying additionally to change and reconstruct theory, the family systems approach in this extended example, so it fits with the needs and characteristics of the family. I think, too, during episodes of practical theorizing about evidence and other feedback from the helping experiences so I can improve the theory for future use.

Finally, everyday thinkers use a pragmatic standard to judge the quality of their thinking. Did it help me achieve desired results? Is my 2003 Toyota Corolla now safe to drive? Practical theorizers consider pragmatic results: Have the theory and thinking about the theory been useful in achieving planned outcomes? In addition, practical theorizers use scientific and professional norms to judge theory use. Did all the elements of my applied family systems theory fit together coherently? Were the theory and my thinking about it consistent with social work values and ethical standards? Did I deconstruct and reconstruct the theory in ways consistent with evidence and valid scientific methodology?

In summary, I argue that practical theorizing involves learning and using many different "theoretical thinking" skills. In the preface, I identified 21 core theorizing skills and eight advanced theorizing skills. During the process of professional socialization, social workers acquire interviewing skills, policy advocacy skills, problem-solving skills, and skills for resolving ethical dilemmas. I am advocating for the inclusion of training in theorizing skills. Mastery of the many theorizing skills will prepare the practitioner to enact adeptly the theorist role and expand significantly his or her toolbox. For example, the work theorist can pull out the "tools of theorizing" necessary to a particular job such as searching for empirically supported theories, examining theoretical assumptions, naming and conceptualizing events, reasoning deductively, classifying human troubles, building and diagramming theoretical models, and thinking critically. The more theorizing skills or tools available, the more likely that the practitioner will consistently choose the suitable tool and act in an intelligent and effective way. Theoretical skills will also enhance the capability of practitioners for making connections. These include connections between theory and practice, classroom and field, scientific knowledge and practice wisdom, formal knowledge and personal knowledge, facts and values, concepts and their theoretical frameworks and between textbook knowledge and theoretical insights derived from immersion in practice situations.

Attitudes (habitual dispositions)

Donald Schön (1995), a renowned innovator in theory application, used the concept intelligence-in-action to refer to a key ingredient in the cluster of attitudes and habits associated with ideal theorists. He argued that social work practice is more than applying academic knowledge to achieve a clear end in a practice setting. Real-world practice problems are complex, messy, poorly defined, and often unique. In many situations, social workers can't ponder at length the best theory- or research-derived course of helping action but must act quickly with familiar or implicit theories guiding their action. Sometimes such actions result in satisfactory solutions. Sometimes we are surprised and need to inquire further into failed or blocked helping efforts. Continual reflection after encountering an obstacle on the theoretical assumptions, theoretical concepts, and theoretical frameworks that influenced our responses will be rewarded by growth in professional intelligence. There are a variety of specific attitudes or habitual dispositions that build this capacity for intelligence-in-action.

Critical thinking

Practical theorizing can become increasingly intelligent and successful when supported by habits of critical thinking. *Critical thinking* is the art of analyzing and evaluating thinking with a view to improving it (The Foundation for Critical Thinking, 2013). Social work theorists can think in a logical and disciplined way. They use careful and systematic reasoning processes when selecting and applying theoretical perspectives. They ask good questions about theories and the degree to which theories meet scientific, pragmatic, and professional standards. They are intellectually flexible rather than rigid and try new theoretical directions when a dead-end looms. They are open-minded and consider alternative theoretical schools of thoughts while enriching their appreciation of preferred theories by comparing and contrasting alternative theoretical perspectives on a helping process (Connolly, 1973; Payne, 2002). Critical thinkers also seek and use feedback from peers and supervisors and accumulated evidence to refine their theoretical orientation and to enhance their theorizing competencies.

Perspectivism

Among theory users, open-mindedness is an important attitude to cultivate: one also referred to as perspectivism (Seigfried, 1996). Adopting this stance, the practitioner acknowledges that there are many possible ways to understand or frame a practice situation or challenge. Any theoretical perspective or frame is often radically different from another perspective. Each perspective will direct inquiry and helping action differently than other perspectives. The intelligent social worker cultivates habits of flexibility when considering conceptualizations of the "person interacting in an environment with a problem" and habits of perspective shifting so he or she can alternate theoretical perspectives using multiple perspectives to enrich the conceptualization of engagement, information gathering, intervention planning, and other phases of the planned change process.

Theoretical self-consciousness

Habits of continual reflection guide the intelligent social worker when collaborating with team members, clients, and members of other professions. Such reflection fosters *theoretical self-consciousness* (Connolly, 1973). This is the awareness of our theoretical assumptions and concepts including their relationship to our professional actions and interventions. Irving (1995) recommends, for example, that we use processes of critical reflection to continually monitor the effectiveness and morality of our practice by questioning our theory use and, when necessary, modifying our assumptions, concepts, propositions, and models to improve our action patterns. He suggests a multi-step cycle of self-investigation. Why did I do that? What outcome did I hope to accomplish? What theoretical beliefs and concepts were operative? What changes are needed in my theoretical assumptions or theory guided practice behaviors to achieve better results?

Theoretical sensitivity

Habits of critical thinking and reflection supported by a solid knowledge base can also foster *theoretical sensitivity* (Strauss & Corbin, 1990). Such sensitivity refers to the capability of the social worker to give insightful meaning to the information acquired about a client system and the challenges it faces. The theoretically sensitive worker can separate information that is pertinent from information that is tangential, and she or he can make sense of the case information using theories and their theoretical concepts rather than everyday terms. Theoretically sensitive practitioners are attuned to the likely relationships between concepts used to understand the case. Theory-informed assessment and intervention hypotheses emerge readily. Theoretical sensitivity also makes possible the development of grounded, rich, and integrated theory about the focal challenge, concern, or problem.

Scholarship

Helping action can become increasingly intelligent and successful when supported by habits of *scholarship*, the continual study of the theories and research studies important in our field of practice. Social work theorists view themselves as part of a larger community of inquiry and make a commitment to life-long learning as members of this group of people. Scholarly knowledge is sought from books, journals, conferences, participation in associations, meeting with supervisors, and websites. However, such knowledge isn't used as revelations of truth about clients, environments, and helping processes but as provisional hypotheses for conceptualizing and changing troublesome person-in-environment configurations.

Ideally, social workers expect a two-way exchange with knowledge production specialists, too, and contribute their scholarship to the community of inquiry. They communicate theoretical discoveries, experiences applying theories, and tests of theory using vehicles such as published articles, workshop presentations, and conversations with colleagues. Scholarly practitioners recognize that the sciences are essential to social work practice. However, social work practice, applied science, also has much to offer back to "the ivory tower" and to laboratory scientists and theory builders employed by universities and research centers.

Scientific inquiry

Helping action can become increasingly intelligent and successful when habits of scientific inquiry or evidence-informed practice are internalized. These include the search for scientific knowledge and protocols to support information gathering, assessment, and intervention processes; the treatment of theoretical propositions and practice directives as hypotheses that must be tested; and the use of single-system design or other evaluation methods harmonious with one's theoretical orientation to appraise effectiveness. Social work theorists are curious like scientists and seek answers to what, why, how, and when questions about social work practice situations. We seek these answers because they will be useful as we try to better understand and help clients accountably and because the answers increase our grasp of complex person-in-environment configurations. Scientific theorists like scientist-researchers monitor their theoretical biases and minimize the influence of unexplored prejudices and preferences.

Reflection

Let's expand on Schön's (1995) proposal that helping action becomes more intelligent and successful when supported by habits of reflection. This is a very important ingredient of practical theorizing, so I will elaborate on this habit. Pedro (2005) defines reflection as "the act of active, persistent, and careful consideration of any belief or supposed form of knowledge in the light of grounds that support it, and the consequence to which it leads" (p. 50). Acknowledging Schön's influential work on reflective professionalism, Pedro adds that reflection involves "a purposeful, systematic inquiry into practice" (p. 51). Habits of reflection are useful at four points in time.

First, before entering the helping situation, the reflective practitioner asks himself or herself: what evidence-supported theories and interventions might be most suitable and most useful with this client system dealing with facing this challenge in this environmental situation?

Second, during the helping process, the reflective practitioner asks what is going on in this helping situation and how well are my theoretical frameworks guiding the helping work? Using reflection-in-action, the social worker can adjust with client input his or her theory-informed helping actions quickly, adapt borrowed theory-based strategies, or try out new theory-based strategies and thus, increase the likelihood of positive outcomes.

Third, theoretical reflection requires a scan of the future and thoughtful planning in anticipation of likely events: obstacles or opportunities. For instance, the practitioner might consider with the help of a colleague, supervisor, or client how to use a theory or set of theories better in the next similar circumstances.

Finally, the reflective practitioner should reflect after the helping session and ask questions such as what worked and why? What didn't work and why? How satisfied was the client with the theory application process? How might I use theories differently next time? Such reflection-on-action is essential to professional growth in our ability to analyze (deconstruct) and use (reconstruct) theories (Payne, 2002; Schön, 1995).

Reflection-on-action can also be used in response to specific questions that emerge during practice work (Grimmett, 1990). Social workers may decide to apply an existing theory or theoretical concept and reflect on possible answers to the question, How do I best use this knowledge to direct my practice? Social workers often deliberate about the possible consequences of alternative theory-based courses of action. Reflection coupled with a review of the relevant research literature can help answer the question, Which theory-informed helping action or actions is likely to contribute to the desired improvements in the client situation? After setbacks, practitioners may need to redesign the helping process and better understand puzzling aspects of the helping situation: the problem definition, the helper role, or the assumptions about directed change. Reflection will assist as the worker searches for answers to the question, How can I approach the next encounter more effectively and more creatively by changing my theory-influenced constructions of problem, role, and change?

Theoretical reflections is especially helpful, Argyris and Schön (1974) suggest, when the practitioner wants to examine the fit between her or his espoused theory, the theory we identify verbally when questioned by others as guiding our actions, and our theory-in-use, the theory that is implicit in our helping work and actually governs how we perceive, appraise, and act during the helping process. We may need to work hard to put this second kind of theory into words. Supervisors can also guide practitioners in reflection of this kind.

Habits of reflection become fortified when a social worker has a genuine interest in understanding the helping process and cultivates an awareness of how theoretical knowledge can effectively enhance this process (Ross, 1992). Additionally, social workers are more likely to become skillful and habitual reflectors when they participate in a community of colleagues, supervisors, workshop participants, and others who provide opportunities for dialogue, discussion, and debate about theories and their effective, responsible use (Papell & Skolnik, 1992).

Theoretical creativity

Finally, intelligent and successful helping action depends on habits of theoretical creativity. Every helping situation is unique in some way. The helping process occurs in a particular time and ecological setting with a certain set of actors. The distinctive and complex quality of each helping act calls for imagination and innovation. Theories don't provide recipes or rules that can be followed precisely and guarantee the production of a predicted Julia Child's-style dinner. Theories provide guidelines. Real-life helping situations present many surprises, unexpected events, and uncertain or hard-to-interpret experiences. Creativity in the forms of imagination, intuition, divergent thought, brainstorming power, and inspiration makes possible the artistry that compliments or modifies the use of scientific theories.

Concluding comments on the theorist role

There are many different phrases used to capture diverse conceptions of the ideal social work practitioner (Rodolfa, Steward, Kaslow, & Keilin (2005). These include terms such as the scientific practitioner, the reflective practitioner, the scholarly practitioner, and the creative practitioner. In my view, the ideal social worker is too rarely considered a theorizing practitioner, a professional who incorporates the role of theorist into his or her set of professional roles and cultivates the knowledge, skills, and habits that make critical, reflective, scholarly, scientific, and creative theory deconstruction and reconstruction possible.

Munson (1983) offers a useful list of suggestions for becoming a first rate theorizing practitioner. I will conclude the commentary for this lesson with Table 1.1, my formulation of his recommendations.

Learning activities and reflections

1   Many people become a social worker because they have strong impulses to help others and a vision of a caring and fair society. This vision often includes images and ideas about how a social worker might contribute to personal and collective well being. Think about and summarize your conception of the ideal social worker.

Use the knowledge-skills-attitudes framework common to social work education. What knowledge does the ideal social worker possess? What skills have been mastered by the ideal social worker? What attitudes have become part of the professional self and personality of the ideal social worker? Refine your profile based on your observations of a social worker that you know and admire.

2   Summarize your thoughts on the characteristics of the ideal social worker in regard to theorizing and theory application, the use of knowledge for understanding and for guiding practice? What theorizing

Table 1.1 Suggestions for becoming a critical and reflective "theorizing practitioner"

Reflect continuously on the congruence between your espoused theory and your theory-in-use

Reflect often on how your choice of a theoretical orientation organizes your information gathering and assessment perceptions and activities.

Focus theoretical reflection and speculation on pressing practice problems (what did you do and why?) not on abstract issues unrelated to your field of practice.

Consider issues of the best timing for theoretical reflections and issues related to the amount of new theoretical material that you are ready to master.

If you are a novice theory user, begin with reflections on your theorizing efforts before and after helping sessions rather than with the more challenging theory reflection during the helping process.

Search for opportunities to make connections between theoretical knowledge, research evidence, and experiential material and to translate difficult theoretical concepts and propositions for practical use.

Alternate your study and discussion of theory knowledge outside the helping context with examination of how your professional actions in the therapy session, meeting room, or advocacy arena are influenced by theories.

Practice the uses of theorizing related to describing, explaining, predicting, critiquing, intervening, and evaluating.

Learn to articulate and communicate your theoretical orientation and how you use it in specific helping situations to clients, colleagues, and supervisors.

Seek and imitate role models who are masters of theoretical knowledge and expert theorizers.

Practice the application of theory-based concepts to practice situations especially the pairing of two theory-based concepts by asking questions like how does concept A relate to concept B for this client system?

Share periodically with your supervisor information about what theoretical frameworks and theorizing skills you have mastered and what frameworks and skills you are exploring.

competencies, theorizing behaviors, and theorizing skills should a social worker demonstrate? What theories and other theoretical content can the practitioner apply to practice? How you can enhance your own progress to realization of this ideal?

3   Social work experts and other commentators often use metaphors related to body parts to characterize social workers. The ideal social worker has a special heart with attributes such as empathy, compassion, caring, and sympathy. The ideal social worker makes special use of his or her hands. This may be to lift up those who are struggling, to pat a grieving person on the shoulder, or to lend a hand in community projects and so on. Expand on imagery and symbolism associated with the head of the

ideal social worker. What adjectives might you use to describe the head? What images might best illustrate the social worker's use of his or her head? What comparisons might you make between engaging in effective social work and mental activities related to the head?

4   Take a life course perspective. Are there optimal stages or seasons for theory and theorizing mastery? At what point in the career should a practitioner attempt to acquire the knowledge, skills, and attitudes/ habits described in this commentary? When might it be too early for mastery? When might it be too late? Imagine that you are at your retirement celebration. Review for the assembled group some of your accomplishments in the areas of theory use, theory development, and teaching theory.

References

Argyris, M., & Schön, D. (1974). *Theory in practice: Increasing professional effectiveness*. San Francisco, CA: Jossey-Bass.

Barsky, A. E. (2010). *Ethics and values in social work: An integrated approach for a comprehensive curriculum*. New York: Oxford University Press.

Boisen, L., & Syers, M. (2004). The integrative case analysis model for linking theory and practice. *Journal of Social Work Education*, 40(2), 205–217.

Brennan, W. C. (1973). The practitioner as theoretician. *Journal of Education for Social Work*, 9(2), 5–12.

Connolly, W. E. (1973). Theoretical self-consciousness. *Polity*, 6(1), 5–35.

Einstein, A. (1936). Physics and reality. *Journal of the Franklin Institute*, 221(3), 349–382.

Foundation for Critical Thinking. (2013). Critical thinking: Where to begin. Retrieved July 17, 2013, from www.criticalthinking.org/pages/critical-thinking-where-to-begin/796

Grimmett, P. P. (1990). The nature of reflection and Schön's conception in perspective. In R. T. Clift, W. R. Houston, & M. C, Pugach (Eds), *Encouraging reflective practice in education: An analysis of issues and programs* (pp. 5–15). New York: Teachers College Press.

Irving, J. A. (1995). Critical thinking and reflective practice in counseling. *British Journal of Guidance and Counselling*, 23(1), 107–114.

Jorgensen, D. L. (1989). *Participant observation: A methodology for human studies*. Newbury Park, CA: Sage.

Lutz, D. S. (1992). *A preface to American political theory*. Lawrence, KS: University Press of Kansas.

Munson, C. E. (1983). *An introduction to clinical social work supervision*. New York: Haworth Press.

Papell, C. P., & Skolnik, L. (1992). The reflective practitioner: A contemporary paradigm's relevance for social work action. *Journal of Social Work Education*, 28(1), 18–26.

Payne, M. (2002). Social work theories and reflective practice. In R. Adams, L. Dominelli, & M. Payne (Eds), *Social work: Themes, issues and critical debates* (pp. 123–138). Basingstoke, UK: Palgrave.

Pedro, J. Y. (2005). Reflection in teacher education: Exploring pre-service teachers' meanings of reflective practice. *Reflective Practice*, 6(1), 49–66.

Rodolfa, E. R., Steward, A. E., Kaslow, N. J., & Keilin, W. G. (2005). Internship training: Do models really matter? *Professional Psychology: Research and Practice*, 36(1), 25–31.

Ross, E. W. (1992). Teaching personal theorizing and reflective practice in teacher education. In E. W. Ross, J. W. Cornett, & G. McCutheon (Eds), *Teacher personal theorizing: Connecting curriculum, practice, theory, and research* (pp. 179–190). Albany, NY: State University of New York Press.

Schön, D. A. (1995). Reflective inquiry in social work practice. In P. McCartt Hess & E. J. Mullen (Eds), *Practitioner-researcher partnerships: Building knowledge from, in, and for practice* (pp. 31–55). Washington, DC: National Association of Social Workers Press.

Seigfried, C. H. (1996). *Pragmatism and feminism: Reweaving the social fabric.* Chicago: The University of Chicago Press.

Sierpinska, A. (2005). On practical and theoretical thinking and other false dichotomies in mathematics education. In M. Hoffmann, J. Lenhard, and F. Seeger (Eds), *Activity and sign—Grounding mathematics education* (pp. 117–136), Dortrecht, The Netherlands: Kluwer Academic Publishers.

Strauss, A., & Corbin, J. (1990). *Basics of qualitative research: Grounded theory procedures and techniques.* Newbury Park, CA: Sage.

Weick, K. E. (1999). Theory construction as disciplined reflexivity: Tradeoffs in the 90s. *Academy of Management Review*, 24(7), 797–806.

Zetterberg, H. I. (1962). *Social theory and social practice.* New York: The Bedminster Press.

<table>
<tr><td>LESSON
2</td><td># Identify and use purposefully different styles of theorizing</td></tr>
</table>

(EPAS 2.1.5 Engage in Research-Informed Practice; EPAS 2.1.7 Apply Knowledge)

As professionals, social workers use various forms of knowledge to guide work with people and social systems. *Research*, the systematic investigation of human behavior and practice effectiveness, provides empirical findings about personal and social problems, assessment and intervention tools, and the quality of theories. *Practice wisdom*, the accumulated and organized lessons about what works to help clients, also directs our understanding and action as professionals. Theoretical knowledge is a third important informational resource. *Theoretical knowledge* involves theory development, the accumulation of theories, and the refinement of these theories.

The meaning of "theory"

The term *theory* and its variants have origins in ancient Greece. The term probably referred to actions conducted by spectators such as gazing on, viewing, and contemplating. Astronomy, for example, the observation and study of stars and their movements, was an activity associated with theory (Craig, 2001).

What theory is

There are many different meanings of the term theory (Abend, 2008). Table 2.1 identifies fifteen different definitions. These terms vary in length, complexity, and philosophy of science assumptions. Social workers need to appreciate that the meaning for the term *theory* is variable. Its use and definition will differ depending on the affiliations of the theorizer, the situation, the purpose for its use, and many other factors. To give us a common reference point, however, I will provide a working definition of theory adapted from the conceptualization of two prominent research textbook writers. A theory is a systematic set of interrelated statements intended to explain some aspect of "person interacting in the environment" configurations, to deepen our understanding of how people find meaning and conduct their daily lives, or to challenge oppressors and empower the members of oppressed groups (Rubin & Babbie, 2008).

Table 2.1   A selective list of definitions of theory

1	"A creative and rigorous structuring of ideas that projects a tentative, purposeful, and systematic view of phenomena" (Chinn & Kramer, 2008, p. 182).
2	"A hunch or a set of untested ideas" (Weis, 1998, p. 2).
3	"A scientific theory is a concise and coherent set of concepts, claims, and laws (frequently expressed mathematically) that can be used to precisely and accurately explain and predict natural phenomena" (Ben-Ari, 2005, p. 24).
4	"A system of concepts that aims to give a global explanation to an area of knowledge" (de Man, 1986, p. xiii).
5	"a systematic way of understanding events, phenomena, and situations. Theory includes a range of explanatory and predictive propositions, such as models, perspectives, and frameworks, and should be applicable to a broad range of situations" (McCracken & Rzepnicki, 2010, p. 211).
6	"A theory consists of one or more functional statements or propositions that treat the relationship of variables so as to account for a phenomena or a set of phenomena" (Hollander, 1967, p. 55).
7	"A theory consists of interrelated propositions that say something general about relations and processes in social reality" (Rueschemeyer, 2009. p. 6).
8	"A theory is a picture, mentally formed, of a bounded realm or domain of activity. A theory is a description of the organization of a domain and the connection among its parts" (Waltz, 1979, p. 8).
9	"A theory is a symbolic construction" (Kaplan, 1964, p. 296).
10	"A transformative activity that views itself as explicitly political and commits itself to the projection of a future that is as yet unfulfilled" (Giroux, 1983, p. 19).
11	"Conceptual system designed to be useful in identifying, organizing, explaining, or predicting some delimited portion of the experienced world" (Jaccard & Jaccoby, 2010, p. 15).
12	"An imaginative grouping of knowledge, ideas and experiences that are represented symbolically and seek to illuminate a given phenomenon" (Watson, 1988, p. 1).
13	Social theory contains an epistemology, a theory of knowledge answering the question of how we know what we know; an ontology, a theory of what reality consists of; a historical location and the influences of the particular place and time on the theory; and a set of prescriptions, directives to the reader on how to behave in everyday life (Best, 2003, paraphrase).
14	"Theories can be regarded as being essentially statements identifying factors that are likely to produce particular results under specified conditions" (Hochbaum, Sorenson, & Lorig, 1992).
15	Theory "refers to a logically interconnected sets of propositions from which empirical uniformities can be derived" (Merton, 1967, p. 39).

What theory isn't

Sutton and Shaw (1995) identify inappropriate uses of the term. Theory is not a list of references at the end of a paper or textbook pointing to existing theory or to theory classics. Theory is not a set of data collected by a researcher to describe an empirical pattern. Theory is not an inventory of variables with their definitions. Theory is not a diagram or other visual display lacking any accompanying verbal elaboration (although a display may be used to help communicate information about a theory). A theory is not a stand-alone hypothesis or a group of hypotheses predicting a specific empirical relationship or a number of relationships. A well-developed theory is more than references, data, variables, diagrams, and hypotheses. Adding to their list, we note that theory is not an ideology, a system of beliefs serving the particular interests of a political group at a particular time—a system resistant to alteration by evidence or reasonable argument (Lutz, 1992).

Terms associated with theory

Current vocabulary includes terms such as *theory, abstract theory, deductive theory, everyday theory, formal theory, grand theory, inductive theory, informal theory, lay theory, meta-theory, middle-range theory, practical theory, practice theory,* and *social theory.* Applied social scientists also use theory as an adjective in phrases such as theoretical approach, theoretical framework, theoretical orientation, theoretical paradigm, theoretical perspective, theoretical school, and theoretical tradition. We will learn about many of these terms in other lessons. In this section, I will attempt to make some important distinctions and clarify the meanings of some of these terms.

Informal and formal theory

A distinction between informal and formal theory is useful (Beder, 2000; Munson, 1983). *Informal theories* are referred to as folk theories, everyday theories, lay theories, implicit theories, and personal belief systems. People use informal theories as tentative answers to perplexing events or circumstances, sometimes with minimal awareness that they are theorizing. Such theories help people make sense of why things happen, how things work, and what follows what in a sequence. A son might develop an informal explanatory theory to explain his grandmother's sudden grouchiness; it's because of health problems or financial pressures or hassles with a neighbor. Societies make available numerous informal theories. Some people create their own odd and idiosyncratic theories. Generally, however, people don't test their informal theories with experimental methods, write about them in journals, or give them fancy names.

Scientists create *formal theories*, theories developed and tested with reference to the methods and standards of science. Generally, formal theories are stated in words or mathematical formulas following the conventions of a discipline. Efforts are made to communicate explicitly about the assumptions, concepts and definitions, propositions, and linkages of propositions in the theory and also the rationale and evidence supporting the choice of these elements and the overall structure. Formal theories are shared with and critiqued by members of the scientific community. Social workers learn major formal theories from the biological and social sciences. These add to our scientific knowledge. Social workers also need to respect and inquire about the informal theories important to their clients.

Empirical theory and normative theory

Theories vary in their relationship to "what is" (McCool, 1995; Rosenau, 1980). An *empirical theory* provides a systematic conceptualization of things as they are if and when they are subjected to human observation. The theorist works hard to think about and characterize patterns and processes that actually exist. Advocates of the evidence-informed practice movement promote the development of empirically supported theories. Section 2 presents lessons for reconstructing existing theories in line with the practitioner's empirical observations.

Normative theory, in contrast, provides a conceptualization of preferences, what ought to be. In a normative theory of justice, for example, the theorist speculates about and argues for the particular kind of society with the particular patterns of resource distribution that could be created assuming the power to manipulate the relevant variables. The ethical practice of social work requires familiarity with the major normative theories of ethics including utilitarianism, deontology, and virtue-based ethics. Section 4 of this book will present a set of lessons for using normative theories and the normative standards endorsed by the social work profession to critically appraise theories.

Explanatory theory and practice theory

There is another important distinction. A theory of human behavior or explanatory theory is differentiated from a practice theory. *Explanatory theory* focuses on "why questions" and assists practitioners as they attempt to understand human behavior, environmental contexts, transactions, cultural backgrounds, and life challenges. *Practice theory* focuses on "how questions" providing guidance to social workers as they work to understand and help clients and client systems. These two types of theory will be contrasted and discussed in Lesson 8.

Scientific theory, schools of thought, metatheory

Scientific theory is a theoretical system supported by a significant degree of evidence that makes sense of some aspect of the natural world. Such theory can refer to the products of the classic scientists and theorists, those intellectual works of theorists from many disciplines such as sociology (Talcott Parsons or Erving Goffman), psychology (Sigmund Freud, John Watson, or Jean Piaget), biology (Gregor Mendel or Charles Darwin), economics (Adam Smith or John Maynard Keynes), and so on. Using theory in this sense assumes familiarity with the schools of thought founded by great theorists such as the Psychodynamic School created by Freud and familiarity with the important advances in the theoretical tradition.

A *school of thought* includes a group of theorists who identify themselves as members of the tradition and who are united by their recognition of the special leader or founder and the distinctive intellectual stance and theorizing inspired by this leader. Adherents to a particular school of thought, Marxism, for instance, study, analyze, criticize, and make use of the school's theories as recorded in classic textbooks, essays, and studies.

Some theories are called *substantive* theories. A substantive theory focuses on a particular topic or substance important to the theorist and others (Layder, 1998). For example, there are substantive theories of drug addiction, juvenile delinquency, mental illness, and many other public problems.

Metatheory is another associated concept. Some theory specialists compare and contrast the assumptions, concepts, strengths, and limitations of different schools of thought. The focus of these theorists is the creation of a very abstract and overarching theory or framework that organizes a set of theories. This is often called the *meta-theoretical approach* to defining theory. Lesson 5 will discuss in more detail the meanings of theory at different levels of abstraction.

Major styles of theorizing

As we have learned, there are many definitions of theory. There are also a variety of approaches to theorizing. In this section, I will profile briefly three major styles of theorizing relating each to its typical research and validation strategies. These are the positivist approach, the interpretive approach, and the critical approach. Each differs by purpose, conception of theory, method of theorizing, type of evidence and theory validation, and overall language.

The positivist approach

This style of theorizing is called the positivist approach, the logical positivist approach, the quantitative approach, or more recently, the post-positivist approach to defining theory.

Purpose

Positivist theorizers aim to create or test formal theory. Theory is used to explain real aspects of human behavior and the social environment: the psychological causes of impulses and decisions to join social movements, the influences on the quality of attachments between a child and mother, or the dynamics of an economic exchange between a tenant and a landlord. Theorizing in this style discovers and identifies the causes, factors, or conditions critical to explaining the specific biological, psychological, social, or spiritual phenomenon of interest to the worker.

Definition

Positive theorizers consider theory to be a set of concepts, the interrelated set of propositions built from these concepts, the formal linkages of these propositions, and the explicit and sometimes mathematical statement of the relationship of these elements in a larger conceptual structure. Theories are like mirrors of reality, and the best theory identifies accurately the correspondence between concepts and observable realities.

Method

Positive theorizers seek sound theoretical knowledge by conducting or supporting rigorous experimentation that organizes the unbiased observation of empirical events, processes, or conditions (Wysienska & Szmatka, 2002). Scientific theory is designed so that its elements can be converted into testable forms (variables with operational definitions and hypotheses). The formulation of clear, precise and operationally defined concepts is highly valued, and these definitions are appraised for validity, reliability, and cultural sensitivity. Reasoning is generally deductive. The theorist starts with a general statement (powerful persons show less motivation to take the roles of and empathize with their less powerful counterparts), deduces a specific hypothesis (25 social work educators at the Harriet Tubman School of Social Work will show less role taking motivation than their 125 students as measured by the Long Perspective Taking Observational Checklist), and tests the hypothesis in specific circumstances. Theory validation occurs as a process of logical, objective, and value-free scientific inquiry. Issues of design validity and of the generalizability of theory-derived depictions of regularities in causal patterns or universal human behavior in the social environment mechanisms are very important.

Evidence

Positive theorizers seek empirical evidence supporting theoretical claims. Results are obtained using statistical procedures, and ideas about probability are used to determine the degree of support for theoretical hypotheses.

Knowledge accumulates thanks to empirical evidence especially when there have been repeated successful replications of studies supporting theoretical claims (Weis, 1998). For positive theorizing, science provides objective knowledge of the events and systems and their relationships common in the real world. Theorists align with researchers and contribute empirical generalizations and scientific laws, statements that apply across time periods and ecological settings to the knowledge base.

Language

Positivist theorizing uses the language of variables and mathematical symbols. Terms such as cause, correspondence with reality, deduction, experiment, explanation, evidence, operationalization, objective reality, reliability, rigor, and validity (design validity and measurement validity) are common to this approach. Positivist knowledge is presented generally in the vocabularies of causal, explanatory statements and middle-range theory (Fay, 1975).

The interpretive approach

This is often called the interpretive approach to theorizing. This slant on theory or theorizing is also called the discursive approach, the qualitative approach, or the grounded theory approach.

Purpose

Interpretive theorizing is a quest for understanding, for "grasping how people in life give meaning to their actions and the social world around them" (Pozzuto, 2007, p. 69). Theorizers aim for *verstehen*, the identification of the meanings and intentions that actors have in relation to particular cultural objects? (Fay, 1975).

Definition

Theory is an articulated and communicated representation of the processes or themes central to members of a specific group or community (Meleis, 1985). It is like a story or text—one constructed by the theorist in collaboration with the members using the words and other symbols significant to the membership group (Pozzuto, 2007). The theoretical story makes sense of how members interact meaningfully in particular environments or across specific phases of the life span. Theory is a way of seeing and comprehending these social constructions. Here, the theorist doesn't seek answers to the question, "What independent variable, x, causes the dependent variable, y?" as positivist theorists do. Instead, the theory is a way to interpret the conduct of group member, and interpretive theorizers start with questions such as "What is the meaning of this pattern of interaction?" and "What do these words, objects, gestures, and actions symbolize to the actors?" The questions are then tailored to the specific theoretical/research project. What meanings do Mexican American gang members on the Eastern Shore of Maryland attach to their preferred tattoos, headgear, and colors, for example? What are the steps by which novice baseball players gain acceptance among their peers as competent Little Leaguers in the Fruitland baseball system? Theories are interpretations of conduct in a social world made from the perspective of the theorizer (Turnbull, 2002).

Method

Interpretive theorizers generally prefer an inductive process of theoretical reasoning. They collect or consider an extensive amount of data that is close to the ground (the natural settings where people live and act) and carefully seek patterns eventually formulating a theory. Interpretive theorizing is supported by a diversity of research strategies. These include participant observation, ethnography, face-to-face interviews, focus groups, and life histories, but each method requires the theorist/researcher to immerse her- or himself in the lived experiences of the group studied. Interpretive theorizers don't prioritize objectivity but assume that much can be learned about life by considering the theorizer's subjective responses. The theorist is not a spectator but an active participant in the social world of the gang members, or the young athletes, or the homeless families. Additionally, interpretive theorizers are wary of claims that theorizing and research can be value-free and independent of historical and cultural influences.

Once an interpretive theory is created, it clues in the theorist and theory users to the standpoints and stories that group and cultural members might share about their own experiences. In a sense, the theory creates a new reality. Kaplan (1964) captures the flavor of this approach with his statement, "A theory must somehow fit God's world, but in an important sense it creates a world of its own" (p. 309). Social work field interns often engage in interpretive theorizing. For example, students who start field placements in a medical hospital must learn a new and complex culture and system of meanings. They observe, listen, ask questions, and try out interpretations until they start to make sense of the biomedical language, a language with an immense vocabulary, unique shorthand, and a set of other distinctive symbols. They become more and more adept also in describing and predicting the ways members of the setting—doctors, nurses, aids, patients—make use of the symbol system.

Evidence

Interpretive theorizers construct specific, situational, and time-bound theoretical understandings and are cautious about making generalizations that claim context-free explanatory power. The theorizers check on the quality of these understandings not by statistical procedure but by member validation. Is their evidence that the gang members, baseball players, or hospital personnel consider the theoretical narrative to include credible, relevant, salient, and useful representations of the group's symbols and social processes? Interpretive theorizers argue that the possibilities for extending scientific generalizations are limited. Knowledge is tied to location and historical period.

Language

Interpretive theorizers make a distinction between scientific language, the language for communicating with other social workers and professionals about clients, challenges and problems, and helping dynamics and member language. An interpretive theory may include some scientific and technical terms, but it will also include the words, phrases, metaphors, and other expressions common to the membership group.

The interpretive language emphasizes quality rather than quantities and meanings rather than variables. Interpretive theorizers use technical terms such as consensus, context sensitivity, credibility, field notes, lived experience, meanings, member validation, natural setting, process, sensitizing concepts, and theoretical sampling.

The critical approach

This style is called the critical approach, the emancipatory approach, or the Neo-Marxist approach to theorizing.

Purpose

Theorizing can refer to a form of social criticism. For the critical approach, theorists are not neutral or free from the influence of values in their work. Theorizing has an important function in the project to liberate oppressed people and achieve just social arrangements. The social worker theorist should take sides and use theories and theorizing to criticize destructive and unjust conditions and to suggest a vision of better alternatives.

Definition

Theory in the critical sense is the analysis of social situations and the features of these situations (status or power differences, economic inequality, systematic exploitation of workers, and so on) that are limiting the possibilities for full participation and growth of some of the members of the situations (Fay, 1975). Theories are weapons created by critical theorizers that oppressed groups can use to resist their oppressors and to prevail in political and ideological struggles (Andrew, 1977).

Method

People are often unaware of the situational elements and forces constraining their actions, and critical theorizing aims to uncover the historical processes, political ideologies, and social arrangements sustaining privation, oppression, or exploitation. Critical theorizers are open to the use of various research strategies to achieve their ends. However, several themes are common to their use of methods. Critical inquiry and theorizing should give voice to those who have been voiceless. Ideally, those with muted voices and limited power are invited to participate in the theorizing or research project. Critical inquiry and theorizing should examine the uses of ideas especially those derived from political ideology and ideological language to maintain unjust conditions. Critical inquiry and theorizing should be aware of how issues of social class, race, gender, and other categorical memberships including the researcher's membership identities can bias knowledge production processes. Critical inquiry and theorizing highlight the historical, economic, and political forces that led to the conditions and structures constraining free and democratic action.

Evidence

Critical theorizers intend to provoke personal and social change. Optimally, there is evidence that the resulting theoretical knowledge functions raised consciousness. Those judging a critical theory might ask some of the following questions (Zavarzadeh & Morton, 1994): Did the critical theory provide insight into the group's place in the social structure, into social relations of dominance and subordination, and into the political economy of labor (who obtains the favored jobs and who doesn't, for example)? Did the critical theory reveal the ways that the government and the dominant classes use information to promote a version of reality favorable to their interests and one asserted to be the universal reality? Did the critical theory increase the understanding of exploited persons of the nature of their exploitation, ways that the exploitation has caused suffering, and personal and collective strategies for resisting exploitation? Did such understandings catalyze activists and social movements in successful acts of liberation?

Language

Critical theorizers have not developed many terms specific to their method of theorizing. However, they tend to use a language with terms such as action-oriented research, critique, advocacy, democracy, empowerment, exploitation, oppression, participatory action research, social justice, and voice.

The pragmatic, syncretic approach to practical theorizing

There are other approaches to theorizing, and my profile of each major approach is a simplified summary. Within each approach, for example, there are variations on the basic themes. Note also that some theorists may combine elements from two or more of the major approaches reviewed here when theorizing.

In this book, I will take a syncretic and practical approach to theorizing. *Syncretic theorizing* means that theorizing practitioners seek a fusion of the major styles of theorizing: positivist, interpretive, and critical in the toolbox of resources for theoretical work (Layder, 1998). Different styles of theorizing are needed for different theory application tasks. Additionally, syncretic theorizing views all approaches to scientific reasoning and the ordering of theory elements (inductive, deductive, and abductive) as tools that have use and should be matched with the requirements of the job. Finally, different theoretical products—the explanatory theories and mathematical models of positivist theorizers, the grounded theories of interpretive theorizers, and the critiques of critical theorizers—have their place in the knowledge base of the profession.

This approach emphasizes the practical aspect of theorizing. Humans need to act to meet challenges related to their environments. Theoretical knowledge makes problem-solving action possible including the implementation of interventions that set in motion processes to achieve desired effects (Stehr, 1992). Theory developers create the intellectual tools used by social workers and other applied scientists to help clients meet life challenges or solve problems. A theory is an "instrumentality" like other tools, a means to an end (Biesta & Burbules, 2003). However, this kind of tool is used to provide a new understanding or perspective on a perplexing practice experience rather than to cut a board or hammer a nail. The theory unblocks our stuck helping action. In this pragmatic conceptualization, a theory is condensed knowledge that has practical consequences and makes a difference in practice, a resource for use in practical situations especially when custom and habit don't provide direction and when action might proceed along multiple courses. A theory's value rests on application followed by the observed and certified results of the application in improving people, relationships, social systems, and the environment.

Professionals build large toolboxes by mastering the basics of many effective theories, and professionals establish multi-theoretical competence by becoming able to choose and use the appropriate theoretical style or tool for each professional job adjusting its use to the features of the job and the job site. Positivist, interpretive, and critical theories have many practical uses.

Learning activities and reflections

1 What is your understanding of the term *theory*? Search for examples of different ways that social workers define the term *theory*. Check with colleagues in your field agency. Look through your textbooks and talk to your teachers. Make use of social work search engines. Interview your field supervisor or some other professional social worker. Find out how he or she defines the concept "theory."

2 Develop a brief summary of several alternate meanings of theory. What definition makes most sense to you? How will this understanding of "theory" help you learn and apply theoretical knowledge about human behavior and the environment?

3 Examine several of the definitions of theory listed in Table 02.1. Attempt to find a definition of theory that can be matched to each of the major approaches to theorizing: positivist, interpretive, and critical. What clues found in each definition did you use to make your match?

4 Think about the different styles of theorizing. Attempt to find a theoretical or research article associated with each of the styles (positivist, interpretive, and critical theorizing). Consider and report on how the theorizing style influenced the theory/research project and how the article contributed to or validated the theory. What are some of the strengths and limitations of each style of theorizing? In which circumstances might different styles be useful?

References

Abend, G. (2008). The meaning of "theory." *Sociological Theory*, 26(2), 173–199.

Andrew, E. (1977). The unity of theory and practice: The science of Marx and Nietzsche. In T. Ball (Ed.), *Political theory and praxis: New perspectives* (pp. 117–137). Minneapolis: University of Minnesota Press.

Beder, J. (2000). The integration of theory into practice: Suggestions for supervisors. *Professional Development: The International Journal of Continuing Social Work*, 3(2), 40–48.

Biesta, G. J. J., & Burbules, N. C. (2003). *Pragmatism and educational research*. Lanham, MD: Rowman & Littlefield.

Craig, R. T. (2001). Dewey and Gadamer on practical reflection: Toward a methodology for the practical disciplines. In D. W. Perry (Ed.), *American pragmatism and communication research* (pp. 131–148). Mahwah, NJ: Lawrence Erlbaum Associates.

Fay, B. (1975). *Social theory and political practice*. London: George Allen & Unwin, Ltd.

Kaplan, A. (1964). *The conduct of inquiry: Methodology for behavioral science*. San Francisco, CA: Chandler.

Layder, D. (1998). *Sociological practice: Linking theory and social research*. London: Sage.

Lutz, D. S. (1992). *A preface to American political theory.* Lawrence, KS: University Press of Kansas.

McCool, D. (1995). *Public policy theories, models, and concepts: An anthology.* Englewood Cliffs, NJ: Prentice Hall.

Meleis, A. I. (1985). *Theoretical nursing: Development and progress.* Philadelphia: J. B. Lippincott.

Munson, C. E. (1983). *An introduction to clinical social work supervision.* New York: Haworth Press.

Pozzuto, R. (2007). Understanding theory, practicing social work. In S. L. Witkin & D. Saleeby (Eds). *Social work dialogues: Transforming the canon in inquiry, practice, and education* (pp. 64–93). Alexandria, VA: Council on Social Work Education.

Rosenau, J. N. (1980). *The scientific study of foreign policy.* London: Frances Pinter.

Rubin, A., & Babbie, E. R. (2008). *Research methods for social work* (6th ed.). Belmont, CA: Thomson Brooks/Cole.

Stehr, N. (1992). *Practical knowledge: Applying the social sciences.* London: Sage.

Sutton, R. L., & Shaw, B. M. (1995). What theory is not. *Administrative Science Quarterly, 40*(3), 371–384.

Turnbull, S. (2002). Social construction research and theory building. *Advances in Developing Human Resources, 4*(3), 317–334.

Weis, D. L. (1998). The use of theory in sexuality research. *The Journal of Sex Research, 35*(1), 1–9.

Wysienska, K., & Szmatka, J. (2002). Positivism and theory construction in group processes. In J. Symatka, M. Lovaglia, & K. Wysienka (Eds), *The growth of knowledge: Theory, simulation, and empirical research in group processes* (pp. 77–96). Westport, CT: Praeger.

Zavarzadeh, M., & Morton, D. (1994). *Theory as resistance: Politics and culture after (post)structuralism.* New York: Guilford Press.

References for theory definitions

Ben-Ari, M. (2005). *Just a theory: Explaining the nature of science.* Amherst, NY: Prometheus.

Best, S. (2003). *A beginner's guide to social theory.* London: Sage.

Chinn, P. L., & Kramer, M. K. (2008). *Integrated theory and knowledge development in nursing* (7th ed.). St. Louis, MO: Mosby Elsevier.

de Man, P. (1986). *The resistance to theory.* Minneapolis: University of Minnesota Press.

Giroux, H. A. (1983). *Theory and resistance in education: A pedagogy for the opposition.* South Hadley, MA: Bergin & Garvey.

Hochbaum, G. M., Sorenson, J. R., & Lorig, K. (1992). Theory in health education practice. *Health Education Quarterly, 19*(3), 295–313.

Hollander, E. P. (1967). *Principles and methods of social psychology.* Oxford, UK: Oxford University Press.

Jaccard, J. & Jacoby, J. (2010). *Theory construction and model-building skills.* New York: The Guilford Press.

Kaplan, A. (1964). *The conduct of inquiry: Methodology for behavioral science.* San Francisco, CA: Chandler.

McCracken, S., & Rzepnicki, T. (2010). The role of theory in conducting evidence-based clinical practice. In W. Borden (Ed.), *Reshaping theory in contemporary social work practice: Toward a critical pluralism in clinical practice* (pp. 210–233). New York: Columbia University Press.

Merton, R. (1967). *On theoretical sociology: Five essays old and new.* New York: Free Press.

Rueschemeyer, D. (2009). *Usable theory: Analytic tools for social and political research.* Princeton, NJ: Princeton University Press.

Waltz, K. N. (1979). *Theory of international politics.* New York: Random House.

Watson, J. (1988). *Nursing: Human science and human care. A theory of nursing.* New York: National League for Nursing.

Weis, D. L. (1998). The use of theory in sexuality research. *The Journal of Sex Research, 35*(1), 1–9.

<table>
<tr><td>

LESSON

3

</td><td>

Identify and use the social work approach to knowledge selection

</td></tr>
</table>

(EPAS 2.1.1 Identify as a Professional Social Worker; EPAS 2.1.7 Apply Knowledge)

When I was educated as a specialist in social work with groups, I learned that a group worker helps each group form a purpose that merges the purpose of the social work profession (the enhancement of social functioning), the agency purpose, and the purpose agreed to by the members. As a social worker, I was helping the group develop an integrative purpose statement. The social work helping group of family members with seriously ill children at the Ronald McDonald House, for instance, would seek different aims than an agency group led by a minister, a nurse, a psychologist, or an attorney. Each of those leaders had an affiliation with a specific and different profession.

The social work purpose and theorizing

Theorizing practitioners also select knowledge that is consistent with the profession's mission. Let's begin with some basic definitions. A *profession* is the umbrella term for an association "covering both discipline and practice that fosters status and respect by establishing entrance examinations, practice standards, and codes of ethics to assure quality and protect the public" (Perlstadt, 1998, p. 268). As a practical profession, social work can also be characterized as an organized community of practitioners committed to the cultivation of its helping practices and technical skills through systematized scientific research, critical reflection, theory development, and theory application (Craig, 2001). Social work has made significant progress in establishing itself as a profession. Other professional groups participating in human services endeavors include education, nursing, law, sociology, and psychology. Each brings its own knowledge base and orientation to theorizing to the helping site.

A *discipline* is "an established field of social science knowledge" (Bentz & Shapiro, 1998, p. 82). A discipline is recognized as such within academic institutions and in society. Disciples of an academic discipline think, theorize, and act in ways characteristic of the discipline in which they were socialized. Social workers collaborate with disciplinary partners from economics, philosophy, anthropology, psychology, political science, biology, mathematics, and many other academic departments.

We can also add the concept, theoretical tradition, or school of thought. This is a perspective for perceiving and understanding and a language for communicating about human behavior and the social environment. Allegiance to a school influences the practitioner's selection of topics of inquiry, approach to scientific research and evidence, conceptualization of "person interacting in environment" configurations, and design and execution of helping activities. Contemporary social workers identify with various theoretical traditions and may collaborate with those who use similar or different approaches derived from behavioral, cognitive, psychoanalytic, family systems, feminist, and other theoretical traditions.

Much contemporary practical theorizing requires cooperation and communication with partners from other professions, disciplines, and theoretical traditions. Effective social workers are able to learn about each partner's culture and interact harmoniously despite differences in background. A clear and confident sense of the profession and our professional identity helps us cross boundaries without losing our way.

Social work's distinctive definition and mission

Professions compete in a society for resources such as status and money. Each makes claims about its distinctive territory, its legitimate professional jurisdiction (Abbott, 1988). For example, social work began to emerge more than a century ago as a profession with the distinctive function of "intersystem translation," that is, facilitating communication between persons with needs and the formal and informal social systems that might help meet these needs (Abbott, 1995). At Hull House, an innovative center of social work activity, Jane Addams and other settlement workers created channels of communication so Chicago's newcomers could become informed, capable, responsible, and active participants in social and political groups and organizations and so Chicago's established citizens could accept and relate cooperatively to their new neighbors.

Theory use and disciplinary status

Cultivation of a scientifically supported and coherently organized base of knowledge is one of the best ways to claim professional legitimacy. As a champion of theorizing, I would like to note that research shows that the most highly regarded "scientific" disciplines tend to be the most theoretical (Simontin, 2006). Physics and chemistry, for example, achieved the highest reputational rank based on numerous indicators of status and scientific achievement. Biology, psychology, and sociology followed in ranking. The highly ranked disciplines possessed many good theories, agreed on central theoretical concepts and the theoretical questions guiding scientific inquiry, generated many theoretical laws compared to their total number of theories, produced many articles and books with theoretical significance, often used visual displays such as graphs to represent theories and theoretical models, pursued theoretical research programs directed to solve theoretical puzzles, and developed innovative theoretical perspectives. Of note, social work was not even included in the disciplines considered by Simontin despite its long presence in hundreds of universities and colleges: a probable judgment of our profession's slow development and articulation of a scientific foundation. Social workers can assist the profession to increase its status and reputation by emulating the prestigious scientific disciplines and fostering more theoretical work and theorizing.

Social workers serve in various countries and as members of different professional organizations. There isn't a unanimously agreed-upon definition and mission statement that crosses the globe. Social workers also differ some in their characterization of the profession. This book won't attempt to summarize or reconcile the differences. Instead, here is one formulation of social work, one that captures the essential thrust of the profession's traditions and one that might help you seek and use knowledge consistent with our profession.

A membership perspective for social work

Hans Falck (1988), a social work professor and experienced group worker, christened his framework "the membership perspective." As presented here, his perspective is not a human behavior theory or a practice theory but another important kind of theory, a theory of social work—a theory that characterizes the profession in terms of what it is, what it does, and what it aims to achieve (Hearn, 1982). According to Falck, social workers are united in their commitment to a shared professional mission. The mission is to understand and help members of various-sized groups and social organizations improve the quality of their membership experiences (Falck 1984, 1988). This includes membership in primary groups such as the family and the friendship group, membership in larger groups such as the community and the organization, membership in societies and in a society's categorical groups related to race, ethnicity, and so on. Here's Falck's definition of our profession: "Social work equals rendering professional aid to clients in the management of membership" (1984, p. 155). Social workers help clients in a variety of ways: to enhance their capabilities for performing membership roles; to restore their membership capabilities after a setback (disease, incarceration, disaster, for examples); and to avoid membership problems that can be anticipated. Social work practitioners also work to change membership organizations (households, workplaces, governments, and so on) into just, democratic, and caring contexts for membership action. Referencing symbolic interactionism as a foundational theoretical framework for the profession, Falck (1988) identified "symbolization ... the fact that members attach meaning to their own behavior and to the behavior of others" (p. 39) as the central membership attribute. Social workers use symbols (appearances, words, images, gestures, objects, sounds) to facilitate communication between members and other members and between members and their membership organizations in the pursuit of shared and ethical ends.

Tenets central to the membership perspective follow. Each person is conceived in holistic, bio-psycho-social terms. Human conduct reflects the influence of seen and unseen membership systems on the total person. The person can't be separated from his or her memberships and membership history (The membership perspective rejects theoretical claims that people are driven by genetic dispositions or by personality traits independent of environmental contexts). The social worker seeks a deep understanding of the client as a member of a variety of interacting relationships, groups, organizations, institutions, and ecologies. Memberships are the foundation for human growth and development. Membership is universal and irreversible (we are always members of our families of origin, for example) and enduring as internalized membership experiences, memories, and patterns. However, people may modify the symbolic meanings (negative social labels, for instance) attached to certain memberships. Clients have the capacity to make choices in consort with their significant others that improve the quality of their memberships, and social workers can enhance this capacity for "social self-determination." The membership perspective is not naïve. In many cases faced by social workers, clients are cast as lesser and stigmatized members, deprived entirely of deserved membership rights, or struggling with challenges that impair their membership performances such as illness or addiction. The membership perspective directs social workers to advocate, organize, and mobilize to change such unjust conditions of membership.

Social work differs, then, from allied disciplines and professions that don't assume and apply a membership perspective (Forte, 2001). For example, sociology is dedicated to the academic study and theories of the social lives of people, groups, and societies but renounced since the 1930s its interest in using knowledge to improve the quality of membership experiences or membership systems. Psychology focuses on the study of the human mind and behavior but doesn't prioritize the study of membership contexts that shape thinking, feeling, and behavior. Physicians are committed to the art and science of medicine and the enhancement of public health but with minimal attention to the bi-directional flow of influence between members and their social membership systems.

Each profession also articulates a different set of core competencies related to knowledge, skills, and attitudes necessary for adept professional action. There are core competencies defined for the social work profession. We have reviewed the current Council on Social Work Education statement of core competencies in the introduction. In a later activity, we will also examine the core values and ethical standards that characterize social work.

Social work's distinctive approach to knowledge

Each profession brings its distinctive definition and mission to the selection and use of knowledge. It develops profession-specific concepts and claims a distinctive frame of reference, perspective, or theoretical domain. This domain includes the aspects of the human condition of focal concern to the profession (Bailey, 1980; Kim, 1983). Symbolic interactionists have studied the notion of domain-specific perspectives on professional knowledge extensively (Forte, 2010). According to interactionists, the *domain-specific perspective* provides a coordinated and shared set of ideas, images, definitions of actions, and guidelines that any member of the profession can use in dealing with the problematic situations common to daily practice. The perspective also helps members of the profession enact roles appropriately in social work settings, make sense of and organize their helping actions, and adjust creatively to unexpected or uncommon professional dilemmas. Newcomers to the profession are socialized to internalize this perspective on knowledge. Masters exemplify the perspective in their work and feed back ideas for its continual improvement and dissemination.

Social workers often refer to our domain-specific perspective as "the person-in-environment" framework. This focus is very compatible with the membership perspective and can be explained in membership terminology. The social worker selects, deconstructs, and reconstructs theories about the person as a member of various social systems in the environment and theorizes about how membership experiences influence key dimensions of being a person (acting, faithing, feeling, sensing, and thinking).

The social worker also selects, deconstructs, and reconstructs theories about the environment. These are the membership contexts and systems in which people behave and develop. The environment includes the community, the culture, the ecology, the economy, the political system, the society, and the global network of societies. Membership problems and membership achievements are transactional; they are manifestations of both member choices and the influences of these contexts.

Therefore, the social worker seeks knowledge and theorizes in ways mindful of the "in." The person or member is understood in his or her particular cultural and historical context, and the member is conceptualized as engaged in continuous transactions and dynamic interplay with his or her salient environmental contexts. Self, social organizations, physical environment, and society are connected by reciprocal action; the person cannot be split from memberships and their influence, and the environmental contexts are continually reconfigured because of membership action. No aspect of the person-in-environment configuration can be specified and described fully apart from the other aspects. In a sense, each human being is like a growing fetus. The fetus is immersed in the mother's womb and dependent on this environment. Humans are embedded in environmental contexts and the human-environment relation is an interdependent one.

Knowledge that focuses only on the person and knowledge that focused only on the environment need adaptation before use by social workers.

Membership work—helping processes designed to prevent future membership problems, to restore damaged memberships, or to enhance current membership functioning—is based intellectually on theoretical, research, and practice knowledge affirming the indivisibility of the member and membership contexts. Membership-oriented social workers direct their practical theorizing efforts toward understanding and enhancing the person's membership capacities, toward understanding and improving the transactions between members and their membership groups, toward understanding and nurturing members' full development within particular environmental contexts, and toward understanding and improving environments so that they support the expression of their members' positive dispositions and potentials.

This membership version of the person-in-environment theory of social work makes possible the creation, borrowing, adapting, organizing, and judging of knowledge suitable to the social work definition and mission. Social workers can apply membership-relevant knowledge to diverse practice situations.

There is one last point about the distinctive social work approach to knowledge. Social work is a profession that carries out its mission in many fields of practice, using many different roles and methods, serving various-sized systems, and addressing a wide range of complex personal and collective challenges (Johnson & Svensson, 2005). Also, social work is a profession accumulating knowledge tailored to our purpose, goals, and normative preferences: affirmation of strengths, promotion of social justice, sensitivity to differences, and so on (We will extensively discuss knowledge selection and appraisal standards in Section 4). Therefore, we must seek, borrow, and incorporate knowledge of human membership from many disciplines, professional groups, and theoretical traditions but deconstruct and reconstruct this knowledge for our practice projects.

Learning activities and reflections

1   Briefly summarize your understanding of social work as a profession. You could check out the website for the National Association of Social Work www.socialworkers.org or for professional social work associations in Canada www.casw-acts.ca, England www.basw.co.uk, Nigeria www.nasowabuja.org.ng or other countries to inform your answer. Talk with non–social work majors to make comparisons between social work and allied professions.

2   How would you define the profession and its mission to a friend, family member, or client? What do you see as the competencies that are critical for success as a social worker? How would you contrast the social work definition, mission, theory base, and core competencies with other

professions: teaching, medicine, the law, clinical psychology, or applied sociology, for examples. What are the similarities of social work to these professional groups?

3   What is your understanding of the knowledge base of the profession of social work? What theoretical knowledge, research knowledge, and practice wisdom are essential to social work activity? How does our knowledge base differ from that of other academic disciplines such as anthropology or mathematics? How does our knowledge base differ from other professions?

4   Synthesize your understanding of our profession. How would you summarize your conceptualization of social work, its distinctive mission, set of competencies, slant on theory use, and other defining elements? How do you compare your understanding to the conceptualization provided by the membership perspective?

References

Abbott, A. (1988). *The system of professions: An essay on the division of expert labor.* Chicago, IL: University of Chicago Press.

Abbott, A. (1995). Boundaries of social work or social work of boundaries? *Social Service Review*, 69(4), 545–562.

Bailey, J. (1980). *Ideas and intervention: Social theory for practice.* London: Routledge & Kegan Paul.

Bentz, V., & Shapiro, J. J. (1998). *Mindful inquiry in social research.* Thousand Oaks, CA: Sage.

Craig, R. T. (2001). Dewey and Gadamer on practical reflection: Toward a methodology for the practical disciplines. In D. W. Perry (Ed.), *American pragmatism and communication research* (pp. 131–148). Mahwah, NJ: Lawrence Erlbaum Associates.

Falck, H. S. (1984). The membership model of social work. *Social Work*, 29(2), 155–160.

Falck, H. S. (1988). *Social work: The membership perspective.* New York: Springer.

Forte, J. A. (2001). *Theories for practice: Symbolic interactionist translations.* Lanham, MD: University Press of America.

Forte, J. A. (2010). Symbolic interactionism, naturalistic inquiry, and education. In P. Peterson, E. Baker, & B. McGaw (Eds), *International encyclopedia of education* (vol. 6, pp. 481–487). Oxford, UK: Elsevier.

Hearn, J. (1982). The problem(s) of theory and practice in social work and social work education. *Issues in Social Work Education*, 2(2), 95–118.

Johnson, E., & Svensson, K. (2005). Theory in social work—Some reflections on understanding and explaining interventions. *European Journal of Social Work*, 8(4), 419–433.

Kim, H. S. (1983). *The nature of theoretical thinking in nursing.* Norwalk, CT: Appleton-Crofts Century.

Perlstadt, H. (1998). Comment on Turner. *Sociological Perspectives*, 41(2), 268–271.

Simonton, D. K. (2006). Scientific status of disciplines, individuals, and ideas: Empirical analyses of the potential impact of theory. *Review of General Psychology*, 10(2), 98–112.

LESSON

4

Identify and use knowledge from varied sources

(EPAS 2.1.6 Engage in Research-Informed Practice;
EPAS 2.1.7 Apply Knowledge)

Theorizing practitioners integrate knowledge from many sources. Doane and Varcoe (2005), for example, report "theorizing involves tuning into and critically considering bodily sensations, intuitive and emotional responses, existing theories and research, contextual forces, and so on" (p. 83). Chambers (1973) wrote a clear and thoughtful profile of knowledge-guided social work practice and asserted that social workers synthesize knowledge from many sources including personal intuition, practice wisdom, and scientific theory before offering their professional judgments.

The professional knowledge base

As professionals, social workers are guided by sound knowledge. We don't read the tea leaves, roll the dice, or consult the stars and astrological charts. A *knowledge base* is "the body of theory, empirical research, practice wisdom, and procedures that are widely recognized and used in a given profession" (Hudson, 2010, p. 83). Social workers have a large knowledge base with knowledge drawn from many different sources.

Be aware, however, that the professional knowledge base is a large, ever-growing, and complex library of information (Payne, 2001). There is not agreement about what knowledge belongs in the storehouse or about the best sources of knowledge. Some social work positivists, for example, prioritize research knowledge obtained through experiments. Other leaders contend that our focus on serving people from diverse cultures requires grounded, interpretive theories. There is no card catalog for accessing every relevant piece of knowledge. There are few "librarians" attempting to bring order to the collection.

Powerful stakeholders such as journal editors, directors of doctoral programs, and funders of researcher often have more influence over the knowledge determination process than relatively powerless stakeholders.

Some journal editors, for instance, consider and publish only research studies. Case reports and papers analyzing or developing theory are rejected. Book publishers often control the production and distribution of knowledge available to social workers. I have noted, for instance, that despite the obvious relevance of markets, financial downturns, the distribution of wealth, and poverty to many clients, publishers rarely support book projects focused on the importance of economics to social work or include chapters on economic exchange theories in theory survey texts. Social work policy advocates and educators have tried unsuccessfully to change this pattern.

The content of the knowledge base changes significantly over time; but the repository may not yet include cutting-edge information. For example, 50 years ago, books and articles capturing psychodynamic approaches to behavior and practice theories were dominant. Now they make up a small portion of our total knowledge. There are missing sections in our library of knowledge. Social work has lagged, for instance, beyond some other professions in incorporating knowledge from the biological sciences and research related neuroscience to practice. In recent years, the profession's leaders have tried to catch up in the accumulation of knowledge on war, war-related trauma, and effective services for soldiers and veterans.

The knowledge considered necessary for all social workers and included in our knowledge base may not include the specialized knowledge needed by a sizable subsection of social workers. Members of the International Association for Social Work with Groups, a vibrant professional society, note the scattered and meager bits of knowledge made available on topics relevant to social work with groups. These members often advocate for the inclusion of content on group theory and group work practice in more curriculums, conferences, and publications.

Finally, gatekeepers of the profession's knowledge base don't always work diligently to ensure that the base includes knowledge responsive to members of diverse membership groups and their experiences. Do our books, journals, and conferences include content useful in understanding and helping members of the lesbian, gay, bisexual, and transgender community, members of newly formed immigrant communities (from Cuba, Jamaica, the Philippines, or South Korea), members of varied but small religious communities (Eastern Orthodox, Mennonite, or Muslim), or members of the community that you must learn about and serve well in your region or country?

There are many places where useful knowledge can be obtained; our knowledge base is not located in one central location, a Fort Knox of social work wisdom. These sources of knowledge include classes provided by professional education programs, social work conferences and workshops, the written and published literature including books and articles, reports and other documents in agencies, and similar settings reporting on practice knowledge, and websites.

Types and sources of knowledge

Figure 4.1 illustrates the connectedness of several important types of knowledge used by social workers to guide practical theorizing efforts (Osmond, 2005; Trevithick, 2008). These include theoretical knowledge, research knowledge, practice knowledge, and also everyday knowledge. In this section, I will describe some of the sources of each type of knowledge.

Theoretical knowledge

Theoretical knowledge refers to scientific theories about the social and physical environment, public and personal problems, and intentional change processes. This can be knowledge that we borrow and use from allied academic disciplines—anthropology, biology, ecology, economics, political science, psychology, sociology—or knowledge that we borrow and use from allied professional groups such as nurses, counselors, applied sociologists, and educators. This can also be knowledge created by social workers.

In most social work programs, the courses associated with "human behavior and the social environment" emphasize the provision of such knowledge. Social work professional groups also sponsor many theory-specific workshops at national, regional, and local conferences and

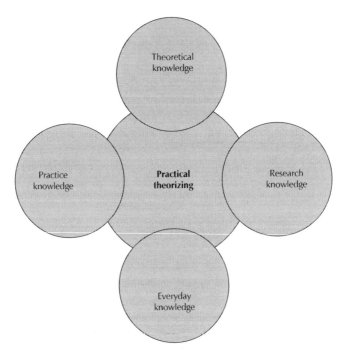

Figure 4.1   Sources of knowledge for practical theorizing

continuing education events. At these events, specialists explain and teach the use of various theoretical approaches and the relevance of these approaches to particular practice challenges. The policy sequence in your social work program will alert you to the theoretical knowledge necessary to analyze policies and to advocate for policy changes.

Social workers and social scientists share what they have learned about theories and theory application by writing and publishing their discoveries. You can make use of these resources. For example, some social work writers have written surveys of the major theoretical traditions. Social work encyclopedias typically include profiles of major practice theories. You can learn more about theoretical traditions, theories, and theoretical concepts commonly used in our profession by joining in theory-specific web conversations. The World Wide Web includes numerous sites devoted to particular theoretical orientations and schools. These may include biographies of key theoreticians, archives of articles on the theory, links to related sites, and chat rooms where participants can discuss issues related to using the theoretical framework.

How else might you find the best and most relevant written theoretical knowledge? There are many computer-based tools that can help you search through millions of books, articles, dissertations, and unpublished presentations to identify information about theories and their application. Your college or university probably has a set of academic search engines that you can use. *Social Work Abstracts*, for instance, facilitates searches for books and articles collected by social work and other relevant knowledge producers.

Mentors are people who guide us and help us develop our potentials as students, workers, and people. Mentors can be teachers, supervisors, senior social workers, or colleagues. Many seasoned social workers are experts in a particular theoretical framework. Even if they are modest and downplay their expertise, they can help mentees learn about theory. Novice theory users can turn to mentors in the same way that those learning a new language turn to native language speakers. You can ask your mentor to explain theoretical terms used in the practice setting. You can work with the mentor to create a list of the most frequently used theoretical terms and begin studying the meanings. You can ask your mentor to observe you and provide feedback when you use a theoretical concept to discuss a case at a meeting. A mentor might review your process recording or case notes and then help you reflect on your articulation of the critical incidents in a session.

Unfortunately, as I indicated in the Preface, much theoretical knowledge created in academic and research settings has limitations for practical theory users (Dreyfus & Dreyfus, 2009). Theoretical knowledge is often abstract rather than tied to particular examples and cases. Theoretical knowledge aims for universality and, thus, suggests what holds across situations but not necessarily what is relevant to a particular helping situation. Traditionally, theoretical knowledge is context-free. However, social work practice is grounded in specific contexts, and knowledge of the constraints, pressures, and opportunities faced in these contexts is critical to effective practice (Alexander, 2010). Theoretical knowledge is often presented in the form of deductive logic—particular conclusions derived from general theoretical principles or statements (Craig, 1996). Much practice follows inductive logic: observing case details and generating theoretical patterns. Until knowledge producers, including social workers, create more knowledge for practice, practical theories (Cronen, 2001), practitioners may need help from knowledge translators such as scholarly practitioners, theory-wise supervisors, or experienced field instructors. Practitioners may also need to use translation tools such as models, metaphors, and maps to grasp academic and textbook theories (Forte, 2006). Additionally, practitioners will need to become adept at blending theoretical knowledge with other sources of knowledge such as practice wisdom and creatively adapting what they know to the concrete aspects of the helping circumstances.

Research knowledge

Research knowledge refers to the accumulated set of scientific studies relevant to the achievement of professional social work purposes. This knowledge includes theory-specific outcome or effectiveness studies. These may be systematic reports on empirical tests of the usefulness of a theory for practice purposes. *Research on Social Work Practice*, for instance, is a journal that publishes many such studies. This type of study sometimes compares the effectiveness of practice based on different theories in solving specific problems. Other research studies might compare the effectiveness of practice based on one theory to practice based on multiple theories or practice based on no theory.

Many social workers, especially those associated with the qualitative approach to scientific inquiry, believe that case studies are another form of important research knowledge. Theory-based case studies are detailed and comprehensive reports on the use of a particular approach with a particular client in a particular setting. These can be very helpful because they illustrate the actual decisions and actions of a practitioner, and they demonstrate how theories and interventions are adapted to client, context, and circumstance.

Research knowledge also includes evidence, facts, records, statistics, and other data about personal and public problems and interventions and programs designed to solve these problems. Often, such knowledge is collected and archived at websites, in university libraries, and by government agencies.

The research sequence in your social work program will help you increase your ability to identify, retrieve, and appraise scientific-based knowledge. It is likely, too, that courses in the practice sequence have introduced you to the idea of evidence-informed practice and the importance of choosing theories and interventions supported by evidence. Conferences and continuing education events often include presentations informed by research, and there are numerous web-based created by knowledge-archiving collaborative organizations that summarize scientific evidence about "what works."

Practice knowledge

Practice knowledge is another important type of knowledge. This is also called "practice wisdom" and refers to the ideas, techniques, generalizations, and guidelines developed through observation and reflection on practice experiences. The wisdom has been passed down across generations of practitioners. For example, social group workers have a long history and much knowledge about the use of program activities (drama, dance, song, games, art, and sports) to help small groups and their members achieve desired goals. Practice knowledge includes agency and social policies, legal precedents and laws, insights into challenges specific to a field of practice, and widely shared procedural information about agreed-upon steps for undertaking professional activities such as referral and foster care placement.

Not all practice wisdom has been transformed into formal theory or confirmed empirically. However, these patterns of conceptualizing "person interacting in the environment" configurations and thinking about helping processes and procedures are often very valuable. They have been generated by social workers during interaction with clients in actual helping settings and have been certified by peers as useful for "getting the job done." The practice sequence and your field internship will expose you to the profession's accumulated practice wisdom. Certain journals focus on practice reports, such as the *Clinical Social Work Journal*, *Families in Society* and *Social Work with Groups*, that might guide work with individuals, families, or small groups. Moreover, whenever you have the opportunity to confer with a social work teacher or colleague, you can give and receive lessons from practice.

Everyday, personal knowledge

Everyday knowledge refers to the information that we acquire as a member of a cultural or sub-cultural group and the common sense understanding permeating our community and social organizations that we absorb over the life course (Lindblom & Cohen, 1979). This type of knowledge can be learned at home, in school, through the mass media, and during our reflections and reveries.

Our previous life experiences contribute to the accumulation of memories about past accomplishments and defeats (and mini-theories explaining such events), the refinement of our values and ethical code, the development of our political ideology, and the formation of our core self-understandings. Reflections on current life experiences and our personal patterns of thinking, feeling, valuing, and action inform our performance as social workers too.

This type of knowledge doesn't trace its creation, verification, claims to truth, or usefulness to a formal scientific community and their practices but to common sense, casual empirical observations, and the thoughtful speculation and analysis practiced by non scientists. Yet, such personalized knowledge is relevant to practice. Practice can be enriched by the reflective use of intuition, common sense, and cultural knowledge. Such knowledge contributes to our distinctive "use of self" when helping others, and we should monitor continuously the intersection of this everyday knowledge with the other types of knowledge: theoretical, research, and practice.

Conclusion: judging knowledge

Malcolm Payne (2001) recommends that knowledge users take care when borrowing different types of knowledge from the library of professional social work knowledge. Knowledge users should increase their sensitivity to cultural and class biases in any country's knowledge base, recognize that the profession may share a variety of interlocking and overlapping categories of knowledge (rather than one homogenous knowledge base), and learn more about how knowledge is transferred to the base across different countries, organizations, and specialties.

Social workers make use of knowledge from diverse sources. In this book, we will focus on finding, deconstructing, reconstructing, and constructing theoretical knowledge; there are many available resources for readers who want to learn more about using research, practice, and everyday knowledge.

It is important to note that some knowledge is better than other knowledge. Although this is a topic of contention, Chambers (1973) provided standards for comparing the relative value of knowledge from different sources. First, we prefer knowledge explicitly formulated so it can be shared publicly in words and other symbol systems (diagrams, for example) with our clients, colleagues, and supervisors. Our intuitions are important, but often they emerge from tacit and implicit knowledge. It is not enough to say, "I have a hunch that this will work." Professionals must elaborate explicitly on the "hunch." Second, we prefer when there is agreement from the relevant community of inquiry (practitioners in the same field, researchers familiar with the topic, theorists expert in the realm of human behavior) that the knowledge is legitimate. My grandmother taught me that a dried red pepper would ward off evil and harm from enemies. It is unlikely that my colleagues will agree that this is a valid strategy for managing inter-organizational rivalries. Third, preferred knowledge is formulated in a way that it can be validated empirically. The knowledge user can create or find a test supporting or rejecting the knowledge claims. Without the possibility of proving knowledge false by evidence, the practitioner can't correct knowledge-based mistakes. Finally, Chambers proposes that we prioritize knowledge organized into a coherent, logical, and empirically supported network of thought, a scientific theory or practice theory. A research finding independent of theory has value, but Chambers argues that it would be more memorable and useful as a brick in a theoretical edifice. Not all would accept this standard for judging knowledge but, as an advocate of theory use, I endorse it.

Learning activities and reflections

1 Review the commentary and summarize your understanding of the major types of knowledge. Comment on the possible strengths and limitations of each type. Review also the major sources for locating each type of knowledge. Which types of knowledge have you consciously used so far in your social work education or career? To which sources did you turn to locate such knowledge? Which sources of knowledge can you use more often? What made it difficult to use a particular type of knowledge? What facilitated your use of a particular type of knowledge?

2 Check out two different websites devoted to theoretical knowledge or human behavior theories. Describe the website. Who sponsors it? What kind of information is provided? What are some positive and negative features of the website? For example, you might take a look at the *Society for the Study of Symbolic Interaction* website www.symbolicinteraction. org or the *Association for Behavioral and Cognitive Therapies* website www.abct.org/Home.

3 Reflect on what written information might help you apply theory to a practice situation. Go to a website of a bookseller and search for useful theory-oriented books. The books might profile the cognitive behaviorist approach to understanding and helping impulsive children, offer a historical-economic explanation to the increase in global poverty, summarize the queer theory of sexuality, or relate attachment theory to developmental successes and setbacks. Report on your search to your classmates. Summarize your report.

4 Look through social work textbooks. Determine whether they include different theoretical traditions or a profile of a particular theoretical tradition. Borrow a theory survey book from the library at your college. Pick a chapter on a theoretical approach of interest. Carefully examine the title. Look at the headings and subheadings. Skim the references at the end. Identify three or four concepts associated with the theory that you discovered during your examination.

5 Develop a plan for searching the professional literature. Be as specific as possible in identifying what type of knowledge you want to find, what sources might have the relevant information, and so on. Use one of the search engines at your school to conduct the search. Summarize

your experience. For example, check whether your library has a digital version of *Social Work Abstracts* www.naswpress.org/publications/journals/swab.html. This search engine will look through abstracts collected from social work and social work–related journals over the last 40 years. Try it out, and report on the results.

References

Alexander, E. R. (2010). Introduction: Does planning theory affect practice, and if so, how? *Planning Theory, 9*(2), 99–107.

Chambers, D. E. (1973). Three principles of a knowledge-guided social work practice. *Journal of Social Welfare, 11,* 35–43.

Craig, R. T. (1996). Practical-theoretical argumentation. *Argumentation, 10,* 461–474.

Cronen, V. R. (2001). Practical theory, practical art, and the pragmatic-systemic account of inquiry. *Communication Theory, 11*(1), 14–35.

Doane, G. H., & Varcoe, C. (2005). Toward compassionate action: Pragmatism and the inseparability of theory/practice. *Advances in Nursing Science, 28*(1), 81–90.

Dreyfus, H. L., & Dreyfus, S. E. (2009). The relationship of theory and practice in the acquisition of skill. In P. Benner, C. A. Tanner, & C. A. Chesla (Eds), *Expertise in nursing practice: Caring, clinical judgment and ethics* (pp. 1–23). New York: Springer.

Forte, J. A. (2006). *Human behavior and the social environment: Models, metaphors, and maps for applying theoretical perspectives to practice.* Belmont, CA: Thomson Brooks/Cole.

Hudson, C. C. (2010). *Complex systems and human behavior.* Chicago, IL: Lyceum.

Lindblom, C. E., & Cohen, D. K. (1979). *Usable knowledge: Social science and social problem solving.* New Haven, CT: Yale University Press.

Osmond, J. (2005). The knowledge spectrum: A framework for teaching knowledge and its use in social work practice. *British Journal of Social Work, 35,* 881–900.

Payne, M. (2001). Knowledge bases and knowledge biases in social work. *Journal of Social Work, 1*(2), 133–146.

Trevithick P. (2008). Revisiting the knowledge base of social work: A framework for practice. *British Journal of Social Work, 38,* 1212–1237.

Identify and use theory differentially by level of abstraction

(EPAS 2.1.3 Apply Critical Thinking;
EPAS 2.1.7 Apply Knowledge)

Knowledge application (deconstruction and reconstruction) requires an appreciation for theoretical knowledge at varying levels of abstraction. The concept—level of abstraction—refers to the distance between a concrete and felt experience and the symbolization of experience by a scientific community (DePoy & Gilson, 2007). Knowledge can be very abstract as if in the clouds or knowledge can be very specific as if a small object on the ground. The construct "common good" is central to pragmatic theories of democracy and an example of a very abstract idea. A theorizing practitioner guided by attachment theory might note a fairly concrete event—Mina, the mother, gently kissing her daughter, Tessa, on the cheek. Imagine the ladder of abstraction placed on the ground and leaning against a house. Theory users can move up and down on this ladder of abstraction from concrete to abstract. Imagine the ladder placed on the ground starting at your feet and extending 28 feet away. Theory users can look outward shifting from a sharp and precise focus on small-scale aspects of human behavior and the environment near the feet to a large and panoramic view of large-scale aspects of human behavior and the environment at the end of the ladder.

Theorizing and the ladder of abstraction

Let's use the ladder. Figure 5.1 displays the progression upward from least abstract to most abstract theoretical content. We have some very powerful and meaningful experiences that are hard to translate into abstract terms, for example, the birth process. These would be near the bottom of the ladder. At a slightly higher level, we use basic concepts to refer to a living being—a son, Geraldo, or our dog, Atticus. At the still higher level of abstraction, we may use category systems when we refer to a person, object, or experience and others of the same kind—Hispanic American boys or cocker spaniels. Near the top, we may use very intangible and abstract ideas to summarize

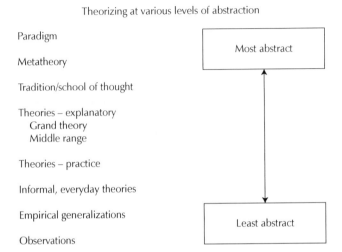

Theorizing at various levels of abstraction

Paradigm

Metatheory

Tradition/school of thought

Theories – explanatory
  Grand theory
  Middle range

Theories – practice

Informal, everyday theories

Empirical generalizations

Observations

Most abstract

Least abstract

Figure 5.1 Theorizing and the ladder of theoretical abstraction

experiences and events like love, Capitalism, or globalization. Theorists provide knowledge to social workers at these various levels of abstraction.

Level of abstraction and scope are related ideas. Theories differ in their *theoretical scope*, the range of phenomena explained by the theory. Some theories have very limited scope, and their advocates claim relevance only to understanding limited aspects of human behavior and the environment, sometimes based on very specific observations. Other theories are very ambitious, and their advocates claim applicability with few limits. Theories of modest scope tend to be somewhat concrete; the few concepts have specific empirical referents. Theories of large scope tend to be very abstract; many concepts lack empirical referents or operational definitions.

The scope of a piece of theoretical knowledge is often not specified explicitly. Moreover, theory experts don't always agree on how to categorize a particular theory by its scope. However, the following discussion attempts to offer a common way to organize theorizing products from those of most limited scope and abstraction to those of greatest scope and abstraction.

Observations

Social workers learn how to make careful and detailed observations of "person interacting in the environment" phenomena in your practice classes and research classes. Reports of observations can be very concrete. Often hard-to-explain, puzzling observations stimulate everyday or scientific theorizing. Observations are like the ground on which the ladder sits and not yet abstracted as elements of a formal theory.

Empirical generalization

At the lower level of this continuum of theoretical scope, there is the *empirical generalization*. This is a summary statement of a biological, psychological, social, or ecological pattern that has been documented through multiple observations as occurring widely. A theorist can summarize a generalization concisely by words, numbers, or graphics (Bass & Wind, 1995). Empirical generalizations specify the uniformity among a group of events or objects and are often presented as a relationship between two or more concepts (Bloom, 1975). Good empirical generalizations are supported by accumulated research evidence. Each empirical generalization synthesizes a large number of specific scientific observations. The generalization has been recorded consistently across different social situations, different populations, or different historical periods. Some theories incorporate or make sense of empirical generalizations.

Here's an example of an empirical generalization confirmed by symbolic interactionist researchers (Forte, 1998). Have you ever felt alone when you noticed that you seem to understand your professor very well, but he has little understanding of you? You are not alone. There is much evidence for the generalizability of the assertion that power and status differences, especially as related to social markers of gender, race, ethnicity, class, and bureaucratic position, affect empathy and role-taking processes in face-to-face social situations. Specifically, *persons in positions of relative powerlessness more fully take the perspective of and empathize with the powerless than do those in positions of power.* Women tend to empathize more than their male husbands and partners. Minority group members generally understand the desires and intentions of majority group members well compared to the understanding of the majority. Low-level employees exert themselves to take the perspective of their employers, whereas employers are often blind to the troubles of their workers. Students try to figure out their professors, whereas professors give less time imagining their student's concerns and attitudes. This is an important and useful generalization about social life. It demonstrates that there is link between two theoretical constructs, social standing, and inclination to understand others and that this patterned relationship has a bearing on many aspects of social life.

Empirical generalizations may be a component of a theory with greater scope. Or the discovery of an empirical generalization may stimulate new theorizing. Generalizations are especially useful for practitioners, Argyris (1996) argues, if they are "actionable." An actional generalization is a generalization that informs the practitioner how to replicate the pattern in a setting beyond those in which it was first identified. The pattern applies both to many cases under different conditions and to the individual case faced. Argyris offers an example of an actionable generalization from psychology: frustration leads to regression, and one consequence of regression is aggression. Such a generalization could contribute to the design of an intervention and thus be used to begin to create positive change in some aggressive clients.

Middle-range theory

Middle-range theories lie between empirical generalizations and the working hypotheses that validate these generalizations and all-inclusive theories of grand scope (Merton, 1968). A *middle-range theory* organizes a set of concepts and propositions in a way enhancing our understanding of a specific aspect of the social world. Middle-range theories are also formulated in a way that makes empirical test possible. They have significantly fewer concepts as part of the theoretical structure than grand conceptual schemes or theoretical traditions. A middle-range theory is not too broad to be useless in specific practice situations but not too narrow to be trivial. However, middle-range theories are less context-free and less generalizable than theories of larger scope (Burr, 1973).

Edwin Sutherland and his successors advanced a differential association theory of delinquent behavior (Matsueda, 1988). This middle-range theory explains a youth's decision to engage in antisocial conduct. I will summarize it in a simple fashion. Sutherland theorized that a person's associates powerfully influence his or her attitudes and behavior. Adolescents who begin to interact frequently with those who consider carjacking, shoplifting, and mugging as acceptable activities soon define these behaviors in the same way. Youths, in contrast, who associate with models of pro-social, responsible thinking and law-abiding behaviors are the youths who tend to refrain from delinquent conduct. Matsueda has extensively tested and confirmed the major propositions of this mid-range theory (Forte, 2006). Such a theory could be used to design group work programs promoting interaction between potential delinquents and identified law-abiding and responsible peers.

Grand theory

A *grand theory* is a very general theory with ambitious scope. Grand theorists attempt, for example, to construct an overall conceptual scheme of social life, history, or human experience (Skinner, 1985). Instead of trying to understand a particular kind of society or one dimension of human experience, the grand theorist builds a framework for understanding social life in all its permutations. Grand theories, Burr (1973) explains, "have great scope and high informative value, and they are not specifically tied to any social context" (p. 280). Grand theories are often very complex, and stated at a high level of abstraction.

A few theorists, Talcott Parsons, for example, have attempted to create grand and comprehensive theories. Parsons, a sociologist, integrated knowledge from various social sciences and from many academic disciplines into one overarching framework. His grand theory includes many very abstract constructs such as adaptation, goal attainment, integration, and latency. This theory explains the totality of social action in societal systems and has been commonly referred to as the functional or structural functional theory.

In nursing, some theorists have developed grand theories, abstract conceptualizations of the whole of nursing (Peterson, 2004). Peterson identified several competitors for the title of the grand nursing theory including Parse's Theory of Human Becoming, Roy's Adaptation Model, Roger's Science of Human Beings, and Newman's Theory of Health. In the social work profession, the eco-systems (person-in-environment) framework is the leading candidate for status as a grand theory. Grand theories can be useful because they provide a discipline-specific frame of reference. They can also provide a framework for organizing a curriculum, an orientation to conceptualizing the relevant aspects of reality, and a foundation for practice

Theoretical tradition

A theoretical tradition or "school of thought" refers to a group of scholars and practitioners who are united by their recognition of a special leader or founder. In linguistic theory, a school of thought could be compared to a speech community, a group of people who share a language and a set of rules for the use of the language (Romaine, 2000). In the social sciences, members of a theoretical tradition speak the same theoretical language. The theoretical tradition often began in a particular ecological setting—Chicago, the University of Chicago, and Hull-House for the symbolic interactionist tradition. Members of a tradition make a commitment to a particular way of understanding social life, conducting scientific inquiry, and talking about theorizing. Tradition promoters develop a teaching network with varied vehicles of communication to spread the language. The vehicles include universities, journals, Web sites, training centers and workshops, and discussion groups. Adherents to a tradition generally regard their framework to be a comprehensive organization of knowledge.

Symbolic interactionism is a theoretical tradition. The tradition's origin is linked historically to George Herbert Mead and Jane Addams. It flourished at the School of Sociology in Chicago, United States during the first half of the last century. It gives central importance to humans as symbol makers and symbol users. It uses a language full of concepts describing communication and interaction, and it endorses a participant observation approach to scientific inquiry. The school has a flagship journal, an annual book, a discussion list, a yearly conference, and a literature of thousands of books and articles. The institutions aligned with the school of thought are like language laboratories where students learn the tradition's language and how to use it.

Theoretical traditions are sometimes called *theoretical frameworks* or *theoretical perspectives*. When a theoretical framework as a collection of ideas associated with a theoretical tradition is used to sensitize or orient social work practitioners to important aspects of reality, it may be referred to as a theoretical perspective. Theory experts often refer to the "strengths perspective" in this way. Here, we are using the theoretical knowledge for its general suggestions and explanations about a practice challenge. We might take the symbolic interactionist perspective on a family dispute and give priority to communication successes and failures, or we might shift to a structural functionalist perspective and think of the family dispute in terms of its function for the whole system.

Some theoretical traditions such as symbolic interactionism or psychoanalysis even include sub-schools or variations on the overall framework. There are communication systems within the comprehensive theoretical language. They can be compared to the wings of a massive building where members develop their own lingo. The idea of sub-school is comparable also to the regional and social dialects or sub-languages found in a large speech community. English-speaking Americans, for example, vary by region in pronunciation, grammar, and vocabulary (Romaine, 2000). Interactionists have identified a Chicago School, an Iowa School, and a Berkeley School. Members of the various schools all understand the base language of interactionism, but members from these competing schools sound slightly different and emphasize different theoretical concepts and theorizing rules. Theoretical traditions subsume the earlier levels of theoretical abstraction and include empirical generalizations, middle-range theories, and grand theories.

Paradigm

Theory experts do not completely agree on the definition of the concept, "paradigm." Kuhn (1970) defines a *paradigm* as a coherent, a worldview or collection of beliefs and theories that has become accepted unquestionably and established as a truthful representation by a scientific community or society. We have been thinking of theory in terms of scope or ambitiousness. A paradigm is knowledge that has the greatest scope of all the forms of theory.

A paradigm is a particular way of viewing and thinking about the world informed by a set of related theories and philosophical convictions, and shared by members of a community. Marshall (1994) defines scientific paradigm as a "consensus across the relevant scientific community about the theoretical and methodological rules to be followed, the instruments to be used, the problems to be investigated, and the standards by which research is judged" (p 376). A paradigm might be compared fruitfully to the culture of a language community. Cultural members agree about the significant symbols and images of the community. There is an agreement also among members of a disciplinary or professional culture that the paradigm offers the best image of the community's focal subject matter.

Paradigms also differentiate one community from another. For example, we might compare the scientific paradigm to the religious paradigm. Atheists from different disciplines such as economics or anthropology and professional backgrounds such as law or architecture see life using a radically different scientific paradigm than devout Catholics laypersons immersed in a religious paradigm. In a society, there is often a dominant paradigm, a system of thought and values widely held and considered standard by societal members. For decades, the Soviet Union and the United States affirmed different dominant political-economic paradigms: communism and capitalism, respectively. The difference was a major source of friction between the two nations. Paradigms for studying people in surroundings may divide Australians. Cooperation across three paradigms will be difficult: the pre-scientific paradigm (the cultural belief systems and patterns of indigenous people, Aborigines); the positivistic paradigm, an approach that guides theorizers, researchers, and practitioners who report on statistical findings from their "objective" studies; and the interpretive paradigm, the approach of theorizers, researchers, and practitioners who use participation to deeply understand the "subjective" aspect of a client subculture (Reid, 2001).

Ritzer (1975), an expert on paradigms, asserts that contemporary science is a multi-paradigm science. There are different scientific paradigms competing for influence, and the champions of paradigms repeatedly question and challenge each other's allegiance. There are many problems, Ritzer adds, caused by paradigm battles. Scientists and practitioners may act according to a paradigm without realizing that they have made a choice and without considering the strengths of alternative paradigms. Blind adherence to a paradigm causes theory users to lose the ability to question their basic assumptions and detect unusual patterns or deviations from paradigm-based expectations. Paradigm supporters often exaggerate the explanatory power and usefulness of their paradigm. Adherents to a paradigm may unfairly criticize their rivals for not using the preferred paradigm to guide research, practice, and theory building. They fail to understand because of this bias why the rival did what she did and what the rival contributed to knowledge-building projects.

I suspect that this discussion of levels of theoretical abstraction may seem somewhat tangential to the needs of practitioners. In the next section, I will provide lessons showing that social workers theorizing in ways close to the lower end and middle of the ladder of theoretical abstraction (concepts, propositions, middle range, and grounded theories) can draw elements from the abstractions of theoretical traditions to create tools for evidence-informed, effective, responsible practice.

Learning activities and reflections

1   Start with a specific and recent experience. Attempt to capture in words some of the features of the experience: related sensations, duration, emotional qualities, associated thoughts, and so on. Next try to use several concepts to characterize more abstractly this experience.

2   Identify an empirical generalization. Based on your experiences and observations of human behavior, what general and empirically sound statements might you make about human beings, about environments, or about transactions between humans and the environment? Provide some generalizations about common life challenges faced at particular stages of the life course.

3   Pick one topic, for example, the causes of eating disorders among middle class suburban high school girls in the United States. Identify and relate three or four variables to form a middle-range theory that organizes knowledge related to one of these topics.

4   What might critics of Talcott Parsons and his grand systems theory argue are the weaknesses of a framework that attempts to explain everything about the person in environment? What might supporters tout as the strengths of the grand theory?

5   Do some research on the Web or in your library. Trace the history of a theoretical tradition that interests you (behaviorism, systems theory, feminism, role theory, or the empowerment approach, for examples)? Who were the founders of the school of thought? What are the core ideas? What branches or sub-schools have developed over time from the foundation? What are some of the concepts, generalizations, and theories contained within the tradition's knowledge library?

6   Compare two persons: one who organizes all aspects of his or her life using a religious paradigm and one who organizes all aspects of his or her life using a scientific paradigm. What are some specific differences in their viewpoints? What might be possible similarities? How might these differences be manifest in action and interaction tendencies? Assume the adherents to the different paradigms engage in a major intellectual fight. How might a mediator reconcile the differences?

References

Argyris, C. (1996). Actionable knowledge: Design causality in the service of consequentialist theory. *The Journal of Applied Behavioral Science, 32*(4), 390–406.

Bass, F. M., & Wind, J. (1995). Introduction to the special issue: Empirical generalizations in marketing. *Marketing Science, 14*(3), Part 2, G1–G5.

Bloom, M. (1975). *The paradox of helping: Introduction to the philosophy of scientific practice.* New York: Wiley.

Burr, W. R. (1973). *Theory construction and the sociology of the family*. New York: Wiley.

DePoy, E., & Gilson, S. F. (2007). *The human experience: Description, explanation, and judgment*. Lanham, MD: Rowman and Littlefield.

Forte, J. A. (1998). Power and role-taking: A review of theory, research and practice. *Journal of Human Behavior in the Social Environment, 1*(4), 27–56.

Forte, J. A. (2006). *Human behavior and the social environment: models, metaphors, and maps for applying theoretical perspectives to practice*. Belmont, CA: Thomson Brooks/Cole.

Kuhn, T. S. (1970). *The structure of scientific revolutions* (2nd edn). Chicago, IL: University of Chicago Press.

Marshall, G. (Ed.). (1994). *The concise Oxford dictionary of sociology*. Oxford, UK: Oxford University Press.

Matsueda, R. L. (1988). The current state of differential association theory. *Crime and Delinquency, 34*(3), 277–306.

Merton, R. K. (1968). *On social theory and social structure*. New York: Free Press.

Peterson, S. J. (2004). Introduction to the nature of nursing knowledge. In S. J. Peterson & T. S. Bredow (Eds), *Middle range theories: Application to nursing research* (pp. 3–41). Philadelphia, PA: Lippincott, Williams and Wilkins.

Reid, W. J. (2001). The role of science in social work: The perennial debate. *Journal of Social Work, 1*(3), 273–293.

Ritzer, G. (1975). *Sociology: A multiple paradigm science*. Boston, MA: Allyn & Bacon.

Romaine, S (2000). *Language in environment: An introduction to sociolinguistics*. Oxford, UK: Oxford University Press.

Skinner, Q. (1985). Introduction: The return of grand theory. In Q. Skinner (Ed.), *The return of grand theory in the human sciences* (pp. 1–20). New York: Cambridge University Press.

Identify and use theory differentially by system level

(EPAS 2.1.3 Apply Critical Thinking;
EPAS 2.1.7 Apply Knowledge)

The social environment is composed of social systems of different size. Generalist social workers learn to understand and help client systems from small to large. Specialist social workers add expert knowledge, skills, and dispositions for serving particular size systems such as the family or the community in advanced ways. Theories and skillful theorizing help generalists and specialists do their jobs.

Systems theory as a framework for organizing all knowledge

According to systems theory, a key component with ecological theory of the common base for practice, there are similarities across systems, whatever the size (Bertalanffy, 1969; Parsons, 1952). Every social system includes elements or subsystems. Every social system has boundaries. Every social system fluctuates between states of stability and instability. Every social system is goal-oriented and inclined to maintain ideal system states. All systems are interconnected so a focal system is influenced by and influences both the smaller subsystems within its boundaries and the larger systems in which it is embedded. The different size systems also have distinctive qualities. Generalist social workers often adopt systems theory as a foundational part of their theoretical orientation and integrate other theoretical traditions depending on the practitioners' systems specialty.

Theory specialization by systems level

Theoretical traditions and their related theory elements vary in their relevance to size-specific social work activities. Social workers select and use theoretical knowledge, then, differentially, depending on the size of the focal system. When theorizing about work with a particular-size system, adept practitioners draw on the theoretical resources best suited to making sense of the system and its dynamics. Some theories such as role theory and interactionist theory provide in-depth understanding of human behavior and environmental issues germane to the small group level, for instance.

The concept of *system level* refers to a particular system's place in the hierarchy of all systems organized by size and complexity. We might also think of the choice of system level as a choice of your unit of analysis. This is a term for the major entity (the who or the what) that you are theorizing about. Social workers often characterize theories in terms of their primary system-level focus: micro-theory, mezzo-theory, and macro-level theory (Dale, Smith, Norlin, & Chess, 2009; Forte, 2006; Van Wormer, Besthorn, & Keefe, 2007). There is not agreement among social work educators about the categorization of social systems by level. The mezzo-level, for example, is often associated with systems of various sizes from small groups to large social networks. Therefore, the descriptions below are offered tentatively. I briefly characterize the focus of theory at each level, identify some roles common to work with each level, and offer illustrations.

Micro-theories

Micro-theories focus on small-size social systems such as elements of the person (biological, cognitive, emotional, behavioral, and spiritual processes), individuals, and couples. When working with micro-systems, social workers might engage in case management, individual counseling, or broker services for a client. Cognitive sciences such as Bandura's social cognition theory and Piaget's theory of constructivism provide various theoretical tools for understanding human thought processes and cognitive development and for helping clients process information more accurately and expand their thinking capabilities. The psychodynamic theoretical tradition illuminates inner psychological processes, especially those related to emotions, ego defenses, and intrapsychic conflicts. The tradition has been the starting point for the development many micro-oriented practice theories, too.

Mezzo-theories

Mezzo-theories focus on intermediate-size social systems such as large work groups, social support networks, and extended families. At the level of mezzo-systems, a social worker might work with an agency coalition or multidisciplinary family assessment and planning team, or the social worker might attempt to activate the strengths available in a family's set of informal helping relationships. Social network theory is an ideal approach for making sense of persons and how they are linked to similar others by various social, economic, communication, and identity channels and bonds. Social network theory also provided directives regarding ways to increase social support and positive network connections.

Macro-theories

Macro-theories focus on large-size social systems that have numerous members and complex structures and may even operate across different geographic locales. Macro-level systems are large-collectives, and this systems level includes organizations, communities, institutions, societies, and global networks of institutions and societies. Macro-oriented social work could involve recommending strategies for improving administrative decision making, serving as a consultant to the president of a corporation's board of directors, mobilizing a social movement to address a public issue, joining with the National Association of Social Workers to influence the national policy-making process, or working for an international organization such as the United Nations. Several theories attend to macro-level issues. Structural functionalism theorizes about the patterns of norms and values shared among members of a society and the socialization processes that produce and reproduce these patterns across generations, for example. Globalization theory provides conceptualizations of the changes in the integration of societies and their economies into the world community following modernization and the subsequent advances in communication, technological, and exchange processes

The idea of systems level helps us select and use theoretical knowledge best suited to our social work roles and tasks. Be aware, however, that some theories such as symbolic interactionism or Bronfenbrenner's ecological systems theory of human development transcend this categorization scheme and provide theoretical understanding of social systems of many different sizes. The systems-level notion also helps us focus our own theorizing work. When theorizing to improve our work with a state legislative body, we select knowledge from theoretical traditions different from when we are theorizing about a family's difficulties coping with an aging and severely ill member.

Learning activities and reflections

1   Summarize briefly your understanding of the concept of systems level including your ideas about how clients are members of interacting and influential social systems.

2   Provide illustrations of actual micro-level systems and the important social worker roles, methods, and tasks associated with this level. Now identify four or more specific micro-level topics or problems that you need to understand when working with micro-level systems. Next, identify three or four examples of the theoretical knowledge that would help you understand these topics or problems and act effectively. If

possible, identify the specific theoretical frameworks, middle-range theories, and theoretical concepts that are relevant to the identified micro aspects of human behavior and the social environment.

3 Provide illustrations of actual mezzo-level systems and the important social worker roles, methods, and tasks associated with this level. Now identify four or more specific mezzo-level topics or problems that you need to understand when working with mezzo-level systems. Next, identify three or four examples of theoretical knowledge that would help you understand these topics or problems and act effectively. If possible, identify the specific theoretical frameworks, middle-range theories, and theoretical concepts that are relevant to the identified mezzo aspects of human behavior and the social environment.

4 Identify three or four examples of theoretical knowledge that would help you when working with macro-level systems. Provide illustrations of actual macro-level systems and the important social worker roles, methods, and tasks associated with this level. Now identify four or more specific macro-level topics or problems that you need to understand when working with macro-level systems. Next, identify three or four examples of theoretical knowledge that would help you understand these topics or problems and act effectively. If possible, identify the specific theoretical frameworks, middle-range theories, and theoretical concepts that are relevant to the identified macro aspects of human behavior and the social environment.

5 Take a life course/developmental perspective and review your participation in systems at various levels. Pick a stage that you remember well. Identify the micro-level systems influential in your development (and that you may have influenced) during this stage. Identify the major mezzo-level systems and also the most important macro-level systems. For each level, identify theoretical knowledge that would help you understand and assess your stage-related development.

6 Take inspiration from Erik Erikson and create a multi-level theory of a person in the middle stage of his or her life. Find and interview a middle-age person. Explore what type of developmental events and factors at the personal, dyadic/intimate relationship, family, community, and societal levels are influencing the person's thinking, feeling, and behaving. How have these changes affected the person's outlook and physical, psychological, social, and spiritual functioning? Ask whether the person has faced a mid-life crisis, and if so, how would he or she describe it? Theorize with the person about the systems (micro-, mezzo-, and macro-) that have contributed most to this crisis. How and why? Theorize also with the person about the systems at each level that have provided support in meeting mid life stage challenges. How and why? What additional challenges and opportunities does the person anticipate in middle adulthood? How are these related to his or her engagement

with different size systems? Finally, summarize the kinds of knowledge that have been helpful in your information gathering and assessment work, and organize your knowledge as a summary of your multi-level theory of the person's stage experiences? Specify the major concepts and theoretical propositions from each theoretical tradition relevant to your profile.

References

Bertalanffy, L. von. (1969). *General systems theory*. New York: Braziller.

Forte, J. A. (2006). *Human behavior and the social environment: Models, metaphors, and maps for applying theoretical perspectives to practice*. Belmont, CA: Thomson Brooks/Cole.

Dale, O., Smith, R., Norlin, J. M., & Chess, W. A. (2009). *Human behavior and the social environment: Social systems theory* (6th edn). Boston, MA: Pearson / Allyn and Bacon.

Parsons, T. (1952). *The social system*. New York: Free Press.

Van Wormer, K., Besthorn, F., & Keefe, T. (2007). *Human behavior and the social environment: Macro level, groups, communities, and organizations*. New York: Oxford University Press.

SECTION 2	Applying theory (deconstructive and reconstructive theorizing)

As previewed in the introduction, I have made the case that practical theorizing by social workers involves two related processes: theory deconstruction and theory reconstruction. Some advanced social workers will construct new theories for their use and for our profession. These projects will be explained briefly in Section 3.

Deconstructing is a process of taking apart or unpacking the elements of a theory about some aspect of human behavior and the environment (assumptions, concepts, propositions, networks of propositions, diagrams) as these are represented in symbols. *Reconstructing* is a process of gathering knowledge of many kinds (theoretical knowledge, research knowledge, practice wisdom, and everyday, personal knowledge), adapting and reorganizing this knowledge as a theory for use in particular helping circumstances. My priority for this section's lessons will be helping readers learn to "make use of ready-made theory in constructing their own theory"(Secker, 1993, p. 78).

Theory deconstruction and reconstruction are followed by supplemental evidence-informed work such as generating theoretical hypotheses about the likely results of theory application, individualizing the theory to fit with the client needs and challenges, trying out the theory as a guide to assessment efforts and/or intervention planning, collecting evidence and reflecting critically on the theory's usefulness, modifying the theory based on this feedback, and resuming the cycle of theory application.

Section 2 includes a set of lessons with knowledge and skills essential to practical theorizing. The lessons can be viewed as a sequence of theorizing steps from lesson 7 to lesson 17. Each lesson can also be viewed as independent and uses as needed by the social work practitioner.

Identify the theoretical aspects of the practice puzzle

(EPAS 2.1.3 Apply Critical Thinking;
EPAS 2.1.7 Apply Knowledge)

Lesson 7 begins the second section of this book. We will focus on the steps of effective theory application. First, let's make an important distinction.

Theorizing versus theory

Theorizing is different from theory (Bengston, Allen, Klein, Dilworth-Anderson, & Acock, 2005a; Bengston, Allen, Klein, Dilworth-Anderson, & Acock, 2005b; Rinehart, 1999). Theorizing is an active process, a process of making sense of and organizing observations, perceptions, intuitions, thoughts, and evidence as we use or create theories to solve practical and intellectual problems. Theorizing is a form of scientific inquiry during which theorists develop ideas that gather, interpret, and explain data (Bengston et al, 2005a; Weick, 1987). Theory, in contrast, is a product, the completed act of theorizing. This product is often shared as a verbal or written summary in the form of concepts and linked propositions answering a "why," "how," "what," "what next," or similar question. Theory is what you read in textbooks and journal articles.

For practitioners on the road to expertise, the notion of theorizing adds a new focus for learning. To the mastery of existing theoretical knowledge, social workers practice and enhance their capacities to adapt theories and use varied theorizing skills to solve different theoretical puzzles. Hoffman (1985) makes a similar but more radical point about theorizing. He argued "in practice, there is no such thing as a theory, there is only theorizing" (p. 366).

Theorizing as puzzle solving

Theorizing can be compared to the process of solving a puzzle. Thomas Kuhn (1970), the distinguished philosopher of science, asserted that "the problems of normal science are puzzles" (p. 37) and "many of the greatest scientific minds have devoted all of their professional attention to demanding puzzles" (p. 38). Theoretical paradigms or traditions, he argued, provide the criteria for choosing puzzles to solve and the tools for solving these puzzles.

The social work profession has taken the initiative in identifying and working on numerous "person interacting in the environment and needing help" puzzles. Social workers on the front line try to solve puzzles every day, and they contribute to the professional knowledge base when they share their solutions to the puzzles encountered in their agencies and businesses. Puzzle solvers are like detectives searching for clues at the crime scene and using the clues and their thinking abilities to figure out the mysteries "embedded deep in the interstices of human relationships" (Rosenau, 1980, p. 23). Puzzle solvers are also like translators trying to interpret the meanings of the sounds, words, gestures, appearance choices, and actions of a foreigner telling a story in her or his foreign language. The best translator creates a translation that accommodates in an English version the essential meanings of the symbolic pieces of communication.

Practical theorizing as puzzle solving

Let's expand on this comparison of practical theorizing to puzzle solving. Figure 7.1 displays the basic phases of the theorizing when considered a puzzle-solving process. The observations or data that we collect during our work with a client system are the *puzzle pieces*. Clients present puzzling challenges, and the details about their bio-psycho-social problems can be understood as sets of puzzle pieces. Each piece of the puzzle provides some useful information, but each piece is incomplete and makes full sense only when fitted into the jigsaw puzzle.

The worker and client are stimulated by the sense of uncertainty or confusion to begin puzzle solving, and they agree to cooperate as theorists— worker as trained theorist and client as novice theorist—and, together, they think theoretically and make choices about where to place each piece into the *puzzle board*. The puzzle board represents the template for knowledge assembly and organization provided by a theoretical tradition.

All the information (puzzle pieces) collected during the helping process is contained in the *puzzle box*, the case files, for instance, of a client. The set of pieces in the box vary in number and complexity. Some puzzles are easy to assemble; there are few pieces. Others take time and require numerous fresh starts; these have numerous pieces or pieces with images that are difficult to decipher.

The worker and client alike take one piece at a time and fit each piece into the *puzzle holes*. They may become frustrated when it is difficult to assemble all the pieces and make out the exact form or shape of a puzzle pattern or

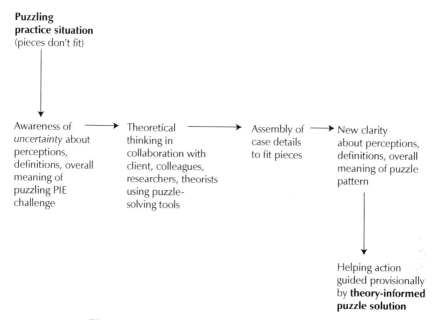

**Puzzling
practice situation**
(pieces don't fit)

Awareness of → Theoretical → Assembly of → New clarity
uncertainty about thinking in case details about perceptions,
perceptions, collaboration with to fit pieces definitions, overall
definitions, overall client, colleagues, meaning of puzzle
meaning of researchers, theorists pattern
puzzling PIE using puzzle-
challenge solving tools

Helping action
guided provisionally
by **theory-informed
puzzle solution**

Figure 7.1 Practical theorizing as puzzle solving

when certain pieces don't seem to fit anywhere. Progress is made as more and more pieces are fit into unfilled portions of the overall puzzle.

The joint completion of the puzzle hopefully reveals clearly an overall *puzzle pattern*. Store-bought puzzles include a picture of the final pattern on the box: an underwater scene, a landscape, a portrait of a famous person, a gathering of animals, and so on. The puzzle solvers can scan this cover picture repeatedly as they assemble pieces. In social work, the final pattern might be thought of as the assessment formulation. For clients with familiar biopsychosocial problems, the picture of the final pattern emerges and serves as a guide to the intervention phase. Sometimes clients present odd or unique problems and challenges. The helping team engages in intervention planning without benefit of total clarity about the final pattern.

Theoretical puzzle solving may also become the stimulus to additional scientific inquiry and research into related puzzles. The agency, mental health clinic, or private practice setting is like *the game room* at a community center where puzzles are completed. Supervisors and colleagues are cheering us on and, at times, recommending steps based on their theoretical knowledge and practice wisdom to solve difficult puzzles. They ask us to record our puzzle-solving successes and failures as guides for other puzzle solvers.

Practical theorizing as different from puzzle solving

Theorizing is different, however, from puzzle solving in several ways. In daily life, we usually work on one puzzle at a time. In professional life, clients often bring multiple and interconnected puzzles to the worker, and workers help many different client systems with their puzzles every week. In daily life, puzzle solving is fun, and the stakes are minimal. In practice settings, clients and others judge social workers on the quality of the solutions to a practice puzzle. The quality or lack of quality has grave implications for life processes. Recreational puzzle solvers proceed in a familiar step-by-step fashion. For professionals, there are many different ways to approach the puzzle pieces of problem-person-transaction-environment configuration; the approach varies, for example, depending on the practitioner's theoretical orientation. Finally, the professional social worker's experience, unlike the game player's act of solving a crossword or jigsaw puzzle, involves a continual process of adjustment to challenges. Puzzle solving is never finished. We can never put away the final puzzle.

The basic features of theorizing as puzzle solving

Let's review some of the features of theorizing. First, theorizing is intentional. Professional theorizing activity is directed to answering a practice question, achieving particular helping goals and objectives, or solving an intervention impasse. Theorizing to solve puzzles then is not happenstance, but it is related directly to our professional purposes, to agency purposes, and to the purposes we negotiate with our clients.

Second, theorizing is a common human process (Bailey, 1980). Giddens (1984) noted:

> all social actors are, it can be properly said, social theorists, who alter their theories in light of their expectations and are receptive to incoming information which they may require in doing so. Social theory is by no means the special and insulated province of academic thinkers (p. 335).

All people engage in theoretical thinking and related cognitive processes such as abstraction, generalization, prediction, and explanation. This is part of the human psyche. People theorize informally, for instance, about life puzzles such as the meaning of "mate," the qualities of the ideal partner, the likely results of dating strategies, and the reasons for rejection or acceptance by the sought-after lover. Scientific theorizing differs from everyday theorizing only in some ways; it aims for systematic, rigorous, and evidence-informed intellectual activity, for example.

Third, theorizing is a social process. Within the social work profession, members of theory development or research program teams theorize together. Within the helping relationship, the worker and client become members of helping system communicating and coordinating their theorizing activities. Collaborative theorizing requires respect for fellow theorizers, an ear open to all the ideas that can contribute to the puzzle solving venture, and an appreciation that different personal and professional biographies lead to different approaches to theorizing. Even when the worker takes the lead and does most of the hard theorizing work in the helping team, any successful theorizing is a collective accomplishment.

Fourth, theorizing styles (positivist, interpretive, and critical) differ in the ideas and rules the theorizer brings to the puzzle-solving process. Additionally, each theoretical tradition (behaviorism, evolutionary science, symbolic interactionism, for examples) focuses on different puzzles and conceives of completed puzzles in different ways. A theoretical tradition is like a lens filtering light so that light shines on some aspects of HBSE puzzles, but the theoretical lens may also place in shadows other important puzzle pieces. When we theorize, we do so with reference to and help from those peers in the theoretical tradition(s) that we have claimed as our own.

Fifth, theorizing involves making explicit our thinking about the puzzle-solving process, reflecting on how the theorizing guides the assessment and intervention processes and articulating our theoretical premises and ideas to others such as clients, client collaterals, supervisors, and agency stakeholders. It is not enough to solve a professional puzzle. We need to be able to talk about what we did, how we did it, and the quality of the effort. Blending metaphors from the finished puzzle metaphor with the narrative metaphor, good theorizers spell out the story or argument created as a result of the theorizing activity, how they arrived at this final story, and the news of evidence increasing confidence that the puzzle pattern has been detected. We also inform and sometimes persuade others during and after our theorizing. By sharing information about our theorizing processes and products, we contribute to the profession's cumulative knowledge-building venture. We provide intellectual resources that other practitioners, teams, networks of service providers, communities of helpers, disciplines, and professions might use in their research, theoretical, and practice puzzle-solving projects.

Sixth, theorizing involves art and science. Theorizing is a creative process, one of disciplined imagination (Weick, 1987), and involves taking the old—existing theoretical knowledge, research knowledge, and practice wisdom—and using it in a new and innovative way, or in some cases, creating a brand new theory. Following the directions of a practice theory cookbook in a rote and non-reflective way won't solve real-life client puzzles. The circumstances that our clients face are usually unique and novel. Thus, our theorizing must innovatively respond to the particular features of the "person interacting in the environment" configuration and of the helping situation. Skillful theory users make use of their life experiences, their practice wisdom, and their refined judgment and intuition to bring a degree of artistry to practice. However, theorizing is a scientific enterprise, too: systematic, tied to the empirical world, subject to correction, and shared with a larger community. Skillful theorizing is a holistic synthesis of art and science: an intellectual process blended with our consideration of bodily sensations, intuitive and emotional responses, cognitions, memories, knowledge of existing theories and research, scientific method, and perceptions and understandings of the client in context (Doane & Varcoe, 2005).

Seventh, theorizing is a political process, and the resultant knowledge has some power. The puzzles chosen may reflect power dynamics. Political forces influence what is communicated to the public about the puzzle-solving processes and products. Who contributes to the cumulative toolbox of preferred solutions to societal puzzles depends on the theorizers' standing in a power and status hierarchy.

Eight, theorizing is a complex set of skills learned by practice. If we engage often in the theorizing process and reflect on our setbacks and our successes using varied skills repeatedly, we can become better theorizers. We can be trained, and we can train ourselves in disciplined theorizing, thus achieving greater rigor in following the steps of puzzle assembly, deepening our insights into the solutions revealed by the final puzzle pattern, and improving our practical judgments about the quality of our theoretical puzzle solving activities (Sears, 2005).

A puzzle-solving approach to the steps of theorizing

We can theorize systematically. Bengston and his colleagues (2005a), Mithaug (2000), and other theory experts offer many useful suggestions for theorizing. I have combined their ideas into a six-step process and paralleled it to the phases of the planned change process identified by the Council on Social Work Education (2013).

Engagement (puzzlement and mutual identification of a theoretical puzzle)

First, the practitioner experiences a discrepancy between what he or she knows and what he or she doesn't know related to the helping process. In other words, the worker and the client recognize that something about the problem or "person interacting in the environment" configuration is puzzling. We call this the *focal problem* or *challenge*. Agency knowledge including standard procedures and routines is inadequate as we try to make sense of the situation (Usher & Bryant, 1987). Our hypotheses about the person, process, or problem serve us poorly: The client continues to act in unexpected ways; harmonious interaction becomes tense and contentious; or two incompatible explanations compete in our minds (Turner, 1980). Weick (1989) notes that the discrepancy or trigger for theorizing has been referred to by many names: question, problem, awareness of ignorance, anomaly, puzzle, or puzzlement.

We decide with the client and members of the client system how to best name and characterize the theoretical puzzle. Is it one of explanation? Does the problem relate to categorization? Are we dealing with a quandary regarding prediction, or is the puzzle about best interventions? We invite the client to join us in practical theorizing and the puzzle assembly can begin.

Assessment: collect and organize data (assemble puzzle pieces)

Second, we start gathering information, attempting to collect all the puzzle pieces, and trying out the fit of each bit into emerging patterns on the puzzle board. We want to transform the indeterminate situation, one that is unclear and perplexing, into a determinate situation, one in which the elements or pieces of the "person interacting in an environment challenge" fit together into a coherent pattern (Stevenson, 2005). Our theoretical frame of reference guides our effort to gather informational pieces from the universe of potential data. We also use existing theoretical and research knowledge to provide tentative clues to how we might fit together the data, the puzzle pieces in our case, into patterns.

Assessment: interpret data (describe puzzle pattern)

Third, we initiate the puzzle assembly process, tentatively moving the pieces on the puzzle board and trying out a few arrangements. These are our preliminary theoretical experiments (Schön, 1987), our attempts to bring coherence to the table strewn messily with puzzle pieces. Slowly we gain confidence in our ability to impose order on the client's past, present, and anticipated future transactions with the environment. Now we begin formulating our hypothesis or guiding conception about the puzzling situation, checking out our hunches about the best fit of pieces and seeking client system validation of the results of this inquiry. As the final overall pattern begins to emerge, we notice a few holes on the overall puzzle board and collect more data, the final pieces. After inserting the missing pieces, we look over the finished puzzle and develop a formulation of what the pattern means. For a mental health worker, for instance, the solution involves a multi-dimensional diagnosis. For the correctional social worker, the pattern includes a prediction about the likelihood of future recidivism.

Intervention (use the puzzle solution)

Fourth, we set goals and objectives, plan interventions, and intervene. For children working on a puzzle, the process ends when the last piece is placed on the puzzle board. The children cherish the subsequent sense of pride and enjoyment. There is still more to do for social workers. After theorizing about the nature of the puzzling challenge, a new puzzle emerges. This puzzle centers on uncertainty about how to conceptualize needed changes or desired outcomes. For clients, the discerned problem pattern is typically one that is troubling or one that doesn't allow for the full realization of potentials. How might the puzzle pieces be reassembled to portray a less problematic or more desirable pattern of person-environment transactions? Additionally, the practitioner and client work together to create a theory of intervention, a solution to the puzzling question: How might the practitioner and client take actions that rearrange and transform the pattern of the puzzling problem into a different and preferred pattern? Having resolved these additional discrepancies or puzzles, we begin implementing with the client the helping actions selected to free the client and make possible new ways of thinking, feeling, acting, and interacting.

Evaluation (appraise puzzle solving work)

Fifth, as we examine the effectiveness of the helping work and client satisfaction, we reflect on the operative puzzle patterns (the pattern or theory of the client problem and the pattern or theory of intervention). We refer, for example, to standards regarding scientific theories to help us judge the quality of our puzzle-solving progress. We analyze whether our formulation of the patterns seem credible and worthwhile. We collect evidence to determine whether action based on the puzzle pattern produced verifiable improvements in the client's social role performances and/or environmental contexts.

We share the results of the evaluation of our puzzle-solving efforts with our clients and seek their final evaluative feedback about the process and product. We may also communicate our theorizing successes and failures so that our experiences might become part of the professional literature on assessment and intervention puzzles and benefit other social workers and clients attempting to solve similar puzzles.

Theoretical puzzle solving and heuristics

Heuristic refers to the study of how to find new ways to solve intellectual puzzles or problems. Theory experts have identified various heuristics, creative strategies for generating or discovering possible solutions to theoretical puzzles (Abbott, 2004; Jaccard & Jacoby, 2010; McGuire, 1997). The use of heuristics stimulates the imagination and reflectivity that characterizes exceptional theorists. Some of the heuristics most useful for social work are summarized in Table 7.1

Table 7.1 Heuristics for theoretical puzzle solving

1	Analyze your own life experiences and behaviors in similar situations for clues to a theoretical puzzle about client's life troubles or accomplishments.
2	Use case studies of helping work with clients with similar characteristics and problems to generate theoretical insights.
3	Conduct thought experiments, the imaginative exploration of possible theoretical solutions, and reflect on the likely value of the imagined solutions for assessment and intervention.
4	Use root metaphors and other metaphors for the person, the environment, and the change process to generate ideas about the possible puzzle pattern.
5	Theorize the opposite. For example, instead of theorizing about why a pattern occurs theorize about why the pattern doesn't occur. Instead of theorizing about how to help the client change, theorize about how to keep the client the same. Instead of hypothesizing that x causes y, try reversing the relationship. Hypothesize that y causes x.
6	Change the level and unit of analysis. Instead of theorizing primarily about the client puzzle by focusing on the personality, switch to a mezzo level (extended family and social network dynamics) or to a macro level (cultural norms or social stratification) focus. Move back and forth from local to distant influences on the client system.
7	Theorize about events and processes rather than about variables and causes. For example, theorize about how the person-interacting-in-environment configuration has been changing over the last month or year rather than about the causes of this change.
8	Freeze frame a puzzling process and theorize about a narrow time frame as if it is static and uninfluenced by the past.
9	Change foundational assumptions. How might different disciplinary or theoretical assumptions change inquiry or theoretical puzzle solving? For example, instead of assuming that self-esteem is a stable personality trait (some cognitive-behavioral approaches), assume that self-esteem is a fluctuating indicator of changing self-society relationships (symbolic interactionist approach), or instead of assuming that the client is a rational actor (exchange perspective) assume that the client is guided primarily by emotions and doesn't analyze the cost of alternative actions (psychodynamic perspective).
10	Apply who questions, why questions, and what questions continually. Who is the client and why does this client do this more or less than other clients? What does the answer mean? Why was this client raised like that? What does "that" really mean?
11	Consult naïve theorists for their theoretical explanations – your grandmother or your five-year old nephew. Then use their ideas and try to develop a scientific theory that solves the focal puzzle more effectively.
12	Combine theoretical explanations from multiple sources (theoretical traditions or research studies) and generate a range of possible puzzle solutions rather than attempting to establish that one puzzle solution is better than the other solution.
13	Create a visual display that summarizes your conception of the solution to the theoretical puzzle. Revise and refine the display continually. Use the display improvements to enhance your theorizing efforts.

(continued)

Table 7.1 Heuristics for theoretical puzzle solving (continued)

14 Theorize using counterfactuals: what if the decision had been different or the event hadn't occurred. Examine how such thinking improves your understanding of what was decided or what did happen.

15 When seeking a solution to a theoretical puzzle, alternate between the position that the client is free and can make autonomous choices and the position that the client is constrained by internal and external forces and compelled to act.

16 Seek solutions to the theoretical puzzle by consulting colleagues, by reviewing the relevant literature, by imagining how exemplary theorists would have approached the puzzle, or by communicating with experts on the theoretical topic or issue.

A brief illustration of theorizing as puzzle solving

Carol Gilligan (1996), the noted feminist theorist, researcher, and counselor, provides an illustration of theorizing as puzzle solving. She noted that "clinical observations, research findings, and epidemiological data" pose a puzzle," and she then developed the following theoretical questions spelling out the explanatory puzzle: "What happens to girls at adolescence? What explains the sudden drop in resilience, the sudden onset of trouble, and the association between vitality and risk?" (p. 239).

Her career-long efforts to solve the puzzle of female developments and their possible contribution to this specific puzzle-solving challenge can only be hinted at here. Gilligan was able to draw on her extensive background as a student and teacher of human development including her collaborative teaching with Erik Erikson and Lawrence Kohlberg, great developmental theorists. As a feminist, she had also reflected and written critically and deeply on male-biased developmental theories. Additionally, Gilligan had conducted extensive qualitative research on the relationships, moral orientations, and development processes of girls and women. She had practice experience, too, through her work with a local club for sixth-grade girls and with a Harvard program designed to strengthen the healthy resistance and courage of girls.

Here is a brief summary of Gilligan's theoretical solution to the assessment aspect of the puzzle of female adolescent troubles. Pre-adolescent girls are developing their voice—the ability to articulate and communicate to others their experiences, desires, identities, and interests, and their inclinations toward human connectedness and relationship. As they approach adolescence within a patriarchal social order, these girls are subject to internal and external pressures to diminish both their voice and their connectedness. Gilligan theorizes that "girls' preadolescent strength and resilience gives way to increasing uncertainty, a hesitancy in speaking, a tendency to doubt themselves, and to dismiss their experience as irrelevant almost before they have said it, or before it can be dismissed by others" (p. 247). To speak out is defined by sexist others as speaking with a "big mouth" and often brings conflict and trouble. The consequent and common disassociation (a psychological defense process) of tendencies toward healthy resistance against sexist and patriarchal others stalls psychosocial development. This disassociation also heightens the exposure to health risks (physical, mental, and social) for many female adolescents. That begins to explain why many girls have troubles during adolescence. What do you think about Gilligan's theoretical puzzle solving? How might Gilligan's identification of an overall pattern contribute to solving puzzles about the best ways to help pre-adolescent girls?

In the remainder of this section, we will learn about a variety of theorizing tools and skills for solving human behavior and practice puzzles. These include the use of existing theories, exemplary theorists, metaphors, assumptions, concepts, propositions, deductive and inductive reasoning, and theory summary and display strategies. For each lesson, we will consider how to deconstruct and reconstruct the theory element for particular puzzle-solving tasks. Figure 7.2 provides a detailed illustration of a recommended sequence for using theory in social work that integrates these theorizing tools and skills. Note that the sequence is an artificially linear depiction. Social workers often change the order to suit particular professional tasks, and they may also, at times, jump ahead or jump back when using theories in practice. Also, there are some variations in the conceptualizations of each phase depending on theorizing style: positivist interpretive, and critical.

Learning activities and reflections

In this activity, we will focus on theorizing, the act of creating a theory. Theorize about one of the items or puzzles on the following list:

1   The processes related to drug use resulting in drug addiction
2   The causes of changing rates of homelessness in the United States
3   The causes of shifts in norms regarding premarital sexual behavior
4   The factors attracting persons to fundamentalist religious organizations
5   The processes related to the development of an attachment disorder
6   The personality factors increasing vulnerability to the formation of an eating disorder
7   The causes of violence against women
8   The cultural factors contributing to debt and bankruptcy
9   The causes of changes in political involvement activity by citizens
10 The changing types of the "family form" over the last two decades
11 The possible differences in autistic children's interaction with their caretakers
12 The vulnerability of adolescent girls to mental disorders and social difficulties

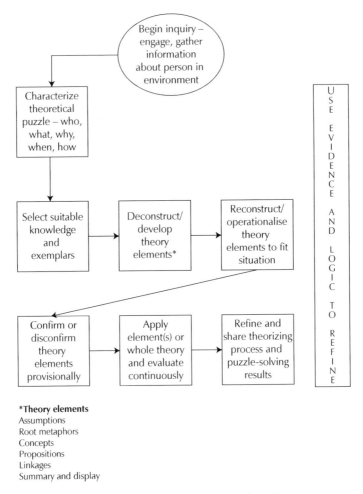

*Theory elements
Assumptions
Root metaphors
Concepts
Propositions
Linkages
Summary and display

Figure 7.2   Using theory in social work

Don't worry about meeting any requirements regarding scientific theorizing. Simply develop a theory about the puzzle, and summarize it in your own words. If possible, follow the puzzle-solving steps identified in the commentary. Identify how you theorized about your "person interacting in the environment" topic. What mental steps did you take? Compare your theoretical product to that of your peers, and comment on the strengths and limitations of the final theory. Reflect on how you might improve your theorizing activity so that a refined product more closely meets standards of evidence-informed practice.

References

Abbott, A. (2004). *Methods of discovery: Heuristics for the social sciences*. New York: Norton.

Bailey, J. (1980). *Ideas and intervention: Social theory for practice*. London: Routledge & Kegan Paul.

Bengston, V. L., Allen, K. R., Klein, D. M., Dilworth-Anderson, P., & Acock, A. C. (2005a). Theory and theorizing in family research: Puzzle building and puzzle solving. In V. L. Bengston, A. C. Acock, K. R. Allen, P. Dilworth-Anderson & D. M. Klein (Eds), *Sourcebook of family theory and research* (pp. 3–33). Thousand Oaks, CA: Sage.

Bengston, V. L., Allen, K. R., Klein, D. M., Dilworth-Anderson, P., & Acock, A. C. (2005b). Controversies and firestorms: An epilogue. In V. L. Bengston, A. C. Acock, K. R. Allen, P. Dilworth-Anderson & D. M. Klein (Eds), *Sourcebook of family theory and research* (pp. 613–630). Thousand Oaks, CA: Sage.

Council on Social Work Education (2013). 2008 Educational policy and accreditation standards. Retrieved July 17, 2013, from www.cswe.org/File.aspx?id=13780

Doane, G. H., & Varcoe, C. (2005). Toward compassionate action: Pragmatism and the inseparability of theory/practice. *Advances in Nursing Science*, 28(1), 81–90.

Giddens, A. (1984). *The constitution of society: Outline of the theory of structuration*. Berkeley, CA: University of California Press.

Gilligan, C. (1996). The centrality of relationship in human development: A puzzle, some evidence, and a theory. In G. G. Noam & K. W. Fischer (Eds), *Development and vulnerability in close relationships* (pp. 236–261). Mahwah, NJ: Lawrence Erlbaum Associates.

Hoffman, R. R. (1985). Some implications of metaphor for philosophy and psychology of science. In W. Paprrotte & R. Drive (Eds), *The ubiquity of metaphor: Metaphor in language and thought* (pp. 327–380). Amsterdam: John Benjamins.

Jaccard, J. & Jacoby, J. (2010). *Theory construction and model-building skills*. New York: The Guilford Press.

Kuhn, T. S. (1970). *The structure of scientific revolutions* (2nd edn). Chicago, IL: University of Chicago Press.

McGuire, W. J. (1997). Creative hypothesis generating in psychology: Some useful heuristics. *Annual Review of Psychology*, 48, 1–30.

Mithaug, D. E. (2000). *Learning to theorize: A four-step strategy*. Thousand Oaks, CA: Sage.

Rinehart, J. A. (1999). Turning theory into theorizing: Collaborative learning in a sociological theory course. *Teaching Sociology*, 27, 216–232.

Rosenau, J. N. (1980). *The scientific study of foreign policy*. London: Frances Pinter.

Schön, D. (1987). *Education the reflective practitioner: Toward a new design for teaching and learning in the professions*. San Francisco, CA: Jossey-Bass.

Sears, A. (2005). *A good book in theory: A guide to theoretical thinking*. Toronto: Broadview Press.

Secker, J. (1993). *From theory to practice in social work*. Aldershot, UK: Avebury.

Stevenson, C. (2005). Practical inquiry/theory in nursing. *Journal of Advanced Nursing*, 50(2), 196–203.

Turner, S. P. (1980). *Sociological explanation as translation*. Cambridge, UK: Cambridge University Press.

Usher, R. S., & Bryant, I. (1987). Re-examining the theory-practice relationship in continuing education. *Studies in Higher Education*, 12(2), 201–212

Weick, K. E. (1987). Theorizing about organizational communication. In F. M. Jablin, L. L. Putnam, K. H. Roberts, & L. W. Porter (Eds), *Handbook of organizational communication: An interdisciplinary perspective* (pp. 97–122). Newbury Park, CA: Sage.

Weick, K. E. (1989). Theory construction as disciplined imagination. *Academy of Management Review*, 14(1), 516–531.

Identify and borrow from relevant theoretical frameworks

(EPAS 2.1.7 Apply Knowledge)

The profession's knowledge base has grown significantly in the last 50 years. Germain (1983) characterized the profession in the 1950s. There were only three models of casework: the Freudian diagnostic model, the functional school, and Perlman's problem-solving approach. Group workers were limited to the social goals, interactionist, and remedial practice models. When I went to graduate school in the late 1970s, I learned two theoretical approaches: ego psychology and humanistic psychology.

Things have changed. Appraising the 1990s, Turner (1999), a theory expert, estimated that there were 30 different practice theories useful to social workers. I suspect that the number has increased significantly since then. There is also evidence that practitioners have been increasingly making use of multiple theories. Reid (2002) conducted a review of knowledge trends in direct practice, for example, and concluded that the dominant theoretical orientation was eclectic. My own review (Forte & LaMade, 2011) of the literature and my survey on field instructors' theoretical preferences also indicated that the vast majority of field instructors and supervisors used multiple theories. Theoretical pluralism characterizes the contemporary knowledge base. This means that our knowledge base includes many different theoretical contributions including theories from a wide range of disciplines, professions, and theoretical communities (Borden, 1999)

My approach to practical theorizing begins with the premise that theoretical puzzle solving is more likely to lead to effective results when the practitioner is knowledgeable and can both deconstruct the major scientific theoretical traditions and their elements and reconstruct selected theories in response to her or his close and detailed observation of a particular case

(Swedberg, 2012). This position is similar to that of several founders of the evidence-based approach to medicine:

> Knowing the tools of evidence-based practice is necessary but not sufficient for delivering the highest quality of patient care. In addition to clinical expertise, the clinical requires compassion, sensitive listening skills, and *broad perspectives from the humanities and social sciences*.
>
> (Guyatt & Rennie, 2002, p. 15, emphasis added)

Selecting and deconstructing theoretical frameworks

Theoretical traditions provide records of solutions to many different puzzling "person interacting in the environment" configurations and challenges. Theory deconstruction begins with the selection of a theory or theories for use in the helping situation. The practitioner must decide which kind of theory is needed. Figure 8.1 summarizes the types of theoretical knowledge available for selective use by the social worker.

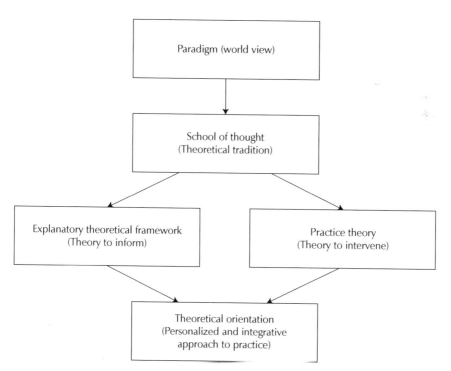

Figure 8.1 Types of theoretical frameworks

Types of theoretical frameworks

Chaiklin's (2004) distinction between basic science or explanatory theories and applied science or practice theories is helpful for categorizing theoretical frameworks. Specifically, he differentiated between explanatory or "human behavior and the social environment" theoretical perspectives and intervention or practice theories. My very broad definition of "explanatory theoretical framework" or "theory to inform" is an organized set of assumptions, concepts, and propositions used by a practitioner to understand human behavior and explain client system problems. Unfortunately, social workers don't agree about terminology. Sometimes, a theoretical framework is referred to as a "school of thought," a "theoretical perspective," a "paradigm," an explanatory framework, and an "orientation." An explanatory framework is useful when the practitioner seeks to explain the nature and causes of a particular client system challenge, recurring transactions, or environmental pattern (Reid, 2004). Explanatory theories of the interpretive kind are useful in identifying and making sense of recurrent social processes, temporal sequences, and meaning systems (Connolly & Harms, 2012). Explanatory theories can contribute much during the information gathering and assessment phases of the helping process.

As a second type of theoretical framework, Chaiklin (2004) identified practice theory or theory for intervention. My working definition of "practice theory" is a theory that describes and justifies a set of processes and procedures used in the attempt to change client system behavior. The concept, practice theory, is also referred to as "applied theory," "a practice model," "a theory of intervention," "a practice approach," and "a practice framework." The practitioner searches for the best practice theory when trying to understand how to change focal person, interaction, and environmental processes and structures (Reid, 2004). Practice theories also provide conceptualizations of change, models of intervention, and specific programs and strategies for achieving desired changes (Connolly & Harms, 2012). Practice theories supply much useful knowledge and directives for action during the intervention planning and implementation phase of the helping process.

Let's be aware that there is not always a sharp distinction between an explanatory theoretical framework and practice theory (Beckett, 2006). A social worker might turn to an explanatory theory from cognitive psychology or feminist theory to guide the information gathering and assessing work and to make sense of client problems. The theory will provide direction on what information should be collected and how the information should be interpreted. However, many interventions are also associated explicitly with an explanatory theory and its larger theoretical tradition. Behavioral interventions fit this description. Reid (2004) asserts that the behavioral theory of operant learning, for instance, fits in the categories of explanatory theory and practice theory. Finally, intervention approaches are often built on conceptions of person and environment that resemble explanatory theories. The "parent" theoretical framework may be implicit, but it is still influential. Empowerment interventions, for example, often start from the critical-feminist theoretical assumption that personal difficulties are the result of oppression in an unequal and unjust society. Change involves realizing and using the powers one has and joining with other oppressed persons to increase and use collective power.

Choice of theoretical frameworks

Though I advocate merging theory-guided and evidence-informed approaches to practice, I must report that the social work profession and our allied professional groups provide limited information identifying the explanatory and practice theories best supported by empirical evidence. For instance, two important journals, *The Journal of Evidence-Based Social Work* and *Research on Social Work Practice*, have published only a modest number of comparative studies of theory-based inquiry methods and theory-based interventions. Also, there are very few studies of the best match of theory-based inquiry methods and intervention strategies to case parameters: client characteristics, challenge or problem features, ecological setting factors, and so on.

Therefore, besides research evidence, the theorizing practitioner should ask and seek answers to a variety of other theory selection questions (Doane & Varcoe, 2005; Englehart, 2001; Spong, 2007). These include questions such as the following: Which theory or theories can the practitioner apply competently and responsibly? What are the client's preferences regarding explanatory and practice theories? Are the theoretical assumptions about the person, interaction, and the environment compatible with social work values and ethical standards? Does the theory provide a focus for understanding or a focus for intervention that is congruent with the mission and knowledge domain of the profession? Will the theory direct the practitioner's attention to salient dimensions of the "person interacting in the environment" configuration? Will the theory help the practitioner ask questions and make observations that deepen understanding of puzzling aspects of the case? Might the theory offer a sound and comprehensive explanation of the relevant causes or processes of the focal challenge? Does the theory suggest helping actions that will be responsive, effective, and culturally sensitive to the client and his needs?

Approach to theory deconstruction

After finding and selecting the preferred theory or theories, the practitioner must decide what deconstruction is necessary, if any (Layder, 1998). The practitioner might adopt the entire theoretical tradition, the ecosystems paradigm, for instance, and use it as an orientation to interpreting and ordering case data and as a toolbox of favored strategies for inquiry and action. Or the practitioner might view the theoretical tradition as a resource with concepts, propositions, models, diagrams, and other theoretical thinking tools to be unpacked from the whole and used as needed in the helping situation. The lessons after this one will cover the second kind of theory deconstruction.

Theory reconstruction

Often, the practitioner considers relevant research, past practice experiences, his or her intuition, and input from clients and colleagues while reconstructing the preexisting theoretical knowledge to increase its usefulness. This might involve modifying the existing theory or its elements (transforming symbolic interactionist concepts about the self and loss into measureable variables), relating the theory to another theory (combining interactionist and role theory concepts to understand the predicaments of persons discharged from mental health facilities), or reorganizing the theory elements in a new way (creating a novel theory of change using interactionist concepts and propositions to support work with homeless families).

The practitioner might carry out the reconstruction work in a fairly systematic way. Starting with a basic familiarity with range of theories and the literature on these theories, the practitioner studies the candidates for theoretical use in depth. Using the criteria reviewed earlier, the practitioner chooses the theory to adapt because of its relevance to puzzling case specifics and because of the evidence for its effectiveness in similar helping circumstances. The practitioner decides whether to attempt to modify the entire theoretical structure (a task best reserved for advanced-level social workers) or to reconstruct particular elements. Then, the practitioner identifies which theoretical elements of the structure to modify (concepts, propositions, network of propositions, and so on.) The practitioner reconstructs and uses the modified theory elements to guide inquiry, assist in action planning, or contribute to some other puzzle-solving aspect of the helping process (Knowledge and skills for the reconstruction of each theory element will be presented in the forthcoming lessons.) Frequently, practitioners appraise the quality of their reconstruction work.

Contemporary theories for deconstruction and reconstruction projects

The social work profession lacks consensus about the theoretical frameworks relevant to practice. I have attempted to include the major theoretical contributions to the contemporary knowledge base, while I recognize that some theories on the lists might not meet formal definitional criteria or be included in the lists of others. Social workers might disagree, for example, about a specific judgment and argue whether a particular entry is a paradigm, a theoretical tradition, a theory, or a model. Table 8.1 lists explanatory theoretical frameworks and Table 8.2 lists practice theories.

Table 8.1   Explanatory theoretical frameworks* used by social workers

1	Attachment Theory	17	Life Stage Theory
2	Behaviorism	18	Marxist/Neo-Marxist Perspectives
3	Classic Psychoanalysis		
4	Cognitive Psychology	19	Moral Development Theory
5	Complexity Theory	20	Neuroscience
6	Constructivism (Piaget's Cognitive Development Model)	21	Object Relations Theory
		22	Phenomenology
7	Critical Theory	23	Postmodernism
8	Ego Psychology	24	Self Theory
9	Ecological Theory	25	Social Learning Theory
10	Economic/Exchange Theory	26	Social Role Theory
11	Existentialism	27	Sociobiology
12	Evolutionary Theory	28	Social Constructionist Theory
13	Feminist Theory		
14	Genetics	29	Spirituality Framework
15	Humanistic Theory	30	Symbolic Interactionism
16	Labeling Theory	31	Other

* An "explanatory theoretical framework" or "theory to inform" offers an explanation of human behavior in the social environment

These lists were created by analysis of many different studies of theories used by social workers (Forte, 2006), a review of the major textbooks presenting theoretical knowledge, and extensive discussion with a group of experienced practitioners (Forte & LaMade, 2011). The lists don't include every theoretical framework used by social workers. The lists don't include all the new theoretical frameworks. Some theoretical frameworks cross categories and include knowledge useful as "theory to inform" and knowledge useful as "theory to intervene." In summary, the lists are not perfect, but they do suggest the range of possible theoretical traditions that might be deconstructed and reconstructed by practitioners, and the lists identify in one place those theories identified as important by theory experts.

Learning activities and reflections

1   Review the lists of explanatory theoretical frameworks and practice theories. Comment on your degree of familiarity with these theories. With which theories are you familiar? With which theories are you unfamiliar? Which theories do you want to learn more about? What theories would you add to the lists? Develop a 2-year plan to increase your understanding of and ability to use a subset of these theories.

Table 8.2   Practice theories* used by social workers

1	Adlerian Theory	17	Narrative Approach
2	Afrocentric Theory	18	Problem Solving/Solution-Focused Approach
3	Behavioral Approach		
4	Bioenergetic Analysis	19	Psychodrama
5	Bio-Psycho-Social Approach	20	Psychodynamic/Psychoanalytic Approach
6	Brief, Short Term Approach		
7	Cognitive-Behavioral Therapy	21	Psychosocial Approach
8	Crisis Intervention	22	Rational Emotive Therapy
9	Eclectic Approach	23	Reality Therapy
10	Ecological Perspective/The Life Model	24	Rogerian/Client-Centered Therapy
11	Ecosystems Approach	25	Self-Help Approach
12	Experiential Approach	26	Spirituality/Religious/Transpersonal Approach
13	Family Systems Approach		
14	Feminist Approach	27	Strengths Perspective
15	Gestalt Therapy	28	Systems Approach
16	Life Stage/Life Span Approach	29	Task Centered Social Work
		30	Transactional Analysis
		31	Other

* A "practice theory" or "theory to intervene" describes and justifies a set of procedures used in the attempt to change client system behavior

2   Focus on the client that you are working with or an acquaintance needing help with some puzzling life challenges or focus on yourself and some difficulty you face related to your environment. Write a summary of your profile of this case (basic system information, developmental history, problems and their characteristics, relevant environmental factors, and so on).

Next, create a large circle (Collingwood, Emond, & Woodward, 2008). On the left side, refer to the attached list and identify all the possible "theories to inform" that you might use. These are the "human behavior and the social environment" explanatory theoretical perspectives covered in HBSE class that help you understand the client system-environment processes and problems.

On the right side, refer to the attached list and identify the "theories to intervene" that you might use. These are the theoretical models and practice theories covered in practice classes (and referred to in HBSE classes) that you might use to guide your helping work with this client (if you were to provide direct social work services).

Next, select from each half of the circle the theories that you think will be most useful in understanding and helping the client. Identify your rationale for selecting each of these theories. Describe how you will deconstruct and reconstruct the "theories to inform" to increase your understanding and the quality of your assessment and how you might deconstruct and reconstruct the "theories to intervene" to guide your intervention efforts and increase your intervention effectiveness.

References

Beckett, C. (2006). *Essential theory for social work practice*. London: Sage.

Borden, W. (1999). Pluralism, pragmatism, and the therapeutic endeavor in brief dynamic treatment. *Psychoanalytic Social Work*, 6(3/4), 7–42.

Chaiklin, H. (2004). Problem formulation, conceptualization, and theory development. In A. R. Roberts & K. R. Yeager (Eds), *Evidence-based practice manual: Research and outcome measures in health and human services* (pp. 95–101). New York: Oxford.

Collingwood, P., Emond, R., & Woodward, R. (2008). The theory circle: A tool for learning and for practice. *Social Work Education*, 27(1), 70–83.

Connolly, M, & Harms, L. (2012). *Social work: From theory to practice*. New York: Cambridge University Press.

Doane, G., & Varcoe, C. (2005). *Family nursing as relational inquiry: Developing health-promotion practice*. Philadelphia, PA: Lippincott Williams & Wilkins.

Englehart, J. K. (2001). The marriage between theory and practice. *Public Administration Review*, 61(3), 371–374.

Forte, J. A. (2006). *Human behavior and the social environment: Models, metaphors, and maps for applying theoretical perspectives to practice*. Belmont, CA: Thomson Brooks/Cole.

Forte, J. A. & LaMade, J. (2011). The center cannot hold: A survey of field instructors' theoretical preferences and propensities. *The Clinical Supervisor*, 30(1), 72–94.

Germain, C. B. (1983). Technological advances. In A. Rosenblatt & D. Waldfogel (Eds), *Handbook of clinical social work* (pp. 26–57). San Francisco, CA: Jossey Bass.

Guyatt, G., & Rennie, D. (2002). *Users' guide to the medical literature: Essentials of evidence-based clinical practice*. Chicago, IL: American Medical Association.

Layder, D. (1998). *Sociological practice: Linking theory and social research*. London: Sage.

Reid, W. J. (2002). Knowledge for direct social work practice: An analysis of trends. *Social Service Review*, 76(1), 6–33.

Reid, W. J. (2004). Contribution of operant theory to social work practice and research. In H. E. Briggs & T. L. Rzepnicki (Eds), *Using evidence in social work practice: Behavioral perspectives* (pp. 36–54). Chicago, IL: Lyceum.

Spong, S. (2007). Skepticism and belief: Unraveling the relationship between theory and practice in counselling and psychotherapy. In S. R. Smith (Ed.), *Applying theory to policy and practice: Issues for critical reflection* (pp. 55-70). Aldershot, UK: Ashgate.

Swedberg, R. (2012). Theorizing in sociology and social science: Turning to the context of discovery. *Theory and Society*, *41*, 1–40.

Turner, F. J. (1999). Theories of practice with vulnerable populations. In D. E. Biegel & A. Blum (Eds), *Innovations in practice and service delivery across the lifespan* (pp. 13–31). New York: Oxford University Press.

Identify and learn from relevant exemplary theorists

(EPAS 2.1.7 Apply Knowledge)

There have been many remarkable scientific theorizers. These have been people of genius who have devised solutions to puzzles about nature, the human body, psychology, or society that daunted all others. In the natural sciences, Nicolaus Copernicus, Marie Curie, Charles Darwin, Albert Einstein, Galileo Galilei, Stephen Hawking, Hypatia, Isaac Newton, and Louis Pasteur have made masterful contributions to the body of scientific knowledge. In the social sciences, there have also been many outstanding theorists. Ruth Benedict, W. E. B. Dubois, Sigmund Freud, Jurgen Habermas, Karl Marx, C. George Herbert Mead, Wright Mills, and B. F. Skinner are a few examples of scientific titans.

Each theoretical "school of thought" and practice tradition has been enriched by the contributions of founding figures and inspirational leaders. The associations and journals of different schools of thought and practice approaches recognize and applaud the work of outstanding contemporary theorists.

Deconstructing the lives of exemplary theorizers

You can learn much about "person interacting in the environment" configurations by studying the lives, theories, and contributions of these exemplars and by learning about how their personal histories and their social contexts shaped their theoretical viewpoints (Meleis, 1985). Such study of the original books, articles, and essays that constitute the theory canon (the collection of classical theoretical works) will deepen your understanding of theories and the theorizing process. You might even pattern your professional thinking and conduct after that of a few of your favorite role models.

Theorists and inner conversations

Social work novices develop over time a professional way of using personal experiences, their own psychosocial processes, and scientific knowledge. This "professional self," symbolic interactionists teach us, learns to make use of an inner forum, a private space where the voices of role models are heard. Here, the practitioner engages sometimes in imagined and unspoken conversations and reflections. We might, for example, ask ourselves questions such as how can I make sense of this person-in-environment configuration or what can I do that will best help this client system? Then, we listen to the voices and echoes of the great theorists for answers.

In a sense, social workers invite imagined others including role models of exemplary theorizing to join this private forum for debates, deliberations, and decision making about important practice matters (see Honeycutt, 2003 for detailed information about the interactionist perspective on imagined interaction and its uses). Using theorists as role models means that we cultivate working relationships with the useful theorists and scholarly practitioners who have founded theoretical traditions and with the creative disciples who have advanced these approaches. We use these imagined others as models, mentors, supports, and allies in our quest for competent, evidence-informed practice, and we learn from our imaginary interactions with these guests in our inner forum to become better social workers.

The benefits of learning from theorist role models

Baretti (2007), Forte (2006), Lengermann and Wallace (1981), Rochberg-Halton (1984), Ritzer (1991), Shalin (2007), and Thompson and Hogan (1996) have identified various benefits of deconstructing the lives of exemplary models. Turning to profiles of exemplars increases our identification with important theorists and our use of theorists as templates for professional thinking, feeling, and doing. Learning from models deepens our grasp of the value of theory and theorizing; shows us how a theory is related to the personality of a theorist and to the context for its development; helps us connect theorists to different schools of thought and practice traditions; and enhances our satisfaction with the theory mastery experience. Learning from biographical materials also helps socialize us to social work as a science-based profession. In summary, familiarizing ourselves with theorists, their lives, and their ideas increases the resources available to us for the private and public deliberations necessary to professional problem solving.

Strategies for learning from theorists who are role models

We can increase our competency as theorizing practitioners by using exemplary theorists as models in a variety of ways. The study of biographies, writings, recorded words, public service histories, theoretical innovations, research studies, and practice application of the masters will increase our appreciation for and mastery of human behavior and developmental theories.

Each theorist has "signature" theorizing strengths, and you can research the signature strengths of a favorite theorist and imagine the particular theorist helping you to learn and develop these strengths yourself. For example, George Herbert Mead was excellent at articulating and explaining the assumptions associated with the premise that person and environment (self and society, in his words) are interconnected. Talcott Parsons specialized in developing a highly regarded "grand theory," an approach to explaining everything about societies, their elements, their functioning, and their development. Carol Gilligan masterfully demonstrated how a theorist can use a critical perspective, feminism, and identify the conceptual and empirical weaknesses of male-centered theories about human development and moral conduct. Albert Ellis was very talented at transforming concepts and principles from the cognitive sciences into easy-to-remember therapy guidelines and techniques.

There are many other strategies that social workers can use to take apart famous lives and bring exemplary theorists into their private forums for imagined conversations. We can seek information that relates a theorist to his or her historical and social context. We can study reports that examine theoretical excerpts from a theorist's opus. We can listen to or read presentations that summarize research extensions of the theorist's concepts and propositions or lectures that compare and contrast different theorists' approaches to the human sciences and to developmental topics. We can impersonate various theorists and engage in role-play activities emulating the stance of different theorists in discussions of various theoretical issues, HBSE topics, and practice challenges. We can join a debate inviting position statements from the perspectives of multiple theorists. We might keep a journal in which we include our reflections on imagined consultations with theorists to understand better and apply more accurately human behavior or developmental theories. We might create and trade a set of theorist baseball cards summarizing basic biographical information, concepts, and theories about our team of theorist "all-stars." For living theorists, we might listen to an interview in which they elaborate on their theories or write an e-mail inquiring about one of the theoretical topics that perplexes us.

Reconstructing aspects of exemplary lives

Boero, Pedemonte, and Robotti (1998) have studied and written about ways to make creative use of the lives and thinking of exemplary theorists. They call their approach the "voice and echoes" perspective; a perspective introduced in the preface. In scientific traditions, *voices* are the verbal and nonverbal expressions produced by historical and contemporary scientists who have built and communicated theoretical knowledge. The theorizing practitioner learns to listen to and integrate into his or her own practice the voices of academic theorists and, also, the voices of supervisors, colleagues, clients, and teachers. Each of these voices has its own perspective, its own validity, and its own narrative weight. The theorizing practitioner can engage in imaginary interaction with the speakers of each type of voice (interactions that transcend time, place, and culture), listen to their voiced utterances, and use these interactions to create new musical scores: for social workers, solutions to theoretical puzzles in contrast to the creative response of composers to sonic impulses. As theorizing practitioners internalize these voices in their minds, they becomes capable of producing their own echoes of influential voices. An *echo* is a link to a scientific voice that a speaker can use in private conversations and can share explicitly in public discourse. Resonant echoes, for example, are the appropriation of scientists' voices to represent the "person interacting in the environment" difficulties presented by the client. Echoes facilitate the use of theoretical content, of methods of theoretical inquiry, and of theoretical languages to create solutions to complex practice problems.

As you listen to the voices and cultivate the echoes of these exemplary theorists, there are many questions that you can ask to reconstruct their insights, theories, and theorizing methods for your own use.

Which theorists do you consider worthy of emulation? Which theorists offer little of appeal or theorized and created theories contrary to your own preferences (these might be negative role models)?

What aspects of a theorist's theory and theorizing resonate best with my own personal and professional experiences? What aspects create dissonance with my experiences and developing orientation? How can I best assimilate and integrate the elements from the theorist's life and corpus that are consonant with my theoretical convictions?

For which helping puzzles will a theorist's theory be most useful? For which puzzles is it likely that the theorist's theory and theorizing approach will be poorly matched?

How might the theorist have interpreted a focal "person interacting in an environment" challenge similar to my client's challenge? What are the similarities and differences between what the theorist theorized about this kind of situation and my understanding of it? In what ways do I need to modify this assessment formulation to suit the details of my case?

What explanatory and intervention hypotheses might a theorist recommend for the case? Is anything missing, outdated, culturally insensitive, or inappropriate about these hypotheses? If so, what modifications can I make to adapt them for inquiry and action planning?

What experiences, arguments, and evidence did the theorist draw on to support his or her theoretical claims? Using critical thinking processes, what claims do I believe have merit still?

What theoretical claims lack adequate support?

How can I more deeply understand the theorist's theory, and how can I theorize more like the theorist? In what ways do I need to adapt these understandings and theorizing processes to the circumstances that I confront in my daily practice?

Below you will find some additional resources for your deconstruction and reconstruction of the lives of exemplary theorists. These include textbooks with profiles of exemplary theorists and websites with detailed biographies. Additionally, I have included lists of exemplary human behavior theorists (Table 9.1) and exemplary practice theorists (Table 9.2).

Learning activities and reflections

1   Develop a profile of an important or founding figure of an explanatory theoretical tradition that interests you (Sigmund Freud, B. F. Skinner, Carol Gilligan, Jean Piaget, W. E. B. Du Bois, or Talcott Parsons, for examples). This will be a biographical profile of a theorist who has contributed to your understanding of human behavior and development within the social environment. Report on how you might model aspects of your own information gathering and problem explanation work on the life of the theorist and his or her theories. Refer to the attached list of human behavior theorists (see Table 9.1) if you need help identifying candidates for your profile. Place a check next to the names of those human behavior theorists that you know and a star next to the name of those human behavior theorists that you want to know better.

2   Develop a profile of an important or founding figure of a practice theory that interests you. (Albert Ellis, Florence Hollis, Salvador Minuchin, Helen Harris Perlman, or Fritz Perls, for examples). This will be a profile of a theorist who has contributed to your understanding of client problems and/or methods for helping clients. Report on how you might model aspects of your own intervention planning and implementation on the practice illustrations of this theorist and his or her theories. Refer to the attached list of practice theorists (see Table 9.2) if you need help identifying candidates for your profile. Place a check next to the names of those practice theorists that you know and a star next to the name of those practice theorists that you want to know better.

Table 9.1 Theorists relevant to social work

1	Bandura, Albert	29	hooks, bell
2	Bateson, Gregory	30	James, William
3	Bertalanffy, Ludwig von	31	Jung, Carl
4	Bourdieu, Pierre	32	Kohlberg, Lawrence
5	Bowlby, John	33	Lewin, Kurt
6	Bronfenbrenner, Urie	34	Linton, Ralph
7	Collins, Patricia Hill	35	Luhmann, Niklas
8	Cooley, Charles Horton	36	Marx, Karl
9	Darwin, Charles	37	Maslow, Abraham
10	de Beauvoir, Simone	38	May, Rollo
11	Dewey, John	39	Mead, George Herbert
12	DuBois, W. E. B.	40	Mead, Margaret
13	Durkheim, Emile	41	Mendel, Gregor
14	Elder, Glen	42	Merton, Robert
15	Erikson, Erik	43	Mills, C. Wright
16	Foucault, Michel	44	Park, Robert
17	Fowler, James	45	Parsons, Talcott
18	Freire, Paulo	46	Pavlov, Ivan
19	Freud, Sigmund	47	Piaget, Jean
20	Geertz, Clifford	48	Seligman, Martin
21	Germain, Carel	49	Skinner, B. F.
22	Gesell, Arnold	50	Smith, Adam
23	Gilligan, Carol	51	Smith, Dorothy
24	Goffman, Erving	52	Thomas, W. I.
25	Gramsci, Antonio	53	Vygotsky, Lev
26	Greer, Germaine	54	Watson, John
27	Habermas, Jurgen	55	Weber, Max
28	Hall, Stuart	56	West, Cornel

3   Consider using the attached topics for your profiles. You might construct the profile like a baseball card to identify relevant information about the theorists (see Table 9.3). Check out the Theory Trading Cards website www.theorycards.org.uk for another example of an interesting way to summarize biographical information about theorists.

Table 9.2 Practice theorists relevant to social work

1	Ackerman, Nathan	16	Kubler-Ross, Elizabeth
2	Addams, Jane	17	Laing, R. D.
3	Adler, Alfred	18	Minuchin, Salvador
4	Beck, Aaron	19	Montessori, Maria
5	Berne, Eric	20	Moreno, Jacob
6	Bowen, Murray	21	Perlman, Helen Harris
7	Denzin, Norman	22	Perls, Fritz
8	Ellis, Albert	23	Reynolds, Bertha Capen
9	Erickson, Milton	24	Richmond, Mary
10	Frankl, Viktor	25	Rogers, Carl
11	Glasser, William	26	Saleeby, Dennis
12	Haley, Jay	27	Satir, Virginia
13	Hoffman, Lynn	28	Schwartz, William
14	Hollis, Florence	29	Sullivan, Harry Stack
15	Horney, Karen	30	Yalom, Irvin

Table 9.3 Suggested format for useful theorists (the theorist baseball card)

Front Side
   Photo (with source of photo in small print)
   Theorist's full name
   Theorist's primary work affiliations
   Theorist's major work positions

Back Side
   Name
   Historical context: birth and death dates, birthplace, personal and historical events
   Major theories, concepts, research findings
   Performance record – articles published, books written, associations formed
   Service or citizenship activities
   Contribution to planned change process (engagement, assessment, intervention), to a specific field of practice, or to theorizing about client problems
   Strengths as a theorist
   Limitations as a theorist

Possible Supplemental Information To Collect
   Audio files or text from interview with theorist
   List of references
   Quotations by or about the theorist
   Timeline with highlights of theoretical advances
   Websites with information about theorist

4   Write a letter to your favorite human behavior theorists or practice theorist. Ask them for advice on a practice challenge that you are facing or anticipate facing. Pose specific and detailed questions in this letter. Tell the theorist also about how you plan to use him or her as a role model for your helping work. Imagine the response to your letter, and write a summary of the theorist's response. Comment on how you might approach the practice challenge using and adapting the theorist's imagined perspective and advice.

5   Create a website dedicated to your favorite theorist. Post resources (perhaps, guided by the baseball card outline) for other social workers desiring to learn more about the theorist and to use the theorist as a role model.

References

Baretti, M. (2007). Teachers and field instructors as student role models: A neglected dimension in social work education. *Journal of Teaching in Social Work*, 27(3/4), 215–239.

Boero, P., Pedemonte, B., & Robotti, E. (1998). Approaching theoretical knowledge through voices and echoes: A Vygotskian perspective. In E. Pehkonen (Ed.), *Proceedings of the 21st International Conference of the Psychology of Mathematics Education* (Vol. 2, pp. 81–88). Lahti, Finland: University of Helsinki.

Forte, J. A. (2006). *Human behavior and the social environment: Models, metaphors, and maps for applying theoretical perspectives to practice*. Belmont, CA: Thomson Brooks/Cole.

Honeycutt, J. M. (2003). *Imagined interactions: Daydreaming about communication*. Cresskill, NJ: Hampton Press.

Lengermann, P. M., & Wallace, R. A. (1981). Making theory meaningful: The student as an active participant. *Teaching Sociology*, 8(2), 197–212.

Meleis, A. I. (1985). *Theoretical nursing: Development and progress*. Philadelphia, PA: J. B. Lippincott.

Ritzer, G. (1991). Biography: A (still) underutilized metasociological method. *Contemporary Sociology*, 20(1), 10–12.

Rochberg-Halton, E. (1984). Object relations, role models, and cultivation of the self. *Environment and Behavior*, 16(3), 335–368.

Shalin, D. (2007). Signing in the flesh: Notes on pragmatist hermeneutics. *Sociological Theory*, 25(3), 193–224.

Thompson, D., & Hogan, J. D. (1996). *A history of developmental psychology in autobiography*. Boulder, CO: Westview Press.

References (profiles of exemplary and useful theorists)

Alligood, M., & Tomey, A. M. (2001). *Nursing theorists and their work* (5th edn). St. Louis, MO: Mosby-Year Book, Inc.

Anderson, H., & Kasperson, L. B. (Eds) (1996). *Classical and modern social theory*. London: Blackwell Publishers.

Billups, J. O. (Ed.). (2002). *Faithful angels: Portraits of international social work notables*. Washington, DC: NASW Press.

Blackwell, J. E., & Janowitz, M. (1974). *Black sociologists: Historical and contemporary*. Chicago, IL: University of Chicago.

Bracey, J. H., Rudwick, E. M., & Meier, A. (1971). *The black sociologists: The first half century*. Belmont, CA: Wadsworth.

Coser, L. A. (1977). *Masters of sociological thought: Ideas in historical and social context*. New York: Harcourt Brace Jovanovich.

Elliott, A., & Turner, B. S. (2001). *Profiles in contemporary social theory*. London: Sage.

Pampel, F. C. (2000). *Sociological lives and ideas: An introduction to the classical theorists*. New York: Worth Publishers.

Ritzer, G. (Ed.). (2000). *The Blackwell companion to major social theorists*. London: Blackwell Publishers.

Schellenberg, J. A. (1978). *Masters of social psychology: Freud, Mead, Lewin, and Skinner*. New York: Oxford University Press.

Sim, S. (1998). *The A-Z guide to modern social and political theorists*. Englewood Cliffs, NJ: Prentice Hall.

Stones, R. (1998). *Key sociological thinkers*. New York: Washington Square Park.

Theorist-related websites

About.com: Feminist Theorists
    http://womenshistory.about.com/od/feminism/tp/feminist_theory.htm
AP Psychology: Important Theorists
    www.scribd.com/doc/89027/AP-Psychology-Important-Theorist-Names
Biography
    www.biography.com
Dead Sociologists Society
    http://media.pfeiffer.edu/lridener/dss/DEADSOC.HTML
Political Theorists and Activists
    www.blupete.com/Literature/Biographies/Philosophy/BiosPol.htm
SocioSite: Sociologists
    www.sociosite.net/topics/sociologists.php
The SocioWeb: Giants of Sociology
    www.socioweb.com/directory/giants-of-sociology
Theory Trading Cards
    www.theorycards.org.uk

Check on and imagine puzzle patterns using theory's root metaphors

(EPAS 2.1.7 Apply Knowledge)

Theory construction and practical theorizing sometimes involve comparing one thing to something else, that is, the use of metaphors and our metaphorical imaginations. Such creative thinking complements the use of scientific approaches to theoretical puzzle solving. I will discuss several ways to deconstruct and reconstruct metaphors in this commentary.

Deconstructing a theory's metaphors

There are two major types of theory metaphors: the root metaphor and the conveyance metaphor. Taking a theory apart to identify its central metaphors provides the theorizing practitioner concrete images and evocative comparisons that deepen his or her understanding of the theory.

Root metaphors

Pepper (1942), a philosopher of science, brought some simplicity to the task of decoding complicated theories. He suggested that each theoretical framework is built on a root metaphor. *Root metaphors* are basic comparisons between abstract theoretical assumptions and ideas and concrete objects. Through such metaphors, theorists attempt to make an overall theoretical framework or disciplinary stance toward human behavior and human development easier to comprehend. The theory and all its branches grow toward the sky, like a tree, thanks to the support and nourishment made possible by the strong root system.

Theorists belonging to each theoretical tradition explicitly or implicitly affirm different root metaphors, that is, they compare their abstract conceptualizations of the person, the environment, the transactions between person and environment, and the change agent to specific objects, events, or processes. When the metaphorical foundation is not explicitly stated, the theorizing practitioner can carefully read key works in each theoretical tradition, or commentaries by experts on the tradition, to find clues about the root metaphors (Forte, 2006).

Human developmental theorists vary, for instance, in their preferred root metaphors. Here are several of my tentative deconstructions of their theoretical products (Forte, 2009). Some theorists such as B. F. Skinner compare the developing person to a machine (the person as relatively passive, lacking intentionality, and acting in response to external stimuli). Some theorists such as Jean Piaget or Arnold Gesell prefer imagery and ideas associated with the metaphor of a living organism (the developing person as a dynamic whole changing qualitatively and predictably during universal stages). Some theorists such as George Herbert Mead and Ken Elder prefer comparing the developing person to a historical event (the person is unique, part of continuously changing processes, and only understandable as situated in a distinct ecological and temporal context).

Conveyance metaphors

Theorists also make use of less ambitious theory comprehension tools called *conveyance metaphors*. Conveyance metaphors are comparisons of more limited scope than root metaphors, which theorists use to make sense of a selective aspect of human behavior or development (MacCormac, 1985). Some family systems theorists, for example, use metaphor-based imagery characterizing the child as an element subject to multiple forces of energy and comparing the parent to an electrician optimizing the flow of electric forces to the child (Forte, 2009). You may also locate conveyance metaphors in substantive theories such as theories about crime that include vivid comparisons: police detective as sleuth, justice as blindfolded, criminal justice processes as a battle between heroes and villains, and police headquarters, courts, and prisons as part of a machine or system.

Many theorists like conveyance metaphors (Forte, 2009). Theorists may make vivid associations between theoretical concepts and war fortifications (ego defenses and military defenses, for example). They may create concepts using metaphoric connections to the ecology (a degree of societal stratification involves a comparison to strata, levels of a rock formation examined from bottom to top). Family changes over time are compared to a "cycle." Some theorists compare systems and helping to things in the world of arts. An agency setting is like a theatrical stage. A small group has similarities to a jazz combo. A qualitative assessment of a client is comparable to an impressionistic painting.

Scholnick (2000) discussed conveyance metaphors common to popular developmental theories and how these metaphors revealed the theorists' gender biases. The theorists often compared developing persons to events and processes associated, affirming masculine symbols. Kohlberg's conception of moral development by argument and dispute, Darwin's bio-evolutionary theory of species advancement by competition where the fittest survived, Piaget's comparison of the developing person to a theoretician making a series of paradigm shifts are frameworks dependent on comparisons tied to the male experience. Critical thinkers might use the feminist slant to investigate how these developmental theorists had slighted the female experience. Critical thinking social workers might also study recent theoretical corrections. These have been made by theorists such as Gilligan, who compare development processes to those associated with friendship and other reciprocal relationships, by symbolic interactionists who characterize development by using images of cooperation drawn from conversations and apprenticeships, and by narrative theorists who compare development to a series of stories shared by community members.

Types of theoretical metaphors

Using your metaphorical imagination means looking for and noticing the similarities or relationships between theoretical knowledge and the everyday world. There are several specific strategies for enhancing your metaphorical imagination. Illustrations will be related to developmental theorizing (Forte, 2009).

A positive comparison explores the linkages between theoretical concepts and everyday objects, processes, events, and places. The theory user answers the question how is the theoretical idea compared to something in the world? A role theory approach to human development suggests, for instance, that the developing person is like a performer acquiring many roles and learning more and more complex scripts across his or her acting career.

Theory learners can develop *analytic comparisons* and explore how the root metaphor (person as system or machine, for examples) reveals information about the theory's assumptions about the developing person, about developmental processes, and about developmental practice. Metaphorical imagination helps the theorizer identify how the root metaphors fit into and influence the overall theoretical architecture (the structured and planned design of how theory elements relate to the whole). The theory user tries to answer the question what does the root metaphor tell me about the theory's foundational assumptions and overall structure?

Embellished comparisons can be used to elaborate on theory-based images and symbols (expanding the interactionist portrayal of human development as like an apprenticeship, for example) and thus, to enrich the depiction of the developing person, the context of development, or optimal developmental outcomes. The theory user asks the question how does the metaphor extend or expand on the basic description and conceptualization of the theoretical element, the core qualities of the developing person, for example?

Practical comparisons can be used to link the theory to phases of the planned change process. For example, we recommend using the theatrical metaphors inherent in role socialization theory to articulate the engagement, data-gathering, problem-formulation, and intervention phases (Forte, 2006). Client problems are understood as difficulties in performing a part in a way earning positive reviews. Here, the theorizing practitioner answers questions about how the root metaphor provides guidance to each specific phase of the helping world.

Every theory has explanatory limitations. *Negative comparisons* are used to investigate how the theory fails to fully or accurately describe the developing person or developmental process. The theory user seeks answers for the question how is the theory or theory element unlike the everyday thing? My summary of the three major root metaphors (mechanistic, organismic, and historical) and the negative comparisons found in human development theories follows (Forte, 2009). The developing person differs from machines, according to critics of the mechanistic world view, because of his or her ability to transcend determining forces, mental and other covert psychic processes, and embeddedness in reciprocal relations with systems in influential contexts. The metaphor of the person as a developing organism, critics of organism theorists contend, neglects the varied individual pathways of development and implies an inevitability, progressiveness, and universality to growth that is not supported by historical and cross-cultural research. The historical act metaphor of human development is limited in that its theorists are unclear about how developing persons differentially use social contexts, and its proponents don't offer a typology of contexts for developments or principles differentiating those aspects of development that are plastic from those that are fixed.

Reconstructing a theory's metaphors

As with any theory and theory element, the practitioner must do some reconstruction work to transform the knowledge for practice use. Such work can help practitioners solve theoretical puzzles and use puzzle solutions to ameliorate troubling situations and to mobilize personal and collective strengths.

General metaphor reconstruction strategy

Here is my recommended starting point for developing our metaphorical imaginations. Try to learn first the specific way each theoretical framework is built on a central metaphor. Remember that a metaphor makes a comparison between two unlike things. Then attempt to discover how theorists aligned to each theoretical framework would fill in the following sentences. The person is like _____. The environment is like _____. The social worker is like _____. Change is like _____. The key assumptions, concepts, and propositional statements for each theoretical framework can often be sensibly linked to these metaphors and adapted to suit the particular helping situation

The following summary of the root metaphors used by some important theorists will serve as a brief introduction to this kind of metaphor-based theoretical reconstruction.

Behaviorists emphasize the commonality between humans and other animals. Much of their early research, for example, examined the learning processes of rats, pigeons, and dogs. Behaviorists conceive of the environment as a laboratory where the major variables associated with learning can be controlled. Social workers are like the laboratory scientists or behavioral engineers who manipulate various contingencies to obtain desired results. Clients are like the animals conditioned by Pavlov and the other behaviorists. Change is like the work of laboratory scientists changing the number or frequency of treats or pellets provided to a behaving animal. The practitioner leading a parenting group for neglectful mothers might reconstruct these comparisons of person to animal, helping setting to laboratory, helping to conditioning, and practitioner to laboratory scientist for use in specific circumstances.

Conflict theorists such as the neo-Marxists see all social processes as marked by contention. The environment is like a battleground where warring groups fight for territory, wealth, prestige, and control of the media. The client is like a combatant in one of two armies: the army of the privileged or the army of those with minimal privilege (power, status, and wealth). Most social work clients are underdogs. The privileged control the machinery for combat and so prevail in almost all struggles. Practitioners are strategists and advocates who try to help the underdogs defy the odds and win some battles. Change relates to the marshalling of troops, the fortifying of the will and means to fight, and the victory over enemies. Social policy practitioners might use and adapt these metaphorical categorizations in a legislative campaign at the state level to raise the minimum wage.

Social systems theorists make use of the root metaphor of a machine with parts. The person or family is one part in a larger machine. The environment is the entire machine. If the parts of the environment work well together, the societal machine will do its jobs well. However, if any part breaks down, the environment or organization (the assemblage of all working parts) will do its job poorly or cease to run. The social worker is like a mechanic trying to find the broken parts and fix them so that the machine returns to a state of efficient operation. Change relates to improving the functioning of a part, removing a dysfunctional part that can't be repaired, or adding a new part that can contribute to the smooth, effective operation of the machine. The social worker serving returning veterans might reconstruct these systems theory metaphors to understand the veterans' experiences in war and to help them adjust to civilian society.

Symbolic interactionists emphasize the capacity for symbol use. The human species has evolved so its members can interact with one another using words, gestures, and sensible actions. Of all species, humans are the best conversationalists on the globe. The social environment is like a massive conversation, one that started centuries ago, one that involves now thousands or millions of people, and one that focuses on numerous different topics. The social worker is the interpreter and discussion leader who helps people converse with one another. For instance, the social worker helps members of language communities that are outside the mainstream (working class Hispanic-American or African-American groups in the United States) join in and influence the national conversation. Change requires learning new symbols (words and sentences to bring to the conversation), learning new ways of symbolic interaction (talking, arguing, and so on during the conversation), and learning how to change topics. The community organizer might reconstruct this interactionist imagery and symbolism identifying language and conversation as central to practice and adapt these metaphors for use in a community center serving members of diverse immigrant groups.

Specific metaphor reconstruction strategies

Metaphors are imaginative structures of understanding that provide words and images to represent theory creatively and communicate about complex and abstract "person interacting in an environment" configurations. Cornelissen (2006) suggests that theorizers use metaphors suggested by theoretical literature reviews, by preliminary case information gathering, and by their own intuitions during "thought trials." Such mental experiments can help the theorizing practitioner try out various representations of the puzzling PIE challenge and various representations of possible interventions. Cornelissen suggests three specific strategies for metaphor reconstruction. Each blends information from the theory and from data about the case. I am adapting his strategies for reconstructing theory metaphors for professional purposes. Specifically, I will show the usefulness of the interactionist theory and its metaphor of jazz for understanding and changing organizations.

Strategy of composition

Composition involves comparing the theoretical metaphor to the practice puzzle or target. Interactionists assert that human interaction has qualities similar to the production of jazz music. Members of a jazz combo alternate between "swing," playing together in accord with the established music, and "solos," improvising on the trumpet or saxophone, for instance, but improvising in harmony with the other musicians. Reconstructing theory metaphors in this way, the practitioner would look at how and how well members of a social work agency follow the same score but support one another's creative embellishments of this score while working together.

Strategy of completion

Completion involves adding details to the comparison identified through composition. For example, we have considered how jazz musicians use both musical structure (a known song or tune) and musical theory to swing together but also to generate new musical ideas. Completing this metaphor, we can think about how the musicians use subtle words and sounds to guide one another during solo and group playing; for interactionists, these are the gestures that actualize group norms. Members excel when they are attuned to the band's code for swinging and for initiating and concluding solos. Completing this metaphor, the practitioner can examine how members of the social work agency act in a way blending conformity to organizational structure and rules with creative enactment of their roles. Additionally, the practitioner can examine how agency members communicate norms of conduct to regulate member participation.

Strategy of elaboration

Elaboration involves theoretical puzzle solving that uses theory metaphors in ways that expand on the basic metaphoric comparison. The theorizing practitioner asks if an organization is like a jazz combo, what are some of the similarities between the organizational member and the jazz musicians? For example, Cornelissen (2006) suggests that the jazz metaphor implies much about the qualities of cooperative work in the social work agency: Members coordinate their actions in ways that are deliberate, collaborative, simultaneous, and creative. Coordination occurs in real time and is guided by social structure, shared understandings, and artistic impulses. Effective organizations recruit members with capacities for "swinging" and for "soloing" and provide opportunities (gigs) for members to refine these capacities. Effective organizations assume that leadership is distributed and each member should be able to solo, take the lead in an organizational project, as their talents dictate.

The value of metaphors for practical theorizing

Theoretical metaphors have a variety of specific uses (Forte, 2006). Using the metaphorical imagination to deconstruct and reconstruct a theory can foster a theory-based synthesis of case information. For example, we may be able to assemble all the information that we have obtained about the client-transactions-environment configuration and summarize it in metaphorical terms as illustrative of "boundary issues" (systems theory) or of "a poor fit" (evolutionary theory).

A practitioner's deconstruction and reconstruction of root metaphors can improve his or her memorization of theoretical knowledge. Metaphors are valuable memory devices. They are often catchy and vivid. The translation of theoretical knowledge into metaphors will help novice and expert practitioners remember a large set of theoretical frameworks by creating associations between the root metaphors and evocative memories. Social systems theorists, for example, often compare society to a human body with inter-related parts; some parts of society and the body function to enhance health, some cause disease and breakdown. This imagery is memorable.

Identifying and adapting the metaphors implicit in a framework can help you appraise the strengths and limitations of any "person interacting in the environment" theory. Think about the social role theory metaphor of life as a drama. Much of the theory is based on the imagery of the stage and of actors learning the lines for their parts in a play. This imagery helps us understand much about the scripted nature of client behavior and socialization across role careers. However, critics note that the metaphor is limited, and many of our role performances are improvised (Forte, 2006). In some ways, life is more like participation in an improvisatory comedy troupe than in a Shakespearean acting company. Also, much human behavior occurs privately with minimal consideration of an audience or impulsively—with no prior reflection on audience reactions. We need to be aware of these negative comparisons when adapting role theory for practical use.

The metaphorical imagination can improve theory application (Duffy, 2005). Practitioners who are stuck and looking for insights into puzzling public problems, client system difficulties, or helping processes might consider the metaphors from alternative theoretical traditions. Shuffling from one to another can lead to new insights, solutions, and discoveries. Switching during family social work, for example, between images of a particular family member as a part of a machine (systems theory), images of the family member as an actor in a play (role theory), images of the member as an investor concerned about returns on emotional and behavioral investments (exchange theory), and images of the family member as a fighter in a war (conflict theory) can enrich our understanding of the client and her family.

Learning activities and reflections

1   Let's practice this theorizing skill by applying the metaphorical imagination to understand the professional social work role. Reflect on different ways of thinking about the client. These could include client as customer, client as patient, client as member, client as detainee. What

are the implications of the metaphorical comparison between service user and each of these roles? What would the expected counter role for the social worker be for each metaphor-based conception of the client? If a client is like a customer, for instance, should a social worker act like a sales clerk? What other comparisons between clients and social workers and everyday roles or types of persons might be helpful?

2   Let's practice thinking metaphorically in a bigger way. The movie, *American History X*, documented the organization of "skinhead" groups in Southern California in the early 1990s. The skinheads attacked viciously anyone in an ethnic-racial minority group, especially Mexican-Americans and the illegal Mexican workers employed in a local grocery store. Offer different metaphorical characterizations of this crime using two of the following theoretical frameworks and their root metaphors: the Behavioral (person like an animal and society like a laboratory), Conflict (person like a fighter and society as a battle between groups for resources), Social Systems (person as a part and society as a collection of smaller social systems), and Symbolic Interactionist (the person as a communicator and society as a community sharing a language).

First, fill in the following applications of the metaphors for each framework. The community where the violence occurred is like _____. The groups causing and affected by the act of violence are like _____. The acts of violence are like _____. Social work intervention would be like _____. Your completion of each statement should integrate ideas and images that vividly expand on each framework's root metaphor. Expand also on the meaning of each use of a root metaphor. Play with some conveyance metaphors, too, that will help you understand the pattern of hate crime.

Then, compare and contrast your different ways of explaining attacks on members of minority groups. How did metaphors help you understand the varied theoretical approaches to this phenomenon?

3   Early behaviorists make frequent comparisons of the developing person to animals—rats, dogs, cats, pigeons. Like animals responding to the pairing of meat and a bell, human behavioral patterns change over time because of conditioning. Like animals trying to increase rewards (treats) and avoid punishments (beatings), human behavior patterns change as agents of socialization alter the consequences of the actions. Like animals imitating the behavior patterns of same-species peers, human behavior patterns change as admirable models are observed when the models are rewarded or punished for certain behaviors. Use our tools of metaphorical comparison to appraise the behaviorists' root metaphor and its usefulness for understanding a developing child. Using positive comparison, identify some similarities between the developing person and a growing puppy. Using negative comparison, identify some differences between the developing person and the growing puppy.

Using practical comparison, discuss some ways that the root metaphor might help social workers conducting a group for parent-child dyads focusing on developmental problems.

References

Cornelissen, J. P. (2006). Making sense of theory construction: Metaphor and disciplined imagination. *Organization Studies, 27*(11), 1579–1597.

Duffy, T. K. (2005). White gloves and cracked vases: How metaphors help group workers construct new perspectives and responses. *Social Work With Groups, 28*(3/4), 247–257.

Forte, J. A. (2006). *Human behavior and the social environment: Models, metaphors, and maps for applying theoretical perspectives to practice*. Belmont, CA: Thomson Brooks/Cole.

Forte, J. A. (2009). Teaching human development: Current theoretical deficits and a theory-enriched "Models, metaphors, and maps" remedy. *Journal of Human Behavior in the Social Environment, 19*(7), 932–954.

MacCormac, E. R. (1985). *A cognitive theory of metaphor*. Cambridge, MA: MIT Press.

Pepper, S. C. (1942). *World hypotheses: A study in evidence*. Berkeley, CA: University of California Press.

Scholnik, E. K. (2000). Engendering development: Metaphors of change. In P. H. Miller and E. K. Scholnik (Eds), *Toward a feminist developmental psychology* (pp. 241–254). New York: Routledge.

Check on and specify theory's assumptions

(EPAS 2.1.3 Apply Critical Thinking;
EPAS 2.1.7 Apply Knowledge)

Each theoretical tradition provides us different guidance in describing and explaining "person interacting in the environment" challenges and in scientific inquiry (Colomy & Brown, 1995; Turner, 1983). These differences emerge because of variations in core assumptions and premises about the nature of the puzzles, about the best explanations of such puzzles, and about the best methods for assembling puzzle pieces and testing puzzle solutions. Social work theory users and theorizers should know the assumptions of the theories that they use and be aware of their own assumptions and biases.

Deconstructing theoretical assumptions

Assumptions are "statements taken as given and not subject to direct empirical verification" (Chafetz, 1978, p. 33). They may be *core assumptions*: general scientific assumptions about reality, statements that can't be adjudicated by empirical proof or disproof. For example, scientists assume that there is a reality outside and independent of individual minds, and scientists assume that there is an order to this reality. They may be domain assumptions. *Domain assumptions* refer to theoretical assumptions that are specific to the subject matter of a particular theory (Chafetz, 1978). For example, critical theorists assume that physical force and coercion are the main methods used by the privileged groups to increase and protect their rights and privileges. Although not directly testable, core scientific assumptions and domain assumptions are very influential during the theory application process (Zhang, 2002).

To understand fully and use well the concepts, propositions, and theories associated with each theoretical tradition, we must first identify and understand the assumptions on which they are based (Einstadter & Henry, 1995). Assumptions relate often to the historical roots and philosophical convictions of the theory founders (Slife & Williams, 1995). Assumptions and their implications, however, are embedded in non-obvious ways in theoretical texts, and assumptions tend to taken-for-granted ideas (Yanchar & Slife, 2004). Pozzuto (2007) points to the importance of searching for and identifying hidden assumptions:

> the form of theory often influences practice by implied and often obscured assumptions about the social world. To the degree that these assumptions can be brought to light, the practitioner can reflect upon his or her practice, making a more informed choice in practice approaches. (p. 88)

Focus of theoretical assumptions

As social workers, we need to deconstruct theory and learn about and appraise critically the theoretical assumptions about the person, the environment, and the transactions connecting person and environment.

Assumptions about the person

Theorists differ in their core assumptions about human nature including the dispositions of the person and the human capacity for freedom and self-determination. Some assume that the person is an individual agent capable of action and somewhat independent of environmental influences. Some assume that the person is a product shaped by the environment with little capability for independent action and little control over life trajectories. Some assume that the person and environment exist in continual reciprocal transactions and the person is capable of some creative and self-chosen action but that all human action is influenced by and influences this environment.

Theorists differ in their assumptions about the most important influences on human behavior. Some emphasize biological factors such as genetic dispositions. Others emphasize psychological factors, and some prioritize social factors. Some theorists assume that human beings are multidimensional, but the influence of biological processes, cognitive processes, emotional processes, and social processes varies by person, circumstance, and problem or challenge. As illustration, consider the different assumptions related to contrasting explanations of human emotions (Forte, 2007). Skinnerian behaviorists assume that there is no cognitive activity between stimuli and response; emotions are triggered automatically; and the actor is not an active constructor of emotional reactions to situations. Parsonian functionalists assume that the person is socialized into playing scripted roles within stable institutions. The creative interpretation and use of emotions is minimal. Psychodynamic theorists emphasize the unconscious, instinctual aspects of emotions and assume that emotions such as shame and guilt are controlled through mechanisms of repression. Bio-evolutionary theorists view emotion as a byproduct, not an integral element of interaction, and focus on the equivalence between animals and humans in emotional display.

Theorists also differ in their assumptions about the moral inclinations of the person, the possibility of altruistic behavior, and the nature of morality. Some adherents to religious and political belief systems assert that human beings are basically bad and tend toward hurtful and self-serving actions if free from surveillance; people need societies to control them. Other humanistic theorizers assert that human beings are basically good and will act morally if they are provided supportive environments. Others aligned with behavioral theory argue that the person is born neither good nor bad but learns a moral orientation reflective of social experiences and the consequences of choices. Similarly, some rational choice economic theorists conceive of the person as selfish and inclined to maximize personal advantage whereas others conceive of the person as inclined toward cooperation and mutual aid. Some attribute blame to the person for misdeeds. Others attribute blame to society. Others assume that the person is always responsible for his or her action, but environments can press very powerfully in ways resulting in immoral conduct.

We might also characterize theorists by their place on a continuum of assumptions about human tendencies toward illness. Decay, disease, deficiency, and disorder are on one of the ends, and growth, strengths, resiliencies, and community assets are on the other end. Those at the extremes would bring radically different assumptions about the person and about possibilities for transformation to the helping process. Positive and strengths-oriented theorists on the growth end have attempted to shift our profession away, for example, from the deficit assumptions inherent in some psychoanalytic and family systems theories.

Think about controversies regarding welfare policies, the processes central to policy formation, the nature of policy arenas, and whether particular policies are expected to result in improvements in the behavior and lives of the recipients of government benefits. In relation to policies important to social workers, the differences between competing stakeholders and their arguments about a policy and its likely consequences are often tied to significantly different theoretical assumptions about the poor and how to deal with poverty.

Assumptions about the environment

Theorists differ also in their core assumptions about the nature of the environment. Some structural functionalist theorists assume that each society is characterized by consensus or agreement about the central values that guide action and interaction. Other critical theorists assume that each society is characterized by conflict between different groups competing for resources; consensus and cooperation are rare.

Theorists make different assumptive claims about the stability of the environment. Some such as interactionist theorists assume a process orientation and conceive of the physical and social environment as changing consistently and significantly. Others assume that social arrangements generally are fixed, durable, and very stable; structural functionalists tend to fall in this camp.

Theories vary in their premises about the most critical systems within the environment. Some assume that primary associations related to the family and friendship group have the most formative and lasting influences on clients. Others believe that macro-size social systems, especially those related to the power structure and the economic structure, are the most influential systems. Others take a micro-stance and believe that the human genetic makeup and our evolutionary-based predispositions determine human-created environments and interaction patterns in these environments.

Assumptions about interaction between person and environment

Theorists differ, too, in their assumptions about relationships between person and environment and the power of these relationships. Some argue, for instance, that cause is basically one-directional from environment to person. The person has minimal power to change the environment. Some contend that cause is bi-directional. Environmental factors change human beings, and human choices can influence the environment. Many consider the link between people and environments as multi-directional, recursive, and transactional. Various aspects of the environment influence people, and various human choices and actions impact the environment; the causal processes set in motion feed back on the actors in the environment, increasing the change effects.

Theorists differ in their assumptions about the primary mediator between person and environment. Cognitive scientists prioritize information. Spiritual theorists give special place to faith. Symbolic interactionists consider communication via symbols to be the primary vehicle for person-environment transactions. Economic theorists give weight to currency, money, and other valuable commodities.

Theorists also differ in their location on the individualism-collectivism continuum. Those at the individualistic pole assume that most human action is self-generated whatever the environmental pressures. Those at the collectivistic pole assume that most human action is shaped by and responsive to the collective. Those at the middle assume most human action reflects continual transactions between person and environment and includes, therefore, traces of individuality and traces of groupness.

Human behavior and practice theorists may differ in their assumptions about behavioral consistency. Some assume that a person behaves in patterned and predictable ways across a variety of ecological settings. Some assume that the person behaves differently in each ecological setting. Some theorists assume that it depends on the person, the transaction patterns developed over time, and the environmental contexts; in some ways and at some places, there is significant consistency, but under certain circumstances, there can be much variation from typical behavior patterns.

Assumptions about human development

Theorists make different assumptions about the nature and processes of human development across the life span. Some such as Piaget assumed that development occurs in a predictable series of stages from birth to death, and these stage patterns are universal. Life course theorists such as Glen Elder assume, in contrast, that there are multiple developmental paths, and the sequence of development can vary significantly across cultures, generations, and historical times. Developmental theorists concerned with environmental influences such as Urie Bronfenbrenner assume that there is great variability in developmental pace, process, and outcomes across different cultural, ecological, and social contexts.

Developmental theorists vary, too, in their views of the events or factors that stimulate development. Some theorists believe that developmental changes are triggered by innate biological mechanisms; others prioritize learning experiences in environmental settings; and others assume that developmental progression depends in complex ways on the interaction of forces of nature and nurture. For some, development occurs independently of individual choice. For others, human beings are capable of altering their own fate by purposeful action.

Developmental theorists differ in the temporal horizons they assign to human growth. Some theorists assume that development is essentially complete by late adolescence or early adulthood, and subsequent personality changes are minor. Other theorists argue that human development is a lifelong process, and even older adults can make major changes in their patterns and life trajectory.

Assumptions about the planned change process

Theorists differ also in their core assumptions about the nature of the change process. Some assume that change is rare, and the continuity of patterns—especially personality patterns formed in childhood—is more common than the transformation of these patterns. Some assume that change is constant. Assumptions about openness to change vary. Some assume that people resist change. Personal and social changes are very difficult and painful. Others argue that positive emotions, positive experiences, and positive relations often and easily trigger enjoyable change processes.

Practice theorists differ, too, on their conception of the person's role in the change process. Some believe that we can change a person with or without his or her awareness and choice; bio-medical theorists and practitioners may adopt this premise. Others contend that change starts with the client, and the client's insight and commitment to new and different decisions are essential to the change process. Existential and psychodynamic theorists and practitioners often prefer this premise. Thus, practitioners with certain theoretical orientations accept interventions that "do to the client" whereas practitioners with other theoretical orientations reject any interventions that don't foster "doing with the client."

Practice theorists often differ, too, in their assumptions about the best temporal focus. Psychodynamic theorists tend to assume that past experiences, especially those in early childhood, powerfully influence the present and should be the focus of therapy. Gestalt theorists believe that change occurs when therapists can enhance client contact with his or her experiences and awareness in the here and now. Symbolic interactionist theorists assume that all change work occurs in the present, but successful change requires an active imagination, and, specifically, the construction of better personal and collective futures.

Identifying theoretical assumptions

Theory users need to be clear about their assumptions and other deeply held beliefs. Shoemaker and his colleagues (Shoemaker, Tankard, & Lasorsa 2004) suggest, for example, "identifying and communicating assumptions is a form of intellectual honesty" and "the more scholars can identify the assumptions that underlie their theories and research the more they and others can understand the implications of the theories" (p. 39). This is not an easy undertaking. Some theorists help theory users by including a list of core assumptions in books and articles about the theoretical tradition. Sometimes, we need to do a very careful reading and study such texts for clues to a theory's assumptive base. We can use comparisons, root metaphors, and conveyance metaphors to gain insight into the foundational assumptions of a theoretical framework. We learned about these tools for identifying assumptions in the discussion of the deconstruction and reconstruction of theory metaphors.

Before and while helping clients, the theorizing practitioner should identify his or her theoretical assumptive biases and prejudices, make a conscious effort to minimize any negative impact of these biases, and reflect constantly on how the data from the helping process support or challenge one's assumptive biases (Piercy & Sprenkle, 1986). If the practitioner notices repeated conflict with a colleague or client over assessment formulations and intervention plans, he or she might search for differences in assumptions and for biases.

Reconstructing theoretical assumptions

There are several approaches to reconstructing theoretical assumptions for use in a particular helping situation. Souva (2013) recommends that the theorizing practitioner follow the following steps. Identify the central assumptions inherent in the theories chosen for inquiry and action planning in a particular case. Write out the logic of each assumption in a formal way: If theoretical assumption X is true (people always act to maximize profits), what is the consequence Y that follows (as group worker, I need to help members of this mandated group see how participation advances their interests). Check the logical argument and the evidence supporting the X–Y relationship of premises. If supported, examine in more detail the relevance of the assumption to the case and consider possible circumstances requiring modification of the assumption (times when it doesn't hold, places where it doesn't hold, factors that lessen the likelihood that the predicted consequence follows affirmation of the assumption). Reconstruct the theoretical assumption and one's practice accordingly.

Slife and his colleagues (Slife & Williams, 1995; Yanchar & Slife, 2004) advise practitioners to carefully consider the quality of the defense of any theoretical assumptions before reconstruction work. A theoretical assumption can be defended in many ways: the marshalling of empirical evidence that tested the expected relationship between assumption and implications; the use of logical argument appealing to philosophical or value preferences; the claim that theorizing developments within the theoretical community weaken or strengthen the assumption; or the reference to simulations approximating conditions such as those when action on the assumption will be taken. This team also offers a way to consider the consequences of an assumption. They refer to a consequence as a theoretical implication, the events that will follow logically if a theoretical assumption is put into action and the costs that the theory user is obligated to accept after affirming one assumption in contrast to an alternative assumption. For example, if we assume that the client's behavior is completely determined, Slife argues, the practitioner is obligated to provide consolation. Exploring alternative choices and courses of action is not an option. The basic formula proposed is "According to Theory A in relation to issue Z, it is assumed that _____, and this assumption has the following implications for the person, environment, transactions, or helping process _____, and these implications obligate the worker to try to help by _____." Repeatedly using this formula when considering theoretical assumptions prepares the worker to affirm and act on some assumptions, to reject other assumptions, and to reconstruct those assumptions that need modification in specific circumstances.

Learning activities and reflections

1 Theorizing begins with premises or assumptions about the person, interaction, the environment, and change processes. Theoretical assumptions are general statements assumed to be true such as "human beings are generally _____," or "Societies (and other environments) can be best characterized as _____," or "Individual and collective change most commonly involves _____." How would you fill in the blanks for each of these general statements based on your preferred assumptions?

2 Report on some of your central or core theoretical assumptions about the person, the environment, and the relationship of person and environment. Identify also your assumptions about how people and groups change. If possible, trace these assumptions to their origin in particular theoretical frameworks that you have learned and in your life history. If this is difficult, read the commentary above again and then return to the learning activity. Remember, too, that your "human behavior and the social environment," "human development," "social work practice," "field seminar," and other courses will teach you about core assumptions, how to recognize unstated premises, and how to increase your own awareness of assumptions. Note whether some of your assumptions have sources other than scientific theory—traumatic experiences, your cultural background, and so on. Comment on how you might reconcile your personal assumptions with those of scientific theories.

3 Think about your favorite human behavior theories and practice theories. Which theoretical assumptions make most sense to you? Which challenge your understanding of the order of things? Which theoretical assumptions would you defend? Which will you attack? Which would you modify and in what ways to fit with your preferred understandings of person, environment, transactions, and change?

4 What are your basic assumptions about human development—its nature, its triggers and mechanisms, its predictability, its pathways, its commonality across persons and cultures, its continuity or discontinuity over time, its relationship to the environment, its challenges? Pinpoint three or four of your theoretical assumptions. Trace the assumptions back to their source in your own life, your theoretical knowledge, your research knowledge, or your practice wisdom. Compare your core assumptions with the assumptions of other students or colleagues. Comment on how these assumptions have influenced your helping work and how you might adapt some of these assumptions to fit with particular features of the developing client, the developmental challenge, or the helping setting.

5   Consider how your assumptions might direct your helping work. What are three or four specific ways that your theoretical assumptions have influenced (or will influence) your social work approach and shape your helping activities? Imagine also that you are collaborating with one or more social workers with different assumptions about human behavior, perhaps because they have specialized in different fields of practice such as medical social work, correctional social work, or social work policy advocacy. Provide some illustrations of possible assumption-based conflicts in regards to assessment, problem formulation, or intervention recommendations. Reflect also on how assumptive differences between a client and worker might contribute to impasses in the helping work.

References

Chafetz, J. S. (1978). *A primer on the construction and testing of theories in sociology*. Itasca, IL: F. E. Peacock.

Colomy, P., & Brown, J. D. (1995). Elaboration, revision, polemic, and progress in the Second Chicago School. In G. A. Fine (Ed.), *A second Chicago school? The development of a postwar American sociology* (pp.17–81). Chicago, IL: University of Chicago Press.

Einstadter, W., & Henry. S. (1995). *Criminological theory: An analysis of its underlying assumptions*. Fort Worth, TX: Harcourt Brace.

Forte, J. A. (2007). Using a semiotic metatheory for theory understanding, appraisal, and use: An illustrative social work translation of the affect control theory of emotions. *Advances in Social Work, 8*(1), 1–18.

Piercy, F. P., & Sprenkle, D. H. (1986). Family therapy theory building: An integrative training approach. *Journal of Psychotherapy and the Family, 1*(4), 5–14.

Pozzuto, R. (2007). Understanding theory, practicing social work. In S. L. Witkin & D. Saleeby (Eds), *Social work dialogues: Transforming the canon in inquiry, practice, and education* (pp. 64–93). Alexandria, VA: Council on Social Work Education.

Shoemaker, P. J., Tankard, J. W., Jr., & Lasorsa, D. L. (2004). *How to build social science theories*. Thousand Oaks, CA: Sage.

Turner, F. J. (1983). Directions for social work education: The challenge of developing a comprehensive, coherent and flexible integrating network of theories. In L. S. Bandler (Ed.), *Education for clinical social work practice* (pp. 125–141). Oxford, UK: Pergamon Press.

Slife, B. D., & Williams, R. N. (1995). *What's behind the research? Discovering hidden assumptions in the behavioral sciences*. Thousand Oaks, CA: Sage.

Souva, M. (2013). Fostering theoretical thinking in undergraduate classes. *PS: Political Science and Politics, 40*(3), 557–562.

Yanchar, S. C., & Slife, B. D. (2004). Teaching critical thinking by examining assumptions. *Teaching of Psychology, 31*(2), 85–90.

Zhang, P. (2002). In defense of realistic assumptions. In J. Symatka, M. Lovaglia, & K. Wysienka (Eds). *The growth of knowledge: Theory, simulation, and empirical research in group processes* (pp. 57–75). Westport, CT: Praeger.

Identify and adapt a theory's concepts

(EPAS 2.1.7 Apply Knowledge)

We need to name a thing or process before we can theorize about it and use it as we apply a human behavior theory or practice theory. A theoretical concept gives a name to some aspect of reality, a name with a more abstract and analytical definition than the everyday definitions attached to common objects and events (Swedberg, 2012). The concept helps us answer the question of what to call a puzzling experience, an unusual behavior, an ambiguous interaction, or a perplexing social structure. Concepts are important building blocks in theoretical constructions.

Overview: theory and concepts

A *concept* is a "word or collection of words expressing a mental image of some phenomenon" (Fawcett & Downs, 1986, p. 16). Besides the name, a concept includes a definition. A *definition* is a public and explicit statement indicating a commitment to use a concept in a particular way. In each theoretical or scientific community, a preferred vocabulary of concepts and preferred definitions of each concept in the vocabulary accumulates over time. Novices in that community are expected to acquire the consensual meaning of each concept and, then, to use the concept in line with the community's norms.

Theoretical concepts have certain features (Chinn & Kramer, 2008). Theoretical concepts include a label. This is a symbolic designation, typically a word or set of words, naming the represented experience. Theorists assign names such as ego defense, reinforcement, and xenophobia to phenomenon of interest.

Theoretical concepts have referents. These are the events, objects, qualities, processes, or properties that the concept points to or represents. Anna Freud built on her father's theoretical insights and her own clinical observations to theorize about some specific types of intrapsychic mechanisms as she refined her concept: ego defense. The concept of an ego defense might be signaled or referenced by increases in bodily tension. This became an important part of the definition.

Theoretical concepts are abstractions. We can't smell or hold a concept. Instead, they are ideas that refer to specific experiences, events, objects, or persons. Concepts vary in degree of abstraction from those close to their empirical referents and directly observed such as "height" to those distant from empirical referents and inferred on the basis of direct and indirect observations such as "well-being."

Theoretical concepts are shared. In a particular scientific community, members assign the same or similar meanings to many theoretical concepts—attachment, family boundaries, self-esteem, or institutional discrimination. However, concepts are also social constructions, and when there are many theoretical communities, there may be many different ways of defining the same concept as influenced by the culture, preferred approach to science, overall network of theoretical concepts, and values of the community (Layder, 1998). Theorists and researchers may disagree about the best way to conceptualize some phenomenon, or there may be a high degree of consensus about the best definition. Two sets of family scientists, for example, disagreed on how to define healthy family functioning (Hampson, Beavers, & Hulgus, 2004). Is healthy family functioning best defined as the maximization of processes of cohesion and adaptability (the highest scores on indicators for each variable), or is healthy family functioning best defined as a middle range of cohesion and adaptability; the avoidance of the extremes of "too little" or "too much" on the indicators of these variables. Typically, members of a scientific community communicate with one another about conceptual definitions and work together to achieve precise and good definitions agreed to by the majority of theorists, researchers, and practitioners in the community. By means of logical argument and reference to empirical research, scientists often discard unacceptable definitions, refine workable definitions, and achieve consensus.

Theoretical concepts are useful. They can guide social workers, for instance, in processes of gathering and interpreting information about a client system; an assessment guide includes a list of concepts meriting investigation. Theoretical concepts can serve workers and clients collaborating to achieve desired ends, conceptions of ideal states

Finally, concepts are learned. Successful professional socialization requires the mastery of thousands of human behavior concepts, for example, by the aspiring social work practitioner.

Deconstructing a theory's concepts

The theorizing practitioner needs to identify the concepts of major theories, learn the definitions of each of these concepts common to the theoretical tradition, and break the concept into its constituent parts: label, words, and referents.

Type of definition

There are two major types of conceptual definitions. A *nominal definition* defines a concept with other concepts. For theorists, a nominal definition is like a dictionary definition of an everyday concept. For instance, Barker's (2003) social work dictionary provides nominal definitions for more than 9,000 concepts used in the profession. Start with A and you will find definitions for abstinence, abuse, absolute confidentiality, accountability, activist, and many other concepts used by social workers. Dictionaries of definitions are also available for theoretical concepts developed in psychology, sociology, anthropology, and other disciplines important to social work.

An *operational definition* defines the concept in terms of observable data. This definition specifies both the empirical indicators of the concept and the procedures, the "operations," necessary to measure the phenomenon. Depression, for instance, may be defined by identifying biological indicators, psychological indicators, and social interaction indicators.

A 25-item depression scale with directions for use and scoring might be employed to measure the overall degree of depression and the degree on biological, psychological, and social subscales. For a research study involving a theoretical concept, procedural specification may identify also who will collect the data, when it will be collected, where it is collected, and the method of data collection (survey, observation, the use of existing records, interview).

The most useful theoretical concepts have both nominal definitions and operational definitions. Moreover, there are reports (research studies, theory-oriented articles, and case examples) indicating that advocates have validated the concepts and their definitions by argument, evidence, and useful application.

Distinctions between concepts

While deconstructing a theory's concepts, it will help to know that the definitions of theoretical concepts generally diverge significantly from the definitions of layperson's concepts. David Olson (1989), a family systems theorist, for instance, has defined family cohesion nominally and operationally in ways much more complex and precise than the common usages of the term *cohesion* by family members themselves. For example, he suggests that cohesive families "consult" with one another; family members are unlikely to think of their sense of togetherness in this way.

A theoretical concept is different than a theorist construct. Some theorists make use of the term *construct*. This refers to a concept at a very abstract level that incorporates other concepts that are less abstract for use in a particular theory (Shoemaker, Tankard, & Lasorsa, 2004). For example, social work educators recommend inclusion of content on the construct "at-risk populations" in social work curriculums. This is a very broad concept, one that includes many conceptual elements and covers much "person interacting in the environment" territory. Biologists often make use of the construct "evolution," and cognitive scientists make use of the construct "intelligence."

Note, too, that practitioners using the interpretive style of theorizing are wary of developing and using definitive concepts, concepts operationalized in accord with the conventions of positivist science. Such conceptual practices fail to make reference to the meanings of a concept as understood by a particular cultural group in a particular historical context. Such concepts are not grounded in the group's experiences. Interpretive theorists prefer sensitizing concepts to operational concepts (Bowen, 2006). A *sensitizing concept* lacks the precise specification of attributes found in definitive concepts. Instead, it provides a general sense of reference and guidance in approaching empirical instances. Sensitizing concepts are starting points for grounded theorizing and qualitative studies. Bowen, for example, used the three concepts—community/citizen participation, social capital, and empowerment—in a sensitizing way to study and theorize about social and economic investment in poor Jamaican communities.

Additional strategies for deconstruction

The process of using our mental powers to translate experiences into abstract representations or symbols is called *conceptualization* (Jaccard & Jacoby, 2010). Concepts are often defined nominally as a first step in theory building, testing, or application. Resilience has been defined nominally, for example, as

> a general frame of reference or belief system through which individuals appraise events and situations in the environment. It allows them to define situations from their environment as a challenge and an opportunity to act with understanding, confidence, and persistence in overcoming or rebounding from the consequences of the associated adversities through environmental mastery and individual adaptation.
> (Richman & Bowen, 1997, p. 101)

To better understand a concept and its nominal definition, the theorizing practitioner should look for exemplars of the concept, resilience, for instance, in their own practice or personal experiences (Walker & Avant, 1995). The practitioner might also find contrary examples, real-life illustrations of what the concept isn't. In relation to the deconstruction of a focal concept, it helps to differentiate similar concepts and dissimilar concepts.

After careful conceptualization, nominal definitions are transformed into operational definitions. This process is referred to as *operationalization*.

Indicators and measurement procedures are specified. Operationally, Richman and Bowen (1997) assert that resilience is best conceptualized as a variable ranging from low to high. They don't identify a specific measurement procedure that directly assesses resilience. However, Wagnild and Young (2009) have completed both definitional steps. They propose a simpler nominal definition of resilience than the Richman and Bowen definition. Resilience is the ability to successfully cope with change or misfortune. They have also developed an operational definition. Resilience is the score on a 25-item resilience scale that asks raters to judge items such as "when I'm in a difficult situation, I can usually find my way out of it" and "I usually take things in stride" on seven possible ratings from strongly disagree to strongly agree. These items are the indicators of the concept. Operational definitions are validated by means of research. Good operational definitions have answered concerns about demonstrable validity (do the indicators and procedures measure with accuracy the concept?) and about reliability (do the indicators and procedures measure the concept with consistency over time or across groups? This assumes values of the phenomenon measured have not changed). These two criteria for measurement quality are covered in social work research classes and textbooks.

To better understand a concept and its operational definition, the practitioner might attempt to identify and think about all the empirical referents or indicators of the focal concept (Walker & Avant, 1995). For example, we might examine carefully Olson's (1989) Family Adaptation and Cohesion Evaluation Scale (FACES) starting with the subscale for cohesion. We can look at each of the ten indicators for family cohesion and ask ourselves what each empirical indicator refers to in family functioning. We might also search out and appraise the literature asserting the validity, reliability, and cultural sensitivity of the entire measurement scale.

Reconstructing a theory's concepts

There are thousands of theoretical concepts available to social work practitioners. However, these theoretical concepts often need to be adapted for use in particular circumstances (Swedberg, 2012). The theorizing practitioner might use an existing concept but clarify its meaning in a particular helping situation. For example, my students and I (Forte, Barrett, & Campbell, 1996) were assisting in bereavement group services for family members of persons who had died in a local hospital. We decided that the interactionist concept of loss might help us make sense of their grief experiences. However, the concept had not been developed in a helping context. We summarized the interactionist literature on the seven aspects of loss: loss of a role partner, loss of mundane assistance, loss of linkages to the deceased's social network, loss of confirmation of the self, loss of shared futures, loss of reality validation, and loss of comforting myths created with the family member. We transformed these aspects into interview questions and interviewed group members to learn the meanings of each aspect of loss from their perspective.

The theorizing practitioner might start with an existing theoretical concept but combine it with another related concept in a new way. In a study of comparing battered women to non-battered women, my colleagues and I (Forte, Franks, Forte, & Rigsby, 1996) theorized using the interactionist tradition that role-taking deficiencies were central to domestic violence (the batter was likely to have minimal role-taking dispositions or skills) but also that power and status differences sustained role-taking deficiencies (the more powerful and higher-status person could use various forms of coercion to compel cooperation from the subordinate and needn't take her role). Combining these two notions, we conceived of "asymmetrical role taking" as a novel concept, one that deepened our understanding of the predicaments of battered women and the long-term consequences of being trapped in a violent household.

Chinn and Kramer (2008) suggest a general approach to reconstructing a theoretical concept. The theorizer should become very familiar with the concept and the literature on it (good parenting, for instance), redefine the concept in relation to professional purpose (assessment, clinical decision making, evaluating progress) and the needs of the case, find an exemplar of the concept based on the case or similar cases (specific episodes of mother-child interaction, for example), modify the definition found in the theoretical or research literature, check that the concept's modified definition differentiates it from contrary cases, finalize the conceptual meaning attached to the phenomenon, and test out the reconstructed concept's usefulness. They add that the worker should engage in critical thinking at each state of the reconstruction process. Layder (1998) warns, however, that when extracting a concept from a theory and redefining it, there is danger of watering down or losing the meaning it had within the network of concepts.

In very special circumstances, the practical theorizer may go beyond concept reconstruction and construct a new concept (Walker & Avant, 1995). Perhaps the PIE phenomenon has never been named and defined by theorists (some event during online counseling, for instance), and there has been minimal conceptualization and operationalization work relevant to these instances in the case. The practitioner might then create a new concept by collecting data, clustering the data into attributes, giving the phenomenon a name, constructing a definition, validating the concept and its definition empirically, revising the definition repeatedly based on the data to achieve conceptual precision, and seeking feedback on the concept from knowledgeable colleagues. This strategy should be reserved for advanced practitioners who also have significant research knowledge and skills.

Theoretical concepts are key ingredients in the language of science. DiRenzo (1957, p. 6) characterized concepts as the "irreducible elements of theory or theoretical systems," and he adds, "the more precise and refined the conceptual elements, the more precise and refined the theory." Theoretical development and the growth of scientific knowledge depend on conceptualization work. Effective theory use by practitioners is enhanced by careful work deconstructing and reconstructing theoretical concepts.

Learning activities and reflections

1 The concept "resilience" is familiar to many social workers. If not, read some of the literature on resilience theory. Answer this question: What aspects of the "person interacting in an environment" does the concept resilience attempt to explain? From this starting point, develop a nominal and operational definition of this concept. Briefly discuss the possible use of this concept by a social worker to understand some aspect of micro level behavior and some aspect of the macro-level social context.

2 Try using Max Weber's (1968) way of conceptualizing power: the probability that one actor in a social relationship will be in a position to carry out his or her will despite resistance from the other. Reflect on how powerful you are. Who can overcome your resistance? What are your reactions to submitting to another person's will? Who do you compel to yield to your will? How often do you consider the other person's feelings, intentions, and desires when asserting your power? What lessons might you generalize to the daily experiences of powerless clients? Next, reflect on Weber's nominal definition: What are its strengths and limitations and in what other ways might power be better defined? Finally, what might you recommend as a specific valid (accurate) and reliable (consistent) strategy for measuring the power of each of the members of your social work department, field placement, or place of employment?

3 Identify two theoretical constructs as homework (class conflict, social status, homophobia, family functioning, role overload, significant symbol, irrational belief, moral development, self-esteem) relevant to understanding some aspect of human behavior and the social environment or human development. Do a Web search for definitions of each construct and report on your view of the best definitions. Seek also articles by theorists and researchers commenting on each construct and definitional issues. Identify some of problems associated with the definition or some of the differing approaches to defining the construct. What have you learned about claims regarding the best definition and about the degree of theoretical consensus regarding the definition?

4 Identify a concept that is important to you in your helping work. Compare and contrast various ways of defining the concept. For example, consider a dictionary definition. Look up a definition associated with a

scientific or theoretical tradition. Identify several of these definitions of the concept that differ from your understanding of its meaning. What are these differences? Develop your own definition by listing the key elements or properties of the concept. Create an operational definition of the concept. For example, write three survey statements that might help you measure the conceptualized phenomenon. Use a grounded theory approach, and find out what the concept means to a specific group or subculture of clients. Based on your careful analysis and research, what do you see as the strengths and limitations of the concept?

5   Kurt Lewin created a very useful ecological concept: life space (Marrow, 1969). His idea of life space refers to the physical places where you go often, the people you encounter there, and events that occur there and your feelings about the people and the place. The life space includes places that you enter regularly or everyday, places that you've been to but enter occasionally, and vicarious places, the imaginary world that you travel to through reading, movies and television watching, and conversations with others. Identify three or four professional situations in which Lewin's concept of life space might be useful. Describe specifically how you might reconstruct the concept to understand and help the clients in the kind of situations that you encounter in your practice or volunteer service.

References

Barker, R. L. (2003). *The social work dictionary* (5th edn). Washington, DC: NASW Press.

Bowen, G. A. (2006). Grounded theory and sensitizing concepts. *International Journal of Qualitative Methods*, 5(3), Article 2. Retrieved October 25, 2009, from www.ualberta.ca/~iiqm/backissues/5_3/pdf/bowen.pdf

Chinn, P. L., & Kramer, M. K. (2008). *Integrated theory and knowledge development in nursing* (7th Edn). St. Louis, MO: Mosby Elsevier.

DiRenzo, G. J. (1957). Conceptual definition in the behavioral sciences. In G. J. DiRenzo (Ed.), *Concepts, theory, and explanation in the behavioral sciences* (pp. 3–18). New York: Random House.

Fawcett, J., & Downs, F. S. (1986). *The relationship of theory and research*. Norwalk, CT: Appleton-Century-Crofts.

Forte, J.A. , Barrett, A.V., & Campbell, M.H. (1996). Patterns of social connectedness and shared grief work: A symbolic interactionist evaluation. *Social Work with Groups*, 19(1), 29–52.

Forte, J.A., Franks, D.D., Forte, J., & Rigsby, D. (1996). Oppressive social situations and asymmetrical role-taking: Comparing battered and non-battered women. *Social Work*, 41(1), 59–73.

Hampson, R. B., Beavers, R. W., & Hulgus, Y. F. (2004). Commentary: comparing the Beavers and Circumplex models of family functioning. *Family Process*, 27(1), 85–92.

Jaccard, J. & Jacoby, J. (2010). *Theory construction and model-building skills*. New York: The Guilford Press.

Layder, D. (1998). *Sociological practice: Linking theory and social research*. London: Sage.

Marrow, A. (1969). *The practical theorist*. New York: Knopf.

Olson, D. H. (1989). Circumplex model of family systems VIII: Family assessment and intervention. In D. H. Olson, C. S. Russell, & D. H. Sprenkle (Eds), *Circumplex model: Systematic assessment and treatment of families* (pp. 7–49). New York: Haworth Press.

Richman, J. M., & Bowen, G. L. (1997). School failure: An ecological-interactional-developmental perspective. In M. W. Fraser (Ed.), *Risk and resilience in childhood: An ecological perspective* (pp. 95–116). Washington, DC: NASW Press.

Shoemaker, P. J., Tankard, J. W., Jr., & Lasorsa, D. L. (2004). *How to build social science theories*. Thousand Oaks, CA: Sage.

Swedberg, R. (2012). Theorizing in sociology and social science: Turning to the context of discovery. *Theory and Society*, 41, 1–40.

Wagnild, G., & Young, H. M. (2009). The Resilience Scale Homepage at www.resiliencescale.com (retrieved October 9, 2013).

Walker, L. O., & Avant, K. C. (1995). *Strategies for theory construction in nursing* (3rd edn). Norwalk, CT: Appleton.

Weber, M. (1968 [1922]). *Economy and society: An outline of interpretive sociology*. New York: Bedminster Press.

Identify and reformulate a theory's propositions

(EPAS 2.1.7 Apply Knowledge)

A theoretical tradition is composed of many different concepts. These concepts are typically assembled in theoretical statements or propositions. Propositions are sentences. Elaborating on the theory construction metaphor, they might be likened to an architect's or general contractor's statements about how different construction elements should be joined together. If two-by-four pieces of lumber are connected properly by nails, the carpenter will progress toward the construction of a the specified wood-framed wall.

Deconstructing a theory's propositions

A *theoretical proposition* is a declarative statement about the nature of a relationship between two or more concepts. Deconstructing a theory's propositions requires familiarity with the different types of theoretical propositions (Abell, 1971; Burr, 1973; Meleis, 1985; Walker & Avant, 1995). Knowledge of the research methods for collecting evidence and statistical procedures for judging propositions and their properties is also useful.

Types of propositions

Existence relationships

This simple proposition asserts that some phenomenon exists and can be named. For example, the theory may include the definitional statement,: "A person's subjective feeling is called affect," or the explanatory theory might refer to the existence statement, "There is significant poverty in this town; more than 40% of the references subsist on income less than the poverty level."

Relationships of association

Propositions often specify the nature of relationship between actions, events, situations, structures, or conditions. For example, the theory may identify an association between two variables. As one variable changes in value, the other variable increases or decreases in value. Burr (1973) reports, for example, on the exchange theory proposition, "The amount of interaction between intimates is related to the degree of positive sentiment or liking."

An associational proposition might specify the direction of association between two variables, whether it is the case that a "high" value on one variable is likely to have a "high" value on the other variable or that a "low" value on one variable is likely to have a "low" value on the other variable, also (positive association). The direction of association can be a negative or inverse association also, that is, high values go with low values or low values go with high values. In exchange theory, for example, exchange theorists have submitted the positive proposition, "The greater the interaction between intimates, the higher the degree of positive sentiment or liking." In the negative, inverse direction, exchange theorists have proposed, "The more costly an intimate relationship in the currency of physical or mental effort, the lower the degree of positive sentiment or liking."

The statement of association may suggest the magnitude or strength of relationship, the degree to which changes in one variable are associated with changes in two variables. This kind of theoretical thinking builds on statistics, and measures of strength vary between 0 (no strength) and 1 (the closer to one, the greater the changes in the values of the dependent variable relative to changes in values of the independent variable). Symbolic interactionists, for example, posit that there is a very strong relationship between a husband's low disposition toward empathy and abusive behavior.

A symmetrical association indicates that if change occurs in values for the first variable, there will be changes in values for the second variable, and if change occurs in the second, change will occur in the first. For instance, a biomedical theory might guide a research investigation starting with the propositions that increases in coffee intake is associated with an increase in asthma-related symptoms and that the reduction of asthma-related symptoms is associated with a decrease in coffee intake.

Causal relationships

A theoretical proposition may specify a causal relationship between two variables. One variable, the independent variable, is identified as the causal variable, and the other variable, the dependent variable, refers to the consequences. *Causes* are events that precede effects (that which is caused). Causal propositions involve relations with documented correlations between cause and effect; there is empirical evidence quantified by statistical analysis of this association (As one value—eating fast food—changes, the other value—overall body weight—changes), and causes have been established by research as the best explanation for the effects; alternative, or spurious causal explanations have been ruled out. Theoretical causal propositions summarize concisely much relevant information answering "why" questions. For example, there is growing evidence that family income and the advantages that money buys have a causal influence on school performance including math scores, reading scores, high school graduation, and college enrollment (Reardon, 2013).

Sequential relationships

Theorists may specify the sequence of a relationship; one event or variable follows the other in an identified time order. Life course theorists often theorize about the relationship of certain childhood social experiences (those that damage esteem, for instance) and issues later in life (assigning meanings to food in ways contributing to impulsive eating and weight disorders). Longitudinal research studies test the accuracy of such predicted sequences. Interpretive theorists also develop grounded theories describing typical sequences (steps to homelessness, the careers of heroin addicts) by deriving from data a set of sequential propositions.

Reconstructing a theory's propositions

Propositions as included in a theory may not be ready for practical use. There are some general and some specific strategies for reconstructing a theory's propositions.

A general strategy for theory reconstruction

Walker and Avant (1995) suggest a general approach to adapting a theoretical statement from an existing theory for use in a current helping situation. It involves the following steps. Select a focal theory relevant to the case. Become familiar with the literature on the theory and its elements (concepts and propositions). Carefully identify all the propositions, the type of each proposition, the properties of a propositions (direction and strength, for example), and the content of each proposition (independent variable, dependent variable, and so on). For any complex, multi propositional statement, simplify it and break it into separate theoretical propositions. Reconstruct one proposition at a time, borrowing and adapting the original formulation so it fits with the case specifics. Check the suitability of the arrangement of concepts in the new proposition for use (consulting relevant theoretical and research literature, for example). Transform the proposition into an assessment or intervention hypothesis, and test it out in practice. Revise each proposition based on the evidence of effectiveness or ineffectiveness. Let's expand a bit on this general strategy.

Reconstructing by if-then propositions

Practice theories are often built from propositions specifying the likely effects of an intervention (Specht, 1977). Burr, Klein, and associates (1994) discussed one way to construct a proposition to inform practice. These are "if-then" statements, associational or causal propositions relating some theoretical concept or independent variable to some likely consequence, the results following a planned change of the independent variable. The "if" part of the propositional clause can be reconstructed, for example, to refer to the actions that constitute an intervention. The "then" part of the clause is reconstructed to refer to the probable outcomes of such intervention for the quality of social membership. For instance, an interactionist theory of small group interaction provides propositions that can be transformed into this useful practice directive: "If the practitioner can increase the perspective-taking abilities and propensities of diverse members of a group, then the quality of communication among these members will increase." Theory developers often fail to think about theory application. Therefore, propositions may not be stated in this way. If you do not find such explicit "if-then" propositions, you might try to use a theory's major concepts to generate them yourself.

Theoretical propositions can be used like the small-scale maps that you download from the Web to get from point A to point B. A social worker, for example, might use behavioral learning theory and teach the behavioral proposition "positive reinforcement increases desired behaviors" to help a parent progress in the direction of effective control of an unruly child's conduct. Before use, of course, she or he would adapt the proposition to refer to reinforcements familiar to the parent and to focus on behaviors relevant to the family. He or she would also translate the wording of the theoretical proposition into the client's everyday language.

Reconstructing by theoretical rules of thumb

Turner (2008), an expert on the deconstruction and reconstruction of formal theories, recommends a strategy similar to the "if-then" approach. He suggests that the practitioner might study the relevant theoretical knowledge and pull out the theoretical principles as "rules of thumb" to guide practice. A focal dependent variable is chosen, the target problem. Each relevant principle or proposition is deconstructed so that a set of independent variables, variables that can be manipulated by the practitioner and client, are collected. Turner illustrates his approach focusing on the practitioner attempting to change an organization's structure and culture, reducing inequality and member disengagements with one another. Deconstructing the social network/interactionist theory of solidarity, Turner suggests, will provide directives for such helping work. The theory prioritizes the dependent variable, solidarity. Turner cites theory and research supporting his contention that organizations with high solidarity have high degrees of member equality and consensus. The theory also identifies independent variables that can guide efforts to increase solidarity: common symbols, solidarity-generating interaction, network density, and distribution of authority. Coupling the independent variables and the dependent variable produces the following rules of thumb for intervention. The practitioner should help the organization develop common symbols, create rituals to orient members to the common symbols, and increase communication using these symbols. The practitioner should strengthen network connections and density to increase opportunities for meetings characterized by solidarity-generating interactions. The practitioner should reduce inequality in authority so that workplace authority is distributed more democratically.

Reconstructing with the assistance of relevant research

When transformed into testable form, a focal proposition becomes a hypothesis, and its truth can be affirmed or rejected by evidence. For example, the strengths perspective includes propositions such as the following one: Families, peers, and friends are important sources of interpersonal influence, and their influence can affect a person's commitment to access and use personal strengths. A practitioner might transform the concepts of these propositions into variables and relate the variables in the form of hypothetical predictions for use in the agency, community, or private practice setting. The research literature can assist in this propositional reconstruction by providing illustrations of the transformation of the proposition's concepts into variables, the transformation of the proposition into a hypothesis, and the testing of the hypothesis under controlled conditions with a certain sample. The practitioner can refer to such literature when reconstructing a proposition.

Practical theorizing requires the hard work of learning the nominal definition of many concepts, understanding the historical changes in definitions related to scientific discourse and discovery, learning about the tradition's progress in formulating operational or sensitizing definitions of its major concepts, and learning how to deconstruct and reconstruct the propositions built from these concepts and central to a useful theory.

Learning activities and reflections

1   Select two or three of the concepts that you have examined. Create a proposition stating how these concepts are related to one another. For example, here's a sample proposition that guided my creation of this book: Perceived competency at theorizing increases the likelihood and quantity of theorizing behavior. This connects two concepts—theorizing competency and theorizing behavior—and proposes that as a person's perception of his or her competency increases, the probability and frequency of theorizing behavior increases.

Develop a simple theory-informed hypothesis linking two or more concepts in your proposition as variables. Specify the dependent and the independent variables. Describe how you would measure each variable. Reference the theory from which the hypothesis was derived.

2 Using the life course/human development perspective, reflect on your sense of identity (the concepts associated with your "self" including personality traits, important social roles, and categorical memberships) and your overall self-esteem (your appraisal of your own worth). Review particularly how your self-concept and self-esteem have developed or changed over your life as a result of specific experiences Make some connections between your "self growth" and important social experiences with various-size social systems such as family, peer groups and self-help groups, social networks, formal organizations, and neighborhoods. Present your ideas about the development of your identity and esteem in propositional form. Here's a sample proposition: Experiences being ridiculed for possessing the physical features of minority group members in a high school dominated by majority group members negatively impact a developing person's self-esteem.

3 Start with self-esteem as the dependent variable and identify a client population likely to have concerns about or problems with worth. Identify three independent variables that might influence self-esteem. Based on your reading or your experience with this population, develop three different propositions, relating each independent variable to the dependent variable. Characterize each proposition using your best judgments. What is the direction of the relationship? How strong is the relationship? Is the relationship a relationship of association or causation and, if causation, what proof would support the claim? How might you modify one or two of the propositions for use in serving a group of members of this population?

References

Abell, P. (1971). *Model building in sociology*. New York: Schocken.

Burr, W. R. (1973). *Theory construction and the sociology of the family*. New York: Wiley.

Burr, W. R., Klein, S. R., & Associates (1994). *Reexamining family stress: New theory and research*. Thousand Oaks, CA: Sage.

Meleis, A. I. (1985). *Theoretical nursing: Development and progress*. Philadelphia, PA: J. B. Lippincott.

Reardon, S. F. (2013). No rich child left behind. *The New York Times: Sunday Review*, April 28, 2013, pp. 1 and 4.

Specht, H. (1977). Theory as a guide to practice. In H. Specht & A. Vickery (Eds), *Integrating social work methods* (pp. 28–35). London: Allen and Unwin.

Turner, J. H. (2008). The practice of scientific theorizing in sociology and the use of scientific theory in sociological practice. *Sociological Focus*, 41(4), 281–299.

Walker, L. O., & Avant, K. C. (1995). *Strategies for theory construction in nursing* (3rd edn). Norwalk, CT: Appleton.

14

Identify and reorganize a theory's deductive argument

(EPAS 2.1.3 Apply Critical Thinking;
EPAS 2.1.7 Apply Knowledge)

Effective theorizers are logical and try to create systematic descriptions, explanations, or predictions about puzzling processes and situations. Theorists generally organize their system or network of propositional statements as a structure using one of two forms of logical argument: deduction or induction. In this commentary, I will review deductive theorizing, and suggest ways to deconstruct and reconstruct a deductive theory. In the next commentary, I will discuss inductive theorizing.

Deconstructing a theory's deductive argument

Deduction is an argument or reasoning process in which the conclusion follows from the premises with logical necessity (Skidmore, 1979). A deductive theory or "top down approach" is like a story that the storyteller begins with a general lesson and then completes by filling in the details supporting this lesson. The premise is the general proposition articulated by the theorizer as he or she begins the deductive theorizing process. The conclusion is the hypothesis or prediction that follows logically from the premise. In this form of theoretical reasoning, confirmation for an expected conclusion is expected if all the premises are true and the theorizing practitioner follows the rules of deductive logic.

Here is an example of deduction that a sexist theorist might endorse. It follows the standard rules of logical inference:

All husbands are better navigators than their wives.
Jang is a husband.
Jang is a better navigator than his wife, Hua.

In the deductive form of theory construction, theorists use general premises or statements to explain more specific events. The general premises or theoretical propositions are assumed to be true statements that are broadly applicable. The specific and expected conclusions are then logically deduced from the general proposition. Useful deductive theories are confirmed by scientific research. Evidence is obtained supporting the prediction that the general premise holds for the specified set of events, processes, circumstances, or actions.

Deductive inquiry is generally associated with the nomothetic approach (DePoy & Gilson, 2012). *Nomothetic theorizing* aims to identify common patterns, generalizations, or laws that hold across a wide range of conditions, events, contexts, or time periods. For example, the social work theorist might develop a research-informed theory about traits such as extroversion and openness to experience that are elements of the personality structure of all human beings. Positive theorizers and researchers often use deductive reasoning. They start with a general hypothesis, deduce a prediction of specific occurrences, experimentally test the hypothesis, and use the results to determine whether to reject or support the hypothesis. This approach is called the *hypothetico-deductive method*. Deductive theory is useful because it can provide order to a large amount of information (many propositions, for examples), and it generates predictions about likely behavior, developmental processes, and social changes.

With repeated validation of the deduction, a general theoretical proposition may earn the status of scientific law. A *scientific law* is a verbal or mathematical statement of a relation derivable from a theory that expresses a fundamental principle of human behavior and the social environment. A scientific law must always apply under the same conditions, and the law implies a causal relationship between its elements. The law has been confirmed and broadly accepted. For example, Stephan (2009) claims the following is a sociological law: "Social structures evolve in such a way as to minimize the time required for their operation." Newton's law of universal gravitation is an example of a scientific law associated with the physical sciences.

Deconstructing like Sherlock Holmes, an exemplary deductive theorizer

Sherlock Holmes is one of the most famous fictional detectives. He was noted for his observational talent, reasoning abilities, and forensic skill. He often coupled careful observations with inferences from general principles to specific conclusions. In the accounts of his investigations, his use of the deductive approach was instrumental in pinpointing and capturing many criminals and solving many puzzles about human behavior. For example, in the story called "A Scandal in Bohemia," Holmes deduces that Watson had gotten very wet recently and that he had "a most clumsy and careless servant girl" (Wikipedia, 2010). When Watson, in amazement, asks how Holmes knows this, Holmes answers with a demonstration of his deductive method. Based on the deductive tenet that if the general principle holds, the specific conclusion should follow, Holmes noted that London doctors generally don't scrape crusted mud collected on their shoes while out in vile weather but assign the task to their servant girls. Holmes reported also that he had observed crude cuts around the sole of Watson's shoes. Holmes deduced that Watson, a London doctor, had been out in bad weather and that his servant girl was clumsy and careless in her efforts to restore the shoes. Watson confirmed the accuracy of the deduction

Deconstructing by identifying the propositions of the deductive theory

Development theorists provide examples of theorizing from a general proposition to specific expected behaviors, processes, or conditions. Many of their theories are familiar to social workers (Forte, 2006). Erik Erikson asserted that a failure to resolve a psychosocial challenge at a life stage (the general proposition) should result in later psychological vulnerabilities and bio-psycho-social difficulties (the specific and testable conclusion). Carol Gilligan argued that young girls often submit to pressures exerted by agents of patriarchal society by stifling their "voice." In her evidence-supported theory, this process of suppression has predictable and damaging results. Role theorists have contended that role transitions (the shift from one role to another role in a role sequence or career) are life course phases resulting in stress. Problems in managing the stress lead to specific identity and behavioral difficulties.

Human behavior theories offer rich examples of deductive theorizing (Forte, 2006). Conflict theory suggests that during times of economic recession, there is an increase in the scapegoating of minority groups and their members by majority groups. Various specific manifestations of this general pattern (such as changes in hate crime, spikes in membership in hate groups, and so on) are associated with the downturn. The feminist theory of gender proposes that cultural standards of beauty influence young girls to take actions bringing their body in line with the standards. Feminists deduce, for instance, that bad eating choices, choices that contribute to eating disorders, are a consequential result experienced by many adolescent girls in the United States

Each of these general propositions has been the starting point for further theorizing of the deductive kind. In each case, investigators have explored the question, What would logically follow if the general proposition were true? Identifying the deductive theoretical argument involves specifying the general proposition or premise, identifying the more specific premises or conclusions that follow if this premise holds, and checking the research that documents the explanatory and predictive power of the deductive theory's hypotheses for a specific population, setting, or focal problem.

Deconstructing by identifying the form of deductive theory

Generally, theorists organize their theoretical ideals into a logical form. A comprehensive deductive theory, for example, consists of propositional statements organized in a hierarchical order so those at the top are the most general (Skidmore, 1979). Statements lower in the hierarchy are more specific and derived from the statements above. Deconstruction work involves taking apart the deductive theory, identifying the propositions, and summarizing the nature of the overall structure of propositions. This may be done as a verbal or written narrative (an approach discussed further in Lesson 16) or as a diagram (an approach discussed further in Lesson 17).

For example, the theoretical research program called affect control theory is formulated in a deductive way (Heise, 2007). I have attempted to make this theory more useful by unpacking its elements and overall theoretical structure (Forte, 2007). Affect control theory is organized in relationship to three general propositions ordered systematically. First, individuals conduct themselves so as to generate feelings appropriate to the situation. Second, individuals who can't maintain appropriate feelings through actions change their views of the situation or work to change the situation. Third, individuals' emotions signal the relationship between individuals' experiences and their definitions of situations. From these propositions, numerous specific hypotheses have been deduced. For example, Britt and Heise (2000) deduced that gay persons who can't (or won't) maintain feelings of fear and self-judgments of worthlessness in response to homophobic reactions take corrective action. This deduction is generated from proposition two. These researchers found support for the deduction. Gay study participants were open and motivated to joining the Gay Liberation Movement, transforming fear and worthlessness into anger and pride, and mobilizing to change the climate of hate and rejection. Affect control theorists have conducted hundreds of research studies confirming a range of deductions associated with the three foundational propositions.

In a theory-testing project, my colleagues and I (Forte, Franks, Forte, & Rigsby, 1996) deconstructed an interactionist theory of battered women's choice of a coping response. We identified the general proposition. In dyadic relationships, the person with less power tends to take his or her partner's role more often due to greater motivation to role take and more accurately due to greater role-taking skill than the person with more power. This premise is supported by the theoretical and research literature. In brief, our theoretical argument then asserted the following specific premises. Battered women generally have less power and status than male batterers compared to women in a non-violent relationship. For survival purposes, battered women will become more motivated to take their partners' role and to accurately anticipate his emotions and his actions than the husband. Consistently taking the role of a physically and psychologically abusive partner has a deleterious effect on the battered women's self-esteem, daily emotions, attribution of blame, and perception of coping options. We conducted an extensive survey of 66 battered women using domestic violence services in Virginia, United States and 80 non-battered women. Research findings provided validation for most of the hypotheses derived from the deductive theory. Battered women's social situations were oppressive and characterized by powerlessness, social isolation, and economic dependency. The husbands and boyfriends of battered women were unlikely to empathize with the woman, and battered women tended to experience more distressful emotions, lower self-esteem, and more constricted coping responses than non-battered women. However, predictions regarding self-blame, the likelihood of accepting the man's contention that relationship problems are her fault, were not confirmed. We wondered whether participation in programs offered in the shelter had influenced the battered women to renounce responsibility for males' violence.

Reconstructing deductive theory and the social work helping process

Deductive reasoning has an important place in the helping process. It is a tool for generating hypotheses that can be tested during work with clients (Edwards, Jones, Carr, Braunack-Mayer & Jensen, 2004). For example, clinicians in mental health settings may attend to initial cues given off by the client about the nature of the mental disorder. The intake worker may categorize the client's condition or clinical syndrome, for example, as a generalized anxiety disorder. This category provides associated general propositions for the direct worker's consideration such as "persons with generalized anxiety disorder are prone to uncontrollable feelings of excessive worry not tied to a specific event." From these useful propositions, the practitioner may generate a testable hypothesis (this particular person will report frequent instances of excessive worry as measured by a self-anchored scale), and the hypothesis formulation could be followed by the systematic gathering and analysis of additional client information (the test of the hypothesis) to determine if the deduction about diagnosis and symptom is related as expected. Thus, the working hypothesis deduced from the general proposition may be confirmed or negated during the clinical sessions.

For the advanced practitioner, reconstructing deductive theory might involve the deduction of hypotheses not identified in the original deductive theory but relevant to the case circumstances. For example, a practitioner reconstructing the interactionist theory relating power asymmetry, role-taking motivation and skill, self-processes related to esteem and emotion, and coping actions might attempt to deduce some other specific hypotheses related to focal puzzles. How should the propositions be adjusted or supplemented, for instance, in a same-sex marriage or relationship? Does one's cohort membership (birth before or after the 1960s wave of feminism) have a bearing on the likely consequences of power differences on role taking? Do forms of disrespect by the powerful person related to class or ethnic memberships of the powerless person, forms other than physical and psychological abuse, have similar negative consequences on interaction and coping?

Or the advanced practitioner might modify an existing theory in a deductive way. Here the practitioner identifies and names the practice puzzle: Why do corporate farm operators expose migrant workers to chemicals causing obvious health problems and deforming babies? He or she will then review the theoretical literature and select deductive theories suggesting general patterns relevant to the puzzle (critical and economic theories are good sources for such theories). Next, the practitioner decides what pattern or proposition seems most likely to generate useful assessment or intervention hypotheses (statements of a general pattern relating class status, political ideology, lax regulation, and exploitation could seem useful). Starting from this pattern or premise, the practitioner specifies the testable hypotheses as part of a reconstructed theory of the puzzling situation deducing likely predictions for these people in this setting at this time period such as "wealthy, corporate farm owners on the Eastern shore of Virginia use laissez-faire economic ideas and government indifference to justify their chemical spraying procedures and to deny unsafe work conditions." The practitioner tests out the related hypotheses during the planned change process or research investigation.

Learning activities and reflections

1   Practice deductive theorizing. Identify some general propositions—perhaps, propositions learned in a research class, a policy class, or a human behavior class.

    Select one such proposition. Think about a specific statement that can be logically deduced from the general starting point. Write down one such specific statement. Comment also on the evidence or logic that supports the validity of this general proposition.

    Transform your specific propositional statement into a hypothesis (a measurable prediction about the relationship between two or more variables about observable phenomena/events). Provide some details about your proposed method for testing your mini deductive theory.

2   Make a general statement that you believe accurately describes most students at your college or at a nearby school. For example, I believe that a sizable number of students at my university prefer flip-flops for footwear. Deduce a specific manifestation of this statement such as "more than 25 percent of students walking into the student center for lunch on Tuesday during the first week of classes will be wearing flip-flops." Develop and implement a research strategy for testing the deduction.

3   Identify a general and universal pattern identified in some human behavior theory. For example, critical theorists argue that persons of color have fewer privileges than persons with skin with a white/pinkish hue. Evolutionary sociologists claim that like our distant ape ancestors, humans create group arrangements characterized by the dominance of many members by one or a few members. Deduce a specific and observable pattern from this general proposition. State how you might reconstruct the proposition as a testable hypothesis to check whether evidence affirms the deduction.

4   Identify a proposition of a general and abstract nature included in a familiar developmental theory such as Erikson's Psychosocial Life Stage Theory, Gilligan's Female Voice Theory, or Kohlberg's Theory of Moral Development. For example, Kohlberg theorized that persons in stage six of moral development more commonly consider universal ethical principles and engage in abstract reasoning when attempting to resolve moral dilemmas than those in stages one, two, three, or four. Use deductive theorizing and state a specific hypothesis that can be derived from the premise of the developmental theory. Explain how you might devise a study to test this specific hypothesis.

References

Britt, L., & Heise, D. R. (2000). From shame to pride in identity politics. In S. Stryker, T. J. Owens, & R. W. White (Eds), *Self, identity, and social movements* (pp. 252–268). Minneapolis, MN: University of Minneapolis Press.

DePoy, E., & Gilson, S. F. (2012). *Human behavior theory and applications: A critical thinking approach*, Thousand Oaks, CA: Sage.

Edwards, I., Jones, M. Carr, J., Braunack-Mayer, A., & Jensen, G. M. (2004). Clinical reasoning strategies in physical therapy. *Physical Therapy*, 84(4), 312–330.

Forte, J. A. (2006). *Human behavior and the social environment: Models, metaphors, and maps for applying theoretical perspectives to practice*. Belmont, CA: Thomson Brooks/Cole.

Forte, J. A. (2007). Using a semiotic metatheory for theory understanding, appraisal, and use: An illustrative social work translation of the affect control theory of emotions. *Advances in Social Work* (Special Issue: A Critical Review of Theories of Human Behavior in the Social Environment), 8(1), 1–18.

Forte, J.A., Franks, D.D., Forte, J., & Rigsby, D. (1996). Oppressive social situations and asymmetrical role-taking: Comparing battered and non-battered women. *Social Work*, 41(1), 59–73.

Heise, D. R. (2007). *Expressive order: Confirming sentiments in social actions*. New York: Springer.

Skidmore, W. (1979). *Theoretical thinking in sociology* (2nd edn). Cambridge, UK: Cambridge University Press.

Stephan, E. (2009). *The division of territory in society*. Retrieved October 26, 2009, from www.edstephan.org/Book/contents.html

Wikipedia (2010). Sherlock Holmes. Retrieved August 2, 2010, from http://en.wikipedia.org/wiki/Sherlock_Holmes

Identify and reorganize a theory's inductive argument

(EPAS 2.1.3 Apply Critical Thinking;
EPAS 2.1.7 Apply Knowledge)

Let's shift to inductive theorizing and start with a definition. Induction or *inductive theorizing* involves reasoning from specific premises or observations to general conclusions. Theorizing as induction might be described in the following way: A specific and detailed set of specific observations of some puzzling event, condition, or set of processes suggests an overall and general pattern that encompasses each of the observations. An inductive theory or, a "bottom-up" approach, organizes these theoretical elements by starting with the observations. Inductive theorizing is like telling a story by reporting on numerous incidents and episodes in great detail and then ending with the lesson or moral derived from reflection on all these episodes.

Both deduction and induction are important to scientific theorizing and research. Wallace (1971) showed this when he summarized the scientific process as like a wheel incorporating both types of reasoning. Figure 15.1 provides a modified and simple version of his display. Wallace described several key aspects of the research cycle: A theory, the most general type of information, is at the top of the wheel. The theory's general propositions are changed into a hypothesis through deductive theorizing. The researcher decides on the best research design and then uses the planned sampling, measurement, and data-gathering procedures to test the hypothesis. Results are analyzed and, by statistical inference, the hypothesis is supported or rejected. The evidence supports or rejects the hypotheses producing the findings or empirical observations. From the bottom, the observations are transformed into general statements about processes or patterns summarizing the key finding by using the logic of induction. These findings can be used to refine and improve the concepts, propositions, or arrangement of propositions in the practical theory. There are other approaches to the theory-research cycle, but Wallace's approach usefully summarizes the interplay of deductive and inductive theorizing.

I
N
D
U
C
T
I
V
E

T
H
E
O
R
I
Z
I
N
G

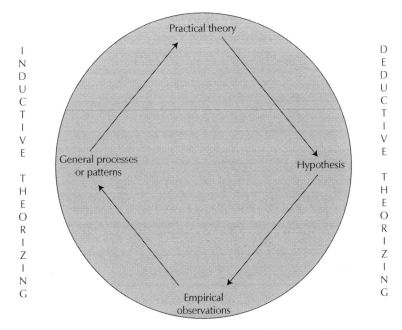

D
E
D
U
C
T
I
V
E

T
H
E
O
R
I
Z
I
N
G

Figure 15.1 Deduction, induction, and practical theory

A note: Deductive theorizers start with the theory and emphasize the right side of the circle using induction sparingly (Lesson 14 reviewed this approach). Inductive theorizers—discussed in this lesson—start with the observations and emphasize the left side of the circle using deduction as a secondary tool.

Deconstructing a theory's inductive argument

Inductive inquiry is generally associated with the *idiographic approach* (DePoy & Gilson, 2012; Fook, 2002). Idiographic research and theory attempt to characterize fully the unique features of one case, condition, or event. For example, the psychodynamic social worker takes an idiographic stance when she or he seeks to discover and portray exhaustively the distinctive childhood experiences, array of defense mechanisms, and symptoms of one particular client. Idiographic theory is useful because it helps practitioners understand comprehensively specific experiences, in particular, historical and ecological contexts. Also, the idiographic approach can take into account individual exceptions to established "human behavior and the environment" generalizations.

Interpretive theorizers generally prefer inductive reasoning to deductive reasoning. Grounded theory, for example, is a popular interpretive theory-building and research approach that emphasizes inductive processes (Glaser

& Strauss, 1967). Rather than beginning deductively by reviewing the literature and developing a theory-based hypothesis, grounded theorists begin with data collection. As the data are collected, a grounded theorist begins to code or make sense of the observations and eventually determines the larger pattern or process uniting all the coded observations. The general theoretical statement or set of statements (the theory) is "grounded" in many specific and up-close observations. This avoids the problem of starting with theory or theoretical concepts in a way influencing the theorizer to fit observations into an "a priori" framework.

Deconstructing like Sherlock Holmes as exemplary inductive theorizer

Sherlock Holmes, the great fictional detective from London, included induction in his arsenal of tools of detection and theorizing about crimes. Careful observations of people and objects, sharp questioning and deep listening, keen attention to sounds and smells, and hands-on manipulation of possible evidence were all trademark activities of Holmes. His detective work assembled and made integrative judgments about the large collection of numerous facts related to each case.

In *The Problem of Thor Bridge* (Public Broadcasting Series, 2010), for instance, Holmes alone can make sense of the various clues associated with a crime: the husband and wife had a fight immediately before the wife's death, there was a gun missing from the house, the wife was noted for her intense temper, a note was found revealing that the husband was having an affair, the wife's rival had become the main suspect, and there was a notch in the bridge to the side of where the wife was found shot. After these and other observations, Sherlock induced the general pattern to the puzzling death: framing a rival for revenge. With this pattern, he went on to solve the mystery of the crime. The wife attached a gun by rope to a stone perched on the railing of the bridge, shot herself, and the gun nicked the concrete as it was drawn into the river by the stone. The wife had hoped to frame the rival as her murderer and obtain revenge against her husband and the rival for their betrayals.

Deconstructing by identifying the propositions of an inductive theory

Let's look at some illustrations of inductive theorizing and imagine how the theorizing practitioner could unpack the argument organizing the elements (observations and broad generalizations) of these and similar theories. In the search for a pattern to understand the risks faced by migrant workers on large rural farms, we might take a critical approach to theorizing and spend a summer making careful observations of the farm activity on the Eastern

Shore of Virginia and Maryland. Over time, we would observe incidents of industrial accidents, continual exposure to pesticides, disease associated with overcrowded housing, harassment by local residents, exploitation by employers in the form of low pay and extremely long hours for physically exhausting work, indiscriminate dismissals, and car crashes resulting from transportation in overcrowded, old, and unsafe vehicles. Our inductive theorizing would have to organize these observations of the specific incidents related to each of the risks into a common pattern. We might conclude, for instance, that "illegal migrants in this region are generally not provided the protections and basic rights provided to long-time residents."

Human behavior theorists often organize their theoretical propositions using an inductive approach. An inductive theory might take the final form of a common theme or pattern, a typology into which all cases fall, or a generic sequence of stages. In my own ecological theorizing and research (Forte, 2002), I used an inductive approach to study a NIMBY ("Not in My Back Yard") controversy related to the location of a shelter for the homeless community members. Some groups wanted the shelter moved miles from the city center; others wanted it kept near the services and resources in the center of the urban area. I was interested in how contestants in the struggle to define the public problem used the media to advance their preferred characterization of their opponents, responsibility for problem, and siting solutions. I monitored newspaper coverage in a southeastern city from 1993 to 1996, a period when the fate of the service center gained regional attention. I collected more than 150 news stories, editorials, photographs, and letters to the editor related to the controversy from four local newspapers. Of the 150 news documents, I conducted a detailed analysis of 79 documents. From the analysis of 266 discrete units of information in these documents, I inductively generated seven themes that seemed to capture the overall set of representations of the pro-shelter and anti-shelter advocates. See Table 15.1 for a list of these themes. For example, theme five summarized the views of many spokespersons. Advocates for the homeless shelter—often associated with community churches—used images and symbols in their media advocacy that could be symbolized by the general notion, "we are all brothers and sisters in Christ" (and therefore, the community has a responsibility to serve its vulnerable homeless members) whereas opponents' views are better summarized by the general notion, "the homeless are outsiders and strangers to us" (and therefore, we have no obligations to them). The shelter should be relocated a great distance from our neighborhoods."

There is one notable limitation to inductive theorizing. Unlike in deduction where laws and rules of logic are used to link general propositions and conclusions in a way ensuring the truth of the conclusions, claims based on induction are less certain. A theorizing researcher, for instance, might have carefully examined the same new stories as I did in my NIMBY study but arrived at a different set of patterns representing the pro-con positions.

Table 15.1 Inductive theorizing – representations of homeless shelter battle antagonists

Pattern of Media Representation			f	%
Anti Shelter	/	Pro Shelter		
1 Prudent capitalists	/	Generous, responsible givers	94	35.3
2 Soldiers at war	/	Defenders of those at-risk in war zone	71	26.7
3 Humans controlling pests	/	Protectors of vulnerable prey	38	14.3
4 Law followers, enforcers	/	Advocates for just, sensitive laws	26	9.8
5 Insiders versus outsiders	/	Brothers and sisters in Christ	20	7.5
6 Unduly burdened	/	Champions of shared burden	12	4.5
7 Competitors in contest	/	Players challenging rigged game	5	1.9
Total			266	100

Reconstructing inductive theory and the social work helping process

Even if they don't use the term, social workers are committed to the practical use of inductive theorizing. For them, professional interpretations and assessments follow only lengthy, up-close immersion in the natural settings inhabited by group members. Social workers make multiple observations and ask many questions. They collect information about numerous specific nonverbal gestures, social behaviors, reported thoughts and feelings, recollected interactions with others, and so on. They conduct home visits and inspect carefully the home, its rooms, its furnishings, and so on. From these specific facts, social workers then speculate about the overall pattern leading to the client's problematic fit with his or her environmental context. As confidence in the speculations grows, practitioners generate broad assessment formulations summarizing the wealth of observational information.

Additionally, practitioners over time may accumulate knowledge of a variety of cases of a similar kind and begin to formulate general statements summarizing knowledge across cases. After years of serving in a Community Mental Health Clubhouse, for instance, I concluded that many persons discharged from our state institutions after lengthy stays tended to communicate in idiosyncratic and unskilled ways. Family, group, and individual services consequently should include work to understand such communications and show the adults returning to the community that they are being listened to and understood. Later, I discovered also that this little bit of practice wisdom fit well with the grounded theories and practice models associated with the symbolic interactionist perspective on the troubles of deinstitutionalized persons.

Social work practitioners might also borrow grounded theories and other theories created by inductive means. They should select theories of relevance to their own practice puzzle or challenge. The theorizer could use theories focused on common social processes such as the processes of adaptation by refugee families to new life circumstances (Weine et al., 2006). The theorizer could use theories focused on themes associated with a public problem such as the common perceptions of child abuse by child protective workers (Kettle, 2013). The theorizer could use grounded typologies such as the varied responses to the experience of chronic illness (Docherty & McColl, 2003) or the different types of crack users (German & Sterk, 2002). The theorizer could focus on intervention effectiveness and theory-generating studies of the patterns of perceptions among homeless young adults regarding program implementation and outcomes (Ferguson, 2008). Of course, the theorizing practitioner should check whether each study situation is similar to the situation where he or she has made observations about similar events, problems, or interventions. If so, the practitioner can identify and modify the generalizations for practical use in the new circumstances.

For example, you might be advocating for the homeless people in your community and turn to my NIMBY study (Forte, 2002). Based on your determination that there were many similarities between my community and your community, you might conclude that allied supporters of the homeless often use religious imagery and symbolism when discussing the challenge of homelessness. You decide to adapt the theme, "In a spiritual sense, the homeless are our brothers and sisters" and use it to guide policy practice in your rural area, town, or city.

Concluding remarks

Induction is a theorizing skill used to generate grounded and other observation-rich theories. Induction complements the use of deduction in many theorizing enterprises. Both contribute to theoretical puzzle solving. Since much scientific inquiry and scientific theorizing involve the use of both deductive and inductive reasoning; the theorizing practitioner needs to understand how to deconstruct and reconstruct each approach to theorizing.

Learning activities and reflections

1   In this activity, we will practice inductive theorizing. Let's attempt to contribute to the work of theorists trying to explain resilience. We can begin with Ungar's (2005) summary of the traditional definition. Resilience is "the individual capacities, behaviors, and protective processes associated with health outcomes despite exposure to a significant number of risks" (p. xvi). We should note that Ungar believes that this definition underestimates the ecological component of resilience. Therefore, Ungar makes another important point about knowledge development. Deductive theories help us appreciate the general aspects and patterns of resiliency, those that are "universal." However, inductive theories are needed to elaborate on general resiliency theory and discover the patterns of meanings and processes actualized in different "local" contexts, ecologies bordered by particular geographic, cultural, and temporal boundaries.

Identify a cultural or subcultural group served in your region. You might focus on runaway street children, migrant workers from a country outside the United States, gay residents of a rural community, members of a youth gang, or recent migrants to the area. Or, if this seems too difficult, focus on your own family during a very challenging time.

Select one of the research questions used by cross-cultural resiliency researchers (Ungar & Liebenberg, 2005). How do members of this cultural group understand the concept of well-being? What do the group members identify as the most significant risks or challenges prevalent in their community? What are the specific "external protective factors" promoting resilience among members of this cultural group? What are the specific "internal resources" promoting resilience among members of this cultural group? What are the stages or steps related to coping with adversity for this group? Or you might ask a life course/human developmental perspective question. What are the specific stage-related risk factors and protective factors experienced by this group?

Supplement the research question with supporting and related follow-up questions. Think through data gathering specifics such as who, where, when, how many, and so on. Then, collect a large set of answers or observations related to your major research question. Create a careful record of your observations.

Next, attempt to group your observations into patterns (consensual definitions of well-being, types of risks or resources, typical coping phases, features of resilient persons, for examples) and, then, into one inclusive pattern. Conclude with your inductive generalization responding to the question: What is your final theoretical statement about resiliency related to this specific local at-risk group?

2   As an alternative learning activity, identify a specific group that you know something about (delinquent youth, teenage girls with eating disorders, drug dealers selling cocaine, international students from countries in Asia, professional athletes in a particular sport, autistic children). Begin a search of a newspaper such as the *New York Times* or an online photo archive. Analyze 30 or more accounts or photographs of the focal group. Take notes on the common themes presented in your data. Use inductive reasoning and summarize your findings as several general observed patterns such as according to the Shutterstock image inventory www.shutterstock.com, male homeless boys are typically characterized as _____ and _____. Reflect on the quality of your method of inquiry, too.

3   Try the following research and theorizing project. (1) Pick a group to observe and theorize about. You might try to learn more about the homeless members of your community, for example. (2) Pick a focus for your observations (you are not trying to observe and theorize about everything related to the group). For example, focus on how the homeless interact on sidewalks with non-homeless persons or how the homeless talk about the concept of homelessness to a social work interviewer. (3) Go observe or talk to some homeless people. Record observations or ask them questions about the focal issue. Keep notes on what you see, hear, and think during this process. (4) Take your observations and/or interview answers and translate the information into a more general theoretical pattern that summarizes most of the data such as "generally, the homeless in my county interact with non-homeless persons in the following way," or "generally, the homeless in my community talk about their homelessness using the following themes or metaphors." This statement is the product of your inductive theorizing and the beginning of an inductive theory of the homeless and their public interaction patterns or conceptions of their homelessness. Reflect on how you might adapt this final generalization for use in your own volunteer service to or helping work with homeless persons.

4   Pick a stage of human development. Identify a group of developing persons who are in this stage of the life course. Pick some focal aspect of development such as physical functioning, behavioral habits, interaction patterns, or engagement with social systems. For example, you might focus on the eating behavior of young adults enrolled in your college. Select a sample and a site for your study. Make numerous observations. Transform your specific and grounded observations into a general statement summarizing the commonalities for developing persons at this stage in relation to your focal aspect of development. Consider how this observed pattern might become the start for further theorizing about stage issues shared by members of this group.

References

DePoy, E., & Gilson, S. F. (2012). *Human behavior theory and applications: A critical thinking approach*. Thousand Oaks, CA: Sage.

Docherty, D., & McColl, M. A. (2003). Illness stories: Themes emerging through narrative. *Social Work in Health Care, 37*(1), 19–39.

Ferguson, K. M. (2008). Conceptualizing outcomes with street-living young adults: grounded theory approach to evaluating the social enterprise intervention. *Qualitative Social Work, 7*(2), 217–237.

Fook, J. (2002). Theorizing from practice: Towards an inclusive approach for social work research. *Qualitative Social Work, 1*(1), 79–95.

Forte, J. A. (2002). Not in my social world: A cultural analysis of media representations, contested spaces, and sympathy for the homeless. *Journal of Sociology and Social Welfare, 29*(4), 131–157.

German, D., & Sterk, C. E. (2002). Looking beyond stereotypes: Exploring variations among crack smokers. *Journal of Psychoactive Drugs, 34*(4), 383–392.

Glaser, B. G., & Strauss, A. (1967). *The discovery of grounded theory: Strategies for qualitative research*. Chicago, IL: Aldine.

Kettle, M. (2013). A question of balance? A constructionist grounded theory study of child protection social work. Retrieved May 3, 2013, from www.baspcan.org.uk/files/Kettle%20Martin%20F45.4%20Wed%209.00.pdf

Public Broadcasting Station (2010). The problem of Thor Bridge. Sherlock Holmes, Public Broadcasting Service, Mystery Series Retrieved August 3, 2010, from www.pbs.org/wgbh/masterpiece/silkstocking/retro.html

Ungar, M. (2005). Introduction: Resilience across cultures and concepts. In M. Ungar (Ed.), *Handbook for working with children and youth: Pathways to resilience across cultures and contexts* (pp. xv–xxxix). Thousand Oaks, CA: Sage.

Ungar, M., & Liebenberg, L. (2005). The International Resilience Project: A mixed-methods approach to the study of resilience across cultures. *Handbook for working with children and youth: Pathways to resilience across cultures and contexts*. (pp. 211–226). Thousand Oaks, CA: Sage.

Wallace, W. L. (1971). *The logic of science in sociology*. New York: Aldine de Gruyter.

Weine, S., Feetham, S., Kulauzovic, Y., Knafl, K., Besic, S., Klebic, A., Mujagic, A., Muzurovic, J., Spahovic, D., & Pavkovic, I. (2006). A family beliefs framework for socially and culturally specific preventive interventions with refugee youths and families. *American Journal of Orthopsychiatry, 76*(1), 1–9.

Summarize the relationship between a theory's elements

(EPAS 2.1.7 Apply Knowledge)

In preparing to construct a house, counseling center, or skyscraper, architects create blueprints. A set of blueprints identifies all the building blocks essential to the construction project and describes how they are assembled into one structure. General contractors, plumbers, carpenters, and other electricians can study the relevant blueprints and learn about the overall design. After the project is completed, architectural critics might examine the finished product, comparing it to the blueprints, and judge the match and also the final structure's strengths and limitations as compared to the planned structure.

Deconstructing a theory

Theory users can engage in a similar process of design examination and review. We can learn to identify a theory's basic building blocks or components and their patterned arrangement. There is a detailed strategy for analyzing and describing a theory in terms of its architectural structure. Fawcett and Downs (1986) call this process *theory formalization*, a tool to "determine exactly what a theory says. It is a way of extracting an explicit statement and a diagram of a theory from its verbal explanation" (p. 15). Turner (1986) calls the process *analytic theorizing*, by which he means identifying how concepts, propositions and, sometimes, theoretical models, are connected in overarching schemes to explain some aspects of human behavior and the environment. I will use the term *theory analysis*.

Unlike buildings constructed in line with public regulations, not all theories come with the architectural blueprints. Social workers, however, can attempt to construct blueprints after the theory has been created. The final product of a theory analysis process is the creation of a written summary of the theory's structure and, often, an accompanying display. Theoretical analysts might create a blueprint of the entire knowledge base of the social work profession and the overall interrelationship of theories. Howe (1997) believes that "mapping out social work's theoretical terrain helps practitioners locate themselves intellectually and invites them to explore new areas of thought and practice" (p. 173). In practice, you will more often need to analyze and display a middle-range theory or practice theory for use as a guide.

Effective language learning necessitates the mastery of the words, phrases, and sentence structures of the language studied (Marshall, 1989). Theory learning is similar. Effective theory learning and theory use involve identifying the elements and structured linkages between the elements of a studied theory. A theory can be analyzed in terms of these elements and the distinctive way that these parts are organized into a whole (Shoemaker, Tankard, & Lasorsa, 2004). Key elements include root metaphors, assumptions, concepts and their definitions, propositions, linkages of propositions, and an overall theoretical argument. If a theory is an intellectual structure for understanding human membership, these parts are the building blocks necessary to create a stable, pleasing, durable, and useful theoretical construction.

Analyzing or parsing a theory

Fawcett and Downs (1986) use the linguistic metaphor for theory analysis like the grammatical metaphor that I am using in this commentary. They contend, "Theory formalization is similar to grammatical parsing of a sentence. Just as parsing identifies nouns, verbs, adjectives, adverbs, and other parts of a sentence, theory formalization identifies the concepts, definitions, and propositions that make up a theory" (p. 15). They add, "Theory formalization may even involve the translation of a verbal theory into a mathematical or computer language" (p. 15).

We can also compare the overall structure of a theory to the design and structure of a written short story. While a fictional story, however, can be deconstructed by studying the unfolding plot and picking out the key plot elements, a scientific theory requires a different kind of deconstruction. A theorizing practitioner analyzes a theory by breaking it into paragraphs and studying each paragraph (the structured ordering of propositions). For each paragraph, he examines the sentences and relationships of sentences to one another (the theoretical propositions and their linkages). For each sentence, he examines the words making up the sentence (the theoretical concepts and their definitions). With careful analysis, the practitioner can also identify and examine the underlying metaphors and assumptions shaping the theory's logic and order. In my second-grade class, we learned to parse the components of a paragraph and diagram how they were connected. For theory deconstruction, however, we will learn to parse the assumptions, concepts, propositions, and relationship of propositions.

List of theory elements

Theoretical frameworks, middle-range theories, and theoretical perspectives including personal practice models and guiding conceptions for practice can be analyzed, summarized in words, and then diagrammed as a pictorial representation (Fawcett & Downs, 1986; Walker & Avant, 1995). Chafetz (1978) reports on the commonly followed components of a narrative of any theoretical structure. Social workers prefer theories with an evidentiary base and, in some situations, test theories. Therefore, to prepare you for theory analysis and summarizing a theory and its elements, I will add an additional component to the list: E. This letter refers to the process of transforming theoretical concepts into operational form and propositions into testable hypotheses. Table 16.1 identifies the total set of the components of a report on a theory.

Past lessons have helped you develop the knowledge and skills to identify a theory's root metaphors and assumptions, specify the theory's concepts, and report on the major propositions of the theory. These theorizing skills will be invaluable as you attempt to analyze a theory.

Theory's argument

Another task of theory analysis will involve reporting on the overall theoretical structure, the ways that propositions are linked to each other (Hage, 1972). Your knowledge of the two major forms of theoretical reasoning, deductive and inductive, will help you here. The theory might use a deductive form of ordering for its propositions. For example, labeling theorists start with general propositions such as social labels influence self-concept and labels influence interaction with others and then, labeling theorists deduce more specific propositions, such as negative labels negatively influence self-concept and negative labels increase punitive and non-accepting behaviors toward the labeled person.

Table 16.1 Summary of components of a theory report

A.	Theoretical assumptions
B.	Theoretical concepts and their nominal definitions
C.	Theoretical propositions 1. Proposition one 2. Proposition two 3. Proposition three 4. Additional propositions
D.	Linkages of theoretical propositions
E.	Empirically verifiable statements 1. Theoretical concepts converted to variables with operational definitions 2. Propositions converted to testable hypotheses

Or the theory might use an inductive form of reasoning and proceed from specific propositions to a more general proposition. A grounded theory of the paths to homelessness might use such an order. For a particular group of homeless persons, the theorists might argue that family conflict preceded homelessness for some. Financial disputes with landlords preceded homelessness for others, and dismissals from work for non-cooperative behavior preceded homelessness for the third subgroup. The overall general proposition would follow: Deterioration in role performance as perceived by important role partners is a common factor in the transition to homelessness. Theoretical deconstruction reports on how concepts and propositions are related—deductively or inductively—and why this arrangement makes sense to the theory developers.

Overall theoretical structure

Theories differ in their arrangement of elements and the complexity of this arrangement (Wallis, 2009). In a simple arrangement, there may be only a list of theoretical concepts. A slightly advanced arrangement might be a list of causal propositions. Formal theories include a more advanced assembly of parts, a system of interrelated propositions, for instance.

A theory's structure becomes more complex as the theorist adds more propositions (for example, more causal statements), more comprehensive propositions (specifying relations between independent, dependent, mediating, and moderating variables, perhaps), more relationships between the propositions (for example, a proposition's link to multiple other propositions), more sophisticated matching of propositions to one another (the linking of every statement of cause with a parallel statement of consequence), or the inclusion of scope conditions, the specific applications or limits to application of the propositions and the contexts where the propositions will be most relevant.

The overall theoretical structure might be best represented by a variety of visual forms (Chinn & Kramer, 2008). There might be a pyramid-like appearance with a foundation of ideas or propositions on which other ideas are added, like Maslow's theory of motivation, the hierarchy of needs. There may be a large circular shape with related sub-circles or areas like Olson's Circumplex model of family functioning. The theory elements might be organized like a continuum with poles at either end like a theory of optimal health and serious illness. The arrangement of the theory might include the differentiation of the entire theory into blocks like a theory with a large block for related independent variables, a smaller block for the focal dependent variable, and several blocks for different sets of moderating variables. The theory might include one structure, or it may be complex and include several structures that constitute together the whole theory.

Conversion of elements for evidence-informed practice

Social workers are committed to evidence-informed practice and, therefore, must focus also on the scientific quality and testability of a theory. Theory deconstruction involves parsing the theory in terms of its operational definitions and hypotheses. The theorizing practitioner should identify each concept and describe how it has been operationalized. Additionally, he or she identifies each proposition and describes whether and how it has been transformed into a testable hypothesis.

Theory deconstruction: an illustration

This "theory analysis" summary includes the essential ingredients of my deconstruction of the original theoretical work of Rogers (1970) and is inspired by Bloom's (1975) brief demonstration of theoretical parsing. I am familiar with many of Roger's original works and with the secondary literature on Rogers, his humanistic theories of human behavior, and his humanistic, client-centered theory of practice. This background was useful. I will briefly summarize the theory in a short narrative form.

Theorist and theory background

Carl Rogers, an American psychologist, was a very influential theorist, researcher, and practitioner. He was one of the founders of the humanistic theoretical approach to understanding people, and he developed a practice theory called the *person-centered approach*, also referred to as *client-centered counseling* and the *nondirective* approach. Many social work interviewing classes introduce students to helping principles and techniques pioneered by Carl Rogers (1970). Rogers also coined the term "Basic Encounter Group" to identify groups that operated on the principles of the person-centered approach, and he developed a related theoretical framework to guide practitioners working with small groups.

Root metaphors and core assumptions

Rogers (1970) brought some of his root metaphors, core assumptions, and central beliefs about reality, people, groups, and helping processes to the project of developing a theory of encounter groups. Experts in Rogerian practice theory indicate that Carl Rogers was committed to several important metaphors. He endorsed an organismic-process vision of the world and the related root metaphors characterizing the person as like other growing, living organisms participating with other organisms in social organizations and characterized by an actualizing process (Ellingham, 1999). In helping sessions, Rogers was prone to use conveyance metaphors associated with

Utopia to craft depictions of the ideal self in terms of the "perfect," "feeling right," "feeling whole, and "accepting self" state achievable by human beings (Wickman & Campbell, 2003).

Regarding human development, Rogers assumed that every person has a tendency to actualize his or her potentials and grow constructively in a way enriching self and society. Additionally, the person is the expert on his or her own life and the decisions that support such self-actualization.

Regarding group work, Rogers assumed and asserted that small groups are vital to the formation of personality and provide opportunities for members to activate self-actualizing processes. Specifically, encounter groups offer an environment stimulating members to open themselves to self and others, an essential step on the path to becoming a fully functioning person.

Regarding the professional group leader, Rogers assumed that the facilitator best promotes the group process by embodying and communicating a set of humanistic attitudes such as empathic understanding, unconditional positive regard or acceptance, and authenticity, also called genuineness. In contrast to other group practice theories, Rogers assumes that the group facilitator does not use a set of structured techniques, demand the performance of particular member behaviors, or press for the achievement of pre-set group outcomes. Instead, he or she helps create humanistic relationships, and he or she trusts the group process. Additionally, the group worker acts on the assumption that participants have the power within themselves to resolve their problems, lessen their defensiveness, heal their psychic wounds, and change in constructive ways.

Central concepts and nominal definitions

In his humanistic theory, then, Carl Rogers made use of constructs including self-actualization, core conditions (empathy, acceptance, genuineness), and the fully functioning person (Bozarth, 1986; Rogers, 1970). You can search the Web or read Roger's books and articles for definitions of these constructs.

Rogers also refined some concepts central to his theory of encounter groups. Following are some of the major ones. The group leader attempts to create a climate of safety. This is defined as a group climate characterized by freedom of expression, mutual support, and confrontations presented in a caring way. The worker makes use of the natural phases of group process. This is conceptualized as movement from superficial expression at the beginning of the group's life through tentative explorations of feelings and, then, to free emotional encounters as the group interaction becomes optimal. Rogers identified a common sequence for this process including milling around, initial resistance to self-exploration, emphasis on past feelings, communication where expressions are mostly negative, the increasing disclosure of personally meaningful material, the increasing sharing of immediate feelings, the development by members of a healing capacity, an increase in self-acceptance, an impatience with defenses that undermine growth, and the sharing of feedback. Feedback is the presentation by one member to another member of supportive and useable information about alternative ways of being. Finally, Rogers (1970) conceptualizes the basic encounter as face-to-face interaction between members typically sitting in a circle during which group participants communicate directly and honestly with one another as full human beings. Rogers's work on encounter group theory didn't include operational definitions of the major concepts.

Theoretical propositions and logical argument

Rogers's general theorizing pattern seemed to be the collection of his life experiences and numerous empirical observations during helping work and the use of descriptive inductive theorizing to convert these into theories. His theory of encounter groups was somewhat informally stated, and it is not clear whether he would have organized the set of propositions in an inductive or deductive pattern. The propositions might be better characterized as a list.

Rogers (1970) did link his theoretical concepts to one another in many specific statements of relationship. Here are a few. As the group moves though the phases of the group process, members begin to drop their defenses and communicate with one another in increasingly genuine ways. After encounters (the revealing of one's real self to others), group members begin to feel greater intimacy with one another, and group members feel a greater sense of trust toward their peers. With the increase of trust among group members, defensiveness decreases. Consequently, members become more open to feedback from others, and members more often try out the new attitudes and behaviors suggested by such feedback. Rogers offered a suggestion regarding effectiveness. The greater the degree to which the group worker communicates the core conditions, the greater will be the evidence of member engagement in the encounter group and the evidence of member personal growth. However, Carl Rogers's original work does not include any discussion of how his theoretical concepts and propositions should be transformed into hypotheses and other tools for evidence-informed practice and research.

Reconstructing a theory

This book doesn't provide knowledge and skills for the reconstruction of a theoretical tradition. Social work specialists in theory or research roles might take on such huge reconstruction projects. However, the theorizing practitioner might parse a specific theory as a start toward understanding, appraising, and reconstructing the elements of the theory (Walker & Avant, 1995). Possible improvements inspired by research evidence, other theoretical knowledge, or practice wisdom might also be recommended.

The practitioner might identify the basic assumptions, the premises on which theoretical reasoning unfolds, and identify which assumptions are explicitly stated. Impressions about implicit assumptions may be recorded, too. The practitioner could judge whether the assumptions would be compatible with his or her own approach to practice and the demands of a particular practice situation or need modification.

The practitioner might identify and summarize the theory's concepts and definitions. A summary might include a count of the total number of concepts, identification of the major and minor concepts, a review of the explicitness of concept definition, and a commentary about the quality of empirical indicators and procedures of each concept. The practitioner might judge which concepts might be useful in identifying interventions and which might better specify target problems. Selected concepts could be reconstructed for practical use.

The practitioner might identify and summarize the theory's propositions. A summary might report on whether the propositions are explicitly stated and what the implied or omitted propositions might be, whether all concepts are included in propositions, and what types of propositions are used in the theory. Specific propositions might be reconstructed into "if-then" form and intervention hypotheses.

The practitioner might identify and summarize the overall logic for ordering relationship statements. The summary might indicate whether deductive theorizing, inductive theorizing, or a combination of both theorizing approaches was used. The logic of a deductive theory might be appraised. The quality of arguments relating observations to general patterns in an inductive theory might be assessed.

Concluding remarks

In summary, theoretical analysis is the effort to identify each component of a theory and present a narrative summary reporting on the components and their relationships. Social workers might then reconstruct the entire theory or salient elements. Theoretical analysis is often supplemented by diagramming the theory, representing the structure of theoretical elements and their relationships visually in a hierarchical manner from A to E, for example. This skill will be reviewed in Lesson 17.

Learning activities and reflections

1   Attempt to summarize the way that I parsed Carl Roger's person-centered theory of encounter groups. Read my report and identify the central assumptions, concepts, and propositions of this theory. Discuss how the propositions were linked to one another. Your parsing can be in the form of a one- to two-page synopsis or a detailed outline. If possible,

develop a visual display showing your analysis including representations of the theoretical elements and their relationships.

As a supplemental step, you might choose to read articles or books identifying ways that the concepts in Roger's theory of encounter groups have been operationalized. You might also check on illustrative studies reporting on the transformation of propositions into hypotheses and the testing of these predictions using research methods.

2   Pick a theory that is very familiar to you. This might be a human development theory: Erikson's psychosocial theory of ego development, Kohlberg's moral development theory, Piaget's cognitive development stage theory, Gilligan's voice theory of female development, or Fowler's stage theory of faith development. Or you might select a theory that focuses on some aspect of human behavior in the social environment: Bowlby's attachment theory, Bandura's social learning theory, Maslow's humanistic theory of motivation, Mead's interactionist theory of communication, Olson's theory of the healthy family, the strengths perspective developed by Dennis Saleeby and others, or the queer theory of sexual orientation and identity.

First, provide a brief overview of the theory. Identify the originators and promoters of the theory. Describe the theoretical puzzle or problem related to the "person interacting in the environment" that the theory was designed to solve. If possible, identify the historical and social context in which the theory was developed and how this might be related to its central features.

Next, parse the theory. Specify the foundational assumptions. Identify the central concepts. Show how the theoretical concepts are related to other concepts by identifying the theory's major propositions. Discuss also how the set of theoretical propositions are related in some systematic way to each other. Offer a few ideas on how the theory might be transformed for scientific testing. How might concepts be operationalized and how might propositions be stated as testable hypotheses?

After the profiling and parsing activities, summarize your overall appraisal of the theory. Comment on its strengths and limitations.

3   Conduct a search of the World Wide Web for information about the labeling theory of deviance. Look for papers by the theory's founder, Howard S. Becker. Download other useful summaries, encyclopedia articles, research studies, and slideshow presentations. Review these materials and attempt to analyze the core elements of the theory—root metaphor, assumptions, concepts, propositions, and linkages of propositions. Provide a summary of your theory analysis. Find and download a visual display showing the elements of the theory and their relations. Study the display and report on how the concepts are linked as propositions and how the propositions are linked together as

a theoretical model. Conclude with some thoughts on the benefits and difficulties of theory analysis and on the ways that you might now use labeling theory and its elements in your practice.

References

Bloom, M. (1975). *The paradox of helping: Introduction to the philosophy of scientific practice*. New York: Wiley.

Bozarth, J. D. (1986). The basic encounter group: An alternative view. *The Journal for Specialists in Group Work, 11*(4), 228–232.

Chafetz, J. S. (1978). *A primer on the construction and testing of theories in sociology*. Itasca, IL: F. E. Peacock.

Chinn, P. L., & Kramer, M. K. (2008). *Integrated theory and knowledge development in nursing* (7th Edn). St. Louis, MO: Mosby Elsevier.

Ellingham, I. (1999). Carl Rogers' "congruence" as an organismic: not Freudian concept. *The Person-Centered Journal, 6*(2), 121–140.

Fawcett, J., & Downs, F. S. (1986). *The relationship of theory and research*. Norwalk, CT: Appleton-Century-Crofts.

Hage, J. (1972). *Techniques and problems of theory construction in sociology*. New York: John Wiley and Sons.

Howe, D. (1997). Relating theory to practice. In M. Davies (Ed.), *The Blackwell companion to social work* (pp. 170–176). Oxford, UK: Blackwell.

Marshall, T. (1989). *The whole world guide to language learning: How to live and learn any foreign language*. Yarmouth, ME: Intercultural Press.

Rogers, C. (1970). *On enccunter groups*. New York: Harper and Row.

Shoemaker, P. J., Tankard, J. W., Jr., & Lasorsa, D. L. (2004). *How to build social science theories*. Thousand Oaks, CA: Sage.

Turner, J. H. (1986). Analytical theorizing. In A. Giddens & J. H. Turner (Eds), *Social theory today* (pp. 156–193). Padstow, UK: Polity Press.

Walker, L. O., & Avant, K. C. (1995). *Strategies for theory construction in nursing* (3rd edn). Norwalk, CT: Appleton.

Wallis, S. E. (2009). The structure of theory and the structure of scientific revolutions: What constitutes and advance in theory? In S. E. Wallis (Ed.), *Cybernetics and systems theory in management: Views, tools, and advancements* (pp.151–174). Hershey, PA: IGI Global.

Wickman, S. A., & Campbell, C. (2003). The coconstruction of congruency: Investigating the conceptual metaphors of Carl Rogers and Gloria. *Counselor Education and Supervision, 43*, 15–24.

Display a theory's elements

(EPAS 2.1.7 Apply Knowledge)

Competent theorizers make frequent use of theoretical models and theoretical displays to make sense of important aspects of "person interacting in the environment" configurations. A model is a small-scale representation of something concrete in the world. There are models of airplanes, railroad trains, cars, and buildings. A model can also be a representation of something more abstract such as the process of reconstructing a social network after a husband dies or a representation of the steps that social workers follow to find knowledge and translate it for use in practice. These theoretical models provide a picture or partial representation of a scientific theory. Shoemaker, Tankard, and Lasorsa (2004) define a *theoretical model* in this way: "A model simply represents a portion of reality, either an object or a process in such a way as to highlight what are considered to be key elements or parts of the object or process and the connections among them" (p. 110).

Theoretical models have some important features (Clement, 2008). First, they are different from the "person interacting in the environment" reality investigated by a social worker. Models are idealized depictions; all aspects of the focal PIE configuration can't realistically be captured in a verbal or visual summary. Second, models can vary in the amount of provided detail from a simple three-variable model, for example, to a model incorporating numerous variables and multiple linkages between these variables. Third, models represent important relationships among elements of the theory topic, not isolated observations or facts. Showing the connections is a key part of model building. Fourth, compared to everyday models, scientists attempt to create theoretical models characterized by qualities such as precision (for example, in the use of concepts), by plausibility (contrasted to questionable leaps of logic associated with some everyday theories), and by internal consistency (the logical and non contradictory arrangement of model components).

Deconstructing theoretical models

A theoretical model serves as an intellectual bridge between the general theoretical framework used by the practitioner and the specifics of the unique helping case. The model transforms the abstract theory into a more limited and concrete form so that the worker use it to achieve practical ends.

Theoretical models serve specific purposes (Shanin, 1972). First, theoretical modeling is an especially useful technique for examining a theory or some aspect of the "person interacting in the environment" configuration, summarizing what concepts are important, and indicating how the concepts are related to each other (Soulliere, Britt, & Maines, 2001). Second, a model provides guidance about what information should be collected. Third, a model offers a synthesis of a set of explanations, interpretations, or critiques of a particular personal or public puzzling pattern or process. A model can identify multiple causal relations, for example, and specify the prediction of certain outcomes assuming the activation of the causal factors. Fourth, theorizers and researchers use models to check empirically on the accuracy of key components of a larger theory. Fifth, theoretical models are good devices for communicating about our theorizing efforts. Models, Britt (1997) argues in his informative book on theoretical modeling, "facilitate continuing dialogue about which concepts are important and unimportant, what their nature is and is not, and how they may and may not be related to one another" (p. vii). Theoretical models also facilitate conversations with partners who use different theoretical frameworks or languages by providing a common and simple mode of communication, and theoretical models facilitate translation within a theoretical language by transforming complex ideas and patterns of ideas into verbal and visual summaries.

Types of theoretical models

There are various kinds of models according to Max Black (1962). The theorizing practitioner needs to recognize, take apart, and make use of various models. The following identifies some of the major types.

Scale models are models such as the fighter planes and bombers designed by my friend. They preserve the relative proportions between the model (the eighteen-inch, balsa wood dive bomber) and the material object (the full-size plane preserved at an Air Force base). The health social worker might use a scale model of the human brain to help the patient understand the biological aspects of an illness.

Mathematical models are very popular in the sciences. These use mathematical logic, symbols, formulations, and equations to illustrate and explain the relationship of variables in some biological, psychological, or social system. These are sometimes called "formal models" (Humphreys, 1998). Advanced social workers might make use of linear regression models to show and characterize the mathematical relationship between explanatory variables and a dependent variable.

Conceptual models use ideas and images expressed as concepts to make intelligible important aspects of some practical problem (Skvoretz, 1998). These are also called semantic or expository models (Shoemaker, Tankard, & Lasorsa, 2004) because the narrative representation is restricted to words (theoretical concepts), and the model is presented as conventional sentences (theoretical propositions) and paragraphs (interrelated statements about the linkage of propositions). Social workers might search for and use many different useful conceptual models: a model of a key helping component such as empathy, a model of a public problem such as homelessness, a model of a social work role such as community organizer, or even a model of the profession of social work such as the membership perspective. We might even consider an entire theoretical tradition, biological evolutionary theory, for instance, to be a large collection of distinct conceptual or theoretical models.

Expository models can be transformed into *research models* when their propositions and the stipulated relationship to empirical data are specified in a form that identifies testable hypotheses. The research model may be simple and identify one cause and one effect, or it may be complex and identify multiple factors causing a specified response (and even feedback loops between the causes and effects). In my own theorizing and research, my colleagues and I have drawn on the interactionist theoretical tradition to create research models of the coping responses of battered women and of the impact of the loss of a loved one on connectedness.

In Section 3, we will describe the construction of middle-range theories. A middle-range theory is a theoretical model blending the features of conceptual and research models but focusing on a topic or concern of limited scope for practical purposes.

The notion of theoretical models has also been adapted for use by practitioners (Mullen, 1983). Mullen proposed that each social worker develop a set of *personal practice models*, "explicit conceptual schemes that express an individual social worker's view of practice and give orderly directions to work with specific clients" (p. 623). These models would summarize what a worker had learned from personal experience, theory, research, and practice wisdom about how to best work with particular clients with particular problems in particular agency settings. Each model in the set of personal practice models would organize its ingredients—theoretical concepts, research and practice generalizations, practice guidelines, and so on—into a concise and usable verbal and visual form. Each model would be continually revised during practice.

Deconstructing theoretical displays

Theoretical displays identify and present visually all the major components of a conceptual or research model and the paths connecting these components. These representations can be drawings, pictures, or diagrams, and they are designed to show in a simple fashion a complex set of ideas. The display is usually created after the theorist has created a verbal statement of the model identifying all the elements of the theory and specifying the way that these elements are organized into a whole.

Theorists create visual representations of their ideas for many different reasons. A display can make clear the logical structure and principles of a theory. A display can represent causes of a focal problem or the phases in a social process. A display can identify the key parts of a whole and show the relationship of these subsystems to the larger structure. The visual aid can offer a shorthand version of the numerous sentences and paragraphs that describe in words the model, a tool that often clarifies theoretical thinking in a way not possible in narratives. Displays can be useful tools for social work problem-solving work enlisted for theory deconstruction, for theory reconstruction during the planned change process, for theory construction, for theory critique, and for communication with clients, colleagues, and team members about theories.

Display conventions

Display conventions are the rules guiding the visual design work of theory users. These conventions can be compared to the grammar that guides language users (Shoemaker, Tankard, & Lasorsa, 2004). Theory deconstruction work requires familiarity with these rules and customary practices.

Here are some common conventions. Short variable names are used. The independent variable is often represented by x, and the dependent variable is commonly represented by y. Variables are placed purposefully on the display. Arrows may be attached to the end of lines to show the direction of influence or causation. An arrowhead at one end of the line indicates an asymmetrical relationship. Arrowheads at both ends of the line indicate a symmetrical relationship. Sets of arrows map a set of relationships.

Line length or line width may be varied to communicate information about magnitude: the thicker the line, the stronger the influence of the independent variable on the dependent variable. Lines may be placed with different angles (for example, a vertical line pointing to a horizontal line) to indicate a conditioning relationship, and lines may be drawn as circling back to a starting point to indicate a feedback loop.

Plus and minus signs might be added over the lines to indicate a positive or negative relationship, respectively. A plus sign indicates a positive association between the variables in which change occurs in the same direction; as one increases in value, the other increases in value or, as one decreases in value, the other decreases in value. A minus sign indicates a negative association between the variables: As one increases in value, the other decreases in value or, as one variable decreases in value, the other increases in value. The absence of a sign indicates no relationship; the variables do not relate in any systematic pattern.

Propositions are usually ordered in levels on a visual display of a deductive theory. The more general propositions are higher than the more specific theoretical statements. A vertical dotted line can be used to connect the propositions from top to bottom. Influence and time are shown by convention as flowing from left to right.

A box or block in which a variety of variables are clustered can indicate that these variables are part of a larger construct. Other abstract shapes including circles and triangles may be used to represent theoretical elements. Colors might be used optionally to differentiate variable or proposition clusters. Words written in the spaces of a shape indicate the concept or variable represented. Insets at the lower corner of a diagram may include a legend explaining key symbols or an identifying date. There may also be conventions for the naming of a display and the placement of this name.

Types of displays

Next, we will present some illustrations of display options for practical models such as middle-range theories. Advanced theorizers might read some of the referenced texts and articles for additional direction on displaying complex theories and frameworks.

Causal displays

A *causal model* identifies causal patterns and relationships by displaying a theory's major variables and the presumed links of influence among these variables (Blalock, 1969). The independent variable (association with delinquent peers, for instance) is placed on the left of the display. An arrow points from the independent variable to the dependent variable (delinquent behavior). The display might use a plus or minus sign to indicate whether the correlation between the two variables is positive or negative.

Causal displays may be simple and portray the relationship of two variables. For example, Rogerian practice theory proposes that the more frequently the social worker uses empathic listening skills, the more often the client will disclose personal information. This can be displayed in an $X \longrightarrow Y$ manner.

Causal displays may also represent the theorized relationship between a larger set of variables. The theory analysis and diagramming might start with focal relationship between two variables (Aneshensel, 2002; Fawcett &

Downs, 1986). Other variable relationships can be drawn. These can include other independent-dependent variable pairs. Additionally, a line depicting the influence of a *moderating variable*, a variable that has a strong contingent effect on the strength or direction of independent variable and dependent variable relationship, can be added (Baron & Kenny, 1986). Sex, race, and class are examples of variables often characterized as moderator variables. Let's review a three-variable model. A social worker in a vocational setting may theorize that there is a relationship between the availability of technical manuals that employees in factories have access to and the number of products that are rejected. Specifically, when workers follow the procedures laid down in the manual, they are able to manufacture products that are flawless. There are no or few rejects. Although this relationship can be said to hold true generally for all workers, it is contingent on a moderating variable, the motivation of employees to look into the manual every time a new procedure is to be adopted. Another kind of variable may be added to a causal display. A *mediating variable* is a variable viewed as a consequence of the antecedent variable and as a cause of the succeeding variable (Shoemaker, Tankard, & Lasorsa, 2004). It comes between or intervenes between the two (Aneshensel, 2002). In some cases, the mediating variable is a mechanism or process that explains the relationship between independent and dependent variable. For example, pre-group orientation of group members (x) leads to knowledgeable and responsible engagement in the group process (the mediating variable), and this kind of engagement leads to achievement of member goals (y).

The theorizing practitioner might also create an inventory of causes (Blalock, 1969), for example, an inventory of all the alleged causes of shoplifting. Such a display could place y, the dependent variable, at the center of the page and then arrange a line with an arrow from each identified cause—x_1, x_2, x_3, to x_i,—at the top of page pointing downward to the dependent variable. Or the display might represent an inventory of effects indicating that a focal independent variable has multiple consequences. For example, the social work practitioner might theorize about the positive effects of upward social mobility for community members. In this display, x is placed at the top center of the page; then, lines with arrows are arranged in a vertical fanning out pattern down from x specifying y_1, y_2, y_3, to y_i. Finally, a theory user might display an inventory of causes, mediators, and effects—the x_s (causes of y) in the top row with arrows down to the m (mediating mechanisms) in the center, and from there, arrows down to the z_s (effects of x; Fawcett & Downs, 1986).

Causal displays may represent complex theories. The display might depict the relationships between multiple variables and add negative or positive feedback loops. This can be shown as a line drawn back to initial variable (s) indicating the effect of information feeding back to increase or decrease the influence of variables making up the initial conditions of the focal system

(Britt, 1997; Abell, 1971). The expert theory user might create elaborated causal models. These attempt to represent visually the relationships of multiple independent, conditioning, and intervening variables. Models with large sets of variables might use displays with the variable grouped into larger blocks such as "individual functioning" (independent variables) and "family functioning" (independent variables) leading to "employment predicament" (dependent variable) with this relationship moderated by a block of "family characteristic" variables. Such complex theoretical models probably exceed the daily practice needs of most social work practitioners.

Process or theme displays

A *process model* summarizes in words the temporal order of development, relationship, or sequence for a set of two or more phases or events, and a process display provides a visual representation of the sequence. For example, symbolic interactionists have theorized that the loved one's death triggers the initiation of a grieving process that triggers the initiation of an identity change and a social network rebuilding project. This sequence can be displayed as a path from the starting point to the final point in the process.

The theorist using a visual display for a process model often arranges events horizontally and uses arrows to connect each event in the sequence with the point of the arrow toward the right. He or she may begin with the starting and termination points of the process and then fill in the steps between these points. The display may also be vertical. Arrows connect events from the first event at the top to the final event at the bottom of the display. The process or path display is often supplemented by a written description of the rationale for the specified temporal order and summarizing the logical relationships between the events in the process (Shoemaker, Tankard, & Lasorsa, 2004).

Complex process models may depict all the tasks that must be completed for a successful social event or team project, a timetable with events ordered by a calendar, or a decision tree representing the ordering of possible decisions and the alternatives associated with each decision (Mullins, 1971). Process displays may also represent steps, phases, or sequences such as the steps leading to homelessness or serious domestic violence, phases in the emotional reactions to the dying process, or the sequence resulting in the development of a gay identity. Typically, process displays represent grounded theories, or other similar interpretive theories supported by qualitative data.

Theoretical maps

Theoretical maps enhance the modeling process. A map can be a very useful visual tool. Let me provide an example of the power of maps from recent history. The Allied forces created huge map rooms during World War II with three-dimensional replications of battle areas. Generals used the maps in these rooms to display the contested terrain, to show the movement of their troops and enemy troops, and to consider alternative strategies for advancing soldiers toward desired objectives. These maps were important contributors to victory over the Nazi Germans. Theoretical maps can be equally useful. Dewey (1902/1990), an educational expert, valued cartography and wrote that the use of the map is

> a summary, an arranged and orderly view of previous experiences, (that) serves as a guide to future experience; it gives direction; it facilitates control; it economizes effort, preventing useless wandering, and pointing out the paths which lead most quickly and most certainly to a desired result. (p. 198)

A theorist might imitate Lewis and Clark. These great explorers attempted to fill in the details of early American maps and describe previously vast and unknown spaces. Theorizing as conceptual mapping accepts a similar mission and tries to fill in the blank spaces in the social work knowledge base, those areas of human's bio-psycho-social functioning in the environment that had not been previously explained.

Theoretical maps have similarities to directional maps that guide travel across a vast system of roads (Giardino, 2010). Both can vary in their scope and detail. A theoretical tradition maps a vast conceptual terrain, an entire world of ideas. Each major tradition might be likened to a geographer's depiction of one continent on the globe. A display of a middle-range theoretical model maps a limited conceptual terrain similar to the map of places in a hometown. Like a roadmap, a theoretical map is holistic and shows elements in relationship to a whole. Both theoretical maps and roadmaps use symbols and signs by convention (shapes, lines, and so on) to create a representation suggesting a correspondence to some aspect of reality. Both theoretical maps and roadmaps must be read and interpreted before they can be used. Neither a theoretical map nor a roadmap offers a complete and exhaustive depiction of the mapped territory. Theoretical maps and roadmaps are practical tools that help map users orient themselves and navigate.

Social workers are familiar with the eco-map and its many uses related to information gathering, assessment formulation, and intervention planning (Forte, 2006). The *eco-map* is a theoretical map and visual tool used to display the central elements of systems theory-based conceptualization of a person interacting in the environment. Figure 17.1 illustrates an eco-map I created depicting a "strengths and resiliency" approach to understanding the teenager, the environment, and transactions influencing choices regarding sexual activity.

Eco-map: positive social work and teen sexuality

Name: Child (sexuality issues)
Date: Today

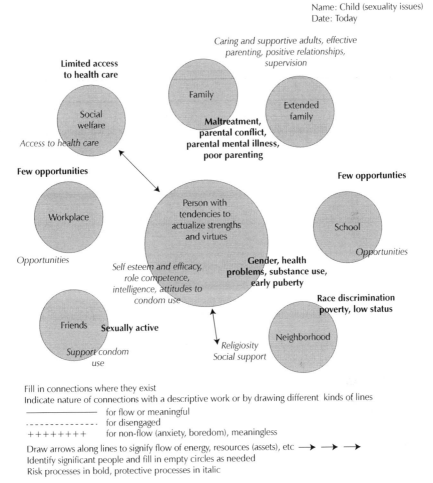

Figure 17.1   The positive social work (strengths and resiliency) eco-map (based on Kirby and Fraser, 1997; Fraser and Galinsky, 1997)

First, let's review the basic conventions for creating an eco-map. The large circle in the center of the map represents the unit of attention: the individual, the couple, or the family who is using the services of a social worker. The eco-map was developed specifically to help workers in public child welfare agencies. Many social workers follow this tradition and place the family or the household in the center circle. Members of this focal system can be also symbolized by genogram conventions—a small box for a male, a small circle for a female, and lines connecting marital partners and parents to children. The focal system might even refer to a larger social system that the worker intends to help: a social organization, a community, or perhaps even, a society.

The entire eco-map figure represents the environment or life space of the client or client group. The circles surrounding the unit of attention are the major social systems. These are the groups, organizations, and institutions that influence and are influenced by the client(s). Social systems included on an eco-map may identify school, friends, the workplace, health care providers, recreational facilities, and cultural or religious organizations by small circles. Circles without names are available so the practitioner can identify and label distinctive or unusual social systems. Two circles of moderate size are included on the standard eco-map to indicate the importance of the social welfare system and the extended family network to most social work clients. A contemporary eco-map creator might include even larger circles to represent the macro-level social systems such as corporations, governments, or labor markets that affect many clients' life chances.

The circles on an eco-map are drawn with solid lines to indicate the boundaries between one system and external systems. Dashed lines could be used to convey the ecosystems notion that all groups of living organisms have permeable boundaries.

The worker must add to the eco-map form by drawing in lines suggesting the connections between the focal system and external systems. These connections have been referred to in various terms as the exchanges, interfaces, relationships, linkages, and transactions between the client system and its environment. The nature or quality of the connection is represented visually in three different ways. A solid or thick line indicates a strong or positive connection. A dashed line indicates a tenuous connection or weak connection, and a line made up of crosses indicates a conflict ridden or stressful connection or relationship. Transactions between the systems are described as the transfer of resources including energy, opportunities, and interests. The direction of the flow of resources is mapped as an arrow placed alongside the connecting line.

There are several other ways to increase the utility of the eco-map. The date on the eco-map records the time when the ecosystems assessment was completed. However, the worker and client or clients can select the most useful temporal focus for their purposes. The eco-map might depict life-space systems and processes in the present, or the eco-map might be retrospective and attempt to capture client-environment exchanges at an earlier historical period. Finally, the eco-map might be prospective and attempt to depict visually a future or ideal ecosystem.

The fact that different members of the focal system construct social reality differently can also be depicted. When all members of the family have connections to the same external system, a line connecting the family boundary and the system boundary is used. However, if the focal system includes multiple members rather than one client, the practitioner might use a color code during mapping and draw lines of different shades from each member to the salient systems for that person.

The eco-map is based in the ecosystem's theoretical framework. However, it can be adapted to display theoretical models from other frameworks. The social worker creating a theory-based eco-map should answer a set of eco-map translation questions (Forte, 2006). How would adherents to the theoretical tradition label the elements of the conventional eco-map, fill in connecting lines, and add descriptive words? A theory-specific eco-map will explicate the notion of the connectedness of clients to varied groups (and specifically how the theorist talks about connectedness and isolation); the theoretical conception of the linkage; the issues and resource-need discrepancies central to client problems given prominence in the theory; and the theoretically varied recommendations for helping clients meet challenges and change transactional patterns.

Based on this information, the social worker creates an eco-map using the terminology of the focal theory. For example, the social worker depicting a "client interacting in the environment" configuration might do so by using a critical-empowerment theoretical framework (Forte, 2006). The entire environment might be characterized as "society under the conditions of political inequality," with this label placed to the left and below the eco-map's name. The central circle depicts the focal client: the person as a citizen or as a group of citizens. The surrounding circles are organized into three spheres. The private sphere includes circles for the family, the extended family, and friends. This sphere is somewhat removed from the daily public engagement of active citizenship work. The dominant sphere includes circles representing politicians and their parties, corporations, the state, and the mass media. From the critical perspective, this sphere includes elite leaders and their agents who actively dominate the social workers' client and these leaders attempt to acquire and protect a disproportionate share of the society's privileges. The third sphere is the oppositional sphere. This includes circles for systems committed to increasing the citizen's power, access to resources, and life chances: social movements, cooperatives, alternative media, and alternative schools. Positive connections are characterized as civic action especially public speech and policy advocacy between the citizen and systems that expand democracy and human rights. Negative connections are characterized as manipulative, dishonest, and distorted public actions that undermine democracy and perpetuate inequality and exploitation of the vulnerable groups. Resources are conceptualized as all the communication and political resources that the citizen can bring to bear on public conflicts, arguments, and political battles with the elite leaders and their agents. Words for specific resources are placed over connecting lines. The theory also suggests an ideal eco-map to contrast with the client's actual eco-map as one characterized by social systems in all spheres governed by democratic and humanistic principles, the full participation of all citizens in public deliberation and decision-making processes, the prevalence of mutual help rather than exploitation and conflict, and active, informed citizen work. The theorist might find creative ways to represent these ideas concisely on the ideal eco-map.

Reconstructing a theory as a display

McGuire (2004), an expert on theorizing, suggests that the novice theorizer can deepen his or her knowledge of theories and sharpen theorizing skills by reconstructing a theory using varied modalities. The theorizer might translate a theory into natural language, perhaps as a story. The theorizer might imitate some of the great scientific theorizers of history and transform the essential ingredients of a theoretical model into an object or picture such as Linus Pauling's wooden representation of a triple-strained DNA. The theorizer might transform a theoretical model supported by research into a set of mathematical symbols.

We have reviewed the conventions for reconstructing theories as causal diagrams, flow charts of processes, and eco-maps. Swedberg (2012) adds that there are many other approaches to visually representing theoretical content. These include tables like a fourfold/2 × 2 table, decision trees, figures of social networks, and logic models. By experimenting and practicing the deconstruction, reconstruction, or construction of visual displays, the theorizing practitioner can enrich her or his grasp of a theory, increase her or his appreciation for the theory's implications, recognize more astutely similarities and differences between the focal theory and other theories, detect the theory's gaps and limitations, and use the theory to guide helping work.

Judging displays and other visual representations

How do we determine whether a visual representation of a theory is weak or strong? Kulpa (1994) offers three criteria. First, we should consider expressiveness. Does the display communicate all the theory elements that the creator wants to communicate without communicating elements not included in theory? Second, we should consider effectiveness. From the perspective of the display's users, is it easy to perceive the theory elements and relationships? Finally, we should consider the degree of match with the goal of the presentation. Is the representation suitable for the creator's purpose: summary of theory, use of theory, critique of theory, and so on?

When deconstructing and reconstructing visual representations, social workers should proceed with some caution. Remember that diagrams are not reflections of an independent reality but an aesthetic creation used for theorizing about and influencing "person interacting in the environment" processes. Do your homework. To "read" a diagram successfully, the interpreter needs extensive background including disciplinary and theoretical knowledge. Finally, be humble. As a representation, a theoretical display is open to multiple interpretations by diverse interpreters including interpretations not intended by the creator.

Learning activities and reflection

1   Identify a personal or community change goal (dependent variable) related to some aspect of "person interacting in the environment." Find or create a middle-range theoretical model specifying some interventions that you might use to facilitate the attainment of this goal. The theory should also identify conditioning factors that might weaken or strengthen the relationship between the independent and dependent variables. List and define the major concepts selected from this theory that you can use for specifying your goal, assessing your progress, and implementing a system-change intervention. Create a diagram depicting your theory's building blocks, their connections to one another, and their connections to your target goal or problem. Briefly summarize your thinking about the display. Next, review the display options discussed in the commentary section above. Return and revise your display.

2   Using theoretical knowledge that you have acquired in the social work program, your field internship, or your general education courses, identify a familiar sequence—the stages of human development, the process of becoming an addict, the flow of work for a group or organization, the transformation from new gang member to gang leader, or the path for career advancement in an organization, for examples. Create a process display of this sequence displaying each step or phase in the sequence and briefly summarize your thinking about the display.

3   Construct an eco-map translated into the theoretical vocabulary of the behavioral approach for your self, your transactions, and your environment. What are some of the behavioral patterns that characterize your transactions (connections) with others in the learning environment? Which social systems (peoples, groups, and organizations) are the sources of reinforcement, punishment, and behavioral models? What is being transmitted between you and other social systems that condition or modify your behavior, and that condition or modify others' behavior? Characterize specific connections with some of these persons and systems as reinforcing, punishing, modeling desired behaviors, or modeling undesired behaviors? What contingencies (related prompts, antecedents, behaviors, or consequences) would you like to change to create an eco-map depicting the ideal person-in-environment configurations from a behavioral perspective? How might you display these contingencies visually?

References

Abell, P. (1971). *Model building in sociology*. New York: Schocken.
Aneshensel, C. S. (2002). *Theory-based data analysis for the social sciences*. Thousand Oaks, CA: Sage.

Baron, R. M., & Kenny, D. A. (1986). Moderator-mediator variable distinction in social psychological research: Conceptual, strategic, and statistical considerations. *Journal of Personality and Social Psychology, 51*(6), 1173–1182.

Black, M. (1962). *Models and metaphors: Studies in language and philosophy.* Ithaca, NY: Cornell University Press.

Blalock, H. M. Jr. (1969). *Theory construction: From verbal to mathematical formulation.* Englewood Cliffs, NJ: Prentice-Hall.

Britt, D. (1997). A *conceptual introduction to modeling: Qualitative and quantitative perspectives.* Mahwah, NJ: Erlbaum.

Clement, J. J. (2008). *Creative model construction in scientists and students: The role of imagery, analogy, and mental stimulation.* New York: Springer.

Dewey, J. (1990 [1902]). *The school and society and the child and the curriculum.* Chicago, IL: University of Chicago Press. (Original work published 1902).

Fawcett, J., & Downs, F. S. (1986). *The relationship of theory and research.* Norwalk, CT: Appleton-Century-Crofts.

Forte, J. A. (2006). *Human behavior and the social environment: Models, metaphors, and maps for applying theoretical perspectives to practice.* Belmont, CA: Thomson Brooks/Cole.

Fraser, M. W., & Galinsky, M. J. (1997). Risk, protection, and resilience: Toward a conceptual framework for social work practice. *Social Work Research, 23*(3), 131–139.

Giardino, V. (2010). The world in maps: Looking for treasures, neurons, and soldiers. In O. Pombo & A. Gerner (Eds), *Studies in diagrammatology and diagram praxis* (pp. 145–165). London: College Publications.

Humphreys, P. (1998). Sociological models. In A. Sica (Ed.), *What is social theory? The philosophical debates* (pp. 253–264). Malden, MA; Blackwell.

Kirby, L. D., & Fraser, M. W. (1997). Risk and resilience in childhood. In M. W. Fraser (Ed.), *Risk and resilience in childhood: An ecological perspective* (pp. 10–33). Washington, DC: NASW Press.

Kulpa, Z. (1994). Diagrammatic representation and reasoning. *Machine GRAPHICS & VISION, 3*(1/2), 77–103.

McGuire, W. J (2004). A perspectivist approach to theory construction. *Personality and Social Psychology Review, 8*(2), 173–182.

Mullen, E. J. (1983). Personal practice models. In A. Rosenblatt & D. Waldfogel (Eds), *Handbook of clinical social work* (pp. 623–649). New York: Wiley.

Mullins, N. C. (1971). *The art of theory construction and use.* New York: Harper and Row.

Shanin, T. (1972). Models and thought. In T. Shanin (Ed.), *The rules of the game: Cross-disciplinary essays on models in scholarly thought* (pp. 1–22). London: Tavistock.

Shoemaker, P. J., Tankard, J. W., Jr., & Lasorsa, D. L. (2004). *How to build social science theories.* Thousand Oaks, CA: Sage.

Skvoretz, J. (1998). Theoretical models: Sociology's missing links. In A. Sica (Ed.), *What is social theory? The philosophical debates* (pp. 238–252). Malden, MA: Blackwell.

Soulliere, D., Britt, D. W., & Maines, D. R. (2001). Conceptual modeling as a toolbox for grounded theorists. *Sociological Quarterly, 42*(2), 253–269.

Swedberg, R. (2012). Theorizing in sociology and social science: Turning to the context of discovery. *Theory and Society, 41*, 1–40.

<table>
<tr><td>SECTION
3</td><td></td></tr>
</table>

SECTION 3

Constructing practical theories

In this section, Section 3, we will learn how to use theorizing skills to construct practical theories. Construction work will involve varying degrees of theory deconstruction and theory reconstruction. We might, for example, derive a theory in the middle range from a major theoretical tradition by deconstructing or unpacking concepts, propositions, and linkages useful to approaching the puzzle and, then, by reconstructing these theory elements to fit the practice situation, we might, in contrast, derive a theory in the middle range from a practice theory, deconstructing and reconstructing the practice theory's elements as needed. We might borrow and reconstruct a theory in the middle range developed by another social worker or developed by theorizers associated with a discipline such as nursing, psychology, or sociology; this assumes a congruence of the theory's basic elements with social work mission and values. In some cases, we might construct a new middle-range theory grounded in the particulars of the puzzling case or our understanding of relevant research studies.

In the first lesson, Lesson 18, I will provide an overview of middle-range theorizing. In Lesson 19, I will describe how to construct a causal theory, a middle-range theory preferred by positivist theorizers. In Lesson 20, I will describe how to construct a grounded theory, a theory of the middle range preferred by interpretive theorizers. The section will conclude with Lesson 21, a lesson dedicated to providing the knowledge and skills necessary for translating and sharing a practical theory.

Construct practical theories in the middle range

(EPAS 2.1.7 Apply Knowledge;
EPAS 2.1.10 Engage, Assess, Intervene, Evaluate)

Theorizing in the middle range

A middle-range theory is a theory that lies "between the minor but necessary working hypotheses that evolve in abundance during day-to-day research and the all-inclusive systematic efforts to develop a unified theory that will explain all the observed uniformities of social behavior, social organization, and social change" (Merton, 1968, p. 39). Middle-range theories are very useful tools for social work theorizers.

On the ladder of theoretical abstraction, theories of the middle range are not at the ladder's bottom: the empirical generalizations and working hypotheses that emerge during daily practice. For example, the policy advocate summarizes her or his recent experience and makes the theoretical assertion that the frequency of making scapegoats of minority group members increases during an economic downturn. Theories of the middle range are not at the top of the ladder either: the all inclusive and systematic theoretical tradition designed to explain all "human behavior and the environment" content important to the profession such as the ecosystems perspective. Middle-range theories fall near the mid-point of the ladder's rungs. I will briefly profile theories of the middle range.

Common features of middle-range theories

Middle-range theories are often built with a limited number of theoretical assumptions, a limited number of concepts (fewer than seven, for instance), and a limited number of relationships between these concepts (Stehr, 1992). A middle-range theory might include five propositions characterizing its important relationships. Typically, the middle-range theory has a name indicating its modest level of abstraction, its topical focus, and its allegiance to a discipline or profession (Liehr & Smith, 1999).

Middle-range theories also specify their concepts in concrete rather than abstract ways. For example, one middle-range theory of relative deprivation defines the concept "deprivation" as the tendency to decide how materially deprived we are not by reference to an absolute standard but by the economic circumstances of people with whom we compare ourselves (Runciman, 1966). Middle-range theorists believe that concrete and specific concepts are easier to attach to empirical indicators and to operationalize using valid and reliable measurement procedures than very abstract concepts.

The elements, relationships, and overall structure of a middle-range theory are often captured in a diagram or other display. The accurate and detailed specification of the theory and its way of resolving a theoretical puzzle or problem in both narrative and visual form increases its usefulness to practical theorizers.

Compared to grand theories, middle-range theories have limited applicability and scope relative to historical time, ecological space, system size, and social problem specification. For many practitioners, there will be an affinity to the narrow, modest, and practical aims of middle-range theorizers. The theoretical products, middle-range theories, focus more closely on the particular aspects of the "person interacting in an environment" configuration causing client and worker puzzlement. Stated differently, middle-range theorizing addresses theoretical problems of manageable scope—not so large that the social work theory users' resources and time will be inadequate but not so small that the focal issue must be a trivial one. Moreover, middle-range theories are not so frugal with their concepts that they prohibit any generalization of findings or testing of hypotheses.

Uses of middle-range theories

Merton (1968) considered middle-range theories very suitable for those professions and disciplines engaged in practice. Middle-range theories are useful because they identify a manageable number of key variables, present a few clear propositions, have limited and manageable scope, and can easily lead to the derivation of testable hypotheses about change processes (McKenna, 1997).

Middle-range theories are essential tools for knowledge building and use by the profession of social work. They can guide scientific inquiry, for example, by suggesting hypotheses. These might include assessment hypotheses, intervention hypotheses, and practice/program evaluation hypotheses related interventions to benchmark achievements. Such hypotheses can stimulate productive empirical investigation.

Middle-range theories are also useful in making theoretical connections between empirical observations and highly abstract, very broad, hard-to-test theories such as Freud's theory of civilization and human discontent.

A middle-range theory could link a theory about inner psychic conflict to specific consequences. A Freudian/Psychoanalytic middle-range theorist might theorize in a focused way, for instance, about the contemporary societal trends influencing a Mennonite community in Pennsylvania and how the reactions of the parental generation to these trends increase the psychic conflicts between sexual impulses and prohibitions experienced by the adolescent members. Such unresolved conflicts might be theoretically related to the teenagers' mental health and conduct problems.

Middle-range theories are constructed to guide practice and do so well because of their limited scope and clear theoretical focus. Compared to the use of a theoretical tradition, middle-range theories increase the likelihood that practitioners can deconstruct the theory with modest effort and make use of its concepts, propositions, and overall theoretical argument to figure out puzzling patterns and discover realistic solutions to person-in-environment puzzles.

Illustrations of middle-range theorizing

Unfortunately, social workers need to engage in more middle-range theorizing and to make greater use of theories in the middle range (Loewenberg, 1984). Our profession lacks a body of middle-range theories on a range of personal and public challenges. In an illustration of the type of study rarely conducted by social work professionals, Stone and McKenry (1998) tested a middle-range role-oriented theory of father involvement in their children's lives after a divorce. This theory identified four independent variables and one dependent variable. The social work researchers confirmed that the independent variables—a father's role identity as a parent, the father's clarity about the father role, the quality of the father-child relationship, and father's satisfaction with the legal system—were related in predicted ways to the dependent variable, level of involvement with children who lived with the mothers. They discussed how the theory could guide practitioners with members of this client group.

Unlike social workers, nursing theorists have developed many middle-range theories. Nurses collect these theories in anthologies and in many journals and use these theories in numerous realms of nursing research and practice (Liehr & Smith, 1999; Meleis, 2010: Peterson & Bredow, 2004; Smith & Liehr, 2008). Their knowledge base includes middle-range theories addressing puzzles related to acute pain management, care giving dynamics, chronic sorrow, comforting processes, cultural marginality, deliberative nursing practices, factors contributing to resilience, health promotion, hopelessness of homelessness, illness uncertainty, internalized HIV-related stigma, life after a liver transplant, music intervention for agitation, pain management in children, unpleasant physical symptoms, symptom management, the peaceful end of life, the transition into a nursing home, and women's anger. Generally, these theories have been tested, and used for specific guidance in nursing practice.

Social work might emulate such industrious theorizing. Our professional challenges could be met more successfully if our theoretical toolbox included many practical theories: middle-range theories that are "empirically sound, coherent, meaningful, useful, and illuminating" (Liehr & Smith, 1999, p. 81).

Learning activities and reflections

1 Social workers refer to cutting-edge knowledge to understand clients who are members of "populations-at-risk" such as persons identified with lesbian, gay, and bisexual orientations. Queer theory, for instance, is a theory used by practitioners to prioritize issues of identity and the creative ways persons resist or subvert gender and sexuality categorizations imposed by others. Develop a middle-range theory relevant to an at-risk population. For example, theorize about the "identity threats" experienced by a group of people with an alternative sexual orientation. Or construct a middle-range theory explaining the use of reference groups by youths in poor city neighborhoods to support pro-social behavior. For your middle-range theory, identify several relevant concepts and define each concretely. Relate these concepts to one another in the form of propositions. Discuss how the various propositions relate to one another. Propose a measurement strategy for each concept and a testable hypothesis about some specific positive or negative life outcome that might be deduced from a general premise in your theory. Summarize your middle-range theory here.

Share some ideas about how the middle-range theory might guide social work efforts to help members of this at-risk population. Specifically, relate the theory to the information gathering, assessment formulation, and intervention planning processes.

2 Begin with the life course/family developmental perspective that you have learned in a psychology course or a social work human behavior class. Use "family quality of life" as your dependent variable. Identify a manageable set of relevant independent variables. You might select frugally from individual factors such as those related to mental health, cognitive beliefs, and perceived stress; family system factors such as degree of family adaptability, collective satisfaction with family relations, and family communication dynamics; ecological factors such as resource availability in family's neighborhood, job market opportunities, and access to family support programs; and family developmental factors such as family stage in family life cycle, family and family member abilities to meet stage-specific tasks, and the division of family roles to perform stage tasks. If you feel ambitious, identity relevant moderating

variables such as level of family member education or family cultural background.

Create a middle-range theory organizing relations between your selected independent and moderating variables and the dependent variable, family quality of life. Identify any foundational assumptions to your model. Attempt to define each concept and specify how you could transform it into a variable. Specify how the variables are related to one another by listing your major theoretical propositions. Write a short narrative summarizing how the propositions are linked to one another. Discuss also how your middle-range theory, if supported by research, could guide your helping work with a family system.

References

Liehr, P., & Smith, M. J. (1999). Middle range theory: Spinning research and practice to create knowledge for the new millennium. *Advances in Nursing Science, 21*(4), 81–91.

Loewenberg, F. M. (1984). Professional ideology, middle range theories and knowledge building for social work practice. *British Journal of Social Work, 14*(4), 309–322.

McKenna H. P. (1997). *Nursing models and theories.* London, Routledge.

Meleis, A. I. (2010). *Transitions theory: Middle-range and situation-specific theories in nursing research and practice.* New York: Springer.

Merton, R. K. (1968). On sociological theories of the middle range. In *Social Theory and Social Structure* (3rd Edn). New York: The Free Press.

Peterson, S. J., & Bredow, T. S. (2004). *Middle range theories: Application to nursing research.* Philadelphia, PA: Lippincott Williams and Wilkins.

Runciman, W. G. (1966). *Relative deprivation and social justice.* Berkeley, CA: University of California Press.

Smith, M. J., & Liehr, P. R. (Eds). (2008). *Middle-range theories for nursing* (2nd Edn). New York: Springer.

Stehr, N. (1992). *Practical knowledge: Applying the social sciences.* London: Sage.

Stone, G., & McKenry, P. (1998). Nonresidential father involvement: A test of a mid-range theory. *The Journal of Genetic Psychology, 159,* 313–336.

LESSON 19

Construct a middle range theory about causes

(EPAS 2.1.7 Apply Knowledge;
EPAS 2.1.10 Engage, Assess, Intervene, Evaluate))

For this lesson, we will focus on theorizing about causes and effects and constructing a causal theory. Generally, positivist theorizers construct causal theories; see Lesson 2 for a summary of this style of theorizing.

Nature of puzzles and theorizing purposes

Causal theorizing helps practitioners and their clients fit the pieces of "why," "what next," and "what will change the pattern?" puzzles. Social workers engaged in policy analysis and advocacy, for example, assemble and read the literature on the theory and research-based investigation of the causes of public problems such as urban poverty, homelessness, migration, substance misuse, crime, unemployment, war, and hunger. Synthesizing this knowledge with their practice experience, these theorizing practitioners might formulate theoretical explanations of why a particular troubling condition, pattern, or process has started or is maintained (Linder & Peters, 1984; McCarty, 2008).

Social workers also use causal theories and research to predict the likely changes over time if a policy is enacted, an intervention tried, a program implemented, or the client's life circumstances allowed to unfold uninfluenced by an agent of change (Walt, 2005). Social workers in correctional settings, for example, use causal theories and research studies to make predictions about the likely careers of ex-prisoners.

Social workers also use empirically supported causal theories to decide on suitable interventions and programs (what works in changing undesired patterns and processes), and to champion their use. Based on familiarity with alternative solutions to housing problems in the recession era United States, McCarty (2008), for instance, concluded, "only theoretically sound and demonstrably effective housing programs can be successfully defended in the current political climate" (p. 85).

Positivist theories offer *causal explanations*, sense-making statements presented as an organized and logical set of cause-effect relationships. The explanation may focus on the physical, psychological, social, or interrelated causes of some event or pattern related to human behavior and the environment. The causal explanation also identifies the effects of a particular cause. In the policy arena, for instance, the causal policy theory might identify the likely consequences or effects of a new "Stand Your Ground" law on the public problem of hate crime.

These explanations help the practitioner make sense of a variety of types of causes (Clemons & McBeth, 2001). These include *accidental causes*, the unintended and unguided actions of nature or fate such as those associated with an earthquake, flood, or car crash; *intentional causes*, actions that are purposeful and with intended consequences such as those of political leaders colluding with developers to overcome opposition to building in an environmentally sensitive area; inadvertent or *unintentional causes*, actions with unintended consequences and purposeful actions that have unforeseen side-effects, sometimes due to carelessness (the corrupt politician's community development policy leads to soil erosion that contributes to serious flooding and the destruction of many homes); or *mechanical causes*, influences related to technological innovations—sometimes controlled by humans, other times uncontrolled or barely controlled by people. The increasing use of computer-driven trading tools in stock markets, for instance, is causing a variety of new economic risks.

Elements and a definition of causal theory

Recall our comparison of theory to language. Causal explanations are like paragraphs. Paragraphs are constructed from words and sentences organized into propositional statements. These statements are linked together in a coherent way. Let's begin with review of some of the elements of a causal theory or paragraph. The elements and strategies for deconstructing and reconstruction each have been introduced in earlier lessons.

Theoretical concepts and variables

Causal theories are built from *concepts*. These are "ideas derived from experience and expressed through symbols" (Bloom, 1975, p. 38). Concepts point to or represent something in empirical reality. Theorists work hard to define important concepts in precise and valid ways. Often, theoretical concepts are used to begin to identify causal patterns.

Variables are definitions of concepts in terms of variation in quantity or qualities. A causal concept is also called an *independent variable*, an action, event, process, or pattern that influences or causes changes to happen. The effect is called a *dependent variable*, that which is influenced or changed by the operation of the independent variable.

Theoretical propositions

The words of a theoretical explanation are organized into sentences or explanatory propositions, statements of relationship between two or more concepts. Punctuation breaks up the flow of a set of propositions into manageable bits. A social worker, for example, might teach the behavioral proposition "positive reinforcement increases desired behaviors" to help a parent progress in the direction of effective control of an unruly child's conduct. Propositions can be transformed also into causal hypotheses relating measureable variables and tested scientifically.

Linkages of propositions

Causal explanations are constructed by organizing a set of concepts and propositions in ways that show the linkages. Concepts are often organized into propositions with symbols indicating the relationship of concepts and the linkage of propositions. For the example above, shorthand may be used. Positive reinforcement is symbolized as x (the independent variable or causal concept). and desired behavior is symbolized as y (the dependent variable or effect). The relationship between cause and effect might be shown as x → y.

Causal propositions may indicate direct or indirect relations (Jaccard & Jacoby, 2010). In a direct causal relationship, the mother's repeated statement "no" frustrates the child and influences aggressive crying and throwing behaviors. In an indirect causal relationship, the focal variable—the mother and teenager's high-quality relationship—has an influence, but not an immediate one, on the dependent variable or effect, the teenager's use of illicit drugs.

Definition of causal theory

By identifying and organizing causal propositions and indicating carefully how they are linked together to explain the causes of some aspect of human behavior and the social environment, we are creating a causal theory. Bell (2009) defines a *causal theory* as concepts, definitions, and propositions that describe the application of causal logic to an empirical context. "Person interacting in an environment" configurations are very complex, and causal theories typically identify multiple causes and in some cases, various consequences of the many different causes.

Theorizing method

Like the building of a new home by Habitat for Humanity residents and future homeowners, theory construction projects require the completion of a variety of tasks. Positivist theorizers and interpretive theorizers must complete the same task. Figure 7.2 in Lesson 7 provided a visual display of the common theorizing process. The task definitions and task sequences differ, however, in many ways (Lynham, 2002).

Causal theorizing: basic tasks

I have framed these tasks using the metaphorical comparison of theorizing to puzzle solving. Many of these tasks will seem familiar. We have discussed them in the lessons in Section 2.

Identify the explanatory puzzle

The theorizing practitioner must transform a vague sense of puzzlement into a specific statement of the theoretical puzzle. For causal theorizing, this requires the formulation of a guiding question regarding what needs to be explained. Typically, this specifies the focal challenge or dependent variable, and the question often begins with "why." For instance, we might start the causal theorizing process by asking, Why do some battered women return to volatile partners and unsafe situations? A review of the relevant literature will help the causal theorizer.

Develop the elements of causal theory

The theorizing practitioner must deconstruct (if the theory is derived from an existing theoretical tradition) or construct (if the theory is an original creation) the elements of the causal theory. These are the tools necessary to assemble pieces explaining the puzzling cause-effect pattern, process, or condition. As indicated above, these elements include concepts, propositions, and a logical argument linking the elements into a framework of concepts.

Transform the causal theory's elements into operational form

The theorizing practitioner must transform the causal theory's elements into a form amenable to research testing and evidence-informed practice. For causal theorizers, this is a process of operationalization. It involves converting the concepts into variables, specifying empirical indicators, and developing measurement procedures for each concept. For instance, the theorizer might operationalize wife battering by using a 25-item self-report measurement instrument with a physical abuse and a psychological abuse subscale. Operationalization also involves converting the propositions into hypotheses and organizing the converted elements into an operationalized theoretical framework (Lynham, 2002). The framework would identify causal variables, predicted effects or consequences, and the mechanisms, if known, by which the causes produce the effects, and the framework would organize these into a testable system. Pilot tests increase the practitioner's confidence in the theory.

In a study with a group of colleagues (Forte, Franks, Forte, & Rigsby, 1996), we identified economic dependency, marital power differences, and social isolation as key causal factors in relationships characterized by intimate violence. We theorized that relationship violence had a variety of negative consequences for the female partner including distressful emotions; self-esteem difficulties; and constricted coping responses. We also speculated that asymmetrical role-taking by the wife was the key mechanism linking the causes with maladaptive choices to stay in the relationship. Measures were identified for each variable, and a set of explicit hypotheses were tested.

Apply the causal theory

The theorizing practitioner applies the causal theory to the practice situation. In the assessment phase, this means using the causal theory to gather relevant information and to formulate an assessment summary (an answer to the explanatory puzzle). For example, our interactionist theoretical model of women's choices in oppressive social situations could serve as an assessment framework directing workers to gather information about social/cultural factors influencing the relationship situation, face-to-face interaction factors, self and emotional psychological factors, and coping actions. In the intervention phase, this means using the causal theory to identify independent variables, causes that can be manipulated (changed in value) and to select an intervention that will increase or decrease the independent variable as needed to achieve the desired consequences (a reassembly of the puzzle pieces into a preferred pattern). Most hypotheses in our theory-testing study were supported. Possible worker actions following from the theory included changing social norms tolerating violence against women; enhancing the social status and relationship power of battered women; educating battered women about the dangers to emotional strength and esteem associated with persistently taking the partner's role perspective, and challenging male batterers to increase their ability and motivation to take their partner's role and experience her pain and sense of humiliation.

Evaluate the use of the causal theory

Committed to evidence-informed practice, the theorizing practitioner evaluates the effectiveness of the application of causal theory. Before the helping work, this could involve a careful review of the research and theoretical literature on the focal problem to determine the degree of empirical support for the causal theory and its theoretical claims about causal relationships. During the helping work, this should involve the use of single-subject practice evaluation procedures to judge the effectiveness of the intervention presumed to change the dependent variable(s), the target problem (s), and the responsiveness of the theory to the client's concerns (Moen & Coltrane, 2005). Has the helping process replaced the sense of puzzlement and uncertainty about the perplexing "person interacting in the environment" challenge with clarity about the causal forces and ways to take control of these forces? Did the new certainty and understanding enable the client to act in preferred ways? Was the client satisfied with the puzzle-solving processes and results? After the helping work, the theorizing practitioner might blend previous research literature on the theory and results from the evaluation of practice. By such critical reflections, a key knowledge accumulation question can be answered. Should the theory be confirmed as a trustworthy, relevant, and useful addition to the professional's personal practice model and even the profession's knowledge base; subjected to refinement or disconfirmed and replaced with a different causal theory?

Refine and adapt the theory for future use

Theorizing is never complete (Lynham, 2002). The theorizing practitioner makes use of the experience of applying the formal or substantive causal theory and critical reflection on this experience to refine, develop further, and adapt the theory. Future uses of the theory as a tool to figure out explanatory puzzles will then be more effective, efficient, and satisfying. Improvements might include adding more causal variables: operationalizing variables in more valid, reliable, and culturally sensitive ways; elaborating on the propositions linking causes and effects; identifying and specifying more fully and precisely the mechanisms or processes that occur between the initial cause and the focal effect; delineating the group memberships and conditions that moderate the relationships between independent and dependent variables; and planning how to share the causal theory with colleagues and others so that the knowledge is diffused through the relevant practice communities. The social workers' reflections on their experiences with causal theory construction, the implementation of practical theories, and the effects of theory use especially on vulnerable populations can be feedback improving the processes of assembling applied theories and generating new and needed theories (Walt, 2005).

Summarize and share the causal theory

A causal theory can be summarized in narrative form by paragraphs. For example, Peng (2009) conducted a literature review to summarize the major theories of the social causes of mental health disorders among racial and ethnic minority populations. These included social stress theory, social capital theory, eco-social theory, and the political economy of health theory. For the narrative, she provided a four-page summary of her integrative causal theory. The summary included an overview of the literature relating social capital to health, to strong communities, and to protection against stress in ethnic minority populations. The summary offered a statement of the definition of social capital (the resources and opportunities that come to people through mutually recognized relationships and membership within various groups and communities) and its major types (bonding social capital, bridging social capital, and linking social capital). Peng presented, too, a discussion of the major variables included in this integrative theoretical approach to mental health disorders: participation, reciprocity, trust, social norms, common resources, and pro-activity. She specified three pathways linking social capital to mental health problems. First, social capital influences the health behaviors of neighborhood residents by promoting the spread of health-related information and increasing the adoption of healthy behaviors. Second, socially cohesive communities facilitate the information spread among their members at much higher rates than non-cohesive communities. Third, access to services is greater in socially cohesive areas, increasing the likelihood that residents will form coalitions and create social organizations. Peng concluded with her major causal explanation: the low quality and quantity of "social capital bonding," (the relationships between families, friends, and individuals that provide a foundation of identity, belonging, mutual support, and understanding), among socially minority ethnic and racial populations are the major causal factors in explaining serious and persistent mental disorders. Unfortunately, Peng didn't include a diagram of her causal model.

A causal theory can also be summarized as a visual display. Figure 19.1, for example, depicts a research-generated cognitive-behavioral theory of the causes or "triggers" of relapse by substance abusers in a residential treatment program (Munson & Schmitt, 1996). This theory also identifies the cognitive processes, the covert behaviors, occurring in the typical causes-processes-responses sequence.

Recall the discussion in Lesson 17. The display summarizing a causal theory may be an inventory of causes—boxes for all the causes of hate crime—X1, X2, X3, X4, and so on at the top level with the effect, Y (verbal and physical assault) on the level below. Each X is connected to the Y by an arrow pointing downward, and each X-Y connection is the symbolization of a proposition (Fawcett & Downs, 1986). Or a causal theory can be displayed as a causal diagram, a visual display of the elements of a theory with each independent

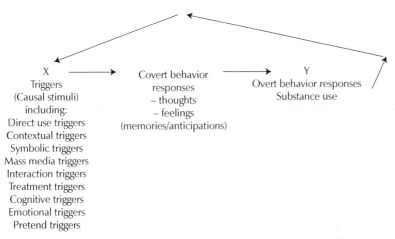

Figure 19.1 A behavioral theory of causes of substance abuse (based on Munson and Schmitt, 1996)

variable–dependent variable proposition layered on top of the other. Arrows connect the variables for each proposition, and signs indicate whether increases in the independent variable result in increases (+ for positive relationship) or decreases in the dependent variable (– for negative or inverse relationships). Typically, moderating or conditioning variables, variables that change the influence of the cause on the effect, like the educational level or age group of the participants, would be included in the diagram too.

Evidence and verification

There is no perfect or total causal theory. Theoretical explanations are always limited, and questions about the rigor of the method used to arrive at a causal explanation are common. Causal theories and their claims can be judged by their logic, evidence, and alignment with social work values (McCarty, 2008).

Criteria for establishing causality

To confirm a causal theory about some aspect of human behavior and the environment, we need to show that our explanation meets the criteria for causality (Shoemaker, Tankard, & Lasorsa, 2004).

First, the theorist must demonstrate prior temporal order. The presumed cause is associated with and must occur prior to the presumed effect. Changes in community attitudes assumed to induce violent acts must have happened in the time order before the increases in violence. Theorists look for the common factor that occurs before every instance of the effect. This search is also called the *method of agreement*.

Second, the theorist must demonstrate statistical co-variation. When the values of one variable increase or decrease (a cause of hate crime, for example), the values of the other variable change (rates of assaults go up or down). In the lingo of causal science, this is sometimes referred to as the method of *concomitant variations* (Argyris, 1996).

Third, the theorist must demonstrate that spurious or false explanations have been ruled out. This is very difficult and requires proof that no alternative explanation more plausibly explains the causal relationship between the independent variables and dependent variables. A theorist points out that the community properly identified X1, X2, and X3 as causes for a rash of acts of social disorder (all causes focused on stereotypical patterns assigned to Mexican-American residents), but a critic claims that this theory ignored a commonly alleged and powerful cause, X4, the shooting by a Caucasian police officer of an unarmed member of the minority group. The claims buttressing a causal theory and reducing concerns about spurious relationships may be supported by the *method of difference*. When a given factor is assumed to play a causal role, the theorist arranges to take away that factor, holding everything else constant, and to see whether the effect still occurs. Let's shift to a new example. One group receives the experimental drug, the other group—a control designed to be identical to the first group—receives the placebo. If the healing effect doesn't occur for the control group but occurs for the experimental group, the causal claim is supported.

Finally, the theorist developing a causal theory attempts to identify the mechanism or process explaining the correlation between alleged cause and effect (Ben-Ari, 2005). For instance, evidence of changes in lung tissues (the mechanism) caused by the carcinogenic agents in cigarettes solidified the causal argument that cigarettes cause health problems.

Learning activities with reflections

1 Let's practice theorizing in a causal way. In 2009, the Southern Poverty Law Center (2010) documented an increase in the number of hate crimes and an increase in the recruitment of members by hate groups. An excellent movie, *American History X*, depicted the organization of "skinhead" groups in Southern California in the early 1990s. The skinheads attacked viciously anyone in the different ethnic group, Mexican-Americans, and the illegal Mexican workers in a local grocery store.

Here's the scenario for your consideration. In a small town 40 miles north of my social work department, there has been an increase in verbal and physical assaults over the last six months. The victims are typically migrant Mexican workers employed by the large local farm businesses. Pretend that you work at the town's community center. This agency has convened a task force of agency workers, neighborhood residents, representatives of the migrant community, and others to assess the situation and identify likely causes of the spike in hate crime.

Imagine, too, that you have been a careful and longtime observer of social processes and member interaction in the town (optionally, you might do this activity with some other students). Offer a causal explanation of the changes in the hate crime rate. Identify the three or more causal concepts that help you explain this phenomenon. Attempt to provide a good definition of each of your concepts. Develop two or more propositions using these theoretical concepts. Comment on how these propositions are related.

To develop your causal theory, you might use a person-in-environment perspective. For example, you could focus on how community factors and processes contribute to such acts of violence. Or you might explain how small social groups create conditions supportive of hate crime. Or you might identify personality and self-concept characteristics associated with assaults on Mexican-Americans. If you are ambitious, you could draw concepts from environmental, transaction, and personal levels.

2   Use a human development perspective. Theorize about how development processes, experiences, and contexts are relevant to understanding the causes of hateful violent behavior. Use the knowledge of racism, discrimination, stereotypes, prejudice, and inter-group conflict acquired in your human behavior and diversity courses to identify relevant concepts.

3   Reflect on the practice implications of your theory. Based on your analysis of the major PIE or development causes of hate crime against Mexican workers, what should the community do to change this pattern? Reflect on how you might transform your concepts into variable and your propositions into hypotheses and design a study to test your causal theory.

4   Consider the causal theory about hate crime that you created or focus on any familiar causal theory (theories about the relationship of cigarettes to cancer, vaccines to autism, human activity to climate change, and so on). Specify clearly the causes and effect(s). Imagine that you are arguing with a skeptic about the causal theory. How would you prove that the alleged causal factors do cause change in the dependent variable? What arguments would you use? What evidence would you supply, and how much evidence would be necessary? What specific challenges to your claims about causation would you anticipate, and how might you respond to these challenges?

5   Take a life course perspective on young adulthood. Stress and depression may be related to mental health and health risks for young adults. Review your life experience, theoretical knowledge, and research knowledge about this life stage. What are some of the possible causes of the widespread experience of stress and depression during the transition to adulthood? Identify several particular hazards that many young adults face. Identify

particular vulnerabilities that may increase the impact of these hazards on particular young adults. Develop a causal theory relating the ideas of developmental stage, hazard, vulnerability, and developmental problems (chronic stress or depression) experienced by young adults. Show how your theory plausibly meets the criteria for causality. Starting with this causal theory, what coping strategies might a social worker recommend to a young adult client seeking help for severe depression?

References

Argyris, C. (1996). Actionable knowledge: Design causality in the service of consequentialist theory. *The Journal of Applied Behavioral Science, 32*(4), 390–406.

Bell, D. C. (2009). *Constructing social theory.* Lanham, MD: Rowman and Littlefield.

Ben-Ari, M. (2005). *Just a theory: Explaining the nature of science.* Amherst, NY: Prometheus.

Bloom, M. (1975). *The paradox of helping: Introduction to the philosophy of scientific practice.* New York: Wiley.

Clemons, R. S., & McBeth, M. K. (2001). *Public policy praxis theory and pragmatism: A case approach.* Upper Saddle River, NJ: Prentice-Hall.

Fawcett, J., & Downs, F. S. (1986). *The relationship of theory and research.* Norwalk, CT: Appleton-Century-Crofts.

Forte, J.A., Franks, D.D., Forte, J., & Rigsby, D. (1996). Oppressive social situations and asymmetrical role-taking: Comparing battered and non-battered women. *Social Work, 41*(1), 59–73.

Jaccard, J. & Jacoby, J. (2010). *Theory construction and model-building skills.* New York: The Guilford Press.

Linder, S. H., & Peters, B. G. (1984). From social theory to policy design. *Journal of Public Policy, 4*(3), 237–259.

Lynham, S. A. (2002). The general method of theory-building research in applied disciplines. *Advances in Developing Human Resources, 4*(3), 221–241.

McCarty, D. (2008). The impact of public housing policy on family social work theory and practice. *Journal of Family Social Work, 11*(1), 74–88.

Moen, P., & Coltrane, S. (2005). Families, theories, and social policy. In V. L. Bengston, A. C. Acock, K. R. Allen, P. Dilworth-Anderson & D. M. Klein (Eds), *Sourcebook of family theory and research* (pp. 543–565). Thousand Oaks: Sage.

Munson, M. A., & Schmitt, R. L. (1996). Triggering and interpreting past drug-related frames: An insider's view of a treatment modality at an adolescent drug treatment facility. In N. K. Denzin (Ed.), *Studies in symbolic interaction* (Vol. 20, pp. 39–72). Greenwich, CT: JAI Press.

Peng, C. J. (2009). Sociological theories relating to mental disabilities in racial and ethnic minority populations. *Journal of Human Behavior in the Social Environment, 19*(1), 85–98.

Shoemaker, P. J., Tankard, J. W., Jr., & Lasorsa, D. L. (2004). *How to build social science theories.* Thousand Oaks, CA: Sage.

Southern Poverty Law Center (2010). SPLC's intelligence report: Hate group numbers rise again. Retrieved August 2, 2010, from www.splcenter.org/blog/2009/02/28/intelligence-report-hate-group-numbers-rise-again

Walt. S. M. (2005). The relationship between theory and policy in international relations. *Annual Review of Political Science, 8*, 23–48.

<table>
<tr><td>LESSON

20</td><td># Construct a middle range theory about processes or themes</td></tr>
</table>

(EPAS 2.1.7 Apply Knowledge;
EPAS 2.1.10 Engage, Assess, Intervene, Evaluate)

Let's shift from causal theorizing to the interpretive theorizing. Grounded theorizing is the major approach to constructing interpretive theorizing and one used quite commonly by social work theorizers and researchers. Like causal theories, grounded theories focus on the middle-range level of abstraction. However, advocates of grounded theory use the term "middle-range theory" with qualification. They want to differentiate their approach from positivist middle-range theorizing. Because grounded theorizers endorse assumptions about reality, science, and theorizing methodology unlike those of causal theorizers—assumptions not yet fully explained in this book—this lesson will take more time and space to review the theory construction basics than Lesson 19 on constructing causal theories. However, the same organizational structure will be used.

Nature of puzzles and theorizing purposes

Interpretive grounded theories help practitioners and their clients assemble "sense-making" puzzles related to the meaning of uncertain and ambiguous situations by deciphering the symbols and the interaction common to these situations. They develop answers to a question such as what is the meaning of an action or set of actions as experienced by the actors in the particular historical and ecological context (Forte, 2008)? For example, a military social worker might use a grounded approach to interpret a series of similar and puzzling acts of suicide by soldiers on and near a military base. Grounded theory can also be used to answer practice evaluation questions such as what particular experiences during the helping process were significant to the clients, what were the clients' interpretations of the overall success of the helping work, and in what ways did the clients perceive the worker as effective and ineffective? Grounded theory can be especially useful in novel circumstances where existing theories have failed to determine the puzzle pattern, relevant theories are incomplete, the applicable theories lack empirical support, or common sense indicates that available theories don't fit well to the "person interacting in an environment" configuration (Eisenhardt, 1989).

The symbolic interactionist theoretical tradition is the foundation for grounded theorizing. Like interactionist theorizing, grounded theorizing focuses on understanding meanings, subjective experiences, social processes, and socially constructed realities. Grounded theories offer interpretive explanations, detailed or thick summaries of the meanings that a situation's stakeholders assign to self and the events, people, and objects in the particular social situation. Such explanations of how people assign meanings to challenges in real-world contexts can increase practitioners' confidence in their ability to help clients address their concerns (Simmons & Gregory, 2003). Grounded theories also develop process explanations, detailed summaries of action or interaction sequences as they change over time. Temporal changes may be characterized as steps, phases, stages, or turning points, the important moments in an individual or social process (Dey, 1999). Less commonly, grounded theories offer causal explanations although the terminology used differs from positivist theorists. Strauss and Corbin (1990), for example, suggest that grounded theory can be used to build a theoretical interpretation of specific phenomena including the core conditions (called *causes* in the positivist approach), the expression through action and interaction of the influence of these conditions, and the consequences of these conditions.

Elements and definition of interpretive theory

Interpretive theoretical explanations are like stories. An interpretive story is typically a descriptive narrative about a group of people making sense of a situation (Strauss & Corbin, 1990). The story line is the abstract conceptualization of the lived story, the core concepts or category identified by the theorist. Strauss and Corbin compare the core category to the sun. They suggest that interpretive storytellers use propositions to characterize the relation of the planets (the additional categories) to the sun (the central category). Grounded theory involves the continually shifting back and forth between theorist and researcher roles, so I will use the term *theorizer/ researcher* in this lesson. A grounded interpretive theory includes the following elements (Corbin & Strauss, 1990).

Meanings

Interpretive theorizing requires the theorizer/researcher to immerse her- or himself in the lives of group members. Such immersion helps the social worker grasp the interpretations that the members create and use to represent their experiences and environments (Strauss & Corbin, 1994).

Concepts

Concepts are the basic units of analysis in an interpretive theory. The theorizer/researcher examines data and assigns a name to similar phenomena. Grounded theorists prefer the term *sensitizing* concept to *operational* concept. A sensitizing concept provides a meaningful and vivid picture of people in the situation as the situation is seen and heard from their perspective (Glaser & Strauss, 1967). The focus is on qualitative perceptions, not quantitative orderings. Recall the lesson on concepts and discussion of the qualitative approach to their use. Bowen (2006) exemplified this approach. He studied a community-based antipoverty project in Jamaica, and his theorizing/ research work generated sensitizing concepts such as community/citizen participation, social capital, and empowerment.

Categories

A category involves theorizing at a higher level of abstraction than conceptualization. The theorizer/researcher organizes concepts into groups based on perceived similarities. Each group or category has certain properties. For example, the grounded theory might specify "perceptions of relationship loss" as category and identify the varied "rationales for the loss" as a property of the category. The grounded theorist might characterize the category by its dimensions. For example, a theory of the experiences of hospital patients might generate the category machine-body connection (Strauss, 1987). This category has the dimensions: connections external to the skin and connections internal to the skin. The internal connections category has sub-dimensions such as discomfort, hurt, fear, and safety.

Propositions

A grounded theory includes a set of propositions. These are plausible statements of relationships between a category and its concepts and statements of relationships between different categories. For example, Pandit (1996) constructed a grounded theory of organizational recovery based on his examination of a large amount of archival data from two empirical cases of organizational turnaround. The theory identified concepts including management change, improved controls, decentralization, and restructuring finances. He grouped concepts into the core category— recovery strategy—and also identified some related process categories including management change, retrenchment, stabilization, and growth stages. He reported on varied theoretical propositions relating the core category and the process categories. For instance, the theory includes the proposition "recovery strategic actions vary in appropriateness according to organizational growth stage."

Definition of interpretive grounded theory

According to Strauss and Corbin (1990), a *grounded theory* is a theory

> that is inductively derived from the study of the phenomenon it represents. That is, it is discovered, developed and provisionally verified through systematic data collection and analysis of data pertaining to that phenomenon. Therefore, data collection, analysis, and theory stand in reciprocal relationship to one another. (p. 23)

The completed grounded theory emerges during the inductive reasoning of the theorizer and comprises the theorizer's interpretation of a core category, related categories, and the framework of propositions specifying these relationships (Strauss & Corbin, 1994).

The grounded theory may be substantive or formal (Dey, 1999). A *substantive interpretive theory* is the summary of a study of key aspects of a single case (person, group, organization, community) in one specific time and place. For example, a grounded theorist might study and theorize about the careers of the scientists working at the Los Alamos National Laboratory in 2013. Findings apply only to the specific context. A *formal interpretive theory* is a summary at a higher level of abstraction, a comparison across cases, studies, or theories resulting in an interpretive explanation that transcends the boundaries of time and place. For example, the grounded theorist might study and theorize about cases across French institutions and create a comprehensive theory of career commonalities derived from comparing those in the law, medicine, and science. These findings apply in various contexts.

Theorizing method

Interpretive theorizing differs from positivist theory construction projects that start with theorizers reviewing the theoretical blueprint and general propositions, deducting hypotheses, and testing specific manifestations of the propositions. The interpretive theorizer may be more like an artist than a homebuilder. She or he doesn't want to impose an architect's blueprint on the theorizing work. Instead, the interpretive theorizer considers all the available materials and inductively decides on the best, most coherent way to arrange all these "person interacting in an environment" materials in one structure

This different stance to theory construction reflects the holistic and naturalistic orientation of interpretive science (Forte, 2008, 2010). The interpretive philosophy of science dictates that the theorizer/researcher respect the nature of the empirical world and organize a methodological stance to reflect that respect. Because humans are distinctive in their symbol-creating and symbol-using capacities, theorizing about human life requires a methodology radically different from that used by the physical sciences (and positivistic theorizers). Interpretive theorizers/researchers prefer a naturalistic methodology; one that captures the qualities of lived experience: complexity, immediacy, symbolic richness, uniqueness, and wholeness. Naturalistic inquiry calls for the collection of naturally occurring data in naturally occurring situations for natural time spans.

Interpretive theorizing: basic tasks

As in Lesson 19, I have framed the basic theorizing tasks using the metaphorical comparison of theorizing to puzzle solving. However, for interpretive theorists, the pieces of the puzzles of life are never assembled into one final pattern. Life is continual change, so theoretical resolutions of life puzzles are only provisional products. As life patterns change, the theory must be revised.

Identify the interpretive puzzle

As indicated earlier, interpretive theorizers/researchers attempt to put aside a priori theoretical assumptions, expectations, hypotheses, and frameworks as they begin a theory construction process (Coady, 1995). The theorizer/ researcher begins at the ground level, the empirical particulars of the focal situation, not by imposing a template on the situation. Dey (1999) indicates that this doesn't mean that the theorizer/researcher is oblivious to previous and relevant theory and research. The theorizer/researcher strives to achieve an open mind, not an empty head.

For social work, grounded theorizing might begin with the recognition that the voices, viewpoints, visions, and versions of participants in a social situation or the helping situation have been ignored or obscured. Effective progress at detecting the patterns of explanatory puzzles or intervention puzzles necessitates stepping back, immersing oneself in the lives of these participants, and working toward "verstehen," the empathic understanding of members' salient meanings and culture.

Develop the elements of interpretive theory

Interpretive theorizers follow an identifiable sequence in developing the concepts, categories, and propositions of the ground theory. The terminology may seem odd, so I encourage interested theorizing practitioners to study further by reading some of the books on grounded theory identified in the reference list.

Briefly, this sequence involves collecting data often from multiple sources and using a range of data gathering strategies including interviews, observations, questionnaires, and analysis of existing data. The theorizer/ researcher quickly takes copious notes to record impressions including those about the research process and theoretical ideas. He or she initiates theoretical sampling, the choice of additional incidents, episodes, or cases that illuminate emerging concepts or clarify the relationships between categories of the developing theory (Glaser & Strauss, 1967).

Concurrently, the theorizer/researcher begins coding: transforming interpretations of observed events, actions, and interactions into theoretical concepts and categories. *Open coding* involves asking many questions related to the what, where, how, when, and how much features of the situation; labeling and categorizing the data produced by this process of questioning; and comparing constantly the emerging theoretical patterns or themes to the data to improve the categorization work. *Axial coding* involves making connections between a category and its sub-categories. It may use Strauss's scheme—phenomenon, conditions, actions and interactions, and consequences—for relating the categories. The inferred relationships are tested against the data. *Selective coding* involves the theorizing work of uniting all the categories around a core category, the main analytic idea of the theory. Categories needing further specification are filled with additional descriptive detail.

The theorizer/researcher continually refines the theory until achieving a point of theoretical saturation or sufficiency; there will be minimal new learning and diminishing returns if analysis is continued (Glaser & Strauss, 1967). She or he uses theoretical memos, notes written while coding to capture ideas about categories and their relationships. She or he engages in more continual comparison of data and emerging theory to improve the fit of the theory to data. He or she also deals with deviant cases, observations and other exceptions that don't fit neatly with the theoretical category system. Finally, the theorizer/researcher begins to write the grounded theory report.

Transform the interpretive theory's elements into operational form

In this phase of theory construction, the theorizer/researcher explicitly communicates how the theory elements have been translated into observable and confirmable elements (Lynham, 2002), and, ideally, how to use the theory to guide assessment formulation and intervention planning. According to Strauss and Corbin (1990), interpretive theory is grounded empirically (operationalized in the positivistic language) when the theorizer/researcher has specified each concept and its indicators (not as definitive concepts with fixed and specified measurement procedures but as sensitizing concepts), identified and described the categories, described the relationships between concepts and categories and categories and other categories, indicated likely variations in the relations, and provided a detailed description of conditions under which variations by people or circumstances will be found. Grounded theorizing is an iterative process. This means that through the entire theory constructing process, the theory/researcher is relating data to theory and theory to data and confirming continuously the quality of the emerging theory.

Apply the interpretive theory

Grounded interpretive theories can increase our practical understanding of client's life situations and our ability to guide the processes in these situations (Glaser & Strauss, 1967). In relation to understanding for assessment purposes, for instance, interpretive theorizing can characterize the particularities of the challenging and perplexing experience of client groups such as those related to initial participation in a feminist social movement, chronic illness, pregnancy, the aging process, and collaboration between social workers and physicians. Riessman (1994) and Sherman and Reid (1994) have edited collections of grounded theories useful for assessment.

Grounded interpretive theories can also guide the practitioner's intervention planning. For example, grounded theories incorporating axial coding identify a range of conditions leading to certain consequences or outcomes. The practitioner might use such theories to figure out which conditions are most influential and to identify strategies for changing these conditions. Simmons and Gregory (2003) have developed a grounded action approach that uses interpretive theorizing in particular helping circumstances to construct an explanatory theory of the practical problem and an operational theory for planning and implementing an intervention. In their study of and theorizing about anger management issues addressed by the social services agency, they identified core explanatory categories related to power and respect issues and an operational theory directing work with clients by focusing on increasing knowledge and skills useful in dealing with these power and respect issues. As a general strategy, social workers might search and find a grounded theory relevant to the helping circumstances, identify the grounded theory generated propositions, adjust these propositions to fit the new helping situation, derive intervention hypotheses, try out, and test the interventions derived from these hypotheses.

Evaluate the use of the interpretive theory

The founders of grounded theory, Glaser and Strauss (1967), recommend a variety of questions for guiding efforts to evaluate the quality of a particular interpretive grounded theory. Some deal with the quality of the theorizing process. Was the theory generated in a credible way from the observations recorded in the field notes, records of contacts, and transcripts of interviews with informants? Were the theory-constructing decisions sensible in light of the theoretical memos? How sound were the theorizing logic, inferences, and arguments employed by the theorizer to go from data to concepts to categories to propositions to final theory?

Many evaluative questions deal with the usefulness of the interpretive theory? Does it serve as a good guide to understanding the situation and directing helping action (Glaser & Strauss, 1967)? Is it relevant to the needs of the practitioner and the client system? Does it make sense? Does the theory offer sensitizing concepts that can direct inquiry in helping settings and realistic recommendations for helping action? Can it be modified for use in diverse helping situations?

Eisenhardt (1989) also recommended "enfolding the literature" as part of the theory evaluation process. How does this interpretive theory compare to the existing literature (interpretive theories on the same group, challenge, or situation)? What is contradictory and why? The theorizer might think critically during this comparison and conceive of ways to correct and improve the definitions of concepts, the description or categories, and the overall framework of propositions. What is similar across grounded studies? If there are many similar theoretical conclusions, the comparison can be used to identify ways that the theory's generalizability can be extended.

Refine and adapt the theory for future use

In interpretive theorizing, there are several options for *theory elaboration*, "the process of refining a theory, model, or concept in order to specify more carefully the circumstances in which it does or does not offer potential for explanation" (Vaughn, 1992, p. 175). For example, Chenitz and Swanson (1986) recommended a theory elaboration project for nurses and other professionals working with addicts. Theorizers could explore in grounded ways the specific intervention processes used in a particular agency or institution and identify, describe, and analyze the elements of these specific intervention processes. They described the helping processes central to one methadone clinic: dispensing, distributing, attending, monitoring, evaluating, protecting, and dispatching. Then, they recommended that the theorizer use comparative analysis to identify the intervention processes in similar situations (mental health centers, day treatment programs, in-patient psychiatric units). Based on such constant comparisons, the theorizers could develop a broad theory of psychiatric helping processes, processes common across the range of helping settings.

Summarize and share the interpretive theory

Interpretive grounded theory may be summarized in narrative form or by a visual display. A grounded theory can be represented as a story with concepts, categories, and propositions organized in inductive form, interspersed with quotations from participants, supplemented by an addendum with the evidence supporting the theoretical claims about the connections between empirical data and the grounded theory

An interpretive theory might also be summarized with a visual representation. This may be a process diagram or a flow chart indicating chains of action or temporal sequences (Strauss & Corbin, 1990). For example, Figure 20.1 shows a process model of socialization to the volunteer

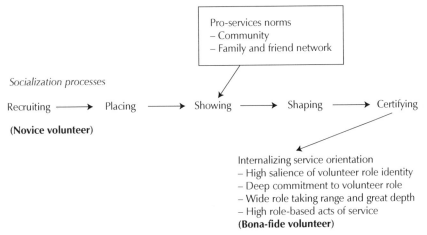

Figure 20.1 A process model of socialization to the volunteer role

role that my colleagues and I used to guide a class on service to the homeless (Forte, 1997; Piliavin & Callero, 1991). Using the process model, we organized the class and socialization processes into six distinct phases.

Interpretive theorizers might use a variety of visual tools—boxes and arrows, summary tables, or network diagrams—to illustrate the grounded theory's categories and/or the relationships between these categories. For instance, Karp (1996) did extensive participatory research interpreting the experiences of chronically depressed persons participating in mutual aid groups in the Boston area. Figure 20.2 illustrates the core category, interpretive dilemmas, that emerged in his grounded theory of the "interpretation of depression" and the four sub-categories of interpretive dilemmas: the meaning of the physical, emotional, and psychological aspects of depressive experiences; the meaning of responsibility for the condition; the meaning of alternative treatments, and the meaning assigned to experts.

Evidence and validation

Interpretive theorizers use a language for judging evidence about an interpretive grounded theory quite different from the language of positivist theorists. However, grounded theory experts have provided some useful translations of the positivist terms (Dey, 1999; Diaz Andrade 2009; Lee, Mishna, & Brennenstuhl (2010).

Instead of *construct validity*, the specification of the correct operational measures for concepts and the testing of these measures, interpretive theorizers refer to the authenticity of the concepts, their fidelity to the meanings held by the participants in the situation. The proper and extensive analysis of data increases this authenticity. Interpretive theorizers are also

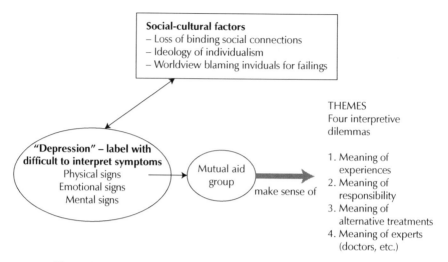

Figure 20.2   Interactionist theory of depression and mutual aid (key themes)

concerned with the confirmability of concepts, the ability to show a logical and reasonable link between the data and the theoretical concepts. Careful observation and categorization processes and detailed note taking increases confidence in the theoretical concepts.

Instead of *internal validity*, the truthfulness of inferences about cause-effect relationships, interpretive theorizers seek consistency; the parts of the emergent theory fit with one another and explain the data well. Careful and explicit coding increases consistency. In relation to this criterion, interpretive theorizers also value credibility; the theoretical conclusions seem believable to the people studied. Continual and critical reflection on data gathering, coding, and analysis increases a theory's credibility.

External validity is the ability to generalize findings to other groups, times, and places. Interpretive theorizers refer, instead, to transferability. Much grounded theorizing is idiographic and focused on the in-depth examination of one case. Therefore, claims to generalization beyond the studied situation aren't made. In formal interpretive theorizing, the comparison of multiple cases, the social work theorizer may be able to demonstrate that the theory can be transferred to understand similar people in similar situations facing similar challenges.

Instead of *replication*, the ability to demonstrate that the study procedures can be repeated with similar results, interpretive theorizers use terms such as dependability or trustworthy. These terms means that there is a chain of evidence and a paper trail documenting the theorizing work from beginning to end. Data are described vividly and with the careful use of quotations. Procedures are explained fully and clearly, and there are detailed reports on the emergence of key theoretical ideas. The processes of inductive reasoning and the logical derivation of conclusions from data are documented carefully. Because the researcher becomes part of the researched situation and because situations constantly change, exact replication isn't possible. However, advocates of a grounded theory should be able to show that the method was used in a dependable and trustworthy way.

Learning activities with reflections

1   When might interpretive theorizing be useful to a social work practitioner? Identify several sub-cultural groups or communities that you might need to better and more deeply understand by reading grounded theory reports on their meaning systems. Identify several social processes or action sequences that might be illuminated well by grounded theory. Finally, identify some social systems or some aspect of human behavior or human development that are very complex and might be helpfully broken by grounded theorizing into major types. Specify how you might locate and use grounded theories relevant to your topics of interest.

2   Find a grounded theory study relevant to social work. For example, pick one from a reader of grounded theories such as those listed in the commentary. Review my discussion of the basic tasks of interpretive theorizing. Attempt to pinpoint in the study how the theorizer/ researcher completed each task. Note tasks that aren't discussed fully. Use some of the criteria for appraising a grounded theory discussed in this lesson. What is your overall appraisal of the quality of the study and the reported theory? Elaborate on how you would use the grounded theory to inform your assessment work or intervention planning.

3   Reflect on two or three ways that you could use interpretive grounded theorizing to help judge your effectiveness with a particular client group and the clients' satisfaction with services. Specify in detail how you would organize a research project and construct a theory of effectiveness and a theory of satisfaction grounded in the perceptions, feelings, thoughts, and experiences of your clients.

4   Compare and contrast two approaches to theory construction: the positivist causal approach and the interpretive grounded approach. What are the strengths and limitations of each? In what specific circumstances would you make use of a report on a causal theory? In what specific circumstances, would you make use of a report on a interpretive theory?

References

Bowen, G. A. (2006). Grounded theory and sensitizing concepts. *International Journal of Qualitative Methods*, 5(3), Article 2. Retrieved June 17, 2013, from www.ualberta.ca/~iiqm/backissues/5_3/pdf/bowen.pdf

Chenitz, W. C., & Swanson, J. M. (1986). Surfacing nursing process: A method for generating nursing theory from practice. In W. C. Chenitz & J. M. Swanson (Eds),

From practice to grounded theory: Qualitative research in nursing (pp. 24–38). Menlo Park, CA: Addison-Wesley.

Coady, N. (1995). A reflective/inductive model of practice: Emphasizing theory-building for unique cases versus applying theory to practice. In G. Rogers (Ed.), *Social work field education: Views and visions* (pp. 139–150). Dubuque, IA: Kendall/Hunt.

Corbin, J., & Strauss, A. (1990). Grounded theory research: Procedures, canons, and evaluative criteria. *Qualitative Sociology, 13*, 3–21.

Dey, I. (1999). *Grounding grounded theory: Guidelines for qualitative inquiry.* San Diego: Academic Press.

Diaz Andrade, A. (2009). Interpretive research aiming at theory building: Adopting and adapting the case study design. *The Qualitative Report, 14*(1), 42–60.

Eisenhardt, K. M. (1989). Building theories from case study research. *The Academy of Management Review, 14*(4), 532–550.

Forte, J. A. (1997). Calling students to serve the homeless: A project to promote altruism and community service. *Journal of Social Work Education, 33*(1), 151–166.

Forte, J. A. (2008). Symbolic interactionism: Artful inquiry. *Patient Education and Counseling, 73*(2), 173–174.

Forte, J. A. (2010), Symbolic interactionism, naturalistic inquiry, and education. In P. Peterson, E. Baker, & B. McGaw, (Eds), *International encyclopedia of education* (Vol. 6, pp. 481– 487). Oxford: Elsevier.

Glaser, B., & Strauss, A. (1967). *The discovery of grounded theory: Strategies of qualitative research.* Chicago: Aldine.

Karp, D. A. (1996). *Speaking of sadness: Depression, disconnection, and the meanings of illness.* New York: Oxford University Press.

Lee, E., Mishna, F., & Brennenstuhl, S. (2010). How to critically evaluate case studies in social work. *Research on Social Work Practice, 20*(6), 682–689.

Lynham, S. A. (2002). The general method of theory-building research in applied disciplines. *Advances in Developing Human Resources, 4*(3), 221–241.

Pandit, N. R. (1996). The creation of theory: A recent application of the grounded theory method. *The Qualitative Report, 2*(4), 1–15 Retrieved June 6, 2013, from www.nova.edu/ssss/QR/QR2-4/pandit.html

Piliavin, J.A., & Callero, P.L. (1991). *Giving blood: The development of altruistic identity.* Baltimore, MD: Johns Hopkins University Press.

Riessman, C. K. (Ed.). (1994). *Qualitative studies in social work research.* Thousand Oaks, CA: Sage.

Sherman, E., & Reid, W. (Eds). (1994). *Qualitative research in social work.* New York: Columbia University Press.

Simmons, O. E., & Gregory, T. A. (2003). Grounded action: Achieving optimal and sustainable change. *Forum: Qualitative Social Research, 4*(3), 1–17. Retrieved June 6, 2013, from www.qualitative-research.net/index.php/fqs/article/viewArticle/677/1464

Strauss, A. (1987). *Qualitative analysis for social scientists.* Cambridge: Cambridge University Press.

Strauss, A., & Corbin, J. (1990). *Basics of qualitative research: Grounded theory procedures and techniques.* London: Sage.

Strauss, A., & Corbin, J. (1994). Grounded theory methodology: An overview. In N. K. Denzin (Ed.), *Handbook of qualitative research* (pp. 273–285). London: Sage.

Vaughn, D. (1992). Theory elaboration: The heuristic of case analysis. In C. C. Ragin & H. S. Becker (Eds), *What is a case: Exploring the foundations of social inquiry* (pp. 173–202). Cambridge, UK: Cambridge University Press.

Translate and speak theory with clients and colleagues

(EPAS 2.1.1 Identify as a Professional Social Worker;
EPAS 2.1.3 Apply Critical Thinking;
EPAS 2.1.7 Apply Knowledge)

Social workers can attempt to dissolve the boundaries that separate theorists, researchers, and practitioners. Optimally, the construction and use of theories of the middle range can do so and affirm the best in theory, research, and practice. Lynham (2002) summarizes this position. She applauds practitioners appreciative of

> the virtuous, systematic nature of interaction among three elements critical to applied theory building, namely, the development and accumulation of a system of coherent, disciplined, and rigorous knowledge and explanation (theory); the conduct of focused and disciplined scholarly inquiry (research): and the resulting informed and improved action that ensues from the application of the outcomes of the first two elements in practice. (p. 228)

In our discussion of the tasks related to constructing causal (Lesson 19) and interpretive theories (Lesson 20), we have recommended practical theorizing enriched by the interplay of existing theory, research (especially practice evaluation), and practice wisdom. Practitioners can also promote this virtuous cycle when they translate their practical theories, talk about them with clients and colleagues, and share in verbal or written communication pilot projects of theory deconstruction, reconstruction, or construction.

Scientific theory as a language

Theorizing is an essential part of scientific inquiry. From the semiotic and discursive perspectives, science is a complex system of signs (indices, icons, and symbols that stand for or represent something material or conceptual), and scientists use many different signs, modalities, and channels when talking and doing science (Sarukkai 2002). Scientists record their progress and communicate with one another by using complex symbol systems including some words and phrases from Standard English but many from technical vocabularies. For example, cybernetics, niche, deoxyribonucleic acid, schemas, catharsis, unconditioned stimulus, sociality, salience hierarchy, externalities, and praxis are theoretical concepts. The dictionary meanings of these concepts may evade you at this point in your career. Applied scientists, psychodynamic practitioners, for example, link concepts together into complex theoretical sentences such as "maintaining a position of aesthetic distance during the working though of the emotional response cycle is associated with adaptive grief management" (Forte, 2006). Beginning social workers find such sentences hard to understand.

Besides symbols, scientists use many other signs including concrete objects, images, gestures, diagrams, and mathematical formulas to represent aspects of human behavior and the environment. You may have encountered some mathematical formulas in a statistics class. Scientific theorizers also use various modalities (written, oral, action, and combined modalities) and many communication channels (blackboards, computers, face-to-face interaction, overhead projectors, audio conferences, reports, and textbooks) to make sense collectively of reality and to communicate about their preferred theories, their research studies, their use of theory to guide helping processes, and empirical findings about effectiveness.

The theory-fluent and literate social worker

Language mastery is one way to think of professional socialization (Forte, 2001). The expert social worker can "do" social work but he or she is also able to "talk" and "write" social work. She or he can participate intelligently and articulately in scientific conversations with colleagues, supervisors, and allies from related professions. This fluent social worker has an extensive professional vocabulary and can organize theoretical concepts into well-ordered and clear sentences. Hr or she can "speak the language of theory" during case conferences, supervisory meetings, consultations with experts, orientation meetings for new clients, and so on. This fluent theory user can define theoretical concepts, explicate the theoretical propositions explaining a client problem, state the theoretical assumptions and principles guiding the selection of an intervention, and communicate the ingredients of and justification for a preferred practical theory. The expert social worker is also literate. She or he can read the theoretical literature including books, articles, and essays. She or he can write about theory, theorizing, theorizing skills, and theory use. She or he has attained a degree of visual literacy, too, and can read and understand many kinds of theoretical displays. Process recordings, case notes and reports, workshop proposals and presentations, articles, and books are vehicles for sharing her theoretical experiments and insights with others in a fluent and literate way.

Scientific and practice communities as multi-lingual

Science is a pluralistic language community. Distinctive groups and networks form with reference to discipline, profession, theoretical allegiance, role (researcher, theorist, practitioner, clients or consumers), and work project (Sarukkai, 2002). There are many different communities of discourse; each like a distinctive foreign society with its own language. Each community develops a unique vocabulary (a shared set of concepts), rules of grammar, pronunciation, and habits of communication. Referring to scientific specialties, Morris (1946) summarized this notion:

> Each science expresses its results in a terminology and system of laws largely unrelated to the terminology and laws of the other sciences. Continuous collaboration among members of an interpretive network results in an order and communication predictability. This facilitates within group interaction but differentiates the network from others. (p. 509)

Becker and Geer (1973) added to this line of inquiry with their studies on professional subgroups. They discovered that every professional group develops a distinctive culture, "a somewhat different set of common understandings around which action is organized, and these differences will find expression in a language whose nuances are peculiar to that group and fully understood only by its members" (Becker & Geer, 1973). They posited about group members, "we can't assume that we understand precisely what another person, speaking as a member of such a group, means by any particular word."

The process of contemporary professional socialization, then, is especially complex and demanding. Competent social workers must master multiple languages: the common language of social work practice, the theoretical languages used in their agency settings and their practice specializations, the theoretical languages of frequent collaborators from allied professions and disciplines, and the language of scientific research

Early in a career, it should become easier for new practitioners to talk with other social workers about their theory-research-practice projects, but conversation may halt sometimes between collaborators from different professions. In my first social work job, for instance, I was an aide in a school for emotionally troubled and developmentally challenged youths. I faced a daunting language mastery challenge. The psychologist who trained us spoke the language of behavioral theory and referred often to the values of behavior modification and to behavioral studies. The part-time therapist was conversant in psychoanalytic theory and advised us about psychic conflicts and ego development. The classroom teachers socialized in the pedagogy of special education and talked of lesson plans, learning styles, and individualized education. The administrator lectured us on efficiency and cost-benefit ratios using business jargon. For a year, I had to listen very hard, study the school's diverse languages after work, and try to catch quickly my misunderstandings and speaking mistakes.

Language use not only differs by discipline, profession, and theoretical tradition but also by generation, specialization, and role (Zetterberg, 1962). A social worker trained in 2013 attempting to understand a description of a practice incident recounted by a colleague trained in the 1950s and using the psychodynamic language of that decade might have difficulty. Social workers in different areas of specialization (casework, community organizing, group work, and administration, for examples) also talk different languages, and this may lead to communication problems (Specht, 1977). Generalist social workers integrating theory, research, and practice roles must communicate, nevertheless, with theory specialists, research specialists, and practice specialists: each using an advanced version of their respective languages. Social workers and clients speak different languages. Social workers in the role of applied theorist must frequently translate their theoretical understandings from the technical vocabulary of scientific language into the common sense, everyday language of the client.

The value of mastery of theoretical languages

Watch two seasoned doctors talk to each other about a patient, or two experienced social workers exchange opinions about a social service case. They are able to communicate quickly and economically. They use theoretical concepts and technical abbreviations as a shorthand communication system (Cohen, 1980). They waste no words. The assumption of fluent use of a common theoretical language saves the speakers from restating elements of an entire theoretical tradition when referring to an aspect of that tradition (systems theory concepts or premises, for example) or to a theory-oriented research study. Their sentences are packed with information (Zetterberg, 1965). They don't need to divert energy or time to communication breakdowns but instead achieve a speedy consensus about the appropriate assessment or course of action). Their shared theoretical vocabulary allows a degree of precision not available with everyday English terms.

To summarize, the competent social worker must be theoretically fluent. Roberts (1990) asserts: "In justifying their actions, social workers are required to invoke theory of one kind or another" (p. 23). He or she works with a mixture of well-articulated theory (clearly and systematically described, tested knowledge) and practice wisdom (not fully articulated knowledge informed by imagination). This accomplished professional works consistently to make implicit theoretical ideas explicit and to transform unstated theories into words and sentences (McCutcheon, 1992).

Such translation work makes possible the examination and improvement of guiding theories using evidence-informed techniques. The translation work also increases awareness of theoretical assumptions or biases that might undermine effectiveness. Finally, the development of theoretical language and translation capabilities enables practitioners to communicate the concepts, propositions, theory clusters, and practical theories that guide their work in ways comprehensible to important others (clients, collaterals, colleagues, consultants, and supervisors).

Learning activities and reflections

Please put on your "ethnographer" hat. Ethnographers are social scientists who observe and report on the members of a cultural group, their symbols, and their patterns of interacting. Theory users often belong to "schools of thought," societies alien to novice social workers. Theory users are like members of a strange culture. Your job is to observe, listen to, and make sense of a teacher, a researcher, or practitioner who communicates using a theoretical language unfamiliar to you.

First, find a site for your ethnographic research, a place where you can safely observe and learn how an expert theory user communicates and interacts. For example, you might participate in an interdisciplinary team meeting at your field internship or a local agency. In a nursing home where one of my field interns was placed, there were weekly interdisciplinary meetings. Each meeting included the social work director, a nurse speaking a biomedical language, a nun talking in the language of the Catholic religious tradition, a psychologist committed to the cognitive-behavioral jargon, and a representative of the agency administration using economics and business terms. Other possible sites for your ethnographic inquiry include a courtroom, a place where social workers must understand the language of judges, lawyers, probation officers; a school, a setting where social workers learn to translate the talk of principals, teachers, and guidance counselors; or a team conference room where social workers versed in different theoretical languages—family systems, feminist, and ego psychological, for instance—converse and collaborate despite their communication differences.

Next, decide on what interaction at this field site you will sample. Pick a segment of the event where participants articulate, defend, or even argue about their respective theoretical positions. You might observe and take notes for an entire meeting. You could focus on one participant, a doctor, for instance, and record his or her conversation during a ten-minute discussion of a client's bio-psycho-social assessment. You might attend to a disagreement between two members of the field site using different theoretical perspectives and languages: the probation officer with a punitive legal frame of reference and the court-appointed special advocate with a humanistic, family-centered vocabulary.

Record accurately the conversation during the chosen sampling period. For this activity, focus on the verbal exchange rather than the nonverbal content. Use a statement-by-statement recording method. Underline the words, phrases, sentences, and paragraphs that you don't understand, especially those that seem based in the foreign theoretical language. Finally, attempt to translate or decode the meaning of this cultural exchange. You might bring your notes to the persons whom you observed and ask their help; or you could seek the help of a native informant, a cultural member with expertise as a user of the theoretical language. You could make use of a theory survey chapter with a glossary of theoretical terms. Perhaps, you could bring your report to a supervisor or professor who is fluent in multiple theoretical languages and enlist their services as a translator.

Summarize finally what you have learned about theory and language. For example, what difficulties related to cross-language communication did you observe? What were some of your impressions about "fluent" theory speakers? How might you plan to learn a language of an unfamiliar theoretical culture?

References

Becker, H. & Geer. B. (1973). Participant observation and interviewing: A comparison. *Human Organization, 16*, 28–32.

Cohen, B. P. (1980). *Developing sociological knowledge: Theory and method.* Englewood Cliffs, NJ: Prentice-Hall.

Forte, J.A. (2001). *Theories for practice: Symbolic interactionist translations.* Lanham, MD: University Press of America.

Forte, J. A. (2006). *Human behavior and the social environment: Models, metaphors, and maps for applying theoretical perspectives to practice.* Belmont, CA: Thomson Brooks/Cole.

Lynham, S. A. (2002). The general method of theory-building research in applied disciplines. *Advances in Developing Human Resources, 4*(3), 221–241.

McCutcheon, G. (1992). Facilitating teacher personal theorizing. In E. W. Ross, J. W. Cornett, & G. McCutheon (Eds), *Teacher personal theorizing: Connecting curriculum, practice, theory, and research* (pp. 191–205). Albany, NY: State University of New York Press.

Morris, C. (1946). The significance of the unity of science movement. *Philosophy and Phenomenological Research, 6*, 508–515.

Roberts, R. (1990). *Lessons from the past: Issues for social work theory.* London: Tavistock/ Routledge.

Sarukkai, S. (2002). *Translating the world: Science and language.* Lanham, MD: University Press of America.

Specht, H. (1977). Theory as a guide to practice. In H. Specht & A. Vickery (Eds), *Integrating social work methods* (pp. 28–35). London: George Allen & Unwin.

Zetterberg, H. I. (1962). *Social theory and social practice.* New York: The Bedminster Press.

Zetterberg, H. I. (1965). *On theory and verification in sociology* (3rd Edn). Totowa, NJ: Bedminster Press.

Critical thinking about theoretical knowledge using scientific, practical, and professional standards

Section 4 provides lessons related to the Council on Social Work Education critical thinking competency and to the theory application competency's practice behavior *"critique knowledge used to understand person and environment."* Lessons focus on topics such as critical thinking about theory; the appraisal of theory by scientific standards such as explanatory power, parsimony, and usefulness; and the appraisal of theory by social work standards such as ethics, diversity, and justice. In these lessons, we shift our attention from the deconstruction, reconstruction, and construction of explanatory and practice theories. Instead, the reader will learn how to engage in normative theorizing. A *normative theory* specifies a set of resources such as ethical standards and value convictions, useful when appraising the "goodness" of a theory and justifying the use of theories and their components. The social work profession has work to do in developing formal normative theories. However, there are a set of scientific norms, pragmatic standards, and social work conceptions of ideal theory and responsible practice that guide our normative thinking and theorizing about theory application issues such as the desirability of theory-specified goals, the proper implementation of theory-informed directives, the possible intended and unintended consequences of a theory's use, and the quality of evidence for theory-guided assessment and intervention alternatives. This section will focus on the critical appraisal of theoretical knowledge using these norms, standards, and conceptions.

LESSON	Think critically
22	about theory

(EPAS 2.1.3 Apply Critical Thinking;
EPAS 2.1.7 Apply Knowledge)

Theories vary in quality, and theories vary in their usefulness for particular social work tasks. Therefore, critical thinking is a necessary part of practical theorizing. Theorizing and critical thinking are like twins. Effective, scientific theorizing is a major part of the critical thinking expected of informed and engaged citizens (Schneider, 2006), and critical thinking makes possible judgments about the quality of a theory and its best applications followed by remedial actions (Oko, 2008). Gambrill (2006) makes the case for critical thinking about theories eloquently: "If we do not critically evaluate our theories (assumptions), they may function as prisons that limit our vision rather than as tools to discover what is false" .... " a theory believed too soon stifles further inquiry" (p. 154). Gitterman and Knight (2013) commenting on evidence-informed practice, assert, "While both theory and research findings about a broad range of variables are essential to social work practice, they are not sufficient. The application of theory and research to practice requires critical thinking" (p. 73).

Theorizing and critical thinking: definition and habits

Critical thinking is the "art of analyzing and evaluating thinking with a view to improving it" (Paul & Elder, 2009, p. 2). Critical thinkers use established standards and ask sharp questions when appraising the quality of theoretical claims, especially claims that are taken for granted by others (Gambrill, 2006). If we fail to think critically about theories and our theorizing activities, we are likely to apply knowledge that harms rather than helps our clients.

In relation to theory appraisal, critical thinkers need to develop certain habits. Social workers who are critical thinkers work hard to monitor and improve their awareness of the theories and theoretical ideas that influence their practice. They engage in self-reflection: appraising and questioning continuously their theoretical assumptions, guiding conceptions, and biases. They develop the predisposition to think in an open-minded way about specific case challenges with an awareness of their own preferred theoretical assumptions and the assumptions of the client. Critical social work thinkers refine inclinations to gather and weigh relevant theory-derived information, raise vital assessment questions, and formulate these questions and their answers precisely. Critical thinkers make a habit of seeking well-reasoned theory-guided conclusions about the client's problems and needs and checking these conclusions against relevant standards. Critical-thinking social workers use evidence to judge possible theory-guided intervention strategies and to select with client input the best and most suitable intervention.

Critical thinking, like theorizing, has social aspects and requires the cultivation of certain habits of interaction. The critical thinker cooperates and communicates with others in finding or generating sound theory-guided strategies of inquiry to understand complex bio-psycho-social challenges and empirically supported theory-based interventions to deal with these challenges. Thinking critically includes looking for evidence with colleagues and clients to support sound theories and to challenge dubious theories. Moreover, the social worker applies critical thinking standards during conversations and arguments about theory deconstruction, reconstruction, construction, and application.

Theorizing and critical thinking: core elements

Experts in critical thinking identify eight elements in the critical thinking process (Elder & Paul, 2007; Paul & Elder, 2009). These elements will be described in relationship to theory selection, use, and critique. First, the critical thinker generates a clear purpose for the particular use of knowledge. For example, the social worker might state, I intend to use theory A (Kohlberg's moral developmental theory) for a particular end (to understand and categorize the adolescent members of a rehabilitation group by moral decision making level) in particular circumstances (the community corrections agency and its combined group and individual counseling rehabilitation program). Lawrence Kohlberg created a very influential theory of moral development. Here is a brief summary of this knowledge. Moral reasoning capacities, the basis for ethical behavior, develop through six identifiable developmental stages, each more adequate for responding to moral dilemmas than the previous stage. Kohlberg argued that the process of moral development was principally concerned with justice and that people can continue to develop morally throughout their lifetime. The stages of moral development are obedience and punishment orientation (How can I avoid punishment?), self-interest orientation (What's in it for me?), interpersonal accord and conformity (How can I meet community expectations?), authority and social-order maintaining orientation (What are the relevant and compelling laws and rules?), social contract orientation (How can I reconcile different rights and values to do good for the general welfare?), and universal ethical principles (How can I use principles that transcend particular times and places as a guide for my conscience?). In this theory, progress in moral reasoning emerges sequentially and by the stages. Each stage-based achievement provides a new understanding, one more comprehensive than its predecessors but integrated with them, and the new understanding is necessary for moral growth. Under certain circumstances, the person may regress from a higher to an earlier stage. Kohlberg's ideas have stimulated many other theorists, researchers, developers of assessment instruments, and practitioners.

Second, the critical thinker begins to raise relevant questions. These are based on a careful review of the information needed in the focal helping circumstances. Related to theory selection and consideration, the worker might formulate the following questions. Does Kohlberg's theory, for instance, appear suitable for use with these particular clients as they face the difficult cognitive, emotional, and behavioral challenges addressed in this agency context? Can the theory be used in a responsible, ethical way? What evidence supports such an application of the theory? What are the specific strengths and limitations of the theory when used for the chosen purposes? Are there competing theories that could be more useful?

Third, the critical thinker checks assumptions. He thinks critically about core theoretical assumptions. For example, in the case of Kohlberg's moral development theory, the social worker might investigate the following topics. What does Kohlberg assume about the nature of morality? What are his assumptions about the processes and dynamics of moral development? What "person, interaction, or environment" events are likely to stimulate or retard moral development? What does Kohlberg assume about moral deliberation, decision making, and action? After identifying such assumptions, the critical thinker considers whether they are reasonable and justifiable. Finally, the critical thinker might check his or her personal assumptions, for example about adolescent moral development, and reflect on how these interface with the theoretical assumptions.

Fourth, the critical thinker considers various viewpoints on the relevant knowledge about the "person interacting in the environment" configuration and reflects on these viewpoints. The social worker considers carefully and critically, diverse theoretical and practical perspectives related to the knowledge for use. In reference to Kohlberg's theory (Kohlberg, Levine, & Hewer, 1983), the worker might do a literature search and consider the viewpoints of human development theorists, researchers, and practitioners who have become expert on Kohlberg's theory. The worker might give special attention to those social workers who have used, tested, or adapted Kohlberg's ideas for practical use. The critical thinker also considers the viewpoints of colleagues and organizational leaders. Most important, the worker confers with the client and solicits his or her views about the suitability of Kohlberg's theory. Finally, the worker attempts to synthesize these multiple perspectives into a personalized theoretical orientation, one that can be incorporated into thinking (mind) as well as feeling (heart) and acting (body).

Fifth, critical thinkers make use of available and relevant information. What information is needed to use the selected knowledge effectively and responsibly? Sources might include Kohlberg's own books and articles on the theory, evidence from research and practice evaluation studies, information from case studies and other reports on practice in the realm of moral development, and practice wisdom accumulated by the profession or the agency about the theory and its use. Critical thinkers attempt to form firm opinions on a topic without bias about the relevant information. Information both supporting and opposing the selection of Kohlberg's theory, for instance, should be considered objectively and with an open mind.

Sixth, critical thinkers identify and use concepts that can help them appraise knowledge and its potential usefulness. For example, the social worker considering Kohlberg's stage theory of moral development might review the meanings of "theory." Concepts related to scientific standards for theory appraisal such as parsimony, explanatory power, empirical support, and so on can be used to judge the knowledge. Social work standards and related concepts associated with affirmation of diversity, promotion of justice, and adherence to ethical principles also merit consideration.

Seventh, critical thinkers make inferences. They think systematically about the logic of their theoretical analysis and the potential usefulness of the analysis. Questions from the study of logical reasoning can be used. For deductive theories, do the theoretical conclusions follow logically from the premises? For inductive theories, do the empirical observations lead logically to the theoretical conclusions? Has the analysis of the selected knowledge avoided logical fallacies or errors? Is the practitioner's theoretical thinking consistent?

Eighth, critical thinkers generate and consider implications. The social worker, for example, thinks critically about the likely consequences of the use of knowledge. What are some of the possible positive consequences for the client and his significant others of using Kohlberg's theory? Are there any likely negative consequences of the use of this theoretical knowledge? What are some of the possible positive or negative consequences for your development as a professional social worker? For the agency? For the profession?

Practical theorizing and logical fallacies

Theory users and theorizers learn from mistakes. In the area of critical thinking, social workers might watch from and correct thinking based on logical fallacies. A *logical fallacy* is a case of unsound or non-scientific reasoning during an argument (Gambrill, & Gibbs, 2009). For instance, a practitioner arrives at a conclusion that doesn't follow from the premise. In Table 22.1, I provide a list of ten of the major fallacies (Ben-Ari, 2005, Richardson, 2012), and I describe and illustrate each in relation to theorizing and theory use.

Table 22.1   Practical theorizing and major logical fallacies

Fallacy – Definition and Example

1. The Ad Hominem – critics challenge the theory by attacking the theorist or theory advocate rather than the theoretical concepts and propositions. Freudian theory is useless because Sigmund Freud used cocaine.

2. The Appeal to Authority – the debater uses the opinion of an authority figure or an institution of authority instead of evidence or a sound argument to defend a theory. My wise and experienced supervisor has told me that the past life regression approach to practice theory works terrifically. That's all that I need to know.

3. The Appeal to the Bandwagon – advocates of a theoretical position assert its validity by arguing that many people believe and act according to the theory. Educational theorists claim that the rapid shift to online classes by a large number of colleges and universities prove that this modality effectively teaches students curriculum content.

4. The Appeal to Ignorance – a theory is true according to its advocates because it hasn't yet been proven false. Astrological theory is sound because scientists have never proven that the stars can't affect human behavior.

5. The Appeal to Tradition – a theory is justified by appeal to the wisdom of earlier proponents. Astrology is useful because it was founded and valued by the ancient and wise Greeks. I still should cherish and affirm my grandmother's theory of the use of dried red peppers to ward off evil.

6. The Argument by Anecdote – the theorizing practitioner uses personal experience or an isolated example to dismiss evidence supporting a theoretical claim. Sure, there is much empirical evidence linking sexist attitudes, power, and control needs to violence against women but I doubt the Duluth Theoretical Model of Partner Violence because my dad was a dominating patriarch in our Italian-American family and he never hit my mom.

7. The Argument to Logic – the thinker assumes that if an argument for some conclusion is fallacious, then the conclusion itself is false. John Dalton, the father of modern chemistry, theorized in the 18th century, that atomic elements combine in integral proportions to form molecules. Critics claimed that his theoretical premises were false, but experts in the field have shown that his theoretical conclusions are still basically sound.

8. Correlation Not Causation – the person using this argument asserts that X happened then Y happened; therefore X caused Y. Two events occur together or one occurs after the other, so there is evidence of a causal relationship. For example, an agency director has an affair with a worker and then the agency's sexual harassment policy is made more lenient. Feminist critics of the director formulate a causal theory and assert with full confidence: the affair caused the policy revision.

9. The False Dilemma – the debater claims that there are only two theoretical possibilities for understanding any situation. Human change over time can be understood by either using the Darwinian evolutionary theory or by using the creationist model. The idea behind the false dilemma is to set up a system in which a disproof of the opponent's argument is automatic proof and support for the attacker's argument.

10. The Straw Man Argument – the critic misrepresents a theory or the theory's elements and structure to make it easier to attack. Critics of intelligent design theory, a theory asserting that the initiation of life was caused by an intelligent planner, who make false claims that the approach refutes evolution and supports creationism are setting up a straw man argument.

Optimally, social work professionals work in agencies or businesses where a culture supporting critical thinking has been created and maintained. The organization expects, for example, that its members think critically about theory selection and theory use (Gibbs & Gambrill, 1999). The organization provides frequent opportunities for employees to increase their knowledge about theory and about critical thinking processes and common logical fallacies. As participants in such cultures, practitioners fortify their habits of critical theorizing.

Critical thinking about theory: questions to ask

Wallis (2011) proposes a set of critical thinking questions tailored specifically to the appraisal of theory and theorizing activity. These could be fruitfully incorporated into a social worker's critical thinking processes. How clearly and precisely are the concepts of the theory defined? In what ways has the historical or cultural context influenced the theory creation or theory use processes? To what degree does the theory provide explanations ranging across system levels: micro-, mezzo-, and macro-level? In what writing style (academic, literary, mathematical, formal-propositional, or logical) is the theory presented, and how well does the theorist use the style? To what degree does the theory achieve its purpose: description, explanation, prediction, critique, or design of intervention? How well does the theory fit with empirical observations? How well does the theory fit with existing theories? Is the theory useful in many common practice situations or only a few helping situations? How well does the theory assist the social worker-client system as they work together to achieve desired results, and how useful is it compared to a rival theory? Does the theory offer a novel or innovative perspective on human behavior and the environment? In what positive or negative ways has the theory changed over time? Does the theory and its use affirm value preferences important to the social work profession related to diversity, justice, strengths, and so on? How economically does the theory use concepts, propositions, and explicit linkages between propositions? From how many sources does the theory draw supporting evidence? I will comment more on some of these questions in the upcoming lessons on theory critique.

Learning activities and reflections

1   Use the critical thinking framework and pick a familiar theory that you might use to help a client or significant other. Think about the theory and whether you should use it critically and report the highlights of how you will follow each of the eight steps in the appraisal process.
2   Develop a critical thinking approach to the claims of a conspiracy theorist. For example, how might you prepare a critical and evidence-informed counterargument to 9/11 conspiracy theorists. These theorists make an

odd claim. They claim that United States government agents destroyed the World Trade Center buildings in New York City on September 11, 2001. Terrorists were not responsible for this crime.

3   Do a scan of the website or media publications for recent controversies about human behavior theory (Creationism is a viable scientific alternative to Darwinian evolutionary theory, for example), policy issues (President Obama should direct police officers to find and deport every undocumented alien), medical or psychosocial interventions (homeopathic remedies work as healing agents for many physical ailments), or ethical conduct (the news corporation of Fox News has not acted improperly in influencing British officials and detectives and in hacking into phones). Expand on my examples or pick a contemporary controversy that interests you; a controversy where there is much coverage of pro and con arguments. Follow the details of the arguments carefully, and identify several illustrations of logical fallacies. Specify the nature of the fallacy and how the critical thinker might have challenged reasoning based on the fallacy.

References

Ben-Ari, M. (2005). *Just a theory: Explaining the nature of science*. Amherst, NY: Prometheus.

Elder, L., & Paul, R. (2007). *The thinker's guide to analytic thinking*. Dillon Beach, CA: The Foundation for Critical Thinking.

Gambrill, E. (2006). *Social work practice: A critical thinker's guide*. New York: Oxford University Press.

Gambrill, E., & Gibbs, L. (2009). *Critical thinking for helping professionals: A skills-based workbook* (3rd edn). New York: Oxford University Press.

Gibbs, L., & Gambrill, E. (1999). *Critical thinking for social workers: Exercises for the helping profession*. Thousand Oaks, CA: Pine Forge Press.

Gitterman, A., & Knight, C. (2013). Evidence-guided practice: Integrating the science and art of social work. *Families in Society: The Journal of Contemporary Social Services*, 94(2), 70–78.

Kohlberg, L., Levine, C., & Hewer, A. (1983). *Moral stages: a current formulation and a response to critics*. Basel, NY: Karger.

Oko, J. (2008). *Understanding and using theory in social work*. Exeter, UK: Learning Matters.

Paul, R., & Elder, L. (2009). *The miniature guide to critical thinking: Concepts and tools*. Dillon Beach, CA: The Foundation for Critical Thinking.

Richardson, J. (2012). The top 20 logical fallacies (or should that be the bottom 20?). *Skeptical Inquirer*, 36(4), 44–47.

Schneider, M. A. (2006). *The theory primer: A sociological guide*. Lanham, MD: Rowman and Littlefield.

Wallis, S.E. (2011). Techniques for the objective analysis and advancement of integral theory. Retrieved June 28, 2011, from http://integraltheoryconference.org/sites/default/files/itc-2010 papers/Wallis_ITC%202010.doc.pdf

Critique theory using scientific and practical standards

(EPAS 2.1.1 Identify as a Professional Social Worker;
EPAS 2.1.3 Apply Critical Thinking;
EPAS 2.1.7 Apply Knowledge)

Critical thinking involves a judgment about the quality of our thinking activity by reference to standards. In the case of theorizing, scientists turn to an established set of scientific standards for determining the worth of theorizing and theories. These are norms agreed to by members of the scientific community. They are useful when deciding whether to use a particular theory, when validating a theory and its claims, and when attempting to theorize well.

Scientific standards for theory appraisal

Scientists and other theory users provide various general standards, criteria for evaluating theories. In Figure 23.1, I identify three types of standards that the theorizing practitioner might use when thinking critically about theory and theorizing activities.

Scientific standards

Let's describe first some of the most important scientific standards for theory evaluation.

Clarity

A theory sacrifices usefulness if it is incomprehensible and can't be communicated to those other than the theory's biggest fans. Good theories define concepts clearly and explicitly. There is general agreement among the scientific community about the nominal definitions (Weis, 1998). Good theories develop valid, reliable, and culturally sensitive operational definitions of central concepts. The assumptions, concepts, propositions, and ordering of propositions of good theories are clearly articulated and can be understood

Scientific standards
Clarity
Internal consistency
Parsimony
Power (explanatory)
Power (predictive)
Scope
Testability

Pragmatic standards
Ease of use (practitioner, client)
Generates new understandings
Readiness for use
Relevance to practice
(by problem, stage, system)

Social work standards
Ethics and values
Evidence-based
Holistic
Justice
Sensitivity to diversity
Strengths orientation

Figure 23.1 Standards for judging theory: scientific, pragmatic, and social work

by the theory users. The theory and its elements can be discussed orally, and they can be written about in ways adequate to the reading capabilities of the common theory user (Hudson, 2010). The overall structure of a good theory can be laid out clearly and with enough detail for the user to understand the logical order of its theoretical argument (Flyvbjerg, 2001).

Internal consistency

A good theory is characterized by internal and logical consistency (Jaccard, & Jacoby, 2010). Concepts are defined clearly and consistently. The use of each concept is consistent with its definition, and each concept is used consistently in various presentations of the theory. Critics have challenged Kuhn's theory of scientific progress, for example, because he used the concept "paradigm" in too many different ways, including as scientific exemplar (noteworthy solution to a problem of science) and as disciplinary matrix (a framework or perspective shared by theorists in a particular theory community; Reynolds, 1971). Each variable in a good theory meets two criteria for consistency: mutual exclusiveness (no different thing can be placed in more than one category) and inclusiveness (all things can be placed in at least one category).

In a good theory, theoretical statements are consistent with underlying assumptions, and the concepts and propositions are linked together logically (Chafetz, 1978). Additionally, the scientific reasoning inherent in the theory—deductive or inductive—follows the rules for proper and logically consistent reasoning. The theory and its elements are arranged coherently as compared to similar theoretical knowledge (Kaplan, 1964). A theory with a great deal of internal harmony is preferable to one with little internal consistency or harmony.

Parsimony

Optimally, the theory's presentation is parsimonious, too. Advocates of parsimony argue that a theory adequately stated with a few assumptions, concepts, and propositions is better than a comparable theory presented more complexly and using a greater number of elements. An ideal theory explains much about the "person interacting in the environment" but without excessive verbiage or mathematical symbolization (Hage, 1972). The standard of parsimony ensures that there is appropriate brevity and conciseness in the statements describing the theoretical elements and overall formulation (Chafetz, 1978). There are no unnecessary elements. For example, if there are two theories of racist behavior in public encounters between strangers, the theory that needs a one-page summarization is preferred to the theory detailed in 42 pages—other things being equal. However, be aware that person-in-environment configurations are often very complex, and simpler theories may not best help social workers understand these configurations.

Power

A good theory has explanatory and predictive power. The theory's explanations fit well with the set of facts known about the relevant phenomenon or processes and provide a comprehensive explanation (explanatory power). Such achievements have been established in the theory's record of explaining past instances (Yearley, 1984). Competing theoretical explanations have been ruled out as inadequate or spurious (Hage, 1972). For social work, good theories, for instance, explain much about the person, transactions, and environment, especially when compared to their competitors.

Preferred theories also have predictive power. They have been specified in ways that relate theory elements to their anticipated effects (in a series of tests, if x occurs, then y is likely to follow 75 percent of the time, for example). This feature of a theory makes precise prediction possible. The good theories have a public record also of predicting future events successfully.

Scope

Theoretical scope is related to explanatory power. A good theory provides a clear statement of the scope of its applicability (Cohen, 1980). The theory creator has answered the question "under what other conditions and in what other situations has the theory been used successfully for explanation or to guide action" (Swedberg, 2012)?

Good theories have wide scope and can be generalized to and used in a wide variety of situations—different circumstances, settings, or populations. Theories with impressive scope have uses that aren't restricted to a particular kind of client, a specific helping setting, a definite historical period, or an ecological setting. Additionally, theories with greater scope than competitors have shown the ability to handle many of the basic theoretical problems and practice challenges of concern to the profession of social work (Hage, 1972). Ideally, the limits of the theory's scope are also identified.

Testability

A good theory has been translated into measurable variables and can be validated (Nugent, 1987; Shoemaker, Tankard, & Lasorsa, 2004). This allows for the derivation of hypotheses that can be tested in the empirical world by researchers and facilitates the appraisal of the fit between theory-based expectations and empirical observations (Aneshensel, 2002; Kaplan, 1964). Popper (1934/1959, 1963) called this the "falsification principle." He questioned the value of any theoretical claim that couldn't be refuted. *Falsification* means that a proposition, theory, or hypothesis derived from a theory is "scientific" only if it can be refuted by data. "God is good" is a statement with spiritual meaning but not a scientific statement; it can't be challenged by scientific inquiry. A theory gains support in the scientific community when it passes multiple attempts by researchers in the scientific community to falsify or refute its major assertions. Ideally, evidence of theory application effectiveness in the same area as the practice puzzle or a closely related area has also been accumulated.

Questions guiding critical thinking about the scientific value of a theory

The standards or norms discussed heretofore and some others have been transformed into a set of questions that might assist us as we think critically about theory and theorizing processes. Shoemaker, Tankard, and Lasorsa (2004), for example, propose that you ask the following questions about a theory. Is the theory testable? Is the theory parsimonious, stated as simply as possible? Does the theory have explanatory power and explain a great deal about the topic or challenge considered by the social work theory user? Does the theory help us make accurate predictions? Does the theory have a large scope and help us understand many important public problems and social work topics? Have the theorists associated with the theory's development taken a cumulative approach and revised the theory whenever new evidence is discovered? Has the theory been constructed formally and precisely; that is, have assumptions, concepts, nominal definitions, operational definitions, propositions, and the linkages between propositions been explicitly articulated? Does the theory have heuristic value and generate ideas for social work practice and research?

Chafetz (1978) adds criteria focused on the communicability of the theory. Are the assumptions explicitly stated? Are the concepts carefully defined and used in a consistent manner? Is the nature of the explanation(s) and the theoretical linkages spelled out clearly and without ambiguity?

Fawcett and Downs (1986) recommend a set of questions related to the theory's suitability for and support by scientific testing. Was the theory developed with reference to a sample representative of the theory user's population of interest? Are the concepts of the theory defined with empirically observable indicators? Are valid and reliable measurements of the indicators available? Are the hypotheses falsifiable? Are the theoretical statements backed up by empirical evidence?

Practical standards for theory appraisal

Pragmatists contend that theorizers, researchers, and practitioners should judge theory by its practical consequences (Doane & Varcoe, 2005). Let's expand on the many ways that a theorizing practitioner might appraise the usefulness of a particular theory and its consequences.

Specific practical standards

A good theory is useful to the practitioner in direct and indirect planned change efforts and supports actions in varied professional roles: advocate, broker, educator, evaluator, leader, therapist, and so on. It contributes to the understanding of puzzling "person interacting in the environment" configurations, and it facilitates the achievement of desired outcomes in many different cases (Webster, & Whitmeyer, 2001). Good theory has several other and specific characteristics.

Generates new understandings and interventions

Gergen (1978) argues that we should judge theories on the capacity to generate something new. Ideal theories provoke debate about conventional human behavior and human development understandings, contribute to the transformation of selves and societies, change the way that people and collectives act, and challenge taken-for-granted assumptions of culture while suggesting alternative and innovative lines of social action. Stevenson (2005) expands on the generative feature of usefulness. Good theories provide the practitioners new ways of describing and conceptualizing their professional selves. They contribute to the effectiveness of helping processes by helping workers understand problematic situations in new ways, by suggesting future scenarios and possibilities for action that enhance the goal setting process, and by identifying innovative helping actions that will lead to desired outcomes. In summary, a good theory is generative. It contributes to the professional work of accumulating sound knowledge. It suggests new lines of inquiry, new understandings, new research, and new applications for varied members of the profession (Hudson, 2010).

Readiness for use

Other practical considerations about theory are important. For example, a good theory is ready for use. The application of good theories is feasible, legal, and possible with a manageable degree of training (Fawcett & Downs, 1986). Worren, Moore, and Elliott (2002) recommend that we judge how friendly a theory is to clients and practitioners. Ideal theories aren't too complicated for practice settings and don't need extensive modification before they can be applied. Ideal theories include operational definitions of central concepts that specify the procedures for use of the concepts in practice, and they include propositions stated in if-then form: If the worker/client takes this action, this outcome will follow. Ideal theories include presentations as narratives such as case studies that are interesting, easy to recall, and involving. Finally, ideally theoretical products make effective use of display conventions and supplement narratives with effective visual representations of the theory and its elements Weick (1987) suggests that the theories most relevant to worker goals and desired outcomes for clients and theories have operationalized variables carefully. Theories with operationalizations that suggest how the worker and client can use the theory's independent variables to effect change are better than theories that have not specified the indicators and operational measurement procedures for its variables. We can add that a good theory can be adapted for use by the practitioner.

Relevance to practice

Contemporary practice-minded theorists have suggested the addition of other criteria regarding usefulness to the core of scientific standards. Many revolve around the theme of relevance to practice. Weick (1987) argues that relevance is a critical factor. Relevant theories describe person-in-environment challenges, life-stage issues, and system-level problems encountered often by practitioners. Relevant theories are timely and will help practitioners deal with contemporary personal and public problems. Relevant theories go beyond the obvious and add understandings that exceed practitioners' common sense and practice wisdom. Ninic (2000) adds that theorists enhance theoretical relevance when they construct practical theories that describe the expected impact of a theory-based intervention or program on desired outcomes in specific contexts. Additionally, the theorists specify the likely direct costs and consequences of using the theory-guided intervention and the possible indirect or secondary consequences and costs. With this information, the theorizing practitioner can judge the usefulness and affordability of a theory application at the practice site. Relevant new theories, we should add, are similar to theories used previously and successfully by the practitioner to guide inquiry and plan interventions—or at least understandable with reference to familiar theories.

Questions to guide critical thinking about the practical usefulness of theory

The theorizing practitioner can transform these practical standards into questions useful during critical thinking about theory and theorizing activities. Several theory experts (Doane & Varcoe, 2005; Stevenson, 2005) formulated questions specific to the issue of usefulness for social work practice. What will a particular theory or theoretical concept lead us to focus on, to attend to, and to do during the helping process? What difference will it practically make to the worker, client, and collaterals if this particular theory is selected and used? In what ways does the theory enhance the practitioner's and client system's efforts to describe, predict, explain, categorize, or intervene in regard to the challenging situation? To what degree does the theory help identify instrumental descriptions of the situation that imply specific actions or means likely to produce a desired change in the situation? What specific improvements in the person-interacting-environment configuration will follow the use of the theory? Does the theory use result in more perceptive understanding of life challenges and more responsive action? How practical is the theory compared to other theories?

Professional criteria for appraising theories

Social workers also use the profession's value commitments to appraise theories critically and determine their validity, usefulness, and suitability for the profession (Vandsburger, 2004). A theory that meets scientific and pragmatic standards may be rejected if the worker judges it as poor in relation to our professional standards, such as ethical soundness, strengths orientation, justice promotion, or affirmation of difference. For example, a bad theory is one that undermines the appreciation of diversity by presenting stereotypical and demeaning ways of understanding culture, members of a culture, and human differences. Standards derived from social work values will be reviewed in the following lessons.

Concluding remarks: using scientific, practical, and professional standards

There is a communal aspect to theory use and theory appraisal. Our scientific standards are very abstract and must be tailored to particular theory use situations. Giroux (1983) follows the pragmatic tradition of Charles Sanders Pierce when he suggests that theory appraisal occurs ideally in open, collaborative, democratic, and critical forums where all relevant stakeholders engage in dialogue and deliberate respectfully about the focal theory, its strengths, and its limitations. The negotiation of differences during theory appraisal sessions will be most successful when organized according to the same democratic and reflective principles and norms that guide scientific inquiry. Specifically, stakeholders should embrace ideals such as unimpeded communication, mutual understanding, the decentralization of power, and freedom from unconscious constraints or force. Stakeholders should also reflect continuously on the ideals, norms, and interactional patterns that characterize their cooperative theory appraisal and use these reflections to improve collective critique and decision-making processes.

Learning activities and reflections

1   It is important for social workers to be alert for articles, books, and debates on the degree to which your favorite theories earn favorable answers to the evaluative questions used by scientists. Review and become familiar with the standards listed in the commentary. Find an article, an excerpt from a book, a research study, or some other document that includes a critical discussion of an explanatory theory, practice theory, or middle-range theory. Briefly identify the standard (s) used in the document and summarize in your own words the details of the critique (s) of the focal theoretical product.

2   Take each of the scientific standards listed in the commentary above. For each, summarize the meaning of this standard in your own words. Additionally, provide for each standard an illustration of how it might be violated by some explanatory theory or practice theory about "person interacting in the environment" configurations.

3   Take each of the practical standards listed in the commentary above. For each, summarize the meaning of this standard in your own words. Additionally, provide for each standard an illustration of how it might be violated by some explanatory theory or practice theory about "person interacting in the environment" configurations.

4   Observe a set of social workers and colleagues, clients, or other stakeholders during a discussion about the merits of a particular theory. Refer to the principles for democratic and dialogical collaboration summarized above. In what ways did the stakeholders conform to

these principles? What are some illustrations of variance from these principles such as intellectual bullying, monopolizing the conversation, poor listening, appealing to one's greater power or status, subtle or overt threats, or the intrusion of impulses and emotions with minimal awareness. Overall, what was the impact of interaction on the quality of the theory appraisal process?

References

Aneshensel, C. S. (2002). *Theory-based data analysis for the social sciences*. Thousand Oaks, CA: Sage.

Chafetz, J. S. (1978). *A primer on the construction and testing of theories in sociology*. Itasca, IL: F. E. Peacock.

Cohen, B. P. (1980). *Developing sociological knowledge: Theory and method*. Englewood Cliffs, NJ: Prentice-Hall.

Doane, G. H., & Varcoe, C. (2005). Toward compassionate action: Pragmatism and the inseparability of theory/practice. *Advances in Nursing Science*, 28(1), 81–90.

Fawcett, J., & Downs, F. S. (1986). *The relationship of theory and research*. Norwalk, CT: Appleton-Century-Crofts.

Flyvbjerg, B. (2001). *Making social science matter: Why social inquiry fails and how it can succeed again*. Cambridge, UK: Cambridge University Press.

Gergen, K. J. (1978). Toward generative theory. *Journal of Personality and Social Psychology*, 36(11), 1344–1360.

Giroux, H. A. (1983). *Theory and resistance in education: A pedagogy for the opposition*. South Hadley, MA: Bergin & Garvey.

Hage, J. (1972). *Techniques and problems of theory construction in sociology*. New York: John Wiley and Sons.

Hudson, C. C. (2010). *Complex systems and human behavior*. Chicago, IL: Lyceum.

Jaccard, J. & Jacoby, J. (2010). *Theory construction and model-building skills*. New York: Guilford Press.

Kaplan, A. (1964). *The conduct of inquiry: Methodology for behavioral science*. San Francisco, CA: Chandler.

Ninic, M. (2000). Policy relevance and theoretical development: The terms of the trade-off. In M. Ninic & J. Lepgold (Eds), *Being useful: Policy relevance and international relations theory* (pp. 21–49). Ann Arbor, MI: University of Michigan Press.

Nugent, W. R. (1987). Use and evaluation of theories. *Social Work Research and Abstracts*, 23(1), 14–19.

Popper, K. (1934/1959). *The logic of scientific discovery*. New York: Basic Books.

Popper, K. (1963). *Conjectures and refutations*. London: Routledge and Keagan Paul.

Reynolds, P. D. (1971). *A primer in theory construction*. Indianapolis, IN: Bobbs-Merrill.

Shoemaker, P. J., Tankard, J. W., Jr., & Lasorsa, D. L. (2004). *How to build social science theories*. Thousand Oaks, CA: Sage.

Stevenson, C. (2005). Practice inquiry/theory in nursing. *Journal of Advanced Nursing*, 50(2), 196–203.

Swedberg, R. (2012). Theorizing in sociology and social science: Turning to the context of discovery. *Theory and Society*, 41, 1–40.

Vandsburger, E. (2004). A critical thinking model for teaching human behavior and the social environment. *The Journal of Baccalaureate Social Work, 10*(1), 1–11.

Webster, M. Jr., & Whitmeyer, J. M. (2001). Applications of theories of group processes. *Sociological Theory, 19*(3), 250–270.

Weick, K. E. (1987). Theorizing about organizational communication. In F. M. Jablin, L. L. Putnam, K. H. Roberts, & L. W. Porter (Eds), *Handbook of organizational communication: An interdisciplinary perspective* (pp. 97–122). Newbury Park, CA: Sage.

Weis, D. L. (1998). The use of theory in sexuality research. *The Journal of Sex Research, 35*(1), 1–9.

Worren, N., Moore, K., & Elliott, R. (2002). When theories become tools: Toward a framework for pragmatic validity. *Human Relations, 55*(10), 1227–1250.

Yearley, S. (1984). *Science and sociological practice.* Stony Stratford, UK: Open University Press.

Critique theory using professional standard of ethics and values

(EPAS 2.1.2 Apply Ethical Principles;
EPAS 2.1.3 Apply Critical Thinking;
EPAS 2.1.7 Apply Knowledge)

Social workers share preferences regarding theory and theorizing activity. These preferences are expressed through our professional language including our declarations of core values and ethical guidelines (Bloom, Wood, & Chambon, 1991). All social workers must confront value and ethical issues during knowledge application, research, and practice processes. Professional values and ethics are very relevant to theorizing and theory use. Theorists create theoretical products with explicit or implicit attention to value issues, and theories include explicit or implicit directives for practical use; these directives have ethical implications (Meleis, 1985). Social workers can learn to take a critical approach to theory and inquire about the consistency of a theory with social work values and ethics (Robbins, Chatterjee, & Canda, 1998).

We are a profession that borrows and reconstructs much knowledge from other professions and disciplines, but we also discriminate about what we borrow. Our values and ethical standards serve as a filtering screen ensuring that we borrow theoretical knowledge consistent with our profession's core convictions. When theorizing practitioners enter universities and research centers and search their knowledge archives to acquire theory for practical use, they should check the material against social work values and ethical principles before making selections. In this way, theorizing practitioners avoid careless or hazardous borrowing and use theoretical frameworks, models, and other elements that will contribute to sensitive, responsible, and successful practice.

Value preferences and theory appraisal

Social work's mission is rooted in a set of core values. These values lead to the profession's central ethical principles. These core values also contribute to our unique perspective and guide knowledge selection and application. A chosen theory, its assumptions, implications, and uses, for example, should be congruent with the core values of the profession (Hudson, 2010). Major values are service, social justice, the dignity and worth of the person, integrity, and competence. Equality and self-determination are also important values (Barsky, 2010).

DePoy and Gilson (2007) call the value judgments, by social workers and others about the acceptability of any theoretical account, *explanatory legitimacy*. An appreciation for explanatory legitimacy directs the theory user to judge "person interacting in an environment" knowledge by consideration of value preferences in addition to the conventional standards of scientific validity and practical usefulness. A competent practitioner, they add, can identify and articulate the values used to appraise the merit of any theoretical account and can select a moral theoretical explanation for a theoretical puzzle.

A value is a standard or quality considered preferable or worthwhile. Each theoretical tradition and its theories include a set of value positions; these may be explicitly stated or implicit to the theory. For example, Barsky (2010) considers Marxist theory in relation to its conception of the preferred person and environment. In this theory, the person is a "cooperative" being, one who works with others for the common good rather than against others in competition for personal gain. The society is one committed to "equality." Each person receives an equal share of the society's resources. This theoretical orientation differs from intellectual systems that endorse the distribution of wealth and resources based on job, status, and entrepreneurial aggressiveness. Critics of Marxist theory associate it with less desirable values such as its endorsement of violent rather than peaceful means to redress injustices and its prioritization of collective over individual good. Because of these value issues and other perceived limitations of the tradition, Marxist theory and its derivatives have been mostly rejected by American social workers.

A theory's values must also be considered in relationship to the society's dominant values. Sociologist Robin Williams (1951) identified values prevalent in the United States. These include individualism (success follows individual effort and initiative); achievement especially as demonstrated by the accumulation of wealth, power, and prestige; hard and challenging work; efficiency (completion of tasks quickly and with minimal wasted effort); technology, especially technological solutions to environmental challenges; progress (continual movement toward "more and better"); material comfort (food and housing and identity-comforting possessions); mutual aid, at least in response to natural disasters; personal freedom; representative and democratic government; equality of opportunity; and group superiority (the conviction that certain groups are more worthy than others). Perhaps many social workers reject Marxist theory because it threatens Americans who embrace social values such as individualism, competitive achievement, freedom, and group superiority. Theorizing practitioners need to consider the consonance of any theoretical candidate for application with the core values of the larger society and the communal site of use.

Ethical standards for theory appraisal

The social work profession is committed to practice in accord with ethical standards related to the client's rights to dignity, respect, privacy, and self-determination. Theoretical traditions that suggest any assessment or intervention practices that humiliate or coerce clients are suspect. Theory-guided practice models that conceive of the worker as controlling rather than cooperating with those who need help deserve a negative evaluation.

Let's quickly review some major ethical guidelines derived from our values and endorsed by the social work profession (National Association of Social Workers [NASW], 2010). These are part of the code that was approved by the 1996 NASW Delegate Assembly and revised by the 2008 Assembly. The relevance to theoretical knowledge is also indicated.

Regarding the value of *service*, social workers' primary goal and ethical obligation are to help people in need and to address social problems. This includes using theoretical knowledge suitable for need meeting and problem amelioration assessment and intervention.

Regarding the value of *social justice*, social workers are ethically obligated to challenge social injustice. This includes efforts to build and spread theoretical knowledge about oppression, inequality, and justice-enhancing strategies.

Regarding the value of *dignity and worth of the person*, social workers are expected to respect the inherent dignity and worth of the person. This refers to a mindfulness of human importance, individual differences, and cultural-ethnic diversity. Mindfulness is enhanced potentially by theoretical knowledge.

Regarding the value given to the *importance of human relationships*, our ethical guidelines expect us to recognize the central importance of human relationships in life and to engage people as partners in the helping process. Effective and ethical engagement requires theoretical understanding about how relationships can foster change.

Regarding the value of *integrity*, ethical social workers behave in a trustworthy manner. This guideline doesn't include a directive regarding professional knowledge. However, we could suggest that social workers are honest about the theoretical orientation that guides their work, disclose information about the evidence supporting this orientation, and openly confer with clients about their adaptations of proven theory-informed helping procedures.

Regarding the value of *competence*, social workers are expected to practice within their areas of expertise and develop and enhance their professional knowledge, skill, and attitudes. Don't use a theory if you don't understand it and know how to reconstruct it for inquiry or action planning. This guideline includes an explicit mandate for knowledge expansion. Social workers should strive continually to increase their professional knowledge, to apply knowledge in practice, and to contribute to the knowledge base of the profession.

Besides judging and critiquing theoretical knowledge for its support of these six ethical principles, competent social workers should become aware of some related ethical issues in the use of theoretical knowledge (Duncan, 1986). These include the requirement to adopt knowledge with proven value for client systems when possible; to refrain from the inappropriate or inept application of knowledge; to decline to make use of knowledge for the exclusive benefit of a special interest group in a way harmful to other groups; and to work hard to avoid any intentional misrepresentations of knowledge.

Illustration of theory appraisal by values

In a chapter on applied symbolic interactionism (Forte, 2008), I examined the interactionist rejection of classic behaviorism and its derivatives. The argument was grounded in perceived value differences. Interactionists focus on the distinctive worth and capabilities of humans: communication by reciprocal perspective-taking activity, and the use of significant symbols. Issues of human purpose, intentionality, and creativity and the complex uses of language such as satire, irony, and humor fall within the interactionist practitioner's purview. In contrast, classic behaviorists are inclined to assume that humans have the same qualities that have been found in rats, pigeons, monkeys, and other nonhumans and treat clients accordingly. This lessens human dignity.

According to interactionists, humans are self-determining creatures; helping work should maximize capacities for choice. The behaviorist recommendation of reinforcement schedules, positive and negative behavioral control, conditioned stimuli, and operant learning may be ideas useful for working with understanding with lower animals. Humans, unlike animals, interpret and choose. Practice theory organized around interventions imposed on a person by an "expert" undermines self-determination.

Interactionists refer to the value of social justice to argue that classical behavioral practice is built on the foundations of an oppressive political philosophy. Clients are treated as captives of their learning history who can gain behavioral flexibility only with the aid of authoritarian behaviorists. Scientific practitioners become oligarchs with a monopoly on the knowledge of psychosocial change. Behaviorist assessment and intervention support the bureaucratic and elitist impulses of social control agents and become an extension of the state's apparatus for defining truth and allocating power. Such behaviorist approaches have been most frequently institutionalized in agencies of control such as correctional boot camps, prisons, mental hospitals, income maintenance programs, and substance abuse programs. In these settings, human lives are often crushed in the name of objective and scientific theory application. Behaviorist practice contrasts significantly to progressive-interactionist practice.

When participating in practice endeavors, interactionists claim to affirm "dignity," "social justice" and the "importance of relationship" values. In contrast to classical behaviorists as profiled by interactionist critics, interactionists relate to people as autonomous actors making meaning of their situations and lives. Information gathering and assessment is a partnership between the worker and the client; both bound by a common humanity. An egalitarian helping dyad or group is created, and members become innovative co-constructors of their own destinies. Social order is accomplished by cooperative and mutually respectful joint action, not by behavioral engineering.

Many behavioral social workers will reject this critique of the behavioral theoretical framework as inaccurate or outdated. However, the lesson here is that social workers should become active in appraising theoretical content using professional values and ethical standards.

Questions to guide critical thinking about theory using ethics and values

There are a variety of questions that a theorizing practitioner might ask when using value preferences and ethical guidelines to think critically about theory and its use. He or she might start with a general question: What are the ethical and value issues, limitations, and strengths, related to a focal theory and its use? A variety of specific questions might also inform critical and reflective theorizing and theory use. In what ways do the theory's core assumptions, root metaphors, and explicit and implicit values (its value base) align (or fail to align) with values of the profession? How well does the value base of the theory align with social work values as compared to other theories? How well do the uses of the theory allow adherence to social work's ethical guidelines compared to other theories? How does the theory compare to other theories in its alignment with ethical guidelines and the degree that likely uses will be ethical? Would theory use increase the likelihood that the practitioner violates an ethical guideline included in the professional code of ethics?

Learning activities and reflections

1   Reflect on some piece of theoretical knowledge that you have acquired in a class or in your career. How would you appraise the quality of the theoretical knowledge? How well does this knowledge meet the evaluation criterion shared by most social workers for good theory? These include a strengths orientation, appreciation for social justice, sensitivity to diversity, a bio-psycho-social or holistic orientation toward its theoretical explanations, an affirmation of social work ethics and values, and empirical support for its effective application. What are some of your personal reactions to the theoretical knowledge? Did it fit or not fit with your own values, theoretical style, and preferences? How might the theory be improved if it were deficient as judged by any of the social work standards or by your personal standards?

2   Imagine that you are considering various possible referrals for a troubled adolescent on your caseload. One is a correctional boot camp. You decide to investigate further and learn that the boot camp's administrators assert that the program makes effective use of a behavior modification theoretical base. The boot camp claims to remove male adolescents from environments filled with negative behavioral models and from stimuli that trigger self-defeating, reckless, or self-destructive behavior. The heads of boot camp residents are shaved, their belongings stored, and their clothing replaced with uniforms. These procedures are viewed as a consequence for past misdeeds and a means to eliminate any rewards for deviant identities. Defiant or disobedient teenagers are punished harshly; punishments are often derived from military training programs. For example, rule breakers are forced to complete lengthy and gruelling physical exercise routines. Fear is often induced in the youthful offenders as a way to scare them straight. The boot camp is organized as a status hierarchy, and new arrivals are treated as worthless and are humiliated often and in public gatherings. Privilege and status can be earned only by meeting standards for appropriate and responsible social behavior as determined by superior camp members. Elevation from the lowest rank to the next rank takes at least six months. After further study, you learn also that teenagers have died at several correctional boot camps in the United States.

    For this learning activity, ignore the question of whether the boot camp is actually applying a behavioral theoretical framework. Many grossly distort the perspective. For example, Skinner strongly argued against punishment as an intervention and for the frequent use of reinforcement to change behavior patterns. Instead, identify possible ethical issues as identified by the social work code that might merit consideration. Review your position on the boot camp program, procedures, and interventions using the social work code of ethics. Conclude with a summary of your decision regarding the referral and your rationale for the decision.

3 Review in your mind the core social work values and the value positions supported commonly by other groups in the United States. Consider the controversy associated with the teaching of evolutionary theory in public schools and the advocates for a curriculum that includes creationism. Darwin theorized that all organisms on Earth, including human beings, are descended from a common ancestor or ancestral gene pool. This theory asserts also that the line of descent for humans can be traced back to great apes. Creationism, in contrast, is the religious conviction that God is the creator of the Earth, human beings, and all other life.

What values might opponents and proponents consider when appraising the Darwinian theory of evolution? In terms of values, what would opponents to evolutionary theory find objectionable? What do proponents mean when they claim that evolutionary theory has been validated by scientific evidence? In what settings providing social work services might agency values concur with the values implicit in evolutionary theory? In what settings would the theory's values and the agency values conflict? What would be a value-based social work stance toward evolutionary theory? Can you imagine a way of reconciling theological beliefs in a higher being or God with scientific confidence in the facts of evolution?

References

Barsky, A. E. (2010). *Ethics and values in social work: An integrated approach for a comprehensive curriculum*. New York: Oxford University Press.

Bloom, M., Wood, K., & Chambon, A. (1991). The six languages of social work. *Social Work, 36*(6), 530–534.

DePoy, E., & Gilson, S. F. (2007). *The human experience: Description, explanation, and judgment*. Lanham, MD: Rowman and Littlefield.

Duncan, J. W. (1986). Ethical issues in the development and application of business and management knowledge. *Journal of Business Ethics, 5*(5), 391–400

Forte, J. A. (2008) Making interactionism useful: Translations for social work and sociological direct practice. In N. K. Denzin (Ed.), *Studies in symbolic interaction* (Vol. 32, pp. 219–249). Bingley, UK: Emerald.

Hudson, C. C. (2010). *Complex systems and human behavior*. Chicago, IL: Lyceum.

Meleis, A. I. (1985). *Theoretical nursing: Development and progress*. Philadelphia, PA: J. B. Lippincott.

National Association of Social Workers (2010). NASW code of ethics. Retrieved August 10, 2010, from www.naswdc.org/pubs/code/default.asp

Robbins, S. P., Chatterjee, P., & Canda, E. R. (1998). *Contemporary human behavior theory: A critical perspective for social work*. Boston, MD: Allyn & Bacon.

Williams, R. M. (1951). *American society: A sociological interpretation*. New York: Knopf.

Critique theory using professional standard of evidence

(EPAS 2.1.3 Apply Critical Thinking;
EPAS 2.1.6 Engage in Research-Informed Practice;
EPAS 2.1.7 Apply Knowledge)

"Show me the money" was a popular phrase in the 1990s; the phrase indicates a skeptical reaction to promises of big salaries and bonuses. Social workers should be skeptics, too, and respond to claims about the quality of a theory or the effectiveness of a theory-derived intervention with the demand: Show me the evidence.

Evidence and its sources

Evidence and theory are not antagonists: "The accumulation of empirical evidence *per se* and the development of theory need not be seen as alternative and competing approaches" (Green, 2000 p. 6, italics in original). Evidence is everything that an impartial judge might consider to determine the truth or accuracy of a theoretical claim. Evidence is also called *empirical support*. Evidence ranges widely and refers to all that can be brought to bear when thinking critically about theory or theory-guided practice (Layder, 1998). Evidence can be found in client reports, notes on practitioner observations, transcripts of sessions and, most important, empirical research studies.

As part of competent theorizing, social workers should be able to find and judge evidence about theories (Anderson, 1976; van Ryn & Heaney, 1992; Whitmeyer, 2002). This includes evidence documenting that the theory guides accurately the assessment of PIE challenges; for instance, the theory-derived assessment tools are valid, reliable, and culturally sensitive. For a good theory, there is evidence that worker and client partners have achieved the desired results adapting and using the theory and its elements in natural helping situations as predicted by the theory. Additionally, the evidence shows that the theory has been applied effectively to deal with similar puzzling situations faced by the worker and the theory has been applied effectively to aid people such as those participating in the current relationship or program. For a good theory, there is also a body of evidence allowing the practitioner to make judgments about its overall explanatory and predictive power.

Evidence is often recorded formally in written documents such as professional notes, single-system practice evaluation reports, reports on program evaluation, randomized controlled experiments, quasi-experimental studies, case reports, systematic reviews of intervention studies, and expert opinion statements. The theorizing practitioner might look for relevant evidence in journals such as *The Journal of Evidence Based Social Work* or *Research on Social Work Practice*. The practitioner might carefully generate a list of theory-specific challenge terms and search Web sites devoted to collecting empirical findings on effectiveness such as the Campbell Collaboration (www.campbellcollaboration.org), a site presenting systematic reviews of research results. The practitioner might also cull evidence from books summarizing accounts related to effective interventions directed to particular size client systems, particular fields of practice, or particular client problems. For example, see the book by Feit, Egan, and Wodarski (2009) called *Evidence-Based Interventions for Social Work in Health Care*.

Evidence and theory appraisal

In relation to the social work standard of evidence, social workers are like courtroom judges attempting to make use of all the information presented by both prosecuting and defense attorneys regarding the guilt or innocence of the defendant. In the case of theory use, the defendant is a middle-range theory, a practice theory, a theoretical concept or proposition, a theory-derived assessment strategy, or a theory-guided intervention.

Theoretical traditions vary in their commitment to developing interventions and testing their effectiveness. Practice approaches derived from theoretical traditions also vary in the quality of their evidentiary base. Some include a set of interventions that are well established and possess clear evidence of efficacy. Behavioral practitioners, for example, have distinguished their approach by accumulating hundreds of studies supporting behavioral interventions. Some use interventions with limited or no evidence of efficacy. The past-life regression approach used for journeys into one's lives before birth has a questionable theoretical base and makes unsupported claims about healing effects. Social workers prefer to use interventions that will work.

Scientific reasoning processes of deductive, inductive, and abductive reasoning can help when weighing evidence. Earlier commentaries reviewed, respectively, deductive theorizing, deriving a specific hypothesis from a general statement, and inductive theorizing, deriving a general pattern from a set of observations. *Abductive reasoning* or logic (DePoy

& Gilson, 2007) is a third form of reasoning. It involves an intellectual and creative process of judging which explanation or interpretation of some aspect of "the person interacting in the environment" is the most plausible one. Abductive reasoning is also useful for thinking critically about theory. When appraising the relative merits of each hypothesized theoretical explanation, the social worker gives attention to the degree of credible evidence supporting the alternatives but also uses her educated intuition.

Social work values and the judgments of colleagues and clients are other important forms of input for validating a preferred explanation. As suggested above, scientific practitioners make certain to consider systematic empirical validations of explanatory theoretical frameworks, practice theories, and theory-informed assessment and intervention procedures (Jaccard, & Jacoby, 2010).

Best practices, best theories, and theory appraisal

How should the practitioner engage in critical thinking about a specific theory element by judging the available evidence? Regarding theory-derived interventions, Chambliss and Hollon (1998) recommend that the worker look for evidence that the intervention has been clearly specified and also shown to be effective in carefully controlled research with a specific population. Questions to guide such a search include Does it work? How do we know it works, and under what circumstances does it work best?

The practitioner might also look for evidence that a theory-derived intervention has achieved the status of a "best practice." Such interventions have been judged as preferred ways for providing competent services to a particular client group with specific problems. These conclusions are based often on empirical studies and the informed judgments of experts. For example, The Child Welfare League of America reported on a youth development theoretical orientation for service to lesbian, gay, and gender-non-conforming youth in out-of-home care settings (Wilber, Ryan, & Markstone, 2006). They identified best practices related to supporting the expression of sexual orientation, providing a safe place for youths to come out, offering nondiscriminatory health care, creating positive recreational outlets, and responding to client-specific concerns.

The achievement of "best practice" status doesn't ensure that the intervention will lead to desired outcomes in a specific case (Thyer, & Pignotti, 2011). The worker and client using an evidence-informed approach should not shortcut the processes involved in searching for and selecting interventions suitable to their circumstances. Supporting this point, Marsh (2004) notes "empirical practice advocates argue for both the utility of multiple theoretical frameworks and the enhancement of practice through the use of evidence *plus* theory *plus* practice experience" (p. 20, italics in original).

Regarding "best" theory-guided approaches, Bledsoe and her colleagues (2007) suggested the consideration of various factors in judging different theory-guided approaches to helping. These included well-established usage, evidence of general efficacy, and research indications of effectiveness as a treatment in specific cases. Here's an illustration of their findings. In a review of three large studies on 23 different approaches, they reported that behavior therapy received three positive checks: well established, clear evidence of efficacy, and solid evidence validating the treatment approach. In contrast, existential psychotherapy received no checks. Of note, there are many practice theories and theory-derived interventions that are not yet supported by a substantial body of supporting empirical evidence. In these cases, decisions about theory suitability may involve weighing client preferences, situational characteristics, and varied types of evidence. Reviews of evidential support, however, can be starting points for appraising the quality of different theories and interventions.

Questions that guide critical thinking about theory using evidence

When thinking critically about theories and theorizing activities, the social work practitioner can ask the following questions. What is the overall evidence supporting the theoretical approach? What evidence confirms the effectiveness of particular elements of the applied theoretical approach such as its assessment tools and intervention strategies? What evidence supports the effectiveness of the approach in specific circumstances—for a specific client system with its values and identifying characteristics, with a particular problem or challenge, by a worker with specific qualities and training, in a particular environmental context, and toward the achievement of definite outcomes? What is the evidence indicating the overall comparative effectiveness of the theory, theory-informed assessment tool, or intervention strategy and also the comparative effectiveness in particular circumstances? How will the working involve the client in weighing evidence and making informed decisions?

Learning activities and reflections

1   Identify several theory-derived interventions that you have added or would like to add to your professional toolbox. Name the interventions that you considered as candidates for inclusion and their theoretical base. Discuss how you have considered this issue of "effectiveness" when selecting interventions from a range of possible interventions. What evidence did you use or might you use to help in the decision-making process? In what other ways, have you attempted to check on the effectiveness of the possible interventions?

2   Develop a detailed plan for seeking evidence about the quality of a possible theory-informed intervention. Where will you search? How might you conduct the search? How much evidence will you attempt to locate? By what standards and in what ways will you consider critically the provided evidence? How will the client participate in this process?

3   Reflect on the assertion by a practitioner: I know that I have made a major difference in the life of this client system. What are some possible arguments that the practitioner might make to support such a claim? Which arguments would you find credible and why? Which arguments would you doubt and why? Which arguments would show that the practitioner based her or his statements about effectiveness on evidence?

References

Anderson, J. D. (1976). Games social work educators play in teaching practice theories? In Council on Social Work Education (Ed.), *Teaching for competence in the delivery of social services* (pp. 1–8). New York: Council on Social Work Education.

Bledsoe, S. E., Weissman, M. M., Mullen, E. J., Ponniah, K., Gameroff, M. J., Verdeli, H., Mufson, L., Fitterling, H., & Wickramaratne, P. (2007). Empirically supported psychotherapy in social work training programs: Does the definition of evidence matter? *Research on Social Work Practice*, 17(4), 449–455.

Chambliss, D. L., & Hollon, S. D. (1998). Defining empirically supported therapies. *Journal of Consulting and Clinical Psychology*, 66(1), 7–18.

DePoy, E., & Gilson, S. F. (2007). *The human experience: Description, explanation, and judgment*. Lanham, MD: Rowman and Littlefield.

Feit, M. D., Egan, M. & Wodarski, J. S. (2009) *Evidence-based interventions for social work in health care*. Washington, DC: Taylor and Francis.

Green, J. (2000). The role of theory in evidence-based health promotion practice. *Health Education Research*, 15(2), 125–129.

Jaccard, J., & Jacoby, J. (2010). *Theory construction and model-building skills*. New York: Guilford Press.

Layder, D. (1998). *Sociological practice: Linking theory and social research*. London: Sage.

Marsh, J. C. (2004). Theory-driven research versus theory-free research in empirical social work practice. In H. E. Briggs & T. L. Rzepnicki (Eds), *Using evidence in social work practice: Behavioral perspectives* (pp. 20–35). Chicago, IL: Lyceum.

Thyer, B., & Pignotti, M. (2011). Evidence-based *practices* do not exist. *Clinical Social Work Journal*, 39(4), 328–333.

van Ryn, M. & Heaney, C. A. (1992). What's the use of theory? *Health Education Quarterly*, 19(3), 315–330.

Whitmeyer, J. M. (2002). Using theory to guide empirical research. In J. Symatka, M. Lovaglia, & K. Wysienka (Eds), *The growth of knowledge: Theory, simulation, and empirical research in group processes* (pp. 149–163). Westport, CT: Praeger.

Wilber, S., Ryan, C., & Markstone, J. (2006). *Serving LGBT youth in out-of-home care: CWLA best practice guidelines*. Washington, DC: Child Welfare League of America.

Critique theory using professional standard of holism

(EPAS 2.1.3 Apply Critical Thinking;
EPAS 2.1.7 Apply Knowledge)

Holism is the idea that the properties of a system can't be determined or explained by its component parts alone. Ludwig von Bertalanffy (1969) championed *holistic theorizing*, thinking systematically about wholes instead of parts. General systems theory, the framework that he founded, was a science of wholeness, and he asserted that the systems expression, "The whole is more than the sum of its parts" means that "constitutive characteristics are not explainable from the behavior of the isolated parts. The characteristics of the complex, therefore, appear as 'new' or 'emergent'" (p. 55). Phillips (1976) discusses holism as involving three related assumptions: parts can't be understood apart from the whole, parts and the whole are in constant and dynamic relations, and the whole can't be understood fully by reference only to its parts. Hanson (1995) uses the mathematical imagery of non-summativity. The contention that the whole is greater than the sum of parts means that we can't understand a whole by adding the qualities of each of its parts. For example, one John Lennon, one Ringo Starr, one Paul McCartney, and one George Harrison didn't add up to one super rock group, the Beatles. The Beatles incorporated the four distinct members and their personalities, but something unique emerged also when they created music: a group chemistry and creativity. These properties of the band as a holistic system differed significantly from the qualities of each member as a musician (and as a leader of his own rock group).

Holism and theory appraisal

Social workers often judge theoretical knowledge and practical theorizing activity using the holistic standard. Let's elaborate on the meaning of this normative standard.

The holistic standard

In its standards for social work with clients dealing with genetic disorders, the National Association of Social Workers (2003) asserts "the complexity of genetic conditions requires a holistic approach to intervention" (p. 13). The Association encourages practitioners to attune themselves to the blend of emotional needs, social needs, and biological conditions, and they recommend multidisciplinary teamwork and theorizing to ensure a holistic assessment and intervention plan. The International Federation of Social Workers in its position paper argues that "social work utilizes a variety of skills, techniques, and activities consistent with its holistic focus on persons and their environments" (spelling in original, 2010, p. 1).

Social workers have called the holistic approach a bio-psycho-social model, or more recently, a bio-psycho-social-spiritual model. Theoretical knowledge that meets the holistic standard focuses on the physical, cognitive, emotional, behavioral, and spiritual dimensions of the person as these are connected to environmental contexts. This whole configuration is theorized as relevant to life success. Parts of the person and parts of the environment may have weight in particular challenging circumstances, but the holistic theoretical lens looks at and clarifies the entire picture. For example, Lee, Chan, Ng, and Leung (2009) developed a holistic framework integrating empirically supported knowledge about body, mind, spirit, and context. They created this theoretical framework for guiding social work practice and illustrated its use with female patients with depressive disorders, female patients with breast cancer, women who have survived traumatic events, and patients with colorectal cancer. The holistic framework directs both the assessment and intervention processes with these client groups. For another example, addiction to substances has a powerful biological base, but holistic theories consider also psychological dimensions, social systems, and other factors (Forte, 2006).

Alternatives to holism: reductionism

The holistic stance can be contrasted to its opposite: reductionism. Holists prefer the imagery of the living organism and assert that a human being or social system such as a living organism can't be fruitfully explained by reduction to selected parts. Reductionists prefer the imagery of machines. Analysis of a part is critical to understanding a machine's functioning or malfunctioning. *Reductionism* in theoretical work assumes that an entire person or social system can be explained by reduction to its parts and that a unit at a higher level of complexity and organization (a society) can be explained adequately by theorizing about the qualities of the lower level and constituent units (individual citizens). Reductionists argue, for example, that societal racism can be grasped theoretically by focusing on the prejudice of the individuals in the society. A gang can be understood if we know the values, aspirations, behavioral tendencies, personality traits, and other characteristics of the individual members. A family and its qualities of cohesion and adaptability can be assessed if we ask each member to complete a survey documenting his or her individual perceptions of family dynamics. Holists reject this approach. Take the last example: Family cohesion, they would contend, is a dynamic property of the family group, not of the individual members. A survey of members tells us only about individual perceptions, not about entire family connectedness.

We can think of reduction going in two directions (Forte, 2006; Wiley, 1994). Downward reductionism occurs when theorists start with a high-level system and then theorize using lower-level factors and processes. Spikes in societal hate crime and minority group scapegoating are explained by changes in individual beliefs and fears. Economic trends and shifting cultural norms are omitted from consideration. Here's a second example. A homosexual sexual orientation is fully explained according to downward reducers by a genetically structured part of the brain. The environment and socialization experiences are left out of the equation.

Upward reductionism reduces complex explanations of the person-in-environment configuration to the pervasive influence of large-scale social systems. The personal dimensions are left out of these equations. For instance, all human behavior is determined, Marxists sometimes assert, by one's place in the larger political and economic structure. Personal choice is irrelevant. Material arrangements—access assigned at birth to wealth, housing, good jobs, and other life necessities—preordain us for prosperity and health or poverty and early death. Human choice and creativity have minimal relevance.

Holism and parts/whole theorizing

Bohm (1980), a scientist and philosopher, reported about his distinguished career "my main concern has been with understanding the nature of reality in general and of consciousness in particular as a coherent whole" (p. ix). The holistic standard urges social workers to judge theories by their appreciation for the irreducible qualities of wholes and by their interest in looking for continuous exchanges between parts and the whole. At times, the social worker may use theoretical analyses or research processes that examine the whole in terms of its components and study a part in isolation from the whole: theories about the woman with qualities independent of her role as wife or the thought processes of the irrational person separate from his or her thought communities (Phillips, 1976). This is similar to everyday theorizing when we single out a family member's face from the family portrait and think about their expressive facial patterns. The social worker committed to the holistic standard, however, uses analyses of a part cautiously with continuous reminders to her- or himself of the part's embeddedness in the whole and a quick return to use of theoretical literature and tools that explicate the indivisibility of biological, psychological, social, and spiritual aspects of the human experience.

Questions that guide critical thinking about a theory considering holism

Holists suggest a number of questions to guide theorizing practitioners as they think critically about a theory or theorizing activities. Is the theory a conceptual system permeated by downward reductionism, claims that all aspects of a higher level system can be explained by one lower level factor or process? Is the theory a conceptual system permeated by upward reductionism, claims that all aspects of a lower level system are determined by the one operation of a higher level system? Is the theory a holistic conceptual system assuming the whole is greater than the sum of the parts and including a continual emphasis on the complex and dynamic relation of parts to the whole, and the reciprocal influences of the whole and its parts? To what degree does the theory incorporate holistic philosophical tenets as compared to other theories, and to what degree does the theory support holistic approaches to information gathering, assessment formulation, intervention planning, intervention, and evaluation?

Learning activities and reflections

1   Reflect on social work with a family and their school-age child. The parents have received several reports from the sixth grade teacher that the child is misbehaving in the classroom and earning grades lower than his apparent potential. Start by attempting to identify "the whole" in this case? What theoretical knowledge might you need to gather information in a holistic manner and to formulate a holistic assessment? Where would you search for such knowledge, and how would you judge the knowledge to determine whether it met the standard of holism?

2   Social workers attempt to enhance clients' performance of important life roles. The bio-psycho-social perspective adopted by social work is a holistic stance. It assumes the interrelationship of basic life and role processes. Reflect on your performance as a student or as worker. How may health problems affect your psychology, your social interaction, and your spirituality and, thus, your performance of the school or work role? How can thinking or feeling difficulties complicate your efforts to stay healthy, to maintain supportive relationships, to affirm your faith beliefs and, thus, your performance of the role? How might troubles or setbacks in your social context (your relationships, networks, or memberships in larger societal groups) contribute to physical troubles,

psychological malfunctions, or doubts related to faith and, thus, your performance of the role? You might do the same kind of analysis of the influence of spiritual challenges (moments of doubt, for example) on the other dimensions of your whole being and on your role performance?

3   Review the following reductionist statements about the "person interacting in the environment." Some psychodynamic theorists have asserted that all human behavior can be understood as manifestations of aggressive and sexual drives and that all environmental patterns can be understood as the collective efforts to channel these instinctual drives. Some theorists aligned with sociobiology make a reductionist claim that all individual and collective action can be understood from an evolutionary perspective as those patterns that were selected over time because they gave the focal human population a survival advantage.

   Pick any one of these theoretical assertions, or identify a similar reductionist generalization. What are your reactions to this claim about human behavior and the social environment? Can you identify counter-examples that might undermine the assertion's validity? What illustrations of topics of concern to social workers at the family, community, organizational, societal, or international levels might not be well explained by the assertion? Pick one human behavior or human development area or topic at a system level higher than genetic inheritance or human drives. Then, offer an alternative, holistic, and non-reductionistic theoretical explanation of this aspect of human behavior and the environment.

References

Bertalanffy, L. von. (1969). *General systems theory*. New York: Braziller.

Bohm, D. (1980). *Wholeness and the implicate order*. London: Routledge.

Forte, J. A. (2006). *Human behavior and the social environment: Models, metaphors, and maps for applying theoretical perspectives to practice*. Belmont, CA: Thomson Brooks/Cole.

Hanson, B. G. (1995). *General systems theory beginning with wholes*. Washington, DC: Taylor and Francis.

International Federation of Social Workers (2010). Definition of social work. Retrieved August 16, 2010, from www.ifsw.org/f38000138.html

Lee, M. Y., Chan, C., Ng, S-M., & Leung, P. (2009). *Integrative body-mind-spirit social work: An empirically based approach to assessment and treatment*. New York: Oxford University Press.

National Association of Social Workers (2003). *NASW standards for integrating genetics into social work practice*. Washington, DC: NASW Press.

Phillips, D. C. (1976). *Holistic thought in social science*. Stanford, CA: Stanford University Press.

Wiley, N. (1994). *The semiotic self*. Chicago, IL: University of Chicago Press.

Critique theory using professional standard of justice

(EPAS 2.1.3 Apply Critical Thinking;
EPAS 2.1.5 Advance Human Rights;
EPAS 2.1.7 Apply Knowledge;
EPAS 2.1.8 Engage in Policy Practice)

The National Association of Social Workers (NASW) defines justice as "the view that everyone deserves equal economic, political and social rights and opportunities," and NASW declares that "social workers aim to open the doors of access and opportunity for everyone, particularly those in greatest need" (2010, p. 1).

The justice standard and theory appraisal

According to Witkin and Gottschalk (1988), theorizing has an important function in the global project to liberate oppressed people and to achieve just social arrangements. They argue:

> a distinctive feature of social work has been its commitment to a value base aimed at promoting a particular vision of social justice. These values help set social work apart from allied disciplines and professions. The evaluation of theories must consider their relationship to these values. (p. 216)

The social worker should use those theories that challenge destructive and unjust conditions and suggest better alternatives. Witkin and Gottschalk (1988) add a specific directive. Social workers should identify and reject the theoretical frameworks that advance the interests of the ruling groups while furthering the exploitation and domination of many other social groups. Politically engaged theory critique can raise the consciousness of social workers and other citizens susceptible to becoming passive victims of the ruling groups. The justice standard for theorizing and for theory evaluation is a necessary tool in the work of justice advocates rebelling against oppressors and promoting human emancipation from circumstances of arbitrary control and domination.

Swenson (1998) recommends the use of the justice standard, too. She rejects the position that a theoretical framework should be considered "value-free" and judged only by references to explanatory power and evidence of positive outcomes after application. Theories are not neutral. Knowledge is socially created, filtered through cultural perspectives, and can be used to protect the interests of groups with disproportionate privilege, power, and status. Social workers, Swenson (1998) adds, should give preference to theories congruent with justice. For instance, she endorses the strengths perspective because it emphasizes human capacities and rejects any "blame the victim" assumptions about humans and their struggles. She also appreciates the feminist theoretical perspective for its critique of power based on domination and subordination, for its assumption that the personal is political (personal experiences are always linked to social, economic, and political structures), and for its development of a methodology for raising the consciousness of vulnerable group members and fostering their liberation.

Lewis and Bolzan (2007) reinforce Swenson's pointed endorsement of critical thinking about theory in terms of justice. They write that

> social work theorists draw on the value base of social work, in particular social justice, as a boundary marking strategy to define itself as a discrete professional group informed by knowledge, practice, and research from other fields of professional endeavor. (p. 139)

Gil's profile of the just society

David Gil (1994, 1998, 2002, 2004), a distinguished social work theorist, has drawn on empowerment theories (critical and feminist approaches, for instances) to develop a vivid conception of the ideal and just person-in-environment configuration. His profile is a useful way to spell out the justice standard. In brief, he imagines the person as an active citizen with a critical consciousness and a capacity for dialogue with others. Transactions between people are I-Thou exchanges with each person treated as an equal, autonomous, authentic subject holding the same rights and responsibilities as any other person. The ideal social environment for Gil is a just society, one free from coercion, exploitation, and oppression and one characterized by wise stewardship of resources, member participation in workplace decision making, and the fair and balanced distribution of goods and service. In this just society, all can meet their basic needs, governance is democratic and nonhierarchical, and there are opportunities for all to develop their human potentials. The practitioner might take this justice-oriented depiction of the ideal "person interacting in the environment" state and use it to think critically about a focal theory and its contribution to the realization of Gil's characterization of the just society.

Justice and theory appraisal: an illustration

Let's take the case of attention deficit-hyperactivity disorder—a diagnosis asserting that a person has difficulty in staying focused and paying attention, difficulty in controlling behavior, and a tendency to impulsivity and over-activity. The underlying biomedical theoretical model for this diagnostic approach suggests that this is a biological disorder and the primary causes are genetic and neurological. Blame is centered on failed bodily processes. We could accept the narrow argument explaining this phenomenon. Or we could theorize about other relevant factors such as crowded schools and classrooms, outdated and poorly written textbooks, inexperienced teachers, family problems, boredom, hunger, preoccupation with text messaging and Web scanning, and inadequate opportunities for physical movement and exercise during the typical class day. We might wonder whether children from poor families are more often diagnosed with this "biomedical" condition as a way to ignore the ways that these families and their schools receive very few resources compared to those in wealthy communities. We might also wonder about collusion between pharmaceutical companies, some doctors, some psychologists, and even some social workers to profit from the recommendation that medications must be bought and used as the primary intervention once the biomedical theoretical explanation of restlessness is accepted. In justice-oriented theorizing, large political, economic, and cultural patterns are allocated responsibility for the unjust and sloppy use of a medical label.

Questions that guide critical thinking about theory considering justice

In order to act on the following conviction—theorizing activities, theoretical frameworks, their underlying assumptions, and their elements should be appraised by the justice standard—the practitioner can ask a series of questions (Anderson, 1976; Swensen, 1998; Witkin & Gottschalk, 1988). What particular interest groups are served by theory and use of the theory, and are those interests aligned or not aligned with the needs of client populations, especially the most vulnerable groups? Do the theory and its uses affirm the self-determination of members of oppressed groups? Do the theory and its uses contribute to the fair allocation of societal resources and to the extension of opportunities to more social groups? Do the theory and its uses contribute to the expression of marginalized voices in public forums and policymaking arenas? Do the theory and its uses expose unquestioned assertions that obscure the structures and processes causing inequality? Do the theory's assumptions, concepts, and propositions affirm human rights, enhance solidarity, and increase economic, political, and social equality and opportunity for all? Or do the theory and its applications support actions and policies that threaten human rights, undermine solidarity, and lessen equality and opportunity for select groups in the society? How well do the theory and its uses promote all forms of justice as compared to other theories?

Learning activities and reflections

1   The Center for Disease Control and Prevention (2010) reported that in 2003, 4 percent of children in the four- to eight-year-old category, 10 percent of children in the nine- to twelve-year-old category, and 10 percent of children in the thirteen- to eighteen-year-old category had been diagnosed with attention deficit hyperactivity disorder (ADHD). Many children were required to take medications prescribed by their doctors. The center noted also that the diagnosis of ADHD had increased an average of 3 percent per year from 1997 to 2006.

How can we explain theoretically this growing epidemic? Debate the statement "Personal problems and relationship difficulties such as classroom restlessness are too often defined using a biomedical theoretical framework that emphasizes medical diseases." What evidence for and against this statement can you present? What are some positive and negative implications of the "medicalization of problems" in relation to the promotion of economic, political, and social justice? What factors besides theoretical convictions and research support might lead a practitioner to use the biomedical model for problem definition and explanation? Do you suspect that children with certain group membership characteristics are more likely to be diagnosed with ADHD than other children? Which groups and why?

2   Take the role of critical thinker and engaged citizen committed to promoting social justice. Examine the proposition promoted by many classical "laissez faire" economic theorists and policy leaders in the United States. They propose that the best financial market is an unregulated market (the concept "market" refers to spheres of activity characterized by exchanges designed to achieve profit, and the concept "regulation" refers to the rules and governance of exchange processes by agents of the government or organizations imposed on the market).

Think critically using the justice standard. What are possible criticisms of this free-market theoretical assumption? How has this assumption advanced the interests of the ruling groups at the expense of most other citizens? Provide three or four examples. In the last 30 years, this economic approach has become increasingly influential in the United States and concurrently, the rich have become richer and the poor poorer: The top 20 percent of our society, for example, control 80 percent of the wealth, and the wealthiest 1 percent control almost 40 percent of the nation's wealth (Norton & Ariely, 2010). What might be a "justice" response to this trend toward inequality? What alternative theories, policies, and arrangements (economic, political, social) would achieve fairer economic consequences for the vulnerable populations served by social workers?

3   A just society provides equal social opportunity and treatment, political opportunity and treatment, and economic opportunity and treatment. Such societies are rare; inequality, differential opportunity, and discriminatory treatment are common. Characterize your salient social and cultural memberships related to age, race, ethnicity, social class, religion, region, and sexual orientation. Using these memberships, place yourself and your family in the societal hierarchy of status (low status to high status).

Describe in detail how, at some point in your family's development, two or three of these membership factors influenced your family's interaction, access to resources, communication patterns, division of labor, rituals, traditions or other family experiences. For example, when my father abandoned our Italian-American family and started to renege on his family support agreement, we changed from a middle-class to a lower-class single mother–headed unit. The effects of this downward mobility were great. We moved to a poor, somewhat dangerous, and mostly African American neighborhood. Each rent day brought fears that we would be evicted. My mother assumed traditionally male and female roles. I began to work part-time to supplement the family's income. For a short time, my three younger siblings had to live in a residential institution. Our relatives blamed my mother for our difficulties; minimal pressure was put on my father to meet his obligations.

Depending on your family's relative status, provide either an example of your experience of positive differential treatment (privilege) or an example of negative differential treatment (discrimination) related to your social and cultural background. What impact did the experience have on your bio-psycho-social development? Organize these reflections as a small-scale theory relating membership, position in a status hierarchy, and family development. How might these reflections help you understand and work with clients placed in a low status by their community and some of the injustices that they confront?

References

Anderson, J. D. (1976). Games social work educators play in teaching practice theories? In Council on Social Work Education (Ed.), *Teaching for competence in the delivery of social services* (pp. 1–8). New York: Council on Social Work Education.

Center for Disease Control (2010). Attention deficit/hyperactivity disorder. Retrieved August 10, 2010, from www.cdc.gov/ncbddd/adhd

Gil, D. G. (1994). Confronting social injustice and oppression. In F. C. Reamer (Ed.), *The foundations of social work knowledge* (pp. 231–263). New York: Columbia University Press.

Gil, D. G. (1998). *Confronting injustice and oppression: Concepts and strategies for social workers*. New York: Columbia University Press.

Gil, D. G. (2002). Challenging justice and oppression. In M. O' Melia & K. K. Miley (Eds), *Pathways to power: Readings in contextual social work practice* (pp. 35–54). Boston, MA: Allyn and Bacon.

Gil, D. G. (2004). Perspectives on social justice. *Reflections*, *10*(4), 32-39.

Lewis, I., & Bolzan, N. (2007). Social work with a twist: Interweaving practice knowledge, student experience and academic theory. *Australian Social Work*, *60*(2), 136–146.

National Association of Social Workers (2010). Issue fact sheets: Social Justice. Retrieved August 19, 2011, from www.naswdc.org/pressroom/features/issue/peace.asp

Norton, M. I. & Ariely, D. (2010). Building a better America—one wealth quintile at a time. Retrieved January 4, 2011, from www.people.hbs.edu/mnorton/norton%20ariely%20in%20press.pdf

Swenson, C. R. (1998). Clinical social work's contribution to a social justice perspective. *Social Work*, *43*(6), 527–537.

Witkin, S. L., & Gottschalk, S. (1988). Alternative criteria for theory evaluation. *Social Service Review*, *62*(2), 211–224.

Critique theory using professional standard of sensitivity to diversity

(EPAS 2.1.3 Apply Critical Thinking;
EPAS 2.1.4 Engage Diversity;
EPAS 2.1.7 Apply Knowledge)

Social workers prefer theoretical frameworks that affirm human differences rather than elevating certain membership groups to a conceptual place of privilege and casting other membership characteristics to the depths of the condemned. From such theories, it is more feasible to develop culturally sensitive interventions. Culturally sensitive interventions are defined as interventions with the following feature: the "target group's culture (i.e., values, norms, beliefs, practices) are incorporated into the design, delivery, and evaluation of an intervention." Such intervention development is done for the purpose of making the intervention "more accessible, congruent, and effective" (Jackson & Hodge, 2010, p. 260).

Diversity and theory appraisal

Professional socialization mandates screening for and training in cultural sensitivity and competence. Gatekeepers monitor, then, the social worker's capacity for taking the perspective of colleagues and clients from various cultural and membership backgrounds. The Council on Social Work Education (2013), for example, expects social workers to understand how diversity shapes the human identity and experience, to be competent in engaging human differences in practice, and to affirm our clients as persons whatever their membership characteristics. Human differences are understood in terms of the intersection of many different factors including age, class, color, culture, disability, ethnicity, gender, gender identity and expression, geographic location, immigration status, political ideology, race, religion, sex, and sexual orientation. Human differences are key to understanding variations in life chances and life constraints for persons, social groups, and communities.

Perspective taking, theoretical pluralism, and diversity

Generally, the development of theorizing competencies contributes to the perspectivist thinking about theoretical knowledge (Guzzini, 2001). Perspective taking refers to the perceptual, cognitive, affective, and imaginative processes used to anticipate, understand, interpret, or infer the covert and private feelings, cognitions, and intentions of another person or group of persons in order to coordinate one's overt conduct, behavior, or actions with that other person or group (Forte, 1998). Perspective taking is conceptualized as multidimensional (Schwalbe, 1988). Perspective-taking competence includes situational accuracy (correct decoding of external communicative signals and predictions of other's likely actions); range (the capacity to take and understand many different types of people and a diversity of perspectives); and depth (the capacity to infer fully the cognitive and emotional patterns and dynamics of an other's perspective). Perspective-taking performance depends on motivational factors and competence factors.

As a profession, social work affirms the proposition that contemporary pluralistic societies operate best when members of diverse cultural and other membership groups work to understand and respect one another, learn to accept and value human differences, and make commitments to cooperate together on community projects. This proposition is relevant to boundary work in multi-theory settings. Practice communities characterized by professionals with different theoretical allegiances are like pluralistic societies. Adept practical theorizers learn that there are multiple theoretical frameworks that are useful for making sense of a particular practice puzzle. Problem solving is enhanced by reciprocal perspective taking cooperation across theoretical, disciplinary, and professional boundaries. So theory users must learn to present their own positions to those with contrary theoretical preferences and explore areas of convergence and possibilities for joint action despite disagreements.

There is a close relationship between theoretical pluralism and social pluralism. When practitioners endorse theoretical pluralism, they grow professionally because of their openness to learning and using multiple theoretical perspectives. Additionally, acting on this endorsement, practitioners can select and use a wide range of theories. Each theory is a new lens. A practitioner with many different theoretical lenses has assorted ways to perceive, understand, appreciate, and respond to the experiences of diverse clients and colleagues (Doane & Varcoe, 2005). Anderson and Wiggins-Carter (2004) agree and contend that "competence in working with and on behalf of diverse populations requires more than just the adaptation of existing frameworks for practice. Clinical social workers must be prepared to expand their theory base and learn new models of practice" (p. 20).

Diversity and strategies for judging a particular theory

Like skilled diplomats in international social work, theorizing practitioners can take a range of theoretical perspectives and interact with the clients, colleagues, and mentors who see "person interacting in the environment" configurations from many different points of view. When judging any theoretical frameworks, the practitioner needs to take first the perspective of the framework and its advocates, understand its foundational assumptions, and grasp its arguments or explanations about the puzzle.

In a pluralistic society, some communities, however, affirm common perspectives, shared understandings, and behavioral norms damaging to members who are different. Social workers learn to challenge the stereotypical thinking and prejudicial actions emerging from these communities. Likewise, in our multi-theoretical practice universe, some theoretical frameworks include assumptions, concepts, propositions, or middle-range theories that distort the lived experiences of minority group members. Social work theory users can identify and reject these frameworks or call for significant revisions. Using such theories without rectifying their flaws will damage vulnerable or at-risk clients.

Appraising theoretical origins and assumptions

The theorizing practitioner should think critically about the assumptions of any theoretical candidate for practical use (McCrea, 2006). Do the assumptions suggest that the theory is sensitive to clients' diverse values and cultural contexts in a way transcending prejudice? Do the assumptions suggest that theory application ensures respectful partnership between workers and diverse clients, partnerships that are nonhierarchical, that promote client autonomy and connectedness, that call for the investigation of stigma and discrimination and their harmful effects, and that focus on protecting client dignity and self-determination. Or, in contrast, McCrea asks, do the theory's assumptions indicate that the theory should be rejected or that the theory needs modification for sensitive use with a particular membership group. For instance, would the theoretical assumptions of a focal theory indicate the theory's suitability for or negation of healing work with a Native American tribe in ways responsive to the tribal members' preferences regarding engagement, goal setting, session scheduling, the location of helping sessions, termination processes, and so on.

Anderson and Wiggins-Carter (2004) propose a strategy similar to the appraisal of theory using the diversity standard. They recommend a critical approach to existing theoretical frameworks, their assumptions, and their core images (root metaphors) of the person and society.

For example, they argue that some theories are built on assumptions common to a deficit model, and these theories "represent people of color, women, gays and lesbians, older people, and those with disabilities as having substantial and continuous difficulties" (p. 20). These social workers also recommend special attention to theories with origins and assumptions tied to Eurocentric cultural principles. These theories may assume that European-rooted values and traditions are superior to all others (to the detriment of African, Asian, and other clients), that patriarchy is desirable and male dominance should be reinforced (to the detriment of men and women), and that capitalism is the best economic approach and its emphasis on individualism and personal responsibility is preferable (to the detriment of those who don't hold this mainstream view and those who are marginalized in the capitalist system). If members of a particular group don't fit these assumptions and related images, Anderson and Wiggins-Carter argue, they are likely to be pathologized, labeled deviant, and ejected from the inside of valued communities by the theory users. Let me offer a few cautions about their line of argument. Anderson and his colleague don't name names and identify the "bad" theories. Nor do they provide evidence backing up this critical profile of "Eurocentric" theories.

Appraising theory-derived interventions

A theory and its theory-derived interventions should be judged for suitability for use with members of a particular membership group (Resnicow, Braithwaite, Ahluwalia, & Baranowski, 1999; Resnicow, Braithwaite, Dilorio, & Glanz, 2002). Optimally, the theory and theory-derived interventions are culturally sensitive. The conceptualization and design of a focal theory-based intervention, for example, affirms the cultural values of the membership group; incorporates concepts and if-then change propositions that reflect the subjective culture (attitudes, expectancies, norms) of the membership group; recognizes the historical, social, and environmental forces relevant to the group; and includes directives for the planned change process congruent with the behavioral preferences and expectations of the members of the group. Ideally, focus group interviews, literature reviews, ethnic mapping strategies, and other methods were used during the intervention design phase to determine preferences. Practitioners need the ability, then, to search, sort through, and select from theoretical knowledge relevant to diverse groups by judging the specific ways that the knowledge suggests interventions that apply sensitively or fail to apply to a given client system and its situation.

Diversity and theory appraisal: illustrations

There are some clear examples of theory problems when judged by the standard of sensitivity to diversity. Antiquated psychodynamic theories characterized homosexuality as a psychopathology, a disorder (Forte, 2006). Heterosexuality was considered the norm and the natural sexual orientation. Such theories included arguments that faulty parenting caused sex role identification with the same-sex parent and a consequent homosexual orientation. This resulted in the psychic pain, emotional and mental disorders, and interpersonal difficulties common to all homosexual persons. From this kind of theoretical base, sexual reconversion therapy became the logical form of intervention. Conversion therapy is an approach to practice that attempts to change the sexual orientation of a person from the "abnormal," homosexual or bisexual orientation, to the "normal," heterosexual orientation. Techniques used to convert lesbians, gay men, and others to heterosexuality have included the application of electric shock to the genitals, nausea-inducing drugs administered at the same time that homoerotic stimuli is presented, visualization, prayer, and intensive group pressure. Research evidence doesn't support the claims of effectiveness (National Committee on Lesbian, Gay, and Bisexual Issues, NASW, 2000). By the social work standard of diversity, psychodynamic theories rejecting the possibility of homosexuality as a mature and healthy orientation and failing to appraise sexual reconversion therapy as an immoral approach fall short.

Erik Erikson's life stage theory has also been appraised by use of the diversity standard. In brief, Cornett and Hudson (1987) took issue with Erikson's original conceptualization of the stage of generativity versus stagnation. In middle life, Erikson theorized, the developing person faces the danger of stagnation but can realize the joys of generativity. The person who can act on his or her capacities for generativity in the form of creative contributions to the next generations by raising their children and who can resist tendencies toward self-absorption will incorporate the ego strength of care. Such adults also develop a sense of responsibility to others. Ego interests expand, and the person devotes him- or herself to other people and wider causes. All social institutions should reinforce the values necessary to the development of familial generativity and the success of generations. Adults who fail to become generative develop instead a sense of stagnation and a basic ego problem: the preoccupation with one's own needs at the expense of the needs of others. Cornett and Hudson (1987) argued that this theory and its early use by practitioners revealed a preference for the conventional family with heterosexual parents fulfilling themselves through contributions to their children. Social workers must adjust Erikson's model of human development and ideas about middle adulthood to expand the meaning of generativity to persons with alternative sexual orientations. These adults may not have biological children, but they still pass on their gifts to the next generation by productive career activities, by creative involvement in volunteer service and hobbies, by artistic endeavors, by political advocacy, and by teaching younger gay and non-gay persons about identity issues and their resolution.

Dowling (2006) provides another example of how the theorizing practitioner might select the theory that best fits the needs of clients by using the diversity standard. The social worker serving disabled children and their families might use the prevalent biomedical model. According to this theoretical approach, disability is a problem that resides in the individual. The disability problem is the result of a mental or physical impairment. The impairment is the cause of the child's and family's stress and coping challenges. Medical interventions such as surgery and medication are preferred. However, Dowling asserts that the biomedical theory doesn't meet the standard of affirmation of differences. She recommends instead the choice of a social model. Difficulties related to the inability to walk are not characterized as indicators of an individual impairment. Instead, the difficulties are caused by the society and its failures to provide accommodations such as transportation accessible to wheelchair users. The child and his or her family experience hardships primarily because of ecological barriers, prejudicial treatment, and poorly conceived and/or supported policies and social programs. From this theoretical base, social workers don't focus on changing the child but on reorganizing the society. The practitioners advocate for policies, programs, and practices that take account of physical differences.

Theoretical contributions to the appreciation of diversity

We have been examining how some frameworks have fallen short of the diversity standard. However, many theoretical frameworks have particular strengths and contribute to our understanding of differences in a variety of ways: the influence of differences on human behavior, human development and life chances; the ecological, social, and psychological factors contributing to differences; and the construction of culturally-sensitive interventions (Dana, Gamst, & Der-Karabetian, 2008).

Let's use the "person interacting in the environment" framework to identify some specific theoretical contributions (Forte, 2006). Several theories illustrate diversity and related patterns. The behavioral theoretical framework informs us about the relationship between variations in learning opportunities, models, and favored rewards and punishments and a person's action patterns. The bio-evolutionary framework has documented the influence of genetic predispositions and physical characteristics (height, weight, skin shade, hair texture, facial features, and so on) on bio-psycho-social functioning. The cognitive theoretical framework theorizes about linkages between the particular characteristics of a "thought community" and notions of rationality, tendencies toward stereotypical thinking, and prejudicial conceptions of other persons.

Symbolic interactionism and pragmatism focus on diversity and interaction between the person and the environment. These approaches have theorized extensively about variations in symbol sets (words, gestures, objects, actions, and so on) and symbol using preferences as related to different cultural and sub cultural groups.

We can use the diversity standard to identify contributions to knowledge about environmental influences on the construction of diversity. Ecological theory specializes in the formulation of ways to characterize variations in the ecosystem, niches, and built spaces as influences on human adaptation in such contexts. Critical and feminist theoretical frameworks focus on the influence of differences in power, privilege, and status on life chances, interaction patterns, and social awareness. The strengths perspective provides insights into community-based differences in the quantity and quality of collective assets and personal strengths as affecting the actualization of member potentials. We might, additionally, identify the practice theories associated with various explanatory theoretical frameworks and list illustrations of guidelines, techniques, and skills for diversity-affirming helping work.

Questions that guide critical thinking about a theory considering diversity

When thinking critically about theories and theorizing activity with reference to the standard, "sensitivity to diversity," the social work practitioner can make use of the questions suggested by McCrea (2006) earlier in this lesson. The following questions also guide critical reflection. Does the theory portray the client, family, or other social system accurately and with appreciation for its membership characteristics, background, and social context? Does the theory limit the worker's ability to know and respond in culturally sensitive and competent ways to diverse clients by including stereotypes or shallow assumptions about human differences? Is the theory built on a narrow set of cultural principles assuming that a particular cultural tradition is superior to the traditions of groups in other continents and countries? Does the theory boldly or subtly make the case that if members of a particular group don't act in accord with the theory's assumptions, root metaphors, and conceptualizations, they should be pathologized, labeled deviant, cast as victims, or ejected from valued communities? How well does the theory affirm human diversity and suggest culturally sensitive interventions as compared to other theoretical approaches?

Learning activities and reflections

1 React critically to the following generalizations made by classical psychodynamic theorists (many decades ago) about diverse members. Religion is a neurosis, an infantile way to deal with family relations and to attempt to control the environment. Homosexuality is the result of pathogenic developmental processes, and homosexuals are characterized by arrested, immature, narcissistic, and undifferentiated capacities for relationships with people and things. Women's biological differences from men condition their psychology and ensure that they are subordinate beings: inferior, incomplete, envious of the male's penis, and preferring submissive interaction patterns.

How do such characterizations fit with the social work approach to human diversity? What problems might practitioners using such theoretical ideas have in customizing their helping work interventions to fit client membership characteristics? What evidence might you use to support or reject these generalizations? What alternative theoretical explanations might you offer for spiritual practices, alternative sexual orientations, and gender-based identity and interaction patterns?

2 Take a feminist theoretical approach toward childhood and gender development (For example, this approach argues that boys have greater opportunities and louder voices in sexist societies. Girls are cast generally as inferior and restricted in subtle and blatant ways from achieving their full potential. Such gender inequalities have identifiable influences on male and female development). Analyze how children were socialized in your family. What different meanings were attached to boys and to girls? How did significant others (your mother, your father, and your siblings) interact differently with boys and girls? What were different behavioral expectations for male and female children? How were the family environments designed differently to accommodate boys and girls? What impacts of these gender-based socialization practices have you experienced or observed later in life on yourself or your siblings (behavior patterns, career aspirations, relationship style, life obstacles and opportunities, etc.)? Appraise this feminist theoretical standpoint on development using the diversity standard.

3 Create a theory about an important human behavior and the social environment topic from a mainstream perspective; for example, the perspective of a white, middle-class, physically able, heterosexual and Protestant male of European descent. Now create a theory on the same topic from the perspective of a member of a minority group (or of multiple minority groups). How do the two theories differ? How are the theories similar? What implications for the application of theory to practice can you derive from this activity?

References

Anderson, J., & Wiggins-Carter, R. (2004). Diversity perspectives for social work practice. In R. A. Dorfman, P. Meyer & M. L. Morgan (Eds), *Paradigms of clinical social work, Volume 3, Emphasis on diversity* (pp. 19–33). New York: Brunner-Routledge.

Council on Social Work Education (2013). *2008 Educational policy and accreditation standards.* Retrieved July 17, 2013, from www.cswe.org/File.aspx?id=13780

Cornett, C. W., & Hudson, R. A. (1987). Middle adulthood and the theories of Erikson, Gould, and Vaillant: Where does the gay man fit? *Journal of Gerontological Social Work*, 10(3/4), 61–73.

Dana, R. H., Gamst, G. C., & Der-Karabetian, A. (2008). *CBMCS multicultural training program.* Thousand Oaks, CA: Sage.

Doane, G. H., & Varcoe, C. (2005). Toward compassionate action: Pragmatism and the inseparability of theory/practice. *Advances in Nursing Science*, 28(1), 81–90.

Dowling, M. (2006). Translating theory into practice: The implications for practitioners and users and carers. *Practice*, 18(1), 17–30.

Forte, J.A. (1998). Power and role-taking: A review of theory, research and practice. *Journal of Human Behavior in the Social Environment*, 1(4), 27–56.

Forte, J. A. (2006). *Human behavior and the social environment: Models, metaphors, and maps for applying theoretical perspectives to practice.* Belmont, CA: Thomson Brooks/Cole.

Guzzini, S. (2001). The significance and roles of teaching theory in international relations. *Journal of International Relations and Development*, 4(2), 98–117.

Jackson, K. F., & Hodge, D. R. (2010). Native American youth and culturally sensitive interventions: A systematic review. *Research on Social Work Practice*, 20(3), 260–270.

McCrea, K. T. (2006). Social work practice diversities: Clients, social workers, and theories about their partnerships for constructive change. In D. W. Engstrom & L. M. Piedra (Eds), *Our diverse society: Race and ethnicity-Implications for 21st century American society* (pp. 201–226). Washington, DC: NASW Press.

National Committee on Lesbian, Gay, and Bisexual Issues, NASW (2000). "Reparative" and "conversion" therapies for lesbians and gay men: Position Statement. Retrieved May 9, 2013, from www.socialworkers.org/diversity/lgb/reparative.asp

Resnicow, K., Braithwaite, R., Ahluwalia, J., & Baranowski, T. (1999). Cultural sensitivity in public health: Defined and demystified. *Ethnicity and Disease*, 9, 10–21.

Resnicow, K., Braithwaite, R., Dilorio, C., & Glanz, K. (2002). Applying theory to culturally diverse and unique populations. In K. Glanz, B. K. Rimer, R, M. Lewis, & F. Marcus (Eds), *Health behavior and health education: Theory, research, and practice* (3rd edn, pp. 485–505). San Francisco, CA: John Wiley and Sons.

Schwalbe, M.L. (1988). Role taking reconsidered: Linking competence and performance to social structure. *Journal for the Theory of Social Behaviour*, 18(4), 411–436.

LESSON	Critique theory
29	using professional standard of strengths

(EPAS 2.1.3 Apply Critical Thinking;
EPAS 2.1.7 Apply Knowledge)

Do you see a glass of juice as half empty or half full, a social or natural disaster as a crisis or a challenge, a family as a mess of dysfunction or a collection of possibilities? Is the theory that you endorse infused with assumptions, concepts, explanations, and imagery emphasizing deficits or potentials? If given the opportunity, advocates of strengths-oriented social work argue, you should pick a positive theoretical framework, one that conceives of the person, environment, and transactions in terms of resources, opportunities, and strengths rather than absences, pathologies, and disorders.

Illustration of a deficit theoretical orientation

In thinking critically about a theory or theorizing activity using the strengths standard, a counter-example helps. Some social workers using family systems theory, for example, have conceptualized the "family in the environment" phenomenon in a way that emphasizes family system dysfunction, surrounding systems characterized by negative norms and role models, and family dynamics prone to chaos and disorganization. Weakness and failure are assumed, and expectations for success are few. Kaslow's handbook (1996) prioritized diagnosis of family dysfunction. The influential Bowen Center (2013) characterized basic nuclear family patterns as marital conflict, spouse dysfunction, child impairment, and emotional distance. Arpin, Fitch, Browne, and Corey (1990) identified 30 percent of families seeking health services as dysfunctional. The following is my creative profile of a deficit-oriented family systems theoretical orientation, a kind of approach to assessment and intervention that I learned during my graduate studies. I present it with once-common and negative characterizations of "multi-problem families."

In such families, the personalities of each member are disordered. An incapacity for empathy, understanding, and sensitivity toward certain family members is the norm. A tendency to deny the severity of family failings is strong, and each member has boundary issues and thus is unable to maintain barriers against physical, emotional, or sexual abuse from the others and outsiders. This approach assumes that criminality, mental breakdown, addiction, suicide, unwanted teenage pregnancy, incarceration, and other tragic outcomes are inevitable for a disproportionately high number of these families compared to those in healthy family systems.

In such families, interaction is problematic. Fighting, arguing, misbehavior, and abuse occur continually and regularly, and members learn to accommodate themselves to such patterns as normal. Unfair and biased exchanges characterize family processes; some members are indulged because of age, gender or personality traits while others are cast as scapegoats and treated with unearned harshness. Trust is rare; deception and manipulation frequent. Negative emotions such as anger, fear, envy, and hopelessness are more often expressed than positive emotions such as love, confidence, pride, and hope. Attachments are few, and promiscuity is favored.

In such families, there is one parent or no biological parents. Fathers have abandoned their children. Mothers can't meet their multiple role demands. If the family system is not broken, the subsystems are. The parents are dysfunctional. Family difficulties result from co-dependent parents or from parental struggling with substance abuse, untreated mental illness, the lingering effects of their own subjugation by their dysfunctional parents, or stalled psychosocial and moral development. Parents have minimal authority over their children and few parenting skills. Sibling dyads are equally dysfunctional, and siblings join together to evade parental surveillance and influence.

In such families, system dynamics are also dysfunctional. Members never spend recreational or social time together. Role assignments are unclear and unstable. Leadership is minimal or tyrannical. Family communication and decision-making processes are primitive. Secrets are common, and threat rather than persuasion is the preferred method for achieving agreements. These destructive family system patterns are transmitted across generations, and the pattern of disorganized, disconnected, and maladaptive system dynamics will be continued in the children's and grandchildren's lifetimes.

Communities with multi-problem families are rife with problems but not with resources. There is little employment in legitimate jobs. Crime, disease, addiction, and violence are rampant. Housing is deteriorating, and the physical environment is harsh, smelly, and noisy. Police are brutal and racist while businesses and professionals have fled to the suburbs. Schools are overcrowded, uncaring, and chaotic bureaucracies. Media images and sounds glorify gangsters, greed, and cruelty. Gunfights find innocent bystanders in harm's way.

Although a caricature, some practitioners see families, their members, and their environments in terms of weaknesses. Adopting a deficit orientation, social workers are likely to lose hope and doubt their ability to stimulate positive change. Committed to a deficit approach, there is no theoretical directive to look for strengths and resilience (despite exposure to numerous hazards), to capture moments of mutual aid and caring interaction, to identify episodes of group cohesion and adaptability, to learn about survival strategies passed across generations, and to search for assets and resources hidden but present in the community and culture. The deficit orientation becomes part of a self-fulfilling prophecy: the expectation of weakness. Helping actions influenced by this bias accelerate the trajectory toward rampant failure.

Strengths and theory appraisal

It is unlikely that you will find a theory as bleak and negative as the family systems theory caricature presented above. Recently, many social work leaders, educators, and practitioners have developed the conviction that the best theoretical knowledge recognizes and promotes human strengths. A strength is "a capacity for feeling, thinking, and behaving in a way that allows optimal functioning in the pursuit of valued outcomes" (Rettew & Lopez, 2008, p. 2). The strengths perspective asserts that social workers can make significant difference in the lives of clients by helping them search for and identify strengths, capacities, and resiliencies (Saleebey, 1992). Social workers also assist in the search for small-group, family, community, organizational, and other environmental strengths and assets that can be mobilized on behalf of clients.

There are several premises central to strengths-oriented theories (Saleebey, 2006). First, every person, group, community, and society has strengths, and these can be identified, respected, and mobilized as transformative resources. Second, adverse life experiences such as illness, abuse, and poverty may be injurious, but they can also be sources of opportunity; people are resilient and find strategies to cope with life's difficulties. Third, theorists and practitioners should not set limits to the capacity to grow. If practitioners and others hold high expectations of clients and affirm client hopes, values, aspirations, and visions, the clients will realize some of their potentials. Fourth, every environment is full of resources. These resources include individuals, families, informal and formal groups, associations, and institutions willing to help others. These people and systems can contribute knowledge, support, special talents, time, energy, concrete aid, and so on to ameliorate or eliminate personal and collective problems. Fifth, human well-being is essentially related to mutual aid and caring relations. Practical theories should facilitate community members' efforts to help and care for each other.

Let me add two more premises. Sixth, the strengths perspective and the theory of risk and resilience are closely related (Greene, 2006). Communities vary by the prevalent risks and hazards, by the protective factors that lessen exposure to the risk, by the degree of resilience of community members, and by the ability of members to recover from participation in risky or hazardous behaviors. Seventh, the strengths standard for diversity directs us to consider the particular meanings community members assign to common events, experiences, and traits (Ungar, 2004). An individual strength in one community may be perceived as a weakness in another community.

Committed to such theoretical premises, Saleebey (2001) even argued that social workers need to create a diagnostic strengths manual as an alternative to disorder-based classification. The *Diagnostic Statistical Manual of Mental Disorders* (American Psychiatric Association, 2000) is an assessment tool used by many practitioners to categorize youths and adults by disorder and associated signs and symptoms. The manual—we will consider its fourth version (DSM-IV)—is rooted in an illness or psychopathological model. Diagnoses based on the manual increase in the likelihood of reimbursement from medical insurance companies and the probability that medication will be included as a preferred intervention. Clients may be categorized by diagnoses such as dementia, male erectile disorder, mood disorder, gender identity disorder, schizophrenia, stuttering, mathematics disorder, and sibling relationship problems and by subtypes of many of the major diagnoses. More than 900 pages summarize the multitude of mental disorders and their major features. Saleeby calls for the construction of a parallel tool cataloguing individual strengths and system resources.

The strengths orientation is a significant departure from the past preferences of many other professionals and some social workers for theoretical and practice orientations emphasizing disease, deficit, deviancy, disorder, disorganization, disturbance, or dysfunction (Saleebey & Longres, 1997). Contemporary practitioners should appraise any theory, theory element, or theorizing activity by examining its foundations and weighing its relative emphasis on the positive aspects of "person interacting in an environment" configurations.

Questions that guide critical thinking about theory considering strengths

Strengths-oriented social workers propose questions to ask when selecting an ideal theoretical framework (Gergen, 1990; Rapp, 1998; Saleebey & Longres, 1997). Does the theory include assumptions that the past conditions but doesn't determine human behavior, that each person has a degree of agency, and that every person can choose and achieve a better future? Does the theory recommend practitioners begin with dysfunction and prescribe remedies, or does the theory begin with aspirations and urge practitioners to invite clients to engage in projects of actualizing desired scenarios? What is the theoretical language like? Is it mostly a vocabulary of pathology and problem, or is it a vocabulary of strengths and accomplishment? Does the theory suggest that certain people and groups are doomed to failure or that all human beings have unrealized potentials and with the right circumstances can learn and grow despite past adversity? Does the theory contend that certain environments are empty terrains with none of the emotional, social, and material nourishment necessary for sustaining life or that all environments include goods, services, relationships, and opportunities that can be used by members to progress toward positive and fulfilling lives? How well does the theory compare to other theories in emphasizing possibilities, potentials, and prospects?

Learning activities and reflections

1 Identify an example of a theory or concept that focuses primarily on negative aspects of human behavior. Identify an example of a theory or concept that focuses primarily on positive aspects of human behavior: strengths, capabilities, competencies, and possibilities. Compare and contrast each approach in terms of explanation and intervention. What are the pros and cons of adopting a strengths perspective compared to a deficit perspective?

2 Think about the diagnostic strengths manual as an alternative to disorder-based classification. What might Saleeby's objections be to the heavy reliance on the DSM-IV? What are negative consequences experienced by a client labeled with a disorder? For the client? For significant others? For the community? What are possible positive consequences associated with a diagnostic label? What might a manual designed to help social workers identify environmental assets and strengths look like? What would be good and bad consequences after practitioners shift to a strengths category system?

3 Watch one of the film portrayals of urban life—*Boyz in the Hood, Menace to Society,* or *Colors*—or watch a few episodes of the television series, *The Wire,* or a similar sociologically oriented and realistic depiction of the experiences of African-American teenagers (or groups of other people of color) in a large city. Focus on several major characters. Use a version of a theoretical framework (behavioral, psychodynamic, or family systems theories, for instances) that is not oriented to strengths and formulate your assessment of the deficits of each of these characters and of their neighborhoods.

   Next, use a strengths orientation for your assessment. Identify protective factors and risk factors prevalent in the characters' community. Discuss perceived strengths and illustrations of resilience in the face of chronic and severe adversity. Summarize your assessment of the characters, their resilient responses to challenges, and the assets and other resources available in their neighborhoods.

Imagine that you could discuss these two different theory-based assessment formulations with the characters of the film or television show or with wise and alert members of their communities. How might they judge the two theoretical interpretations of the same "person interacting in environment" dynamics? What might be the differential impact of social work with such at-risk populations guided by the deficit perspective compared to the strengths perspective?

References

American Psychiatric Association. (2000). *Diagnostic and statistical manual of mental disorders* (4th edn, text revision). Washington, DC: American Psychiatric Association.

Arpin, K., Fitch, M., Browne, G. B., & Corey, P. (1990). Prevalence and correlates of family dysfunction and poor adjustment to chronic illness in specialty clinics. *Journal of Clinical Epidemiology, 43*(4), 373–383.

Gergen, K. J. (1990). Therapeutic professions and the diffusion of deficit. *The Journal of Mind and Behavior, 11*(3–4), 357–368.

Greene, R. (2006). *Social work practice: A risk and resilience perspective.* Belmont, CA: Wadsworth.

Kaslow, F. W. (Ed.). (1996). *Handbook of relational diagnosis and dysfunctional family patterns.* New York: John Wiley and Sons.

Rapp, C. A. (1998). *The strengths model: Case management with people suffering from severe and persistent mental illness.* New York: Oxford University Press.

Rettew, J. G., & Lopez, S. J. (2008). Discovering your strengths. In S. J. Lopez (Ed.) *Positive psychology: Exploring the best in people: Discovering human strengths* (pp. 1–21). Westport, CT: Praeger.

Saleebey, D. (1992). Introduction: Power in the people. In D. Saleeby (Ed.), *The strengths perspective in social work practice* (pp. 3–17). New York: Longman.

Saleebey, D. (2001). The diagnostic strengths manual. *Social Work, 46*(2), 183–187.

Saleebey, D. (Ed.). (2006). *The strengths perspective in social work practice.* (4th edn). Boston, MA: Pearson Education.

Saleebey, D., & Longres, J. (1997). Is it feasible to teach HBSE from a strengths perspective in contrast to one emphasizing limitations or weaknesses? In M. Bloom & W. C. Klein (Eds), *Controversial issues in human behavior and the social environment* (pp. 16–32). Boston, MA: Allyn and Bacon.

The Bowen Center (2013). Nuclear family emotional system. Retrieved October 9, 2013, from www.thebowencenter.org/pages/conceptnf.html.

Ungar, M. (2004). A constructionist discourse on resilience: Multiple contexts, multiple realities among at-risk children and youth. *Youth and Society, 35*(3), 341–365.

Critique theory by reference to moral and technical uses

(EPAS 2.1.3 Apply Critical Thinking; EPAS 2.1.7 Apply Knowledge)

In this book, I have commented repeatedly on the responsible and effective uses of theoretical knowledge. I have linked such use to professional core competencies. The Council on Social Work Education (CSWE) expects practitioners "to apply *theories* and knowledge from the liberal arts to understand biological, social, cultural, psychological, and spiritual development" (CSWE, 2013, p. 6; emphasis added). Several other uses are identified in the CSWE standards. These include applying knowledge of human behavior and the social environment to understand person and environment, critiquing knowledge about person and environment, and using conceptual frameworks to guide the helping processes, especially assessment, intervention, and evaluation.

Immoral uses and theory appraisal

Theorizing responsibly and effectively includes the recognition that theoretical knowledge may be used for immoral purposes or improperly used. In a previous lesson on judging theory by social work ethical and value standards, we explored how social workers can use theory in accord with our code of ethics and core professional values. In this lesson, we will examine other misuses of theoretical knowledge.

Theory use for destructive ends

A theoretical framework often includes premises, concepts, and propositions that can guide the formulation and implementation of social policies. Political leaders, policy entrepreneurs, agents of social control and others who don't accept the bonds of professional ethics have used theories and their elements for evil ends. For example, eugenics theory, a distorted version of the genetic and evolutionary biology traditions, represented the product of theorizing about social actions that would improve the gene pool of human populations. This theory was harmfully influential during the early twentieth century (Penna, 2004). Adolph Hitler and his Nazi followers used eugenics to justify human experimentation, the prohibition of sexual contact across racial-ethnic groups, and the extermination of "undesired" population groups. In the United States, eugenics became a theoretical rationale for administrators of state hospitals deciding what to do with persons diagnosed with mental illnesses or learning disabilities. Theory-justified policies included the forced institutionalization of persons deemed unfit for community life, the use of lobotomies to treat persons diagnosed with mental illnesses, and the compulsory sterilization of many vulnerable adults. Following breeding rationales, those with traits allegedly caused by damaged genes were made incapable of passing on their illness, disability, racial characteristics, or adaptive strengths to the general population. More recently, variations of eugenics theory assuming the superiority of the dominant social groups and the inferiority of rival ethnic or tribal groups have been used to justify policies and programs of "ethnic cleansing" or genocide in Rwanda and Bosnia.

Here's a second example. Marxist theory and Marx's ideas about ideal community were transformed by political leaders such as Lenin and Stalin to serve a theoretical rationale for the creation of a totalitarian state in the Soviet Union. Mass murder, extreme abuses of power, and the complete repression of citizens advocating for rights were excused as necessary steps on the society's path toward a fully developed and communist society (Penna, 2004).

Theory use and knowledge control or distortion

There are other illustrations of the immoral misuse of theories. Dorothy Smith (1990), a feminist theorist, has written of the control of knowledge and knowledge use by male scientists, sociologists, doctors, lawyers, judges, and community leaders. The privileged theoretical and research knowledge ignored women's experience and was used to justify unfair policies and actions. Smith and her feminist associates have documented such misuse of scientific knowledge. Biomedical doctors, for example, used male-biased theories to ignore or disvalue the experiences and stated preferences of women giving birth. Psychiatric theories made possible the judgment by male authorities that women expressing strong emotions in response to overwhelming and inequitable family roles should be institutionalized. If a woman challenged the judgment of these powerful men, this challenge was interpreted as additional proof of her hysteria and poor contact with reality. See Clint Eastwood's film, *The Changeling* (2008), a tale of a mother institutionalized for rejecting the police's false claim to have found her lost son for a vivid dramatization of a real-life abuse of psychiatric theories.

Drug policy experts (Choo, Roh, & Robinson, 2008; Golub & Johnson, 2002) argue that the gateway theory of drug abuse—people start with marijuana use and this leads to the use of hard drugs such as crack cocaine and heroin—has been intentionally misused. First, the research suggests that the theory's central tenets are incorrect for most drug users. Second, the theory has been used to justify the harsh and life-damaging incarceration of many young marijuana users. Third, the theory allows political leaders and policy makers to ignore the risk factors that are much more predictive of hard drug use such as neighborhood crime and drug sales, anti-social peers, and schools that don't evoke student commitment.

Technical misuses and theory appraisal

Theory users may use theory to justify immoral means or to support actions to achieve immoral ends. However, some theory users are inept. There are many improper ways to use theory.

Bias

Bias refers to a process of thinking that gives systematic favoritism to certain theory-based interpretations and interventions over alternatives. Such biased theorizing activities are a hindrance to effective practice; Goldfried (1999) argues to watch for biases because "they lead us to distort information provided, inaccurately fill in the gaps, or selectively recall that which fits with our theoretical construction" (p. 544). For a biased practitioner, the theory directs what one sees, even if these perceptions are not supported by data collected. Additionally, such a practitioner may reject interventions, even those supported by evidence if they go counter to unsupported interventions derived from the favored theory.

Whitaker (1976), a family therapist, is also concerned about theoretical bias. He believes that those who adopt a biomedical theory often emphasize symptoms and focus helping efforts on diagnosing and relieving symptoms even when this stance isn't congruent with a client's needs. Psychodynamic theories of psychopathology bias workers toward attaching abstractions about blocked personality development and infantile character structures to family members. Helping is an art as well as a science, Whitaker believes, and theoretical bias (and any closed-minded theory-guided practice) undermines practitioner intuition and creativity, creates a distance between the worker and the family group, creates therapeutic rigidity, reduces practitioner trust in the helping process, and lessens the use of accumulated practice experience.

Ecological fallacy

The ecological fallacy occurs when the theorist draws conclusions about individuals on the basis of data on groups or other larger-size social systems. Chafetz (1978) provides an example of shoddy theorizing on the relationship between race and voting behavior. In her example, voting records indicated that a majority White precinct voted 75 percent of the time for the conservative candidate whereas the adjacent majority Black precinct voted 75 percent of the time for the liberal candidate. To theorize that White voters prefer and vote for conservatives and Black voters prefer and vote for liberals is an ecological fallacy. All Blacks in the first precinct may have voted, in fact, for the conservative candidate.

Reductionism

Reductionism is a theorizing problem that we have examined in the lesson on the holistic standard. Reductionism occurs when a theorist explains aspects of a complex larger system, a country frequently engaged in war, for instance, by variables associated with lower-level systems, belligerent, and aggressive personality dispositions of citizens and leaders. Though lower-level phenomena may be part of the explanatory framework, the reductionist claims inaccurately that the individual or group variables fully and adequately explain the societal pattern.

Reification

The theorizing mistake of reification refers to the process of attributing the status of reality to a theoretical concept or proposition (Thyer, 2008a). Theories are conceptual creations, not tangible things. Sometimes, theorizers forget this fact. The theorist, for example, may become so enamored of his or her creation that he or she treats the abstraction as if it were a real part of the environment with the abilities and qualities of living beings. The theoretical object has scientific meaning, but it doesn't breathe, move, eat, or die in the way living organisms do.

Tautology

A tautology is a circular form of theorizing. The theorist asserts that something (the subject term) is true by definition (the explanation). The form of a theoretical assertion is such that it can't be falsified (Chafetz, 1978). The inept theorizer claims, for example, that Pedro is smart. High intelligent quotient (IQ) scores on an intelligence test explain his smartness. If smart is defined as high intelligence, a circular argument, IQ scores don't add anything to the theoretical explanation of Pedro's cognitive functioning.

Teleology

Teleology means that the theorist provides a theoretical explanation that offers the result of something as its cause (Chafetz, 1978). For example, a community organizer might theorize about why communities develop a division of labor after reaching a certain size of population. The theorist suggests that the division of labor is created to reduce competition between community members over scarce resources. Chafetz points out that the anticipated result of a community process couldn't have been the cause of the process. In actual cases, it is very unlikely that community members ever convene to discuss how to specialize, to divide labor by specialties, and to do so with the rationale of avoiding within-community competition. The division of labor is more likely an unforeseen result of community growth.

Theoretical overgeneralization

Theoretical overgeneralization occurs when a theorist develops an explanation, prediction, or description based on research on a population with specific characteristics. Then, the theorist extends his or her claims about the relevance of the theory to a different or larger population. For example, critics of Alfred Kinsey's theorizing about patterns of human sexuality complain about sampling issues (Jones, 1997). Kinsey asserted that he was discovering common patterns of sexual activity in the general United States adult population. However, his samples, critics report, included an over-representation of prostitutes, homosexuals, prisoners, and child molesters. Thus, patterns and types suggested by the data might not occur in the larger population. Incidentally, Kinsey and his supporters contested this charge of improper theoretical generalization.

Professionally damaging misuses of theory

There are a variety of ways that inept or irresponsible theory users might damage the profession and their own professional growth and reputation. Theorizing practitioners should use their critical thinking skills to avoid such negative outcomes.

Pseudoscientific theory

Thyer (2008b) warns social workers, for example, against investigating and learning about a bad theory, one without empirical support or positive qualities as judged by our scientific and social work standards. Past-life regression theory and therapy fit this description of bad theory. Such efforts waste the practitioner's precious time and resources. Ben-Ari (2005) refers to such bad theory as pseudoscience, a theory that makes use of the style and conventions of science without any legitimate claim to status as science (Ben-Ari, 2005). Pseudoscience has a variety of identifiable deficiencies: the lack of explanatory mechanisms, the lack of a coherent system of concepts and propositions, and a shortage of empirical support. Ben-Ari identifies alchemy and astrology as examples of pseudoscience and would join Thyer in claiming that their use weakens professionals and their profession.

Using pseudoscientific theory can also result in ineffective and even harmful helping activities (Thyer, 2008b). For instance, the use of a rebirthing theoretical orientation (the approach emphasizes resolving current problems by re-experiencing birth traumas and simulating a trauma-free birth) caused the death of one social work client.

Theoretical monism

Thyer (2008b) advises also against adopting one theory as the only lens for understanding practice challenges and then forcing all observations into a form consistent with the vision provided by this theoretical lens. Such theoretical monism blinds the social worker or professional team to other useful theoretical perspectives and lessens the likelihood of finding a good match between theories and the problems identified during assessment. Plionis (2004) shares this conviction and argues that no single theory can accommodate all the person-in-environment processes and structures addressed by social workers. Moreover, social workers need to discriminate intelligently from a variety of useful theories. Thus, in particular cases, they can pick the theory that is most applicable to the helping circumstances and best supported by the evidence.

Theory cults

Finally, Thyer (2008b) worries about professionals and professional groups that give theory leaders, theory creators, and theory advocates the status of authority figures and, then, create personality cults adulating these theorists. Such adoration reduces critical thinking, increases destructive antagonism toward all who challenge theoretical ideas, and deepens reluctance to subject the theory to scientific and logical tests. Lindblom and Cohen (1979) note also that a cultish embrace of a particular theory undermines the interactive and improvisational problem solving necessary to effective theory application and becomes a noisy distraction during the helping process.

Learning activities and reflections

1   Review your grasp of history, politics, current events, and world affairs. If necessary, spend a week scanning a major newspaper or a Web-based news organization. Identify an example of the immoral use of theory in relation to policy, public programs, or social problem solving. Specify the person misusing the theory. Describe the use of the theoretical knowledge for harmful and destructive means and/or ends. How might a critical thinker challenge the distorted use of theory?

2 Familiarize yourself with each of the inept uses of theory identified in the attached commentary. Summarize the meaning of each in your own words. Pick one and give an illustration of how you might make the mistake in your own application of theory to practice.

3 Talk with social work friends, colleagues, supervisors, or teachers about their observations of theory use in the profession. With their help, attempt to identify an example of a time when a professional has used an explanatory theory or practice theory in a way damaging to the professional's growth or reputation. With their input, attempt to identify an illustration from a profession's long history of a time when the social work profession or an association or subgroup within the profession has used theory in a way that weakened our allegiance to a scientific and accountable knowledge base. Describe each example in detail, and identify some ways that the damage might have been avoided or repaired.

References

Ben-Ari, M. (2005). *Just a theory: Explaining the nature of science.* Amherst, NY: Prometheus.

Chafetz, J. S. (1978). *A primer on the construction and testing of theories in sociology.* Itasca, IL: F. E. Peacock.

Choo, T., Roh, S., & Robinson, M. (2008). Assessing the "gateway hypothesis" among middle and high school students in Tennessee. *Journal of Drug Issues, 38*, 467–492.

Council on Social Work Education (2013). *2008 Educational policy and accreditation standards.* Retrieved July 17, 2013, from www.cswe.org/File.aspx?id=13780

Goldfried, M. R. (1999). Role of theoretical bias in therapeutic interventions: To see or not to see? *Journal of Clinical Child & Adolescent Psychology, 28*(4), 544–547.

Golub, A., & Johnson, B. D. (2002). The misuse of the "Gateway Theory" in US policy on drug abuse control: A secondary analysis of the muddled deduction. *The International Journal of Drug Policy, 13*(1), 5–19.

Jones, J. H. (1997). *Alfred C. Kinsey: A public/private life.* New York: Norton

Lindblom, C. E., & Cohen, D. K. (1979). *Usable knowledge: Social science and social problem solving.* New Haven, CT: Yale University Press.

Penna, S. (2004). On the perils of applying theory to practice. *Critical Social Work, 5*(1), 1–7.

Plionis, E. M. (2004). Teaching students how to avoid errors in theory application. *Brief Treatment and Crisis Intervention, 4*(1), 49–56.

Smith, D. (1990). *The conceptual practices of power: A feminist sociology of knowledge.* Boston, MA: Northeastern University Press.

Thyer, B. A. (2008a). Preface. In K. M. Sowers & C. N. Dulmus (Eds), *Comprehensive handbook of social work and social welfare: Volume 2, Human behavior in the social environment* (pp. xiii–xxvi). Hoboken, NJ: John Wiley & Sons.

Thyer, B. A. (2008b). The potentially harmful effects of theory in social work. In K. M. Sowers & C. N. Dulmus (Eds), *Comprehensive handbook of social work and social welfare: Volume 2, Human behavior in the social environment* (pp. 519–541). Hoboken, NJ: John Wiley & Sons.

Whitaker, C. (1976). The hindrance of theory in clinical work. In P. J. Guerin, Jr. (Ed.), *Family therapy: Theory and practice* (pp. 154–164). New York: Gardner Press.

Critique theory in historical and cultural context

(EPAS 2.1.3 Apply Critical Thinking;
EPAS 2.1.7 Apply Knowledge;
EPAS 2.19 Respond to Contexts)

Genealogy is the study of families and the tracing of their lineages and history. Genealogists use oral traditions, historical records, genetic analyses, and other methods to obtain information about a family and to demonstrate the kinship and pedigrees of its members. Results are often displayed in charts or written as narratives. Social workers conduct genealogies when they work with family systems to construct and interpret a genogram, a tool for deepening insights into past influences on current patterns. Genealogies can enrich our understanding and appraisal of a theory and its parent theoretical tradition.

Contextual analysis places a client system in a particular ecological, social, and cultural context. Such analysis identifies relevant systems, connections between systems, and the reciprocal influence of the focal client and the salient social systems. Social workers conduct ecological analysis to learn more about the context for client system patterns when they construct and interpret an eco-map. Likewise, contextual analysis can deepen our understanding and appraisal of a theory and its parent theoretical tradition as developed in a particular place.

Historical and contextual factors and theory appraisal

Theorists often construct theories by assembling metaphors, images, and concepts that best characterize the selected aspect of the "person interacting in the environment" configuration. Theory construction is a rational and scientific process insulated from the biasing effects of personal preferences and political influences—at least, in theory.

Influences on theory construction

However, theorists are human beings who live in particular historical times and specific contexts. and they acquire ways of seeing, thinking, feeling, and valuing shaped, at least to some extent, by their experiences in the stream of history and an ecological setting. Theory creation doesn't occur solely in the conscious mind. Theorists, for example, may respond with or without awareness to societal and political conditions when theorizing (Stehr, 1992). Tyrannical governments are likely to flavor the theorist's work in ways different than beneficent and democratic governments. Changes in social norms such as those related to shrinking numbers of two-parent, two-children families or increased rates of premarital sex might influence a theorist. Unexpected and non-normative historical events such as the World Trade Center attacks on September 11, 2001 or the British Petroleum oil spill in 2010; ecological shifts such as climate change and increases in unusual weather events; and technological changes such as the creation of the World Wide Web might challenge theorists to think in new ways about human behavior and the environment.

The tenor of the times and larger context may also directly influence the personal decision making of the theorist deciding on a theory project. The availability of funding related to social work with older persons, for example, might attract some theorists. The perceived popularity and prestige attained by certain theorists may evoke an urge to emulation. Theorists are influenced also by charismatic theory developers, by their scientific peers, and by their perceptions of the possibility of sharing a theory and its ideas with others via books, journals, websites, and other vehicles (Germain, 1983).

Influences on theory reception

Dimaggio (1995) noted that "the reception of a theory is shaped by the extent to which a theory resonates with the cultural presuppositions of the time and of the scientific audience that consumes it" (p. 394). In some contexts and historical periods, for example, cultural trends, theoretical enthusiasms, and the characteristics and interests of theory users result in a warm reception for a particular social work theory while another theory fades from the public realm quickly. In the United States, theories affirming individualism and self-interest have had popularity in the recent past whereas theories emphasizing our involvement in and dependence on membership organizations gained less support. Theory reception may also be affected by the cultural membership groups and social movements (civil rights, female liberation, gay pride) that advance justice and cherished social causes and promote certain theories as social change tools.

History and theory appraisal: illustrations

Any theory has a genealogical lineage, and it is important to know its history, especially its record of success and failure in solving theoretical problems. I am fond of interactionism partially because of its creation by social workers and sociologists working together at Hull-House in the early twentieth century and the expansive range of human experiences it addresses.

Policy theories

Social work educators may include a historical review in their theory survey courses to enhance appreciation of changes in theoretical thinking. For example, policy instructors often cover theories of policy influential in different historical periods (Nagel, 1990). These include the political theories of the ancient Greeks, especially around the fifth century BC, Machiavelli's theory of political power in the sixteenth century, utilitarian theories of Bentham and Mill developed in the eighteenth century, Pareto's theory of wealth distribution at end of the nineteenth century, the pragmatist theory of John Dewey formulated at the beginning of the twentieth century, and the theory of justice created by John Rawls in the 1970s. Classroom lectures and activities might help students appraise the contemporary relevance, if any, of each of the important historical theories.

Social theories of aging

Theory users and theorizers should learn about how theory appraisals change over time. Bengtson, Burgess, and Parrott (1997) propose that many disciplines and professions experience growth across generations in theorizing preferences. They examined the field of social gerontology. The first generation of theorists in social gerontology built a theory of disengagement, for instance. This emphasized age-related decreases in social interaction, psychological involvement, and physiological functioning. These decreases were explained in terms of the individual's withdrawal from social engagements because of lessened ego energy and the anticipation of death. Second-generation theorists discovered that research findings didn't support many of the claims of disengagement theory. New theoretical frameworks were constructed such as social exchange theory, social breakdown/competency theory, and age stratification theory. These borrowed selectively from and improved on first-generation theories. In the third and current generation, theorists interested in aging have shifted to theorizing that is supported by multidisciplinary partners and that limits its scope to one level of analysis such as the micro level rather than spanning multiple levels.

Family development theories

We have seen changes in theoretical notions about family development. When I was completing my dissertation in the late 1980s, the family life cycle theory was popular (Forte, 1990). This focused on the cycles of birth, growth, maintenance, shrinkage, and death experienced by all families.

Family changes were commonly grouped by seven family life cycle stages: the newly married couple stage, the young couple with a newborn stage, the family with school-age stage, the family with adolescent children stage, the launching stage when children begin to leave home, the empty nest stage, and the post-retirement stage. The family was conceptualized as a system of roles and relationships that changed in predictable ways with each stage. Three criteria for demarcating the boundaries between family life cycle stages were shared by many theorists. The first criterion gave central importance to the life course of the first child as a "catalyst" or pathfinder stimulating change for the entire family. It was believed that family interaction and needs are strongly influenced by the age of the oldest child and the oldest child's evolving social involvements, especially the school. The second criterion, changes in composition, recognized that a central emphasis in family development is the effort of the family group to manage changes in family group composition. The entry and exit of children influence entire family relations and the experience of each family member. As family size increases, family interaction becomes more complex. Membership changes necessitate family reorganization to accommodate the requirements on the family related to changes in number of members and organization. The third criterion focused on the work career of the man in the family. Reflecting an increasing life expectancy, this criterion permitted consideration of later stages of family life including the period after the departure of children from the home, when the major wage earner retired. The role transition has effects on family life for all family members including the retiring person.

Since the 1980s, theorists, researchers, and practitioners have identified many limitations to the family life cycle theory (Forte, 1990). The framework was biased toward the intact nuclear family, a type of family structure increasingly rare in the United States. The framework didn't fit the experiences of different family forms such as multigenerational and one-parent family households. Gender, ethnic, cultural, and sexual orientation differences were not accommodated well by the theory. Contemporary theorists have shifted to notions of the multiple and intersecting careers of family members. Theoretical models of family change over time have become more complex and now recognize the great diversity of family forms and the many variations in the scheduling of family events such as childbearing, marriage, and retirement.

Theories of cultural competence

Kohli, Huber, and Faul (2010) provide a social work example of historical developments in theorizing about human differences and cultural competence. They contrasted the changing theoretical emphases of the 1950s (melting pot imagery and ideas), the 1980s (cultural pluralism and variations on identity development), and the early 2000s (the social construction of ethno-cultural distinctions). Distinctive notions of cultural competence are associated with each theoretical emphasis. Unfortunately, the authors don't identify possible historical or contextual factors contributing to these advances in theorizing or comment on the current perceived value of these different theories.

Context and theory appraisal: illustrations

Malcolm Payne (2002) investigated how the cultural context for the use of knowledge in a profession affects theoretical development. He focused on trends and changing theoretical preferences in Great Britain.

Systems theory

Systems theory became very popular among social workers in Great Britain in the 1970s especially for understanding and guiding services to families. Payne argued that this was not because of the strength of systems ideas. The theory had been available for several decades. Specifically, the theory's growth in popularity wasn't because it added something new and needed to the social work knowledge base. The theory became popular because of changes in the cultural, political, and historical context for practice. Systems theory made it possible for social workers to work in the large organizational structures emerging in England at the time. Increases in the complexity of social service departments, in the demand for social services, and in the power, prominence and public visibility of social workers stimulated the theoretical shift from psychodynamic approaches to system approaches. Systems theory also helped reduce the fragmentation of services by providing ways of unifying specializations such as child care and mental health (the shared systems orientation), unifying workers trained in different methods such as casework, group work, and community organizing (the common systems methodology), and unifying diverse roles in common action (shared systems interventions including social networking, the provision of informal support, and community care). Systems theory fitted with the cultural preference of British social workers to maintain some continuity with traditional helping approaches such as ego psychology. Systems theory offered an integrated approach to guide rationing resources, setting priorities, and dealing with problems in this cultural context. Social workers shifted to systems theory, Payne concluded, not primarily for scientific reasons but for historical and contextual reasons related to advancement of the profession, of their organizations, and of their careers.

Individualistic theories

Cultural context also influences the theorist's likelihood of creating individualistic or communally oriented theories (Falck, 1988). North

American theorists tend toward theories that conceive of society's individuals as free agents pursuing self-selected goals and unique preference sets often in resistance to societal pressures. Other theorists (Asians and European theorists, for example) more often conceive of society's members as bound by responsibilities to the collective and as able to realize potentials through shared activity and commonly endorsed values (Askeland & Payne, 2013).

Concluding remarks

Practitioners must consider ecological and temporal contexts when thinking critically about theories and selecting a theory for use. For example, they might ask whether there is there an identifiable similarity in the context for the theory's development and the context for the theory's application? Or are the contexts very different: the academic setting versus the community center, for example? As a general rule of thumb, social workers might assume that the more similar the contexts of theory development and use, the more likely the theory will be appropriate for helping work. Additionally, theories created by social workers in common practice contexts and created with an appreciation of the specific features and complexity of such contexts are more likely to be useful than theories created at great distances from the field by academicians or researchers unacquainted with social work concerns and issues.

Learning activities and reflections

1   Reflect on your current place and time. What are the features of your environment that shape knowledge creation and adoption? Think about political, economic, cultural, social, and technological features? What are some of the contemporary events, trends, fads, and patterns that might possibly influence your theorizing or a theorist's construction of a theoretical system? If you were creating a theory, how might these features and events influence your theorizing work?

2   Select a theoretical proposition from a theory developed more than 50 years ago such as Sigmund Freud's psychoanalytic theory of personality development, Max Weber's theory of bureaucracy, or Adam Smith's invisible hand theory of economic processes. Summarize your views of how the proposition makes sense or fails to make sense of contemporary manifestations of the focal topic. How would the theory have to be modified to serve current social work practitioners well?

3   Conduct some interviews. Find a social worker from a very different region in your country or a different country. Engage that person in a discussion. You might use a Web-based tool to find and converse with this partner. What are the two or three most important theoretical frameworks or theories in that place? According to your partner, in

what ways does this theoretical knowledge reflect the influence of the region or country? Is any preferred theoretical knowledge universal and transcendent of place? How so?

4   Find and interview a social worker from a generation earlier than yours: your parents' or your grandparents' generation, for examples. Ask him or her about the theory or theories that were most popular early in their career? What were some of the perceived influences on the theory creator, the characteristics of the theory, and its popularity? How were these influences associated with the time period? How has your respondent seen the profession's preferred and valued knowledge change over his or her lifetime?

5   In the past, male theorists typically developed human behavior theories and practice theories. How might shifts in theory preferences and evaluations relate to changes in gender roles and the greater involvement of women in research and scholarship? Identify a specific theoretical tradition, theoretical proposition, or concept associated with a "founding father" and critique it with reference to gender biases.

References

Askeland, G. A., & Payne, M. (2013). What is valid knowledge for social workers? Retrieved July 23, 2013, from www.scie-socialcareonline.org.uk/repository/fulltext/74815.pdf

Bengtson, V. L., Burgess, E. O., & Parrott, T. M. (1997). Theory, explanation, and a third generation of theoretical development in social gerontology. *Journal of Gerontology, 52B*(2), S72–S88.

Dimaggio, P. J. (1995). Comments on "What theory is not." *Administrative Science Quarterly, 40*(3), 391–397.

Falck, H. S. (1988). *Social work: The membership perspective*. New York: Springer.

Forte, J. A. (1990). Men's personal, dyadic, and family well-being across the family life cycle. Unpublished doctoral dissertation, Virginia Commonwealth University, Richmond, VA.

Germain, C. B. (1983). Technological advances. In A. Rosenblatt & D. Waldfogel (Eds), *Handbook of clinical social work* (pp. 26–57). San Francisco, CA: Jossey-Bass.

Kohli, H. K., Huber, R., and Faul, A. C. (2010). Historical and theoretical development of culturally competent social work practice. *Journal of Teaching in Social Work, 30*(3), 252–271.

Nagel, S. S. (1990). Introduction: Bridging theory and practice in policy/program evaluation. In S. S. Nagel (Ed.), *Policy theory and policy evaluation: Concepts, knowledge, causes, and norms* (pp. vii–xxiii). New York: Greenwood Press.

Payne, M. (2002). The politics of systems theory within social work. *Journal of Social Work, 2*(3), 269–292.

Stehr, N. (1992). *Practical knowledge: Applying the social sciences*. London: Sage.

LESSON	Critique theory
32	considering long-term impact

(EPAS 2.1.3 Apply Critical Thinking;
EPAS 2.1.7 Apply Knowledge)

How do we judge the impact of scientific theoretical tradition? How do theoretical ideas make a difference? These aren't questions solely about the effectiveness of an application of theory in specific helping circumstances only but about the long-term impact of theoretical ideas and intellectual systems.

Likely impact and theory appraisal

Several criteria have been suggested for judging theoretical impact. These are based on the notion that theories with impact add something new to the professional and social knowledge base.

New understandings

First, we may judge theoretical knowledge in terms of its contribution to a new understanding of the "person interacting in the environment" (Feyeraband, 1978). Such theoretical breakthroughs offer an innovative way of seeing and thinking. Many philosophers of science relate this criterion to the value of knowledge accumulation: the "new work somehow meaningfully incorporate and build upon earlier work" (Rule, 1997, p. 27). The innovation occurs sometimes in an unanticipated yet important way. Sigmund Freud, for example, offered a theoretical lens that opened the eyes of social workers to the influence of childhood experiences and sexuality on human development.

New languages

Second, theoretical knowledge may be impactful because it provides a new language, a way of scientific talking (Alexander, 1988). Queer theorists, for instance, argued that the theoretical language of heterosexuality and homosexuality and the public derogatory language of "faggots," "queens," and "dykes" inadequately captured the life experiences of persons with diverse sexual identities and orientations. Queer theorists took control of language about sexual orientation back, for example, by embracing and promoting an affirming meaning for the concept queer. This linguistic advocacy contributed to the ability of theorists and laypersons to articulate in new ways aspects of human behavior in the environment related to sexual orientation and discrimination. Specifically, this new theoretical discourse lessened communication distortion among theory users, gave meaning to complex experiences, enriched the interpretation of previously misunderstood social worlds and cultural groups, provided for persuasive theoretical arguments, and enhanced the society's conversations about the subject matter.

New ways of coping

Third, theoretical knowledge may have a lasting impact because it increases the coping ability of community members as they adjust to changing environmental conditions (Feyeraband, 1978). A theory might provide useful insights into the possibilities of "better social relations" and of "a social world which all concerned could acknowledge as superior" (Rule, 1978, p. 173) while also providing demonstrations of the effective means for realizing these possibilities. The application of an impactful theory reduces human miseries, increases enlightened patterns of personal and social action, lessens the degree of disagreement and debate about social polices and practices, and helps social workers solve urgent problems in line with our values and visions of social justice (Rule, 1997; Witkin & Gottschalk, 1988).

James Rule (1997) suggests that social work theory users should judge theoretical knowledge by this standard of coping. Has the theory become a base of action for helping practitioners cope with professional challenges faced in the world? Does the theory identify the contingencies (events, states, meanings, or arrangements that are connected to one another) that hold across a variety of contexts relevant to community interests? Has the identification of such contingencies reduced our vulnerability to destructive biological, psychological, social, political, and ecological processes? Has the theoretical knowledge better equipped practitioners with intellectual strategies and intervention tools for ameliorating destructive processes and enhancing positive processes?

Knowledge accumulation

Finally, we can consider the likely impact of theoretical knowledge by the criterion of cumulative progress. Ideally, new knowledge refines existing knowledge and stimulates theory-building work. The theorist is like a brick mason adding a brick to a major construction project: the building of the library of social work knowledge. The artful theorist inspires other brick masons, too.

Laudan (1977), for instance, discusses the usefulness of *theoretical research programs* for knowledge accumulation. Such a program is a theory-driven enterprise involving multiple theorists and researchers working together to accumulate knowledge in a given "person interacting in the environment" area. In social psychology, for example, there are theoretical research programs related to role-based emotional experience (affect control theory), power and bargaining processes, social exchange networks, rational action, and social comparison (Berger, & Zelditch, 1993a). Much effort has been expended testing and refining the theories of interest to these theorist/researchers. Such work has increased the impact of these theories. The interplay between theorizing and research promoted by theoretical research programs resulted in substantial knowledge accumulation (Berger, & Zelditch, 1993b; Shelly, 2002)

Advances in theoretical knowledge help theorizers transform anomalous, unsolved, and significant theoretical puzzles into solved ones. Additionally, impactful theoretical programs refine theories so they mature as tools for solving the tough theoretical puzzles. Eventually, such theoretical knowledge becomes part of the canon. The *canon* is considered the fundamental theories in the discipline or profession: the basic knowledge, for example, considered a prerequisite to a genuine and comprehensive understanding of "person interacting in environment." The professions' accrediting and licensing associations mandate that every legitimate social worker master this profession's canon. The canon changes slowly. So theories accepted into the theory "hall of fame" may have influence on generations of social workers.

Cumulative and systematic theoretical work to increase theory impact can take several paths (Berger, & Zelditch, 1993b). *Theory elaboration* occurs when a theory becomes more comprehensive in its scope and ability to explain aspects of human behavior and the social environment. Symbolic interactionism, for example, has expanded its explanatory power to cover social structures and biological processes. *Theory proliferation* refers to the expansion of the practical use of theoretical knowledge. For example, behavioral theory has extended its range of application to many different social work helping situations.

Long-term impact and theory appraisal

Practitioners may find it difficult to make judgments about the long-term impact of theoretical knowledge. Has a given theory contributed to the thinking, communicating, and coping abilities of social workers and the profession in a lasting way? The answer often depends on the values, standpoints, and interests that the judge brings to the evaluation process. Reflect on the impact of the feminist theoretical tradition. Many social workers have viewed this theory in a positive way.

However, those with deeply held and fundamental Christian beliefs have arrived at different judgments. The Jeremiah Project (2010), for instance, argues that feminism has had long-lasting and damaging effects on many spheres of society, especially the family. The feminist theory and its advocates have undermined favorable societal beliefs about God, capitalism, birth, heterosexuality, males, and family structure. Feminists have irreversibly alienated many women from men. Because of feminist theorizing, the home and traditional family values are no longer a source of identity and moral guidance for most Americans. Adultery, lesbianism, divorce, and selfishness have increased as a direct result of the dissemination of feminist thought. The pillars of American society—private property, the state, and the family—are under attack by feminists, and feminist theorizers and their organizations have championed unrestrained sex, rights for deviants such as homosexuals and transgendered persons, and abortion on demand. Since the 1960s wave of feminist theorizing and theory application, women have also been stripped of many economic and legal protections. Displaced and abandoned housewives and their children have become a new and large underclass. This extremely negative appraisal of the feminist theoretical tradition illustrates the value-based nature of judging long-term theoretical impact.

Learning activities and reflections

1   Galileo's sun-centered theory of the relationship of the planets to the sun, his ideas about observation methodology, and his other theory-based discoveries such as the telescope revolutionized science, changed astronomy, physics, and mathematics, and provoked a transformation in the dominant paradigm in Europe. The impact of his theorizing work has been great.

   Let's consider more deeply an important and controversial theoretical tradition discussed in the commentary. In the early 1960s, several feminist theorist-activists reignited the flame of feminism lit earlier by the Suffragists fighting for women's property, sexual rights, and the right to vote in the nineteenth and early twentieth centuries. Betty Friedan (1963), for example, wrote a book titled *The Feminine Mystique*. She theorized that lives organized only around child rearing and domestic activities and the internalization of the beliefs about femininity that identity was inextricably linked to the mother and wife roles unfairly closed off other roads to fulfillment and caused unhappiness. The Women's Liberation Movement began the next year. Feminist theorists have added significantly to the theoretical tradition in the last 45 years.

   Has this line of theorizing make a positive difference? Reflect on your own life experiences and developmental history as a man or woman. Confer with your mother, your grandmother, your aunts, and other women. Confer with some of your teachers. Do some research on the impact of feminism on American society, families, norms, patterns of interaction, and self-conceptions. What evidence might you assemble to argue that early and contemporary feminist theories have been influential? If you believe that the tradition has made a significant difference, what values might you use to argue that the influences have been either positive or negative? What evidence might you use to argue that feminist theory made no difference or had a destructive influence? How might social workers in 2050 look back and judge the impact of the feminist framework?

Add some specificity to your reflections. Select and address several of the following questions. How has our knowledge of human behavior and the environment changed because of feminist theorizing? How have public policy and problem solving changed because of feminist theorizing? How has social work practice changed because of feminist theorizing? How have research methods and procedures changed because of feminist theorizing?

2   Take this activity a step further. How might you use what you have learned about the impact of a theoretical tradition to appraise the scholarship of a school of thought: behaviorism, symbolic interactionism, cognitive psychology, Marxism, or queer theory, for examples. To what degree has the focal tradition had a positive impact? What is your evidence for this appraisal? In what ways has the focal tradition negatively impacted human beings, society, the environment, or the profession of social work? What is your evidence for this appraisal?

References

Alexander, J. C. (1988). The new theoretical movement. In N. Smelser (Ed.), *Handbook of sociology* (pp. 77–100). Newbury Park, CA: Sage.

Berger, J., & Zelditch, M. Jr. (1993a). *Theoretical research programs: Studies in the growth of theory*. Stanford, CA: Stanford University Press.

Berger, J., & Zelditch, M. Jr. (1993b). Orienting strategies and theory growth. In J. Berger & M. Zelditch, Jr. (Eds). *Theoretical research programs: Studies in the growth of theory* (pp. 3–22). Stanford, CA: Stanford University Press.

Feyeraband, P. (1978). *Science in a free society*. London: Verso Editions.

Friedan, B. (1963). *The feminine mystique*. New York: W. W. Norton & Company.

Jeremiah Project (2010). The impact of feminism on the family. Retrieved August 20, 2010, from www.jeremiahproject.com/prophecy/feminist2.html

Laudan, L. (1977). *Progress and its problems: Towards a theory of scientific growth*. Berkeley, CA: University of California Press.

Rule, J. B. (1978). *Insight and social betterment: A preface to applied social science*. New York: Oxford University Press.

Rule, J. B. (1997). *Theory and progress in social science*. Cambridge, UK: Cambridge University Press.

Shelly, R. K. (2002). How scope and initial conditions determine the growth of theory. In J. Symatka, M. Lovaglia, & K. Wysienka (Eds), *The growth of knowledge: Theory, simulation, and empirical research in group processes* (pp. 115–130). Westport, CT: Praeger.

Witkin, S. L., & Gottschalk, S. (1988). Alternative criteria for theory evaluation. *Social Service Review*, 62(2), 211–224.

<table>
<tr><td>SECTION

5</td><td># Conclusion</td></tr>
</table>

The final section summarizes my approach to practical theorizing and the theorizing skills necessary for competent, evidence-informed social work. The coda identifies the major themes infused across 32 lessons, themes that might stimulate your thinking about how to meet the professional, career-long challenge of theory-practice integration.

Coda: principles for practical theorizing

Theorist, theory, theoretical, theorizing, and theory-practice integration are words and phrases used often in this book. Practical theorizing is the construct that I have created to unite these terms and characterize the activity central to competent practice. The first section of the book built a foundation for practical theorizing by identifying features of the theorist role, three theorizing styles, a social work filter for knowledge selection, and theorizing variations related to source, system size, and abstraction level. Section 2 explicated a systematic process for deconstructing and reconstructing theory elements for practical use. The section included lessons focused on theory summary and display. Section 3 demonstrated how to model "person interacting in the environment" configurations by constructing middle-range causal and interpretive theories. The section also elucidated how to share such theory construction projects with others. Section 4 developed a critical thinking approach to theory use and showed how practitioners might use scientific norms, practical considerations, and professional standards to appraise theoretical knowledge and theorizing activity. In this final chapter, I will review the principles that have guided my efforts to explicate the "Practical Theorizing" approach to social work. I have used the mnemonic phrase "I Theorize" to organize the chapter's content.

I

Identify as a theorizing practitioner. *Practical theorizing* identifies theorizing as central to professional social work. This is an emphasis common to the definition of the profession found in the mission statements of many social work associations. I have suggested adding "theorizer" to the basic roles of generalist practice and encouraged readers to incorporate the key attributes of the associated role identity of theorizing practitioner to their professional self. Doing so, practitioners are joining a long tradition committed to theory-practice integration. Useful theorists and scholarly practitioners associated with varied schools of thought can serve as role models, and, ideally, this book will motivate readers to begin a career-long project emulating these models and progressing in mastery of theoretical knowledge and refinement of theorizing skills.

T

Think theoretically. *Practical theorizing* involves theoretical thinking, the purposeful use of a system of concepts with scientific meanings to reconstruct or construct a theory. Practical theorizing also involves critical thinking about the quality of theory in terms of scientific norms and other standards. Theoretical thinking is compared to puzzle solving: an enterprise of identifying a puzzle (the client problem or challenge), selecting a puzzle solving strategy (a theoretical or paradigmatic style of theorizing), assembling the puzzle pieces (empirical data and other evidence about the case), fitting the puzzle pieces together (the assessment formulation), recognizing and naming the pattern detected (problem statement for intervention plan), and testing the fit of puzzle pieces (practice evaluation).

In my approach to *practical theorizing*, I make the case that a significant obstacle to past theory-practice integration has been the conceptualization of theorizing as a monolithic activity. Theorizing is conceptualized instead as multi-dimensional—a complex thinking-feeling-acting process—and as a process that can be differentiated into a large set of distinct but related core and advanced theorizing skills. Table 33.1 lists these skills and identifies the lessons providing content and learning activities for each skill.

Practical theorizing is an open and continual process. Theorizing produces a theoretical product (a theory of the problem, of change, of intervention implementation, of evaluation, and so on), but the theorizer recognizes that the product is incomplete, unfinished, imperfect, and potentially revisable. The provisional theory can always be improved with time with the client, with work with similar clients with similar problems, with new evidence regarding the theory's usefulness, or with theoretical insights from colleagues or supervisors.

H

Habituate for intelligence-in-action. *Practical theorizing* in an intelligent, accountable, and effective way requires the cultivation of a set of dispositions. These include habits of thinking critically; considering openly many theoretical perspectives on a case; exploring theoretical assumptions and biases; scholarly study of relevant theories and research reports; scientific, evidence-informed inquiry; reflection before theory use, while using theory, and after theory application; and creative imagination. Acquiring

Table 33.1   **A matrix relating theorizing skills to lessons**

	Theorizing Skills	Lesson
	Core	
1	To analyze causes	13, 19
2	To classify	20
3	To conceptualize	12, 19, 20
4	To contextualize	31
5	To critique theory	19, 20, 22, 23, 23, 25, 26, 27, 28, 29, 30, 31, 32
6	To display theory	02, 17, 19, 20
7	To explain	13, 19
8	To form propositions	13, 19, 20
9	To identify processes	20
10	To make theoretical assumptions	10, 11
11	To model a theory	02, 09, 16, 17, 18, 20
12	To name	12, 21
13	To predict	13, 19
14	To use metaphors	10,
15	To reason deductively	14, 19
16	To reason inductively	15, 20
17	To search and select theories	04, 05, 06, 08, 09
18	To speak about theory and elements	01, 03, 07, 10, 12, 16, 19, 20, 21
19	To synthesize theory elements	18, 19, 20
20	To test theory	13, 19, 20
21	To translate theories	10, 21
	Advanced	
1	To apply theories differentially	02, 05, 06
2	To deconstruct theory and elements	08, 09, 10, 11, 12, 13, 14, 15, 16, 17, 18, 19,
3	To differentiate theory strengths and limitations	02, 04, 10, 22, 23, 24, 25, 26, 27, 28, 29, 30, 31, 32
4	To integrate into varied professional roles	01, 03, 09, 21
5	To synthesize theoretical frameworks	19, 20
6	To transfer across helping contexts	25, 31
7	To use specialized theories	19, 20
8	To use theories for comprehensive assessment	07, 16, 17, 18, 19, 20

and strengthening these habits increases the practitioner's sensitivity to theoretical puzzles and readiness to solve these puzzles.

E

Excel. *Practical theorizing* argues that superb social work performance follows the transformation by drill, rehearsal, and experimentation over a significant period of time of discrete theorizing skills. Eventually, these skills are synthesized into a holistic style of theory use and theorizing activity. Using these skills repeatedly, considering evidence of effectiveness in skill usage, and reflecting critically on the trials will hasten the practitioner's advancement toward competent and then excellent social work practice.

Practical theorizing identifies and specifies the theorizing skills to accompany the practice behaviors associated with many of the 2008 core competencies of the Council on Social Work Education. Relevant competencies include identify as professional social worker (2.1.1), apply critical thinking (2.1.3), engage in research-informed practice (2.1.6), apply knowledge (2.1.7), and respond to contexts (2.1.9). Practical theorizing provides guidance to practitioners progressing toward the demonstration of their expertise in competent, critical, evidence-informed, reflective, accountable, and theory-guided action related to each of the competencies.

O

Overcome dualisms and related obstacles. *Practical theorizing* requires the rejection of dualistic thinking (practice versus theory, academy versus field, theory versus theorizing, theorist versus practitioner, theory-guided versus evidence-informed practice) and the affirmation of unity within differences. For example, the divide between practice and theory is crossed purposefully. During practical theorizing, the separation between theory and practice is minimized. Theory and practice are distinct human activities but linked on the continuum of scientific problem solving. All professional helping work contains a mix of knowing and action although with different emphases at the poles. Effective practitioners learn to alternate between moments of theorizing and moments of doing while engaging in scientific practice. Theorizing improves doing. Doing improves theorizing.

Practical theorizing is also conceptualized as a continuous process, one that is integral to practice and with relevance to each phase of the planned change process. Practical theorizing begins before the first helping session, informs the entire helping process, and continues after the helping work ends. Practical theorizing is not separate from the helping work.

Practical theorizers must leap over a variety of hurdles impeding the path of theory-practice integration. These include obstacles related to differences between theory creators and theory users in conceptions of ideal knowledge, the proliferation of theoretical frameworks and the complexity of their theoretical languages, the status and power considerations impeding cooperation across disciplines and professions, the organizational pressures to act by routine procedure rather than to infuse action with theoretical thinking, and the deficits in social work education related to theory and theorizing capabilities.

R

Reconstruct knowledge for professional use. *Practical theorizing* assumes that knowledge use is not a technical, rational process of application but involves the worker's creative imagination, embodied reflection, critical thinking, and purposeful adjustment of knowledge to accommodate evidence, the changing dynamics of the helping relationship, and contextual factors. Practical theorizing shows practitioners how to deconstruct preexisting theoretical knowledge (assumptions, concepts, propositions, models) and how to reconstruct such knowledge for the achievement of specific purposes in specific places with specific clients. Practical theorizing counts on the synergy between accumulated knowledge and new thinking (emergent knowledge) and calls for continual zigzagging between theoretical ideas, data, and critical reflections during the creation of novel theory.

Practical theorizing, therefore, prioritizes the reconstruction and construction of modest theories: middle-range theories including causal and interpretive theories. Such modest and practical theories can illuminate the specific "person-interacting in an environment" factors relevant to the focal client system puzzle and key aspects of perplexing client life processes. Middle-range theories can also illuminate episodes of "being stuck" during helping processes. Advanced practitioners may even construct new practical theories in those situations where existing theories are not suitable.

I

Integrate knowledge and styles of theorizing. *Practical theorizing* synthesizes knowledge from many sources, including theoretical knowledge, research knowledge, practice wisdom, and personal knowledge. Practical theorizing involves the interaction among four processes critical to theory use: the reconstruction or construction of a system of coherent, disciplined, and rigorous knowledge (theorizing); the conduct of focused and disciplined scientific inquiry into the use of the knowledge (research); the tempering of the theorizing and evaluation by imagination and intuition (personal reflection); and the informed and improved helping action (practice) that ensues from the interplay of the first three processes and feeds back to each.

Practical theorizing takes a pluralistic stance. Borrowing and using knowledge from diverse theoretical traditions increases the practitioner's ability to explain diverse client system challenges and her or his flexibility in devising action plans to improve complex and varied "person interacting in an environment" situations. The pluralistic stance also supports constructive dialogue between the advocates of each theoretical language, capitalizing on the strengths of each, and recognizing the differences and tensions that must be reconciled in the integration of multiple theories for a particular helping project.

Practical theorizing also endorses methodological pluralism and operates in a syncretic way selecting from the major styles of theorizing: positivist, interpretive, and critical (each with its own conception of data collecting, theory generation, evidence, and validation) as needed for any particular theory application task. Practical theorizers fuse the different approaches to the ordering of theory elements (inductive, deductive, and abductive) into theorizing projects, and they engage in theorizing ventures varying in scope (conceptualization, hypothesis formation, middle-range theorizing, grand theorizing) as called for by work demands.

Z

Zone theorizing projects. *Practical theorizing* necessitates attention to ecological and temporal contexts or zones. For example, effective practitioners appraise the helping context to determine when practical theorizing will be most needed and most useful. These are often circumstances characterized by uncertainty and unpredictability; circumstances where habit and organizational procedure are inadequate to scientific problem solving. Theorizing practitioners must also be sensitive to the ecological and cultural contexts of their partners in collaborative ventures. Partners from the academy, the research center, the practice arena, and the life spaces of clients bring different purposes, theoretical preferences, and theorizing sensibilities to a helping team. Practical theorizers zone into these distinctions.

Temporal context is important, too. *Practical theorizing* appreciates the past and affirms the continuity of current practice with the major theoretical traditions and the exemplary theorists of the basic and social sciences. Members of each tradition have made many contributions to the analysis of "person interacting in an environment" puzzles, and these traditions (the historical stream of theorizing) offer resources for inquiry and action planning. However, practical theorizers must also be attuned to the present and use the research literature and contemporary critiques of theoretical knowledge to select suitable theories. Finally, practical theorizers think about the future, prefer theories that generate new ways of understanding and helping, and construct novel theories in anticipation of the emerging needs of clients and the profession.

E

Explain theory and theorizing in clear ways. *Practical theorizing* recognizes that scientists create much knowledge in sites distant from the lives of our clients and with minimal appreciation for the clarity or usefulness of the knowledge to practitioners. Practical theorizing shows practitioners how to enter "knowledge trading zones," search for and select useful knowledge, and translate academic and research center knowledge so it can be explained and used to help people improve their lives and environments.

Practical theorizing values team collaboration among professionals with different disciplinary, professional, theoretical, and role-specialty backgrounds. Collective inquiry and action planning are facilitated through barrier-bridging translation and communication processes. *Practical theorizing* recommends that effective practitioners learn to translate knowledge back and forth across multiple modalities (words, diagrams, mathematical formulas, objects, pictures, and other sign systems). This increases theoretical fluency and literacy and, thus, abilities to explain theory and theorizing activities to clients, collaterals, collaborators, supervisors, supervisees, and others.

I theorize. You theorize. We all theorize. Practical theorizing invites practitioners to grow in their capacities to theorize responsibly, skillfully, and joyfully.

Index

identification of the explanatory puzzle, 207; independent variables and, 205–6; intentional causes, 205; learning activities, 212–14; mechanical causes, 205; method of agreement, 211; method of difference, 212; refinement and adaptation for future use, 209; reflection, 212–14; summarization of, 210–11; transformation of elements into operational form, 207–8; unintentional causes of, 205

causation versus correlation, 239

cause and effect, 204–14

Chafetz, J. S., 292–3

Chaiklin, Harris, 26, 108

Clinical Social Work Journal, 73

coda, 9, 311–17

cognitive-behavioral theory, 210

communication. *See* language

competencies: CSWE definition of, 3–4; skills for competent theorizing, 5, 6

"competencies movement," 3

concepts: construct and, 144–5; critical thinking and, 238; deconstructing a theory's concepts, 143–6; description of, 142; distinction between, 144–5; identification of, 142–50; interpretive theory and, 217; learning activities, 148–9; nominal definition of, 144; operational definition of, 144, 217; overview, 142–3; reconstructing a theory's concepts, 146–8; reflections, 148–9; sensitizing, 145, 217; theoretical, 142–3, 205–6; variable, 205–6

conceptualization, 145

conceptual models, 185

conflict theory, 127; neo-Marxist approach, 55, 127

construct, 144–5; validity, 223–4

continuum: middle of, 24–5; practice end of, 24; theory end of, 24

conveyance metaphors, 124–5

Corbin, J., 218

core assumptions, 133

correlation versus causation, 239

Council on Social Work Education (CSWE), 2, 3–4, 275, 290; "competencies movement," 3; definition of competencies, 3–4

Cribb, A., 19

critical approach to theorizing, 55–6; definition of, 55; evidence supporting, 56; language, 56; method, 56; purpose of, 55

critical thinking: about theory, 235–41; about theory using ethics and values, 256; about the usefulness of theory, 248; core elements of, 236–8; definition and habits of, 235–6; diversity and, 281; holism and, 267; learning activities, 240–1; overview, 235, 242; practical theorizing and logical fallacies of, 238–40; questions to ask, 240; reflections, 240–1; scientific value of a theory, 245–6; strengths and, 287–8; of theorists, 39; theorizing and, 235–6; using evidence, 262. *See also* critique theory

critical theory, 281; neo-Marxist approach, 55, 127

critique theory: considering long-term impact, 304–8; in historical and cultural context, 293–303; by reference to moral and technical uses, 290–6; using professional standard of ethics and values, 252–8; using professional standard of evidence, 259–63; using professional standard of holism, 264–8; using professional standard of justice, 269–74; using professional standard of sensitivity to diversity, 275–83; using professional standard of strengths, 284–9; using scientific and practical standards, 242–51. *See also* critical thinking

CSWE. *See* Council on Social Work Education

cults: theory and, 295

culture: critique theory and, 293–303; learning activities, 302–3; reflections,

59574331R00191

Made in the USA
Lexington, KY
09 January 2017